Dear Debbie.

Best Regards

Dear Debbie.

Best Regards

THE ARCHITECTURE OF **ADRIAN SMITH**

The SOM Years, 1980–2006

Toward a Sustainable Future

Revised and Updated Edition

images
Publishing

Published in Australia in 2015 by
The Images Publishing Group Pty Ltd
ABN 89 059 734 431
6 Bastow Place, Mulgrave, Victoria 3170, Australia
Tel: +61 3 9561 5544 Fax: +61 3 9561 4860
books@images.com.au
www.imagespublishing.com

National Library of Australia Cataloguing-in-Publication entry:

Creator: Smith, Adrian (Adrian Devaun), author.

Title: The architecture of Adrian Smith, SOM : toward a sustainable future / Adrian Smith.

Edition: Revised edition.

ISBN: 9781864706253 (English edition)

Series: Master architect series.

Notes: Includes bibliographical references and index.

Subjects: Smith, Adrian (Adrian Devaun)—Criticism and interpretation.
                    Adrian Smith + Gordon Gill Architecture.
                    Skidmore, Owings & Merrill.
                    Skyscrapers.
                    Architects—United States.
                    Architectural firms—United States.
                    Sustainable architecture.

Dewey Number: 720.483

Production by The Graphic Image Studio Pty Ltd, Mulgrave, Australia
www.tgis.com.au

Pre-publishing services by United Graphic Pte Ltd, Singapore

Printed by Everbest Printing Co. Ltd., in Hong Kong/China

Contents

Foreword

Many see the presentation of the AIA Honor Awards as a highlight of the American Institute of Architects' annual convention. And it is quite often at this presentation that we also see Adrian Smith. The Adrian Smith, the one so often up on that stage accepting major awards, the Adrian Smith on the 20-foot-square media screen looking politely satisfied, quite humble, and anxious to return to work. What's he thinking? How has he succeeded in contextually integrating large buildings while improving the human performance and the quality of life in each and every one? How has he achieved status as a national treasure in architecture while producing at such a rich and abundant, almost opulent level?

Over the years nearly every one of the projects he has been involved with has achieved international acclaim in one form or another. In fact, at Skidmore, Owings & Merrill, projects under his guidance have earned more than 90 awards for design excellence, including seven national AIA awards. He has been presented the Urban Land Institute's Award for Excellence in Large Scale Urban Development/Mixed Use, the prestigious FIABCI *Prix d'Excellence* Award, the Gold Prize of Shanghai Classic Buildings. Still, while chatting with Adrian, seldom does he discuss or focus on awards. Why? What Adrian really wants is not another award, but to discuss the enhancement of the urban fabric through unique solutions and inspired design. It is for this that he has earned his essence, renown, and respect.

Adrian Smith graduated from the University of Illinois and started working at Skidmore, Owings & Merrill as a student. Following graduation, and after five years with the firm, he advanced to associate and soon developed a global perspective. If you do a little digging in architectural publications and the internet, you soon discover that Adrian Smith has indeed brought design solutions with enduring value to the entire planet. He's designed buildings in China, England, Germany, Brazil, Kuwait, Canada, Korea, Guatemala, Bahrain, Japan, Saudi Arabia, Dubai, and the United States, and, while he has become one of the preeminent architects for design, few realize that he also served as the Chief Executive Officer of SOM, from 1993 to 1995. His expertise covers areas as broad as operations, marketing, finance, and professional services. He is truly one of the few architectural polymaths, a person who has a great diversity of skills and immense intellect.

Adrian is perhaps most recognized for designing exceptionally aesthetic and functional tall buildings. Clients around the world know that he understands scale, community, and context as few others do. He is passionate about (and celebrates) well-designed buildings of all shapes and sizes, of course, but how many other architects have earned accolades for designing the tallest building in the world?

When asked about his favorite projects, Adrian pauses to consider—one can almost hear his brain processing the question. After several ruminant moments, he tells me that a number of projects have indeed proved most gratifying. In chronological order, Adrian's most rewarding projects are: Banco De Occidente, United Gulf Bank, Rowes Wharf, 10 Ludgate, Jin Mao Tower, Burj Khalifa, and Pearl River. Each of these projects amazes in their real and conceptual ability to bring success to the clients' business objectives, while creating communities appropriate to the opportunity.

I've had the chance to visit many of Adrian Smith's SOM projects. Of these, I most admire Rowes Wharf, perhaps because I love the hotel as such a delightful retreat within the city of Boston, or perhaps because, at Rowes Wharf, there is so much design to contemplate.

As Harvard defines Cambridge, I have found over the years that Rowes Wharf, for me, is Boston. It is uniquely Bostonian, and the housing, offices, hotel, and 65,000 square feet of retail space enhance everything truly loved about Boston. I've yet to talk with anyone in or around Boston, or the planet for that matter, who doesn't truly appreciate what this project has done for the life and dimensions of the city.

Adrian Smith has provided truly consummate leadership on buildings that fit their site and enhance their occupants.

Wisdom, extracted from Adrian Smith's vast experience, is found in these pages. Turn them slowly and carefully as you consider what has already transpired and what potential exists for the future of our urban environments. This book provides a clear, thought-provoking read, rich in illustration as well as ideas.

When it comes to important buildings, Adrian Smith and SOM have provided us a beacon by which to steer. In these pages, Adrian Smith illuminates, showing us how to engage, energize, and inspire students, architects, and clients to do and to be their very best.

James P. Cramer
Chairman/CEO, The Greenway Group
Editor, *DesignIntelligence*
Former Executive Vice President/CEO,
The American Institute of Architects

Introduction: state of the art of context

It has been several years since I wrote about the nature of context in my work. I find that it is evolving into a work that is not as rooted in the things that I see in a particular place or region, nor in the familiar references to a place or a group of buildings that define a place, but to attitudes that should define a place. New methods of design and fabrication facilitated by three-dimensional modeling and better tools available to architects to present their intended concepts have resulted in the possibility for buildings to become much more intellectually sophisticated. I find that every structure should respond to its location through how it reacts to sunlight, wind, humidity, temperature variations, soil conditions, and topography as a major driving force. The referencing of physical elements of past buildings in an area is perhaps still important in terms of rooting the building to its cultural heritage and this attitude is still valid in terms of cultural sustainability. In my mind and attitude toward architecture though, I now think that form can and should be given to a work more through the influences exerted on it by wind and weather, by the nature of the functions contained within, and by the feasibility of its structure.

This attitude shift in my work and in my thought process is the result of extensive travel to cities throughout the globe. There is little respect or caring for much of the historic fabric, and indeed the historic culture, of most cities in Asia in the 21st century. Most of the fabric has disappeared from major cities such as Beijing or Shanghai, except for national monuments such as Tiananmen Square, or the Forbidden City, or the Temple of Heaven, all in Beijing. Traditional one- and two-story courtyard houses are being demolished and replaced by 15-story office blocks; where historic references are applied, they are often so distasteful that the buildings would be far better without them. Also, many new cities such as Shenzhen and Seoul are being built from scratch—they have no local history and are subject only to economics and trade. It is hard to imagine that just 25 years ago these two cities had populations of less than 100,000. Now the population of each is more than 10 million, and still growing fast. In Europe, complete new districts such as London's Canary Wharf are emerging as new central business districts that are specifically built for productivity, efficiency, security, and the provision of space that cannot be found in the historic core, with rare exceptions. It is seldom appropriate to design buildings that contain overt references to a place since the nature of that place will change and leave the new contextual piece standing alone and foreign to the very context to which it was endeavoring to relate.

So where do contextual architects go to find contextual influences? I believe we have to use the new tools we now have at our disposal to shape our buildings to take maximum advantage of the climatic environment we are designing for. Further, we need to do this with an attitude of innovation regarding the best use of materials and the most efficient use of available sources of free energy. Harvesting the sun, the wind, the water sources of humidity and rain, the local materials, and the latent geothermal conditions that can be used for heating and cooling are all contextual elements that humanity, in its most basic and indigenous state, dealt with when designing their first dwellings.

We should also be looking to the future of travel and transportation modes. There is about to be a tremendous change in the nature of travel for most societies. The automobile will eventually be replaced with personal air vehicles and highways will become parks for recreation. Buildings will have ports in the sky and elevator systems will be more local. Material technology is advancing the strength of materials and in fact making new materials that were not available for construction a few years ago. Through nanotechnology research, new materials for the future will make structures that most scientists have only dreamed were possible.

Suddenly, the context is the vision of the future, not the memory of the past. But must we all throw our memories of the past away in the architecture we pursue? Is there a place for nostalgia and memory in the architecture of the future? Do we need cities where buildings relate to one another in a sympathetic and respectful way? Is the cohesive physical environment of material similarity and consistency of expression still valid? Is the city analogous to a language where each new piece of work within that language can be a new word or phrase? Is technology alone enough to express the character of a place? What role will art in architecture play and will the familiar be necessary to make a connection with the public? Should the city be ordered and classic, or chaotic? Who will be responsible for such decisions?

I look at many modern cities now and see a kind of disorder and lack of inspiration toward any statement other than creating space for people to inhabit. Yes, there are feature buildings, but the vast majority of the environment is made up of a texture of indifference, a lack of caring. Where will the inspiration come from to make and remake this world a more beautiful and a more logical environment, where everyone is on the same wavelength? In this world of pluralities and idiosyncratic philosophies and no philosophies, it seems that our cities are destined to become a collage of different forms, materials and shapes that bear little resemblance to one another, unless a common paradigm is embraced by those who control our environment and its design.

I hope for an environment where the old and new are connected and where human scale is an important factor in the texture of our public surfaces. I hope that materials are used that enhance the uniqueness of a place. I hope that there is a relationship between buildings that helps to form a sophisticated and harmonious series of public rooms that both excite and bring comfort to the users of those spaces. Above all, I hope there is quality of design, construction, and the art of making cities embodied in what the real estate, construction and design professionals create in the cities of the future.

Let the cities come first and the egos of the individual support, but not overpower, the goals of making our culture one of respect and admiration for each other.

Adrian D. Smith

Further insights into the work of Adrian D. Smith

Tall buildings and sustainability

Paper presented by Adrian D. Smith to the Tenth Annual Conference of the National Council of Structural Engineers Associations, October 2002

The tall building has been a fixture on the American urban landscape since the early 20th century. Initially, these buildings were clustered, to concentrate large groups of people within walking distance of each other and within walking distance from major public transportation systems. Cities grew and buildings became taller as advances in vertical transportation and structural engineering progressed. It was not until the mid 20th century that air conditioning of tall structures began to influence the design of all building systems, including the exterior wall and its glazing, structural framing systems, ceiling systems, lighting and ventilation, exit strategies, and fundamental space allocation criteria. As buildings became more closed to the exterior environment in order to condition the interior space, the more important it became to develop an exterior enclosure that both let natural daylight into the occupied space and reduced the amount of heat coming into or leaving the occupied space.

The movement to develop a sustainable high-rise vocabulary is an important step in the development of this building type. Successful integration of sustainable concepts into all disciplines of architecture and engineering will help promote the continued propagation of high-rise buildings in our society. In the past, progress has been very slow, with only a few examples where a partial development of sustainability has been achieved. It is ironic that from a total building point of view, many of the buildings constructed in the first half of the 20th century were much more environmentally friendly than most of today's tall buildings. In Europe, where most office buildings are designed with operable windows and narrow lease spans, the level of sustainability and environmental awareness generates buildings whose designs are similar conceptually to the buildings of the 1920s and 1930s in America.

The dilemma in the United States is that the user has become used to the space-planning efficiencies of much larger floor plate sizes (in the range of 2500 to 4000 square meters) than is typical of our European counterparts (whose floor plate sizes range from 1000 to 2000 square meters). With floor sizes of 3000 square meters and lease spans of 15 meters it is not possible to satisfy fresh air needs with operable windows or lighting needs with windows alone; therefore, mechanical ventilation with heating and air conditioning is a necessity.

The following is a selected history of some typical building types, illustrating the development of the high-rise building from the beginning of the 20th century, through the transformation of the early 1950s, to today's sustainable design concepts, and where we could go in the future.

1904: Santa Fe Building, Chicago

The Santa Fe Building, designed by Daniel Burnham in 1904, is the prototypical office building of the turn of the century. Its plan is roughly square in shape and it houses a central light and air court to aid in cross ventilation and to bring light into the interior office space. This building has been retrofitted with a skylight at the top of the court, turning it into an atrium; air conditioning systems have been installed to meet today's market standards.

1930: Rockefeller Center, New York/ Empire State Building, NY

In the 1920s and early 1930s elevator technology improved and with it, the need to open up space around the taller buildings to provide more light and air to offices. The high-rise office tower reconfigured itself to a stepped form with a central core and narrow lease spans. The Rockefeller Center and Empire State Building exemplify the best examples of this early type of high-rise. It was still necessary to protect the interior environment from the exterior climate, so masonry cladding was used extensively on the exteriors.

1957: Warren Petroleum Building, Tulsa

The Warren Petroleum Building, designed by SOM, was the first building to incorporate a double glass wall. It also used a tinted glass-shading device at the head of the exterior light of glass to cut down on the heat load and glare to the occupied space. Each light of glass was single-glazed and no attempt was made in this system to introduce mechanical ventilation of the interstitial space between the glass lights. As a result, it was ineffective as a device for controlling heat gain into the occupied spaces of the building.

1957: Inland Steel Building, Chicago

The Inland Steel Building, designed by SOM, was the first high-rise building to use heat-absorbing tinted glass in a double-glazed insulating unit. This building was initially designed as a double wall system but was changed during the design process to a double-glazed system with tinted glass. This was seen as a refinement to the double wall since it took less space and, because the interstitial space was not ventilated on earlier versions of the double wall configuration, it was probably viewed as being more efficient than the double wall. The Inland Steel Building was also one of the first buildings to incorporate a completely modular system of exterior wall mullion spacing, exterior blinds, ceiling tiles, light fixtures, partition systems, and air conditioning systems. It was a clear span structure, allowing the interior complete flexibility. Its glazing system was floor to above ceiling, to bring in the maximum quantity of light into the space.

1962: Occidental Petroleum Building, Niagara Falls

The Occidental Petroleum Building, designed by Cannon, was the first building to use a double wall system that incorporated sun-shading devices in the interstitial space and a form of air circulation to ventilate the hot air from the cavity wall. The sunshade devices were large extruded aluminum horizontal elements that spanned 10 feet and were mechanized to open and close automatically. Unfortunately, many of the motors have since burned out and the system has been compromised because of a lack of parts. The blinds were also monumental and as such blocked views from the interior. As a result, this building, which should have become a prototype for the future of sustainable design in office buildings, was not a success.

1964: BMA Building, Kansas City/Tenneco Building, Houston

The BMA Building and the Tenneco Building, both designed by SOM, are examples of a number of high-rise buildings that have used their structure to provide shading for the glass exterior. In the case of Tenneco, an additional sunshade is provided to screen the more severe sun conditions of Houston.

1970: John Hancock Center, Chicago

The John Hancock Building in Chicago, designed by SOM, was the first true high-rise building to incorporate significant quantities of mixed uses in one structure and therefore became a model for a new form of urban planning and urban architecture, and a new form of sustainability. It provided an alternative to the concept of living in the distant suburbs, commuting into work and then returning to the suburbs at night. It was a model of living and working in the same building, or at least the same neighborhood, saving on both time and energy. The residential units on the top of the building have both mullions that allow natural ventilation and operable windows, although the operable windows are not used because the winds are too great at that height to provide comfortable air circulation in the units. The building is also equipped with a grocery store, sky-lobby, banking facilities, laundry and dry cleaning service, restaurants, mail room, clothing stores, hairdressers, shops, car parking facilities, and health club facilities.

1983: National Commercial Bank, Jeddah, Saudi Arabia

The National Commercial Bank in Jeddah, Saudi Arabia, designed by SOM, is unique in that it took into account orientation for sun control and drew upon indigenous cultural influences to inform the aesthetic of the building's image. Large solid walls with very large multistory holes allow light to reach the exterior glazing, set far back for sun control. The plan configuration allows all interior occupied spaces to have access to shaded natural daylight while being protected from the sun by these deep overhangs. The building also features sky gardens on the roof of each floor where the holes exist, adding to the principles of modern sustainable concepts. In addition, each terrace and opening is connected by a vertical shaft that runs through the entire building and acts like a chimney to draw air through the exterior terrace spaces of the building, cooling the terraces.

1986: United Gulf Bank, Manama, Bahrain

The United Gulf Bank Building in Manama, designed by SOM, uses local and regional materials for exterior walls, structure, and millwork. Vertical heat-absorbing glass sun fins and double-glazed reflective glass provide shading from low sun from the west, and overhangs from deep punched windows shade the glass from southern sun. Translucent glass panels and coved ceilings at the perimeter provide daylight at the work surfaces in the perimeter offices from the top, while the windows provide light from the side. Floating glass terraces divide the atrium light shaft into four "spaces" where light is filtered through the atrium and adjacent office space via glass block floors. These terraces are landscaped with hanging vines, adding landscape features to the interior of the building. The building's architectural expression is derived from the indigenous context of Bahrain and by the image of the local pearl fishing boats—*dhows*—that are so prevalent along the Bahrain coastline.

1995: Commerzbank Competition, Frankfurt, Germany

This competition entry by SOM, although not the winning entry, attempted to reintroduce the principal of the double wall into the modern office building. A 2-meter interstitial space was created to house the structural system for the tower and insulate the interior wall from the exterior through air movement within the cavity, thus making this an active cavity. Exit stairways would also occupy the interstitial space in this scheme, to leave the occupied space column and core free for maximum flexibility. Photovoltaic panels were proposed for the roof of the existing building and multistory interior atria were intended to connect the existing building with the new tower, converting an exterior wall into an interior atrium wall to reduce energy consumption in the existing building.

1996: Samsung Togok Tower, Seoul, South Korea

The Samsung Togok Tower was a feasibility study by SOM, prepared for the Samsung Electronics Corporation to test the validity of housing all of Samsung's office needs in one facility. The concept was to house all of Samsung's space needs in an experimental office tower that would become a showcase for current technology and a laboratory for its future products in the field of energy generation. The proposal used a double wall with photovoltaic panels placed in the interstitial space, positioned to provide shading to the office floors. Air movement would be horizontal within the interstitial space to move the heated air on the south sides of the building to the cooler north side of the building. The energy generated from the photovoltaic panels would power the fans to move this air when the sun was out. The air would move vertically during the summer months when the air on both sides of the building exceeded the design temperature. Large sky holes on the broad face of the mass relieve the wind forces and reduce the vortex action. The holes also capture the downward air movements and funnel them through an array of wind turbines to generate power, useful for evening lighting or to apply to the power grid. The base of the holes would house sky terraces and gardens for use by the building occupants.

1999: Jin Mao Tower, Shanghai, China

The Jin Mao Tower, designed by SOM, is currently the tallest building in China. Similar to the John Hancock Building in Chicago in that it comprises a variety of functions ranging from office uses to hotel, parking, observatory, restaurants, and shopping, its primary contribution to sustainable architecture is in the way it expresses itself as an intrinsic component of the culture of China. Through its use of contextual references and its transformation of these references into a modern language of architecture, Jin Mao attempts to reawaken the spirit of the Chinese people to the delights of their past history, and to be a new landmark for Shanghai. The exterior wall is composed of insulating low-e glass units of varying densities and stainless steel and aluminum projecting vertical and horizontal members that act as shading devices to all exposures of the building's façade. It is also the first major project in Shanghai to use natural gas as its primary energy source and its sewage treatment and water purification systems are self-contained.

1999: Seven South Dearborn, Chicago

Seven South Dearborn, designed by SOM, was designed to be the world's tallest building and to house sufficient antenna and transmission equipment to satisfy the needs of the Chicago metropolitan area for all future HDTV broadcasting. The major elements of sustainable ideology included an 8-inch double-wall cavity design with blinds in the interstitial space and the use of photovoltaics on the top 70 floors of the south, east, and west elevations. This would have been the largest array of photovoltaics to be applied to any high-rise building to date.

2002: Toward a zero-energy building: Mitsui Muromachi Competition/Beijing TV Headquarters Competition/Block 37 Prototype

SOM's Block 37 Prototype is the synthesis of exterior wall technologies previously studied on the competitions for Commerzbank, Mitsui Bank, and Beijing TV Headquarters. In addition, it adds interior architecture and engineering strategies such as enhanced lighting systems, reduced receptacle energy usage, reduced thermal energy, reduced ventilation energy usage, reduced cooling and heating energy usage, and incorporation of renewable energy systems. The combined results of all these features can result in a zero-energy building.

It seems that technology has now developed to the extent that we have the ability to not only create buildings that are benign to the environment, but to create buildings that can actually reverse the negative effects of past projects by adding to the energy grid and replacing more polluting power sources with cleaner ones. It takes a fundamental change in the way we think about our built environment to make any significant moves forward.

Challenges

- What, if anything, can the structural engineering profession do to make structures more sustainable and more responsive to the environment?

- How can building design professionals develop a data bank of research and information from which to learn and teach to the next generation of engineers?

- How can we get our clients to understand the importance of sustainability in our built environment and to invest for the long term?

Relationships in Architecture

Paper presented by Adrian D. Smith as part of the UIC lecture series, November 21, 2005

Architecture is about relationships

Before we talk about architecture and design, I would like to begin with a very simple assertion: architecture is about relationships. I know that seems obvious but I think it's important to reiterate this idea before we move on to discuss some very specific kinds of architectural relationships. Our capacity to design homes, offices, schools, streets—even entire neighborhoods—is as diverse and as abundant as human creativity itself. Consequently, architecture reflects our multifarious, often circuitous, and seemingly infinite quest to manipulate the environment, built and not yet built. These relationships include the way in which humans perceive a need for shelter; they involve our understanding of community as it relates to that shelter, and also how we link that community to culture, science, and art. Architecture synthesizes all of these components, and, as we consider the socio-economic and socio-political forces that shape our architecture, we must also consider how our architecture shapes our society—its economics, politics, and behavior.

Architecture is an expression of our mood as a culture

Contextualism is integral to the way we think about the built environment. I have always maintained that architecture is an expression of our mood as a culture. It reflects our interests and it mirrors the preoccupations of our time. Our built environment must not just reflect our culture and the age we live in but it must also delight those who use it and are affected by it. Our built environment is constantly in transition; it is kinetic and it is at once a reminder of the past and a predictor of the future. It is an expression of our conscious values and the state of our economies. It exposes our egos and reveals the degree to which we are willing to collaborate. Architecture expresses our optimism in the future. Contextualism too is an expression of our mood as a culture. When we look around us, we see that designing within a larger context has been around for many years, although, as a formal, articulated theory, contextualism has been much more present in the last five decades.

Thesis: the architectural vocabulary of a place

We talk about the "architectural vocabulary of a place" quite a bit but I would argue that a place possesses much more than a vocabulary. It has grammar, it has poetics, it has form, metaphor, and a symbolic and literal language. So what do I mean when I say to you that we're building with grammar? Instead of trying to add a new language to that vocabulary of architecture, I strive to discover/unearth words, or expressions, that fit into the existing vocabulary. And that vocabulary only has meaning, both symbolic and literal, because it fits into a larger pattern, or a language. That language is easily discernible to most because it does, in fact, have a formal structure. It possesses a grammar. This is how one thinks about architectural context. The metaphor can be extended to stretch over buildings and our lived spaces. Grammar is by no means absolute. The rules, although strict, are flexible. They demand invention and they evolve through time. The grammar of early Modern English, or of Shakespeare, is enormously different from the grammar of today, as is the vocabulary, and yet we understand both, and both have the capacity of elicit a kind of poetic understanding from us.

In an essay about architects in the *Lewis Mumford Reader*, Mumford wrote: "By his choice of materials and textures and colors, by the contrasting play of light and shade, by the manipulation of planes, by the accentuation, when necessary, of sculpture and ornament, the architect does in fact turn his building into a special kind of picture: A multidimensional moving picture, whose character changes with the hours and the seasons, with the functions and actions of spectators and inhabitants. Similarly, he creates in a building a unique work of sculpture, a form one not merely walks around but walks into, a form in which the very movement of the spectator through space is one of the conditions under which the solids and voids of architecture have a powerful aesthetic effect, not known in any other art."

How then, should we consider Mumford's notion of the building as a picture? Mumford too was talking about establishing context.

TS Eliot's essay, "Tradition and the Individual Talent", examines how one thinks about context in a culture where there is no longer any assurance on the part of the poet (designer?) that the public has a common cultural heritage, a common knowledge of works in the past. A city builds its own body of references, but these are ever changing, continuous, adaptable, and in flux. Why do I insist upon this notion of context? In order to envision, one must first re-vision, re-appropriate, and continually update our understanding of the architectural landscape.

Eliot: *"Yet if the only form of tradition, of handing down, consisted in following the ways of the immediate generation before us in a blind or timid adherence to its successes, 'Tradition' should positively be discouraged ... Tradition is a matter of much wider significance. It cannot be inherited ... What is to be insisted upon is that the poet must develop or procure the consciousness of the past and that he should continue to develop this consciousness throughout his career."*

Representation is much more than a matter of mere repetition. Now it's true that no artist, designer, or building has any meaning in and of itself. We are understood in a certain way because each one of us can be evaluated in and against a certain larger context, by which I mean body of work. However, if I merely examine the history of a place, and seek to design a building that echoes that history, then sure, I've designed something contextually—but all I've really managed to do is repeat history. Constructing meaning through contextualism is about how meaning is constructed through a relationship with everything that has gone before and everything that is to come—the simultaneous existence and simultaneous order—and then adding to it, changing the sequence somehow, having technology and our contemporary awareness inform our designs. Only then does a piece become contextual to both the historical fabric and the contemporary sense of place. It reveals a unique identity that is singular to its own time.

Words only have meaning when viewed against a pattern of other words. And the meanings of certain words change as their contextual landscape changes. And so any discussion of contextualism also has to include that larger pattern, the language itself, and an understanding that as memory changes, the symbolic value changes, as does the literal meaning.

I view the city as a kind of tapestry in which many people over many years have left an imprint and where the structure of the tapestry is inviolate and is similar to the infrastructure of the city. It is this underlying structure that gives the city its lasting memory and it is the manner in which we relate to this infrastructure that forms the character and shape of our building over time. (The infrastructure has parallels to the broader language that both symbolically and literally defines the city.) I believe in cohesive, rational environments where there is a connected sense of consciousness and an evolution within the built environment of the city that reflects the continuity of its culture.

The relationship between old and new is important if we are to take our past seriously and if we covet the values of the context that formed the present. The new must make a connection with the old in ways that respect the essence of a place, a kind of ethos regeneration. A foreign ideology inserted into an environment of strength and harmony can have a cancerous effect on the biology of a city. It may be very apparent in the tapestry, but if it is not the right object, or if it is not placed in the correct position in relationship to the composition of the piece, it can ruin the continuity of a place.

Contextualism and the skyscraper

Postmodernism and new urbanism versus the skyscraper
The super-tall building not only drastically changes the literal landscape, but changes the symbolic landscape as well; the meaning of that landscape is changed through the mutual interaction of images, and the meaning is enlarged by echoes, by the sequence.

As an architect who specializes in tall building design, I am focused on building cities. From that perspective, my architecture has to extend a sense of familiarity—a connection—to the culture of the city. I am not typically interested in jarring the civility of a city with buildings that are aesthetically and functionally challenging to the surrounding communities—unless there's a proper spot and reasoning for it.

Discussion of skyscrapers and context can seem paradoxical but in fact, it is not. The city's built environment is the physical context that future architecture will be seen in and will interact with. It is important to understand not only the physical context that a building will be designed to relate with, but also the nature of the climate, topography, cultural influences, and the history of a place. A new urban building must establish a connection to the fabric of the city and maintain a hierarchical balance between the public and private realms. There are clues in every city that make that city unique from others. These clues are based in the cities' past; they are both physical and symbolic, and they emanate from the culture of the people who inhabit them.

The history of a skyscraper is inextricably linked to its technology

The skyscraper marks time by the use of technologies. If we examine the history of a particular building, we can see how it registers its history, piece by piece, through the sophistication of its systems and its enclosures. The skyscraper records time and human innovation by the use of technologies. It adopts materials, means, methods, and engineering principals. The evolution of technology commingled with design ideas to solve complex problems in intriguing and previously unheralded ways represents a particular breakthrough in the history of architecture.

For instance, at the turn of the century, before the advent of air conditioning, the high-rise was built with a center court/atrium to allow for natural light and air ventilation. The Rockefeller Center, circa 1930, was built with a central core, but the building was very narrow. Air

conditioning came along, and windows didn't need to open as much. Then double glazed windows were invented (double paned, with an air pocket between), meaning that buildings could have more glass, and more light.

Tall buildings and the context of Modernism

The first modern tall buildings, post-World War II, were developed as an innovative counterpoint to the skyscrapers in the 1920s. Their formal departure was based on innovation and the emerging philosophy of Modernism as practiced by the international school. Modernism was based, in part, on the mass production technologies of building components. To accomplish the design and construction of these new modern structures, the building industry had to be re-tooled to accommodate the tremendous building volume that was to take place. The philosophy was in place, but new technologies of building and construction were not as developed. The integration of new building services such as long-span structural systems, automated elevator systems, energy-efficient exterior wall components and systems, air conditioning systems, and modular lighting and wiring systems were all in their infancy and had to be designed and integrated into a building whose components were mass produced. Many architects designing tall structures in this period were obsessed with a manifesto to design for the masses. They utilized the components of mass production and the best of these architects refined their designs through endless study of proportion, scale, and material selections to produce architecture as art and a reflection of a modern civilized society.

This movement produced a multitude of large high-rise structures in America that redefined the image of the city. The first of these buildings were highly refined artistic and beautifully detailed structures and are considered today to be modern classics. Lesser architects quickly began to copy these icons. But tragically, the beautiful details were eliminated through the developers' value engineering process, reducing them to their most basic materials. In the 1960s and 1970s, the American city was characterized by a proliferation of bland, poorly detailed, and poorly resolved boxes of glass and steel, aluminum, or stone. These boxes were rapidly losing their appeal and falling from the favor of the general public and the corporate world.

By the 1980s, Modernism in America was dead. In its place arose a new paradigm whose inspiration came from the fundamental principles of pre-World War II architecture. "Less is more" was no longer the mantra of the day. Decoration was in. The composition of classical elements defining entry, base, middle, and top, centered compositions, mannerist façades, and contextual influences became dominant components. It was the desire of society to give a face and a personality to each of our buildings, and a character to our cities.

This period produced dramatic variety in the world of architecture and unleashed a level of individual creativity never before encountered within a single decade of building. New systems were developed for replicating natural materials and enhancing building envelope performance. Energy-efficient building systems advanced appreciably during this period. During this time anything was acceptable, except a plain glass box and austere Modernism. It was a time of significant expansion in the service sector of America, where the client wanted newness, even if it had an old face. It was a time of experimental and historic recall in tall buildings.

Postmodernism in architecture began with the rejection of Modernism as a valid way of building cities. Postmodernism incorporates a bit of the neo-Classical in that it is a return to the classic pre-Modernism, pre-glass box. It attempts to define these elements that Modernism forgot to define.

Buildings like Rowes Wharf, AT&T, NBC, Neiman Marcus, and Founders Court are pretty literal in their character. I didn't expand the vocabulary of the place, rather used it to add dimension.

I now try to be more inventive about the expression of a building, linking to indigenous elements of the building or the place. Looking at new technology to express these elements, 10 Fleet Street, Jin Mao Tower,

Chemsunny, Manulife, and United Gulf Bank are all examples of this marriage of memory and technology. Jin Mao adds to and revises the language of a place.

All of these buildings share a common language, although each expresses itself somewhat differently. Each responds to its particular context, bringing memory and tradition as well as intervention into the design process. A narrative of memory informs design; examples of this include the Nanjing Tower, the Burj Khalifa, and the 201 Broadgate Tower in London. They all acknowledge certain realities—of climate, culture, politics, and economics—and each expresses those realities by the manner in which they intervene in their contexts. Most importantly, each is clearly a site-specific solution. None of them could be replicated anyplace else, nor should they be.

The glass "thermos" envelope of the proposed Commerzbank or Samsung Togok projects would be totally inappropriate in Bahrain, and the recollection of images from Bahrain would mean very little in London. But in its place, each of these architectural solutions is clearly appropriate in that it redefines context, in much the same way as the work of the "individual talent" in Eliot's essay redefines the "Tradition."

Contextual architecture represents architecture and designing in a particular context, whether historical or vernacular. Often referred to as contextually compatible architecture, this notion can be easily understood through the analogy of "context" in linguistics. "Contextual compatibility" ranges from the superficial repetition of architectural styles or elements or cosmetic treatment of building façades, to the meaningful, inspired designs of a symbolic place in a building. Contextual architecture is different in scope, objectives, and approach than technology-based architecture. Contextual architecture confirms the continuity of the past and extends to the future, depending on the quality of design and understanding of context.

Contextualism in architecture

Adrian D. Smith

Contextual intervention: a sense of place

The streets and public spaces of the city are defined by the façades of the buildings that surround them. The exterior wall is the element that mediates between the two—between the public realm, whose edges it defines, and the private realm, whose domain it encloses.

An urban building has the responsibility of making a connection to the traditional urban fabric by maintaining—or restoring—a proper hierarchical balance between the public and private realms. The exterior wall is the only element that a building has in common with the public realm. If a building fulfills this first responsibility, it can then be developed to fulfill its other responsibilities—possibly a romantic or picturesque silhouette on the skyline, a gateway to the city, a corporate image, a civic symbol—but even the most low-profile "background" building must strive to make a good background by contributing to this definition of public space, enhancing the cohesion of the city as a whole.

In responding to the context in which we intervene, we are free to draw upon the historical, cultural, and regional differences that make one place unique from another. We are not bound by these influences and characteristics, but we can draw upon them for inspiration. TS Eliot, one of the 20th century's greatest poets and critics, wrote an essay more than 80 years ago called "Tradition and the Individual Talent". In this essay he asserts that Tradition—the collected literary "monuments"—exists as a body of work, complete in itself before the arrival of the new work. For order to exist after the intervention of the new work, the whole context is readjusted in the minds of the writer, and the reader, so that it all fits together with a sense of continuity. The contextual architect approaches the new work with the same respect for the traditional city that the poet has for the tradition in which he works. The thoughts one has, the inventions and discoveries one makes, can be additives to the built environment. But they assume their place as part of an assemblage of building, adding to, not disrupting the continuity of the urban context.

Having said this, I think it is worth pointing out that there is always "the exception that proves the rule," or as Robert Venturi said, "To perceive the ideal, one must acknowledge the real." Venturi—who is probably the first architect to introduce the literary criticism of TS Eliot into architectural discourse—never believed that the Modern movement was a bad thing in and of itself. Rather, he thought that the presumption of an "International Style"—a way of making buildings that could and should be applied in all cases and in all contexts—was a wrong-headed approach. He admired individual landmarks of the Modern movement such as Ludwig Mies van der Rohe's Seagram Building in New York, as an exception to the pre-existing order; by its contrast with the urban fabric the Seagram Building enhanced the "ideal" quality of that pre-existing order. When imitations of Mies' buildings started popping up all over, however, the urban fabric began to unravel to such a degree that the pre-existing order was in danger of extinction. Moreover, the power of contrast was diminished to the point where even the best of the modern buildings became trivialized. To most of the public, all glass boxes look alike—the significance of Mies is largely unappreciated—and as more of them were built and began to erode the traditional fabric, the less special even the best of them seemed to be. At the same time, there was too little left of the traditional fabric in most of our cities to be perceived as an "ideal" order. Venturi's call for a "complex and contradictory" architecture was as much an attempt to call attention to the real achievements of modern architecture as it was an appeal to stop destroying all that had come before it.

Like all revolutionary movements, the Modern movement became a crusade, complete with moral imperatives. Advances in building technology were, of course, among the major forces behind Modernism, and it was therefore crucial to the movement that the vocabulary of the architectural language reflects those changes. But as Eliot points out in "Tradition and the Individual Talent," we must always take care not to throw out the baby along with the bath water. As Eliot explains, "Someone said, 'The dead writers are remote from us because we know so much more than they did.' Precisely, and they are that which we know." The same can be said of the "dead architects." We do know more than they did, in terms of building technology. But we also know them, and now the Modern movement is also part of our history, we can use all of our accumulated knowledge to create architecture. New technology can offer opportunities to relate to the past while adding another element. It can reinforce tradition by establishing a new methodology for keeping tradition alive, bringing it up to date, making it more efficient and viable, and reaffirming a sense of continuity.

The case studies presented here are not re-creations or imitations of old buildings. They are modern buildings that meet contemporary needs. They relate to the past, but they add another chapter to the continuing evolution of the city. Some of them are clearly "modern" in their expression, but they are all site-specific and do not represent an

"International Style" that can be appropriated for use in other contexts. Some of them, on the other hand, are more evocative of traditional or historicist, rather than modern, architecture, but they are not pale or thin imitations, of older, more expensive materials and craftsmanship. Rather they are rich, expressive, solid, familiar, and reassuring. They use both modern and traditional materials in harmony with each other, to provide efficient construction methods and more economical use of materials than traditional materials and methods alone. In short, they speak of quality, permanence, and commitment. They are not short-term investments, they are long-term interventions.

Contextualism in a multicultural society

The earliest forms of architecture existed some 7000 years ago, when man transformed primitive cave shelters into architecture through embellishment by wall paintings, engravings, and sculpture, thus establishing architecture as what Victor Hugo called "The great book of the human race; Man's principal means of expressing the various stages of his development." Hugo said, "During the last several centuries of the world's history, from the time of the pagoda of Hindustan to that of the Cathedral of Cologne, architecture has recorded the great ideas of the human race. Not only every religious symbol, but every human thought has its page in that vast book ... he who was born a poet became an architect." Hugo's masterpiece, *Notre Dame de Paris*, has as one of its chief aims the advancement of the idea that architecture was a form of literature that expressed national culture. British writer John Ruskin proclaimed in his celebrated *Seven Lamps of Architecture* that a building could become "the embodiment of poetry, life, history and religious faith of nations" through an architect's hands. Like Hugo, Ruskin believed that "all good architecture is the expression of national life and character."

Both Hugo and Ruskin were advocating theories and ideals narrowly focused by the confines of Western culture and civilization, and therefore, limited by comparison to today's broad instant world framework. At the root of the conceptual structure of their thought was the Vitruvian triad of commodity, firmness, and delight or utility of structure. It is necessary to connect elements of art (delight) with elements of utility of structure, mechanicals and enclosure (commodity and firmness) in order to create architecture, which is connected to its place. Contextual architecture embodies utility as well as poetry. Tectonic architecture can be contextual, but not all contextual architecture is tectonic. Culture is complex and contradictory to the Modernist urge to reduce complexity to simplicity and essence.

Architecture critic Joseph Giovannini wrote, "Advocates of one-and-only truths overlook solutions whose complexities are rich matrices of form, philosophy, technology, meaning and culture. Rather than repressing form, architects like Luis Barragan orchestrated the Mexican wall, farm-like troughs of water and courtyards, into a contemporary architecture embedded in traditions of local culture. Barragan's form has beauty and meaning. Form does not preclude culturalism; it acts, in architecture, as an instrument of culturalism." It should also be pointed out that Barragan's architecture is uniquely suited to the place and, like most great contextual architecture, is not literally transportable.

A dilemma exists when designing in an environment increasingly dominated by stylistic diversity brought on by globalization, which has resulted in the replication of universal design thought. No longer are cities being designed for the particular needs of their regions with regard to climate, geography, local and indigenous materials, cultural symbolisms, or cultural mannerisms. Instead, architects and builders are globalizing their practices and designing buildings to their own idiosyncratic styles, regardless of the place or context in which they are placing the work. To some extent this has always been the case; however, materials remained vernacular, as did the concern for solar impacts as Beaux Arts or Colonial approaches were adjusted in order to relate to their new surroundings. In the modern world of urban architecture, cities are losing their uniqueness of place. Many urban structures built in the last 30 to 40 years appear the same, whether they are constructed in Cleveland or Singapore. Cheap energy and efficient mechanical systems for heating and cooling have nullified one of the basic criteria for designing to meet localized climate conditions through architecture. Materials and construction practices have also become globalized. It is now less expensive, and has been for some time, to buy granite in Sweden, Spain, or South America, ship it to Italy for fabrication and deliver it to almost anywhere in the world for installation, than it is to use the local stone traditionally quarried and fabricated nearby. Stone fabrication technology has advanced, making mass fabrication inexpensive, thus rendering local or regional fabrication techniques obsolete.

Culture is a way of life, an ancestral history in which religious beliefs, rituals, economic status, mobility, habitat, and memory all play a role; a continuum from one generation to the next, modified by new technology and invading cultures. Transition occurs as the assimilation of counter cultures takes place. When assimilation is resisted or avoided due to segregation, bias, or irreconcilable belief systems, nullified transformation results in a multicultural social system. Conversely, the basic impulse in multiculturalism brought on by the politics of identity is to break the molds of dominant cultures to allow the many constituent cultures their own space and legitimacy.

Architecture is and has always been a symbol of culture. It speaks about its users. It has become an individual tool of expression, not to build a homogenous society, but to exemplify the designer's perception of its owner's social beliefs. Urban architecture in this era has largely been shaped by the rationales of the corporate user. It has become an economic tool for investment. Its identity has been pacified by the constraints of normality and collective acceptability, largely reduced to universal shelters of glass and stone facings, and void of rooted contextual meanings. From the struggle for social expression an expressionless series of misfits, blandness, and contrivances has emerged. Witness the new cities of urbanism where architecture has no roots in history or memory of the place, no paradigm of influence to draw upon or only transient and fleeting universal stylistic fashions to emulate. The new Tokyo city is like this. In its drive to become a model of Modernism and progress it is void of delight; stripped down to its utilitarian essence, it has become unemotional. It is difficult to find a sense of place outside Tokyo's traditional core. Ironically, Japanese culture can be deeply traditional and thoroughly contemporary at the same time, at home in its contradictory cultural paradigms.

Only by a search for the meaning of a place through its past, its climate and its culture, can we forge an architecture that provides an environment of richness and collective identity—site-specific architecture recognizing its place. Cities can emerge to achieve a connected indigenous vocabulary, constantly enriched by technological innovation, but not overcome by it. By an attitude of additive inventiveness, our cities can re-emerge with personalities expressive of their collective cultures, but not devastated by them. The tall building has always had a key role to play in establishing a city's identity—from the great Tower of Babel, the Pagoda structures of Hindustan, the Islamic minarets, the towers of commerce at San Gimignano, the bell towers of Europe, the spires of Gothic cathedrals, to the super-tall edifices of our corporate culture today. The hope is to establish a set of constant parameters rooted in the history of the place, the memory of its people and especially its specific natural characteristics. Put the city first, above the individual building or architect. Maintain and reinforce

those elements shaped by the city's inhabitants, which have expressed its culture in physical form. Only then should the personalized approaches of the architect be layered to provide a micro-expression within the larger framework of the urban habitat.

My design philosophy is about identifying the nature and the character of a place and the people that occupy that place. Ultimately, I design buildings and environments that attempt to strengthen character by adding context. On one hand, the context identifies with the culture of the surroundings. On the other hand, it brings a new vocabulary to the language of architecture and supports the particular environment.

Many cities have multiple characters. And through time, many architectural styles have been layered over each other. Those things considered, I look for the essence of a place—its spirit, its ethos—and I try to identify the indigenous aspects, both physical as well as cultural, that make it unique and different from other places.

I work to strengthen a sense of place by relating to its memory, a sense of familiarity. Yet, I attempt to develop a building in ways that could only be done in today's world, with today's technology. I try to add time to the familiar and connect past to present, linking the identity of new environments to established ones.

My influences include indigenous materials, forms, and surfaces derived from a region's past. Also, the nature of the climate and the culture of the people are always analyzed. I am influenced by geographic amenities that formed the occupant's livelihood. The quality of light on vertical faces and idiosyncratic forms familiar to the region all have an influence on my architecture in a particular place.

My origins of the contextual approach

The origin of my search for contextual influences and their appropriate adaptation and application to today's needs dates back to my first experiences of Ricardo Legoretta, Raul Ferrera, and Luis Barragán in 1975 when we were engaged with them on the Grupo Industrial Alfa Headquarters project in Monterrey, Mexico. During that time Ricardo would preach contextualism, using influences of simple adobe houses as examples of a distilled architecture where climate, the sun, views and vistas, natural ventilation, local available materials, and topography played significant roles in forming these simple modest habitats.

He pointed out how misplaced the International style glass box was in Mexico's hot and arid climate, and how inefficient this style was in energy conservation. He used the work of Luis Barragán, his mentor and previous employer, as an example of a contextual approach to architecture in the region and how by using today's construction technology, architecture could be modern and have strong relevance to its culture without duplicating examples, but by using indigenous principals to inform its contemporary counterpart. Luis Barragán took us into his house and talked gently about his love of primitive cultures and their influences on his work.

Our approach for the design of the headquarters facility at Grupo Industrial Alfa took each program element one by one and developed rooms with proportions to suit each space. We created window placements to take advantage of the best views from each place, and colonnades to shade users from hot sun. Our courtyard spaces became outdoor rooms with orange groves to landscape side yards. All of our designs were indigenous to Mexico.

The experience of Grupo Industrial Alfa, although the project was never built, was exhilarating. It was completely different from what I had been accustomed to at SOM, where my training was based on international Modernism, and principles developed from the teachings of Mies van der Rohe.

Shortly after this experience, SOM was engaged to design the Haj Terminal in Jeddah, Saudi Arabia and although I was not involved in this project, my partner-to-be, Fazler Kahn, SOM's great structural engineer, started working with Gordon Bunshaft from the New York office. The scheme they developed was both contextual and structurally inspired. The use of tent structures was a perfect fit to the Bedouin tribes who roamed the Saudi deserts and the use of fabric in tension, suspended from cables above, allowed for natural ventilation to cool the 100-acre tent structure and its inhabitants below. Fazler Kahn began talking more about the influences of context in architecture, and its relevance in our architecture.

In the late 1970s, we were commissioned to design a bank building in the historic district of Guatemala for Banco De Occidente. Bruce Graham, initially the design partner on this project and I, as studio head, went to Guatemala City. We saw this project as a great opportunity to apply the principles of contextualism that we had learned from Barragán and Legoretta. During the next several years, we designed two branch banks and a headquarters for Banco De Occidente using local materials, indigenous color palettes, and solar orientation and natural ventilation principles in the design process. Bruce Graham at the time stated that he felt like Bernini. I felt like a Guatemalan using what was at hand; developing new ways to see spaces and enter rooms. It was a wonderful experience, due in large part to our client Herculano Aguierre, who wholeheartedly embraced our concepts. As a result, the banks are able to operate without air conditioning and can function when power failures occur. The buildings need very little maintenance, and they blend into their context in a distinctive, natural way.

Experiencing the process of looking at the place, one designs for and obtains clues from the visual energy and cultural stimulation embodied in the site. It was intoxicating, and it changed my approach to architecture from that point on. No longer would I be bound by a particular style or signature of current practice. I was beginning to see where my buildings would go, learning about the place, what was common and what was unique, studying how a new building could draw upon these influences to add to what was already there.

Through a successive series of commissions in Bahrain, Boston, Chicago, London, and China, with enlightened clients in each city, I was able to practice and expand on the principles of contextual design. I learnt that most contextual design by definition is familiar, if not in all cases, popular to the inhabitants who come into contact with it. The works transcend the familiar in a new way that is readable and understandable. Many of these cities have layers of culture and civilization to their context. The challenge is in distilling these elements of physical history into a subject that can create a contextual approach of innovation and invention.

Interview with Adrian Smith

By Tom Finnegan, November 2003

Mr Smith, what was your role early on at Skidmore, Owings & Merrill?

I started in 1967 while I was still a student at the University of Illinois' Chicago campus. In the early years I was an apprentice architect. I worked with Bruce Graham in the 1960s and early 1970s.

On some of the bigger projects?

I worked on the basement and third floor levels of the John Hancock Center where I detailed some grills and laid out a very tight mechanical room. Later, I worked on the First Wisconsin Center (today known as US Bank Center) as a project architect under Jim DeStefano and Bruce Graham. In 1972, my wife and I decided to move to Europe while we were still highly mobile, and SOM had a project in England—a headquarters for a tobacco factory for WD & HO Wills. It was an interesting project on a very fast track where all stages—design, construction documents, and construction—were all being done at the same time. SOM was associated with a British architectural firm named York, Rosenberg, Mardall, which was primarily responsible for the construction phase services, but needed help. I was offered a position there as a project architect. My wife, Nancy, and I moved to London for two years and I worked on that project from the start of construction to its completion, which gave me some very good technical and field experience.

When I came back to Chicago, I became a studio head, which means I had my own studio here at SOM. I worked on projects like Banco de Occidente in Guatemala, and Grupo Industrial Alfa Headquarters in Monterrey, Mexico where I met Luis Barragán and Ricardo Legorretta and learnt a lot about contextualism from them. I was very interested in following through with the ideas I had learnt, such as designing buildings that fit their time and their place and feel culturally relevant and connected to the location within which they are placed. So I started practicing these new principles on Banco de Occidente. I became a partner in 1980 and since that time I have been responsible for the design and philosophical conception of all work under my direction.

So this was happening just around the time that Postmodern architecture was becoming popular?

Around 1982 I designed Olympia Centre on Michigan Avenue. It was my first mixed-use project, and the Neiman Marcus department store was the element that controlled the nature of the development and its aesthetic character. The Michigan Avenue façade was probably my first Postmodern building. It was trying to be a Modern building with a Postmodern stage set, I guess you could say. The tower was quite rational and contemporary and expressed the fluidity of a concrete tube system with a mixed-use development where different typologies required different lease spans. I worked with Fazlur Kahn on this concept and we were able to open up the structural tube at the top and in the center in order to create some more interesting and open spaces for the residential.

In 1984 I started working on the United Gulf Bank Building in Bahrain and Rowes Wharf in Boston. On both projects I was exploring the contextual approach to architecture, each project having a very different context.

With the United Gulf Bank Building in Bahrain, the context had much more to do with climate and culture. The culture was largely influenced by the nature of the nomadic Bedouin tribes and the pearl divers who until recently had a thriving pearl industry in Manama. They lived on large wooden pearl fishing boats called Dhows, which were pulled up on the beaches in Manama when not in use. They were very interestingly shaped boats with cloth canopies draped over them for sun protection. I drew upon these images for inspiration, and our site happened to look like a boat in its plan. I referenced several elements in the boat form and combined these with elements of solar control and thick, deeply punched concrete walls to form the concept of the building. If the observer really thought about it they could see similar shapes in the Dhows along the coast. Bahrain's setting is dominated by the wonderful emerald green water of the Arabian Gulf and the light beige sand desert, both of which form the basis for the materials used in the design. We used light troughs throughout the building's exterior wall to bounce light into occupied space while using Solex heat-absorbing glass fins to block reduce the solar heat gain from direct sunlight from the west. Although energy was very inexpensive in Bahrain, UGB was interested in finding all means to reduce energy consumption and increase the occupant's comfort through the mitigation of the effects of climate on the building.

At Rowes Wharf in Boston, I was trying to make the design relevant to this city that has a very strong historical context. I delved quite deeply into the history of the place and the city's fabric. The visual approach was very different from Bahrain but the philosophical approach of contextualism was still very similar. I wanted a building that felt like it could only go in that location and in Boston, and that would be so connected to the site that it felt like it had always been there.

There's been a transformation in my work since those days. I found that these buildings, and even NBC Tower and AT&T Corporate Center here in Chicago, were too representational of an earlier era. I started to look beyond location and the physical context for inspiration. This meant trying to relate the buildings to the technologies of the present time, and to add to the vocabulary of a city by using materials in more innovative ways.

At 10 Ludgate in London, a project I worked on in the early 1990s, the granite façade hangs in perpendicular slabs instead of being supported onto the face of the building as is typically done. I chose to express the thickness of the granite and to express it as a real curtain wall, and to open up the building's skin to expose the method of exterior wall construction. By doing so, it not only developed a new language for exterior wall expression, but did so in a manner sympathetic to the British mentality of Constructivism, since it related to their idea of composing the building out of parts rather than sculpting it out of a block. Less organic and more constructivist, the British loved it. I learnt a lot about using materials and construction techniques in unique ways to achieve more meaning than something that replicates earlier work.

That was probably my first significant departure from a traditional approach to contextualism. I don't shy away from the word Postmodernism but I was really looking for something more contextual, and the thing I disliked about most Postmodernism at that time is that it was a sort of cartoon Classicism. Many of the Postmodern buildings of that era took materials and cut them almost like foam core into cartoon shapes, without the richness of detail and shadowing that more traditional architecture embodied. I think the richness of detail is what's so wonderful about most of the older buildings, not necessarily the fact that they have a pediment or a pitched roof or some other thing. I was very interested in using the detail and working the detail into the façade at a human scale, the kind of scale that one could envision a craftsman being able to pick up and place on the building, like a brick or a piece of terracotta.

AT&T Corporate Center was your tallest building in the 1980s, and in the 1990s you designed Jin Mao, the tallest building in China. Between these two buildings there seems to be a very different approach to contextualism. What are some of the motivations that drove your contextual approach?

When we designed the AT&T Corporate Center in 1985 with our site very close to the Sears Tower, I felt that if we did a modern developer-type building it would be overpowered by Sears. I also felt at that time that

Chicago had undergone a long period of excessive modern intervention to the point where the historical fabric of the city was breaking down too much, becoming too eroded, to the point that the modern vernacular was in danger of becoming too commonplace. The city was turning into a collage of buildings rather than a synthesis. With both NBC and AT&T I wanted to rebuild the urban fabric. Not necessarily to make icons out of them but to make them part of a larger whole. NBC, designed in 1985, was probably a clear case because it uses the same materials as the Tribune Tower, 333 North Michigan, London Guarantee Building, and 35 East Wacker Drive. I was trying to make it part of a larger assemblage around the Michigan Avenue Bridge. AT&T was placed in another context where it was meant to connect with the Art Deco buildings of the central Loop, like the Civic Opera Building and the Chicago Board of Trade, and yet to do it in a way that Eliel Saarinen might have done it. It used the idea of contextualism in a fairly literal way, still using today's technology but reminiscent of past forms.

SOM has always been associated with structural engineering marvels such as the Sears Tower and the John Hancock Center. How does structural engineering play a role in the design of your work?

Structural engineering and mechanical engineering are both integral to the design of my work. I always start a project by having brainstorming sessions with my partners Bill Baker in structural engineering and Ray Clark in mechanical engineering. What I don't do is let them lead me into a solution where a structural engineering paradigm becomes the predominant idea of what the structure should be, because that approach is not always sympathetic to the context and use of a building. One of the significant challenges of the 21st century for architects will be to recognize the important contributions that can be made to architecture through the total integration of sustainable building concepts achievable by integration of HVAC systems with structure and architecture.

One of the complaints I have about buildings like the Aon Center is that here you have one of the world's tallest buildings, and yet the windows are only 5 feet wide at the top floor. You have height but you are boxed in with walls and can't really see out. It was the same with the World Trade Center. So I said, "Why not design towers with as much viewing capacity as possible, making them glassy and open?" It's been my challenge to engineers to devise structural systems that allow permeability. It started as far back as Olympia Centre, but at that time I hadn't learnt the flexibility that I'd have with structural engineering concepts. When Fazlur Kahn and

I were designing a building, as we designed it up toward the top I asked, "Can't we open some of this up and reduce the structure as we go higher where the gravity loads are less?" And Kahn said, "Yes, we can make it more like a basket as it gets toward the top; we can thin it out." So I put in some duplex units with much larger windows, which produced the unique open top of that building.

There was also a project that did not get built called Dearborn Center in Chicago, designed in 1989. Its structural system had a solid concrete core with eight super-columns around the perimeter so its views opened up as it rose to the 85th floor. This project expanded on the structural idea and massing attitudes we used for AT&T. Also, on the exterior wall we proposed the use of textured glass over mirrored surfaces to get a type of modern ornament for the spandrel surfaces, and we faceted the walls to orient the views subtly in one direction or another and to accentuate the center of the building.

Although the Dearborn Center project wasn't built, it had a strong influence on the Jin Mao Tower, designed in 1993. Except for the top, the fundamental shape and the floor plates are very similar. One of the main massing attitudes that Jin Mao borrowed from the Dearborn Center and AT&T was the way the building wall steps back as it rises to the sky. On AT&T there's a step at the 15th floor and at the 30th and 45th floors; it looked really appropriate on the model, on elevation studies and from the air, but when it was built I was disappointed because surrounding buildings block the first two setbacks. One only sees the last step, and so the composition of the tower doesn't appear to complete itself very well.

On Jin Mao, I tried stepping it back in eight-floor segments but I determined that this was too static. Then I tried modulating from larger stepped segments at the bottom of the tower to progressively shorter segments at the top. This approach solved for me the issue of the tower feeling complete even when the views of the lower levels were blocked by adjacent structures. The side effect of this stepping system is that, in some ways, it resembles the characteristics of the ancient pagoda forms used in the Chinese culture as burial towers. These were actually the first form of high-rise building.

A lot of people have made that comparison, which I suppose comes as no surprise. The comparison is direct. It wasn't meant to look like a pagoda but it was intended to invoke the memory of pagodas, in much the same way as the pyramid in the Louvre is a modern depiction of the ancient pyramids in Egypt.

How does contextualism relate to Trump Tower and Burj Khalifa?
That's a good question. On Trump Tower the heights of the surrounding buildings have an influence on the massing. The first setback relates to the Wrigley Building, the second setback relates to the height of Marina City and River Plaza, and the third setback relates to the IBM Building.

The texture of IBM influenced the texture of Trump, as did the rhythm and lightness of the Wrigley Building. I think the challenge in making this a contextual piece is that it's located in the middle of several dynamic buildings that each have their own importance to the city and to the field of architecture in general, so I was trying to synthesize the surrounding architecture by taking the IBM Building's delicate simplicity and yet rejecting its darkness.

In your interview on Chicago Tonight *you mentioned that the spire was decorative and was designed to help "uplift" the building.*
Yes, to give it a higher visual aspect ratio. I want to make the spire more dominant than it is as we move forward on the design.

There was a prior rendering that had a taller spire than what is on there now.
Yes ... well, we're going to make it taller than it is now.

What's the color of the skin going to be when finished?
It's going to be stainless steel and natural anodized aluminum.

Sort of like the Inland Steel Building?
Yes, it's going to have textured stainless steel spandrels with horizontal polished stainless steel tubes projecting about a foot out from the façade. The anchorage system for those tubes will be intricate, and the shadows and reflection from the tubes will give the skin a very lattice-like or lacy quality, similar to what was done at Jin Mao but not nearly as vociferous. I wanted Jin Mao to read as a solid metallic building, and I used as much metal as I could get away with.

Here I think it's all right to be glassy but I wanted an expression of depth to the wall and a lacy filigree appearance. With a glass wall that's fairly reflective, one can use the reflective nature of the glass to increase the sense of depth by hanging elements away from the glass and have those elements reflected in the glass to give the illusion of depth. In this case, it will reflect the projected tubes that surround the building, so it will seem as though the wall is 2 feet thick. The depth will give it a more solid but delicate appearance. I wanted to be neutral to the palettes of both IBM and the Wrigley Building.

Burj Khalifa is an interesting project because there is very little context for a building of this height to draw from in Dubai. The city has a lot of the same heritage as Bahrain—it's a historic Middle Eastern trading port with lots of desert and the same water conditions, but here I tried to build on a more cultural aspect of Dubai, relating to the desire of Dubai to create iconic local buildings and creating something very different. You know the onion dome shapes that you see in mosques and other buildings in Dubai, for example; we used these shapes but in plan, not in elevation. When seen by looking up from near the base from certain angles, one will see the onion dome shapes.

At the setbacks?

Yes, so if you point it out to someone who doesn't know about it they may say, "Ah-ha! I see what you're talking about!" The other aspect that relates to Dubai is the desert flower—the shape of the desert flower has three major petals and three minor petals. This is seen in plan and is a central organizing force in the building.

Will the building have lobes that might be seen from the top view?

Yes, the lobes at the base of the building are the entry vestibules to the various functions. From the sky looking down one will be able to see these elements and from directly over the tower one will be able to discern the shape of the flower. The base of the building will be very dense with a stainless steel latticework, which will have characteristics similar to the traditional moucharabie screens used in Islamic architecture. The traditional screens are typically made of wood, and they are used to block a lot of light and heat from coming into the spaces that they contain, giving this a filtered light quality to the interior space. Usually one can open pieces of the screen if you want to look out. The base of Burj Khalifa will be heavily screened on the first three or four levels to give it a dense metallic texture.

Will the building be a mix of concrete and steel?

The structure is 100 percent concrete below the spire but with a lot of steel reinforcing bars. The spire above the observation floors will be steel. Architecturally, the building will move from a solid base expression to a vertically expressed middle section of polished stainless steel projected metal fins. I wanted vertical elements here because of the extreme dust in Dubai's air. Sandstorms are frequent so this tower will have virtually no horizontal ledges to collect dirt. I learnt that from Jin Mao where there are so many horizontals that they had difficulty washing the building.

Burj Khalifa is going to be an incredibly tall building from the renderings I've seen. Can you tell us how tall you're going to build it?

Well, we want to keep it purposely under wraps so that nobody knows the height until it's finished. EMAAR, our client, definitely wants Burj Khalifa to be the tallest building in the world upon completion. We may include elements that can grow during construction, if needed. You know from the history of the Empire State Building and the Chrysler Building that height can be added during construction.

When you're building that tall, what kinds of challenges do you face? Because it seems to me that when you take it to that next level the economic challenges must be astronomical compared to other super-tall buildings such as Sears Tower?

Economics is a very important issue, and I'll get back to that but from a structural engineering perspective I believe we're pushing the limits of the height at which structures can be built profitably at this time. This one happens to be a concrete core with concrete arms going out toward the three legs of the building. We do believe that we have a project here that can make money for the developer at the time of completion because we are offering terrific condominium units of the highest standard with incredible views and at a very high efficiency of net to gross area. The combination of residential and hotel makes this a viable project economically. We have learnt this both from Tower Palace III in Seoul, South Korea and with the Trump Tower Chicago, both very tall buildings that are predominantly residential.

Is there any similarity to the bundled tube concept of Sears Tower and One Magnificent Mile?

No, and the structural concept being used in the Burj Khalifa structure could only be used in residential and hotel-type buildings because of the cellular nature of the floor plan. But it happens to be a very efficient and cost-effective structure because it's all concrete. Concrete is the cheapest and most rigid material for tall buildings. If this were done in steel it would move too much in the wind for a residential building.

I suppose it's no coincidence then that the highest residences you could have in a steel structure are those within the John Hancock Center?

Well, one could go taller than the Hancock in steel but the economics of the steel structure would be prohibitive given the stiffness that the structure would have to achieve. Super-tall building engineering is all about trying to eliminate the perception of movement within the building and getting the loads to the foundations.

Does that have to do with the better quality of concrete?

Well, that's interesting. This building has been engineered very carefully, and on super-tall buildings there are all sorts of factors that affect how the structure will work. For example, a building with the same shape of floor plate all the way up and down is not as good as a shape that changes as it goes up and down. And there's a phenomenon when the wind blows on a building: let's say the wind is blowing from the west—it will hit the west façade and it has to get around the building, so it starts moving up the wall, down, and around the sides. So the wind actually accelerates because it has to move not only the air that's blocked by the façade but also the air by the two sides. It's actually compressing the air as it's moving around the tower. This compression at the tower's edge and subsequent decompression on the back side of the tower creates eddies, or vortexes that can create stronger forces on the building then the wind itself and these forces tend to pull or rock the building from side to side and it is this acceleration of movement that we design to alleviate.

Was there anything remarkable about the way your design for Tower Palace III, Tower G in Seoul was designed to handle wind loads?

Yes. Basically the shape and skin texture of the building play an important role in vortex shedding because they can help to prevent the forces from building up in a harmonious way. The three-legged shape of the floor plan on Tower Palace III and Burj Khalifa give the building significant width to withstand horizontal movement and depth to buttress against the wind forces.

We've been through three wind tunnel tests on Burj Khalifa. One of the important things we learnt was that the taller legs that step back at a higher floor need to be on the sides of the prevailing wind rather than the front face because that sheds the vortexes more effectively. The texture of the façade and the weight distribution also affect how wind impacts the structure—for instance how much weight is at the top of the building, and where the columns are placed. We're still fine tuning it a lot.

Both Dubai and Chicago are cities where skyscrapers are not a real necessity, as in cities like Hong Kong where land constraints force their construction. What do you think drives these cities to build tall?

Well, the Burj Khalifa is being built for two reasons that I know. One, it's part of a much larger development where they're putting many smaller housing towers, hotels, and a very large shopping center into a 300-acre master plan, and they want the tower to create a critical mass for that whole development, which will add value to the rest of the parcels. They're also doing it as part of the country's desire to become a major tourist attraction. The city of Dubai wants to become a major hub in the Middle East and a tourist hub as well as a financial and trading hub.

More so than it already is I suppose?

Oh much more so, yes, they have big plans and the Emir of Dubai is doing everything he can to encourage great developments. He can do a substantial amount because he controls all the land.

And Donald Trump is, well, Donald Trump?

Yes, he's definitely in it to make money and they've done incredible business so far; the sales are going very well and it has exceeded everyone's expectations except for Donald's. He knew it was going to be successful. They have already sold a substantial number of units.

Any idea how the commercial portion has been doing since it got scaled back quite a bit?

They scaled it back, and they have a couple of tenants that are in pretty solid discussions now, and I wouldn't be surprised if it grew.

So there's still room to grow for Trump if he starts getting more office tenants looking for space?

Just a little bit. It can't grow that much more because of its structural system, but you could add two or three floors without it being a big problem. It also has a PUD in place that limits the height.

Thank you very much for this conversation.

Tom Finnegan is a Chicago-based Senior Editor of Emporis.com
Emporis is a provider of building-related data, and can be found at www.emporis.com.
Reprinted with permission.

Further insights into the work of Adrian D. Smith

Man of steel: able to leap tall buildings

By Kevin Nance, November 27, 2005

On opposite sides of the globe, and at the same time, two great towers are rising. One is Trump International Hotel & Tower, the most ballyhooed new skyscraper to be built in Chicago in decades. The other is Burj Khalifa, which promises to be the jewel of the United Arab Emirates and, by the way, the tallest building in the world.

These far-flung projects, expected to be complete in 2008, have much in common. Both are luxury hotel/condo buildings designed to appeal to the rich. Both have flamboyant, high-rolling billionaire developers, Donald Trump and Mohamed Ali Alabbar.

But what Trump Tower and Burj Khalifa mainly share is their principal architect: Adrian Smith of the Chicago office of Skidmore, Owings & Merrill.

Adrian who? So you might ask about the designer of two of the most eagerly anticipated building projects in the world today. Compared to peers such as Rem Koolhaas or Santiago Calatrava, Smith is relatively anonymous—partly because of his lack of a signature style, partly because his firm has always emphasized its corporate identity over that of its individual architects.

Who is Adrian Smith, and how did these two career-defining projects come to him at nearly the same moment?

Stretching the vocabulary

Born in Chicago—his father was a national manager for Montgomery Ward & Co.—Smith spent his formative years in San Clemente, California, before making his way back to the Windy City to study architecture at the University of Illinois at Chicago. In 1967, while still in school, he started working at SOM, where for several years he learnt the secrets of skyscraper design directly from Bruce Graham, architect of the Sears Tower and John Hancock Center.

Over the years, Smith steadily climbed up the firm's ladder, becoming a partner in 1980. By that time, influenced by Mexican architect Luis Barragán, Smith had become a devotee of contextualism: the idea that new buildings ought to relate to the geography, the culture, and especially the architecture immediately around them. This was a departure from the modernist ethic of legendary Chicago architect Ludwig Mies van der Rohe, which had produced several generations of boxy steel-and-glass buildings in what became known, tellingly, as the International Style. As the name suggested, such buildings could exist, more or less interchangeably, almost everywhere.

Smith went in the opposite direction. "I wanted real buildings that felt very much a continuation of the fabric of the city they were in," he says. "When I designed a building, I wanted it to look as if it could only exist in this location—it would be out of place anywhere else."

But the trap of contextualism is that an architect can pay so much attention to blending into his surroundings that he fails to develop a design vocabulary all his own. Avoiding the wild eclecticism associated with postmodernist structures by Michael Graves, Robert Venturi and others, Smith produced a series of buildings in the 1980s that worked hard—at times too hard, as he later thought—to fit in. Smith's project for Boston's Rowes Wharf (1982–1987) borrowed so much of the surrounding architecture's scale, historical detail (a neoclassical dome and rotunda) and materials (especially Boston's dominant red brick cladding) that it all but disappeared, absorbed into the cityscape as if in camouflage.

"Some of those buildings added depth and ornamental detail that had not been seen before, but they got uncomfortably close to replication instead of transformation," Smith admits. "I wasn't stretching the vocabulary."

The solution was not to jettison context altogether, but to apply it more loosely, putting it at the service of what began to emerge as a nascent personal aesthetic marked by increasing transparency and sleekness. Since the early 1990s, Smith has produced a series of designs that maintain his commitment to context, but do so within a relatively consistent framework of silver-blue skins of stainless steel and glass, dominant vertical elements and elegant tapering effects.

The most striking of these projects to date is Jin Mao Tower (1992–1999) in Shanghai, China. This 1380-foot structure, currently the fifth-tallest in the world, is a true Janus of a skyscraper. It looks back at Chinese architectural history—abstractly evoking the traditional pagoda with an ascending series of flaring horizontal elements that ring the tower's cylinder like bracelets—while aggressively conveying a sense of the technological present and future.

Which brings us to the Trump Tower and Burj Khalifa—and to the fact that, if not for certain tragic events in 2001, the two buildings might have been battling for the title of the world's tallest.

Very international, very Chicago

In 1999, Donald Trump, known for his opulent buildings in New York, Atlantic City and elsewhere, sent a team of representatives to inspect the Chicago Sun-Times building on North Wabash at the Chicago River as a possible site to build a new tower. His ear to the ground, Smith developed a few preliminary ideas for a building on the site. But nothing happened until the summer of 2001, when Trump announced a deal to go forward with a redevelopment plan.

What happened next was simple: Smith, who had never met Trump, picked up the phone and called the developer, inviting himself to New York to share his ideas. Smith went, Trump liked the ideas, and Smith was hired.

"He recognized that for a very tall tower, he needed a very experienced architect, and few people are," says Smith, 61. "It's a market niche I happen to occupy right now."

As Trump recalls the decision to bring Smith on board, it was both simpler and more complicated than a question of experience. "I loved his work," he says. "I thought it was both very international and very Chicago."

With Trump's blessing, Smith set to work on a design for a roughly 150-story building that would top out at 2000 feet—considerably higher than the world's current architectural peak, Taipei 101 in Taiwan.

It wasn't to be. On the morning of September 11, 2001, Smith was in an SOM conference room in Chicago, preparing to present his design to Trump's team. They were all sitting down to look at Smith's schemes, pinned on a wall, when they got word that an airplane had crashed into one of the World Trade Center towers. They went to a television and watched, aghast, as a second plane hit the other tower.

"Everybody was devastated," Smith recalls. "I remember one of Donald's people saying they'd looked at buying the World Trade Center, but had decided against it because it was a terrorist target."

The meeting broke up without considering Smith's design scheme, and the next day he received a call from Trump, who was adamant that the design had to be significantly downsized.

"I just didn't want to be in a position where I was building a building that was too tall in light of what happened on September 11," Trump says in an interview. "I realized that the great dream of the very tall building in this country should no longer be a dream."

With the new restrictions in mind, Smith's first design for Trump Tower was a stack of faceted parallelograms, which, when shown in a preliminary version, were not well received. He then smoothed away the design's sharp corners, cutting off 60 feet of mostly unusable space on each side, creating elegant curves and dramatic setbacks that divide the building into distinct vertical masses.

It's in those stepping-up setbacks, keyed to the heights of neighboring buildings, that Smith's contextualism subtly expresses itself, although most observers will perceive it subliminally, if at all. The step that defines the top of the tower's base is related to the nearby Wrigley Building. Moving up the tower, the next step connects to buildings across the Chicago River. Finally, the top step relates to Mies' IBM Building.

Later, with the design process well under way, Trump had second thoughts. "I realized I could take the existing building, and with very little difficulty, elevate the height by about 10 stories, and it would be taller than the Sears Tower," he says. "By that time we had passed $300 million in [condo unit] sales, and I wrote the buyers a note that said, 'We are able to create a building that would be the tallest in the U.S. What do you think?' The answer was a resounding 'Please don't do it.'"

Still later, however, Trump toyed with the idea of further heightening the tower by adding an elongated spire that would make it the tallest building in the world. He approached Smith, who put a damper on the concept, in part because he was already working for another developer on the world's tallest building: the Burj Khalifa.

"How tall is it?" Trump wanted to know.

"I can't tell you," Smith said. "It's a secret."

"Well, I'd like to get involved with that," an excited Trump said. "We could call it the Trump Burj Khalifa and make a killing!"

Going "as tall as I wanted"

The height of Burj Khalifa (which translates to "Dubai Tower") was in fact a fiercely held trade secret. Alabbar, Smith says, saw the tallest-building title as one of his main selling points in his drive to make Dubai, capital of the United Arab Emirates, the most sparkling tourist destination in the Middle East.

The focus on height was such that at one point, Smith says, he and Robert Booth, executive director of EMAAR, Alabbar's company, discussed the possibility of a hydraulically controlled spire that could be raised in case some other developer decided to, well, trump Alabbar with a taller building.

As has been often reported, Smith got the commission for Burj Khalifa by winning a design competition held by EMAAR. What isn't as widely known is that Smith himself set the guidelines for the competition. Indeed, Smith had something of an inside track from the beginning. The very day that Alabbar's team interviewed Smith in New York, it received an enthusiastic call from the developer, who had just visited Jin Mao in Shanghai; he also admired Smith's three-legged footprint for Tower Palace, a residential high-rise in Seoul, South Korea.

"We quite simply liked the design," Booth said. "It held the right proportions and was truly elegant and iconic, and would stand as a landmark for the city of Dubai."

But EMAAR had also interviewed several other architects and was unsure how to proceed. The company asked for input from Smith, who was happy to provide it. He proposed a competition with a two-week deadline—long enough for competing architects to come up with an idea, but not so long that they'd spend much money to develop it.

Smith's advantage was twofold: he knew roughly what Alabbar was looking for, and he also knew that as a large firm, SOM could work at warp speed. "We had the horsepower to produce a lot of work in two weeks—probably faster than anyone else."

But the most important ace in Smith's hand was that he had clear vision of what his Burj Khalifa would look like: a slender, tapering, dizzyingly tall building with a tripod-like footprint that EMAAR would eventually compare to a Middle Eastern desert flower. Here, in fact, Smith's contextualism was an afterthought. Since there was almost no geographic or architectural context in the still-emerging city of Dubai, he'd actually been thinking of Chicago's tripedal Lake Point Tower.

He was also thinking, vaguely, of another metropolis: the forest of gleaming towers that is the Emerald City, as glimpsed by Dorothy and her friends from the poppy field in the film version of *The Wizard of Oz*.

"That was in my mind as I was designing Burj Khalifa, although in a subliminal way," Smith says. "I didn't research the way it looked—I just remembered the glassy, crystalline structure coming up in the middle of what seemed like nowhere. The funny thing is, I didn't remember it being green."

After winning the competition, Smith set about developing the design and quickly ran into trouble in connection with its height. EMAAR executives had wanted a building about 550 meters (1804 feet), in part because they viewed anything above that height as of diminishing economic benefit. But the essence of Smith's design was tallness and slenderness; he presented it at around 700 meters (2296 feet), but to Smith, even that felt too short.

"At the very top, it didn't feel like it was resolved properly," he says. "The top three or four layers felt like they were stuck on top rather than an extension of the vocabulary of the rest of the buildings. I kept adding height, and got to a point where it could be a more continuous extrusion of elements of the building below it, instead of feeling like a base and a top with no middle," he says. "Eventually, Mohamed allowed me to go as tall as I wanted."

Kevin Nance is the Architecture Critic at the *Chicago Sun-Times*
Reprinted with permission.

Trump is beefsteak; Dubai is frosting

By Kevin Nance, November 27, 2005

One is a handsome but matter-of-fact and oh-so-muscular skyscraper for the City of Big Shoulders, its elegant sheen barely disguising its underlying assertion of power and practicality—a brawny Teamster in an opera cape. The other is a desert dream, impossibly tall and slender, a dazzling mirage come to life as if from the pages of *The Arabian Nights*.

Chicago architect Adrian Smith's design for the Trump International Hotel & Tower fits perfectly into the ethos of a city that works hard and plays harder: excellent quality but not too fancy, like an expense-account beefsteak cooked just right. His design for Burj Khalifa, in the United Arab Emirates, looks like something Samuel Taylor Coleridge might have conjured up in an opium-induced fugue: mythic, ethereal, Romantic with a big R.

Trump Tower appears brazenly technological, its 60-foot setbacks creating an ascending series of stacked masses—base, middle, top—that may remind viewers of a sleek, stretched-up Cuisinart. Burj Khalifa feels organic and pliable, like frosting extruded from a pastry bag.

Trump Tower is of the here-and-now. Burj Khalifa (as befits a design rumored to have been the inspiration for certain buildings in George Lucas' *Star Wars: Episode III—Revenge of the Sith*) is of some distant past or perhaps never-to-be-arrived-at future.

Trump Tower will be welcomed into the Chicago skyline like an old friend. Burj Khalifa looks like a building that ought not to exist.

How unexpected, then, that the two designs actually have so much in common. Their skins, for example: they share the same silver-blue curtain wall, the same stainless steel spandrels and mullions, the same part-transparent, part-reflective glass (though the Dubai building will appear less transparent and more reflective during the day because of the brighter desert light). They're as much alike, in that sense, as Ludwig Mies van der Rohe's IBM Building and his twin apartment towers at 860–880 N. Lake Shore.

Trump and Dubai are also both structural engineering marvels: massive buildings that float above moist foundations with the help of caissons drilled between 40 and 110 feet into the solid earth, supporting reinforced concrete columns.

Both are complicated, although Burj Khalifa is more so. Because of its extreme height, for example, it required a "sky lobby" system, similar to that of Chicago's John Hancock Center, in which residents will be required to transfer from one elevator to another, sometimes more than once, to reach their apartments. At the much shorter Trump Tower, residents will be able to zip from the ground floor straight to the penthouse, no pitstops necessary.

But the fundamental differences between the two buildings are related to history, vision, nerve, and Smith's own evolving relationship with his contextualist ideals. He designed Trump Tower in the jittery aftermath of the September 11 attacks, a period when American developers were understandably loathe to reach too far into the sky. Mohamed Ali Alabbar, Smith's client for the Dubai project, apparently faced no such constraints, or at least saw his way clear to minimize them.

And where Trump is famous for his determination to stretch a dollar, Alabbar was willing to indulge Smith's desire for extra height for the sake of Burj Khalifa's proportions, even though it wasn't strictly cost-effective.

Then there was Smith's philosophy of adapting to local contexts, which had the effect of guiding the Trump design toward assimilation and continuity with the mainstream of Chicago architecture. In Dubai, a city in which most commercial structures were built within the last decade, there was little context to adapt to; instead, Smith seems to have relied, perhaps more completely than in any previous project, on artistic instincts given free rein to experiment and dream.

The result is that Burj Khalifa is by far the more fabulous (and fabulist) of the two buildings, an aesthetically magnificent, if perhaps less than entirely practical, masterpiece. That isn't to say that Smith's Trump Tower design doesn't have its own brand of genius. Necessity often mothers the best kind of architectural invention, and in this case, given the parameters he was handed, Smith has acquitted himself with considerable style, wit and panache.

He's done us proud.

Kevin Nance is the Architecture Critic at the *Chicago Sun-Times*
Reprinted with permission.

Heritage Projects

Art Institute of Chicago, European Galleries Renovation

Location: Chicago, Illinois, USA
Client: Art Institute of Chicago
Year: 1986

The Art Institute of Chicago has its home in an early 20th-century Beaux-Arts building designed by Shipley and Bullfinch. A series of additions by Shaw Metz in the 1950s modified the character of the interior spaces by removing all moldings and installing a minimal lay-in translucent ceiling or, in some cases, a painted ceiling. On the second floor of the main building, the European galleries contain a very important collection of art ranging from early Renaissance Classical paintings to late Impressionist paintings. The original circulation system for these galleries had been removed and replaced with storage closets and mechanical rooms, leaving the circulation from salon to salon up to visitors. Many of the rooms were dark and illuminated only with incandescent downlights of inferior quality.

Under the direction of James Wood, the Director of the Art Institute of Chicago at that time, we developed a strategy to remove the closets and mechanical rooms on the Gallery floor and replace the circulation system, developing the circulation ring as a series of spaces that would exhibit drawings of the finished Masters' works in the main salons.

We also researched the type and scale of moldings that would have been used in galleries of this scale and replaced the minimalist 1950s base-plates, frameless doors and one-inch lay-in ceiling frames with moldings and panels appropriate to the rooms' scale. In addition, we replaced the acrylic translucent panels with a UV protection layer and a special light-directing lens that filtered the natural daylight and created a more consistent daylight throughout the gallery spaces. Gallery colors were chosen for their suitability to the art in each room. All moldings and frames were painted a mid-tone gray. The result is a gallery space that belongs to this Beaux-Arts building and to the era in which the art itself was created.

The mechanical system was removed from the exhibit space and a new system was installed using the attic space. The air supply and returns were integrated into the frames of the corridor in a seamless manner and are not noticeable in the new renovation.

AT&T Corporate Center/USG Building

Location: Chicago, Illinois, USA
Client: Stein and Company, Richard Stein
Year: AT&T 1986–1989; USG 1989–1992

AT&T chose the team of Stein and Company and SOM from a limited field of developers and architects in a competition process to both design its new headquarters, and consolidate space for its 38,000 employees on an 85,000-square-foot site in Chicago's Loop.

The plan for the site allowed for two phases: the 60-story, 1.7-million-square-foot building to house the 1-million-square-foot AT&T headquarters; and a 35-story, phase II 1.1-million-square-foot building, originally planned for AT&T expansion but later built as the headquarters for USG. The two buildings create a continuous urban façade, with each tower emerging from the 16-story base to form a separate and distinctive profile on the skyline.

At the pedestrian level, the two buildings are perceived as a single composition. A sequence of public rooms distinguishes the ground level with a two-story retail concourse joining the AT&T Corporate Center with the USG Building through an atrium. The lobby space of the ground floor is composed as a series of grandly scaled rooms, finished in oak and marble. It was completed in the grand tradition of the European great hall with a 34-foot-high ceiling in its Monroe Street entrance, and a 26-foot-high Franklin Street lobby. They are clad in Italian marble, gold leaf, satin-finish bronze and American oak wood trim.

The lobbies for the AT&T & USG Buildings are connected to provide a through-block passageway from Monroe Street on the north to Adams Street on the south. This through-block arcade is common to several buildings in the Loop, including the Field Building on LaSalle Street, the Commonwealth Edison Building, Marquette Building, Northern Trust, and many others in Chicago.

When conceiving this complex, it was important to re-establish the traditional texture of stone and glass—used in the Chicago construction boom of the 1920s—as a counterpoint to the black anodized aluminum and bronze glass Sears Tower immediately adjacent to the south. In doing so, a reference is made to the genesis of this style; the design submission for the Tribune Tower Competition in 1922, designed by Eliel Saarinen.

This building was never realized but greatly influenced the entire Art Deco movement. It had a restrained elegance and simplicity about it, and it embodied the kind of detail, scale, and texture that are not found in modern architectural styles. The components of base, middle, and top contain human-scaled features that people can identify with and relate to. By relating this complex to the traditional fabric of the city, it allows Sears Tower to stand as the exception to the predominantly masonry and stone context that surrounds it, thus making the Sears Tower more of a special intervention as a full block user.

Phase I, the AT&T Corporate Center, is a composite structure, with a poured-in-place concrete exterior tube, steel columns at the core, and steel horizontal members. Phase II, the USG Building, features a structural system that is based on an exterior steel frame combined with a poured-in-place concrete core. The tapered building mass reduces the bulk of the building by adding visual relief at the third points.

The corners and centers are articulated to emphasize a layering of the building skins. Night lighting is set on each setback ledge giving a glow to the stone façade above. Special 20-foot-high exterior light fixtures mounted on the central columns at each setback and at the entry help to center the massing of the composition at night. The exterior wall is modulated by two-story punched openings in an effort to increase the verticality. Special extruded aluminum mullions overlap at the top and bottom of each opening and are visually connected by dark granite vertical bands that further emphasize the vertical character of the wall. The two different building crown designs are both executed in aluminum and glass.

AT&T Corporate Center establishes a connection to the memorable towers of Chicago, particularly the massive buildings typical of the business district centered on LaSalle Street. The tower sits on a strong, highly articulated granite base of five stories with a monumental entrance on Monroe Street. The granite tower sets back at the 29th and 44th floors, where 5-foot setbacks relate to historic datum and taper the building

mass. The building changes in color from deep red at the ground floor, to lighter red from floors two through five, to a light rose color from the sixth floor to the top. Recessed spandrels and accent pieces are deep green granite with a decorative abstract pattern.

The AT&T Corporate Center takes full advantage of state-of-the-art structural and mechanical systems and its architecture expresses these contemporary advantages through various means such as the extensive use of glazing.

Interior storefront windows, columns and portals are trimmed in white oak. Three chandeliers illuminate the lobby. The elevator core is unique in this building in that the points of entrance are at two different levels. At grade level, two banks of shuttle elevators take passengers to the 29th floor sky lobby and the 44th floor sky lobby, at which point they transfer to a 15-level local elevator system. To access the first elevator zone of the building, one takes the escalators to the second floor where there is a secured entrance point and reception area for AT&T personnel and guests. When arriving at this level, there are four circular openings that recall the circular features in the 1980 AT&T Headquarters in New York designed by Philip Johnson.

While the silhouette of both the AT&T and USG buildings is evocative of the era of great skyscrapers, the execution of the details is unmistakably contemporary. The material palette chosen for the AT&T Corporate Center is carried through in the USG Building, providing a unified sense of elegance as one moves through the public spaces between the two towers.

NBC Tower at Cityfront Center

Location: Chicago, Illinois, USA
Client: Tishman/Speyer Properties
Year: 1985–1989

The NBC Tower was the first structure to be built within the Cityfront Center master plan, conceived by Alex Cooper with SOM as master architect. As such, it played an important role in demonstrating the physical guidelines for height, density, setbacks, and relationship to the streets surrounding the tower.

The Cityfront Center master plan is a multi-phase, 50-acre development conceived as a link between Chicago's burgeoning near north side and the Loop. Guided by a desire for neighborhood improvements to benefit business tenants, residents, and pedestrians alike, the tower is thoughtfully integrated within the historic Michigan Avenue Bridge District, an area highlighted by the Wrigley Building, the Tribune Tower and Pioneer Court.

The area of the tower is approximately one million square feet. It is 40 stories high and contains a four-story bustle that houses a free-span studio for live and taped broadcasts from NBC. The design of the building is meant to extend the character of the existing 1920s landmarks located at the intersection of Michigan Avenue and the Chicago River through the use of similar setbacks, similar use of materials, human scale details, centered compositions, and a clear reading of entrance, both from close up and from afar. At the same time, the building is not meant to be a pastiche of earlier styles and should be true to its own structural expression and contemporary function within. Previous to this building, developers in the Modern era felt that a building with intricate detail and use of small-scale stone elements over the entire façade was prohibitively expensive and could not be pursued.

When first confronted with the design, Jerry Speyer, the developer of the NBC Tower, was visibly upset by what he thought was an extravagant and unfordable scheme until David Hoffman, the construction manager at Morris Diesel Construction Company vouched for the scheme and confirmed that it was on budget. The budget for this building was $60 per square foot in 1985, and it came in on budget.

The building's formal gestures are reminiscent of the RCA Building at Rockefeller Center in New York, a particularly apt association as RCA is NBC's parent company. There, however, the setbacks are intended to be read as parallel to the central slab, whereas at NBC, the concept is one of a series of parallel planes oriented north–south and articulated by limestone piers penetrating the central east–west mass of the tower. This massing meets the needs of a wide range of tenants by providing a flexible, column-free floor plan, and varying floor areas that range from 29,670 square feet at the widest part of the tower to a 14,920-square-foot penthouse level.

The setbacks in the east–west direction are structurally simple, since one simply stops building the columns and beams as it steps back. However, the setbacks on the north–south direction are major transfers and the exposed buttresses are load-bearing concrete transfer columns that take the load from above and transfer it outward to the wider lease spans of the lower floors.

In addition, the massing at grade conforms to the scale of the street-level pedestrian activity. The series of setbacks that define the tower profile are consistent with earlier Chicago zoning requirements that influenced the traditional Chicago buildings along the Chicago River. Alternate use of limestone piers and recessed double-glazed bronze glass and coated precast panels to resemble terra cotta give the façade both depth and vertical expression. Major entrances on the east and west façades are detailed with bronze metalwork and are accentuated by a bowed central window that extends the entire height of the building. The NBC Building's architectural design and use of materials set the standard for the development of the remainder of the Cityfront Center development.

One particularly key detail of the Tower is the use of unfinished saw-cut small pieces of Indiana Limestone for the entire exterior of all columns. It was initially budgeted as an architectural precast finished exterior; however, I felt that by using a small limestone pattern with a simple saw-cut finish (like the finish of the Tribune Tower next door), instead of the milled finish common on most limestone buildings of the day, I would be able to afford to clad the building in a higher quality material. One problem we ran into yielded an equally inventive solution. The reason all limestone is run through a planer is to give it a constant thickness, which is important in setting it up on the building. I discovered that if we laid the stone flat on a bed and poured concrete into a form on top of it, the problem of thickness would not be an issue since the concrete would form around the varying sizes and depths of the stone and would also become the backup for erection, alleviating the need for tedious scaffolding and masonry work. The precast panels could simply be lifted up off the truck by the tower crane and placed on the column.

Rowes Wharf

Location: Chicago, Illinois, USA
Client: Stein and Company, Richard Stein
Year: 1982–1987

The Rowes Wharf project began as a competition in late 1982 with an open invitation to developer/architect teams to submit their qualifications. Phase two of the competition limited the invitation to eleven teams, including architects Cesar Pelli, I.M. Pei, KPF, The Architects Collaborative, Stubbins, and SOM. These teams all submitted first-stage schemes to the Boston Redevelopment Authority (BRA) and the City, the owners of the land, and three teams were shortlisted for further consideration and development. The shortlisted teams, I.M. Pei, Cesar Pelli, and SOM, all developed their concepts to a more complete level and each gave verbal public presentations.

The team of the Beacon Companies and Skidmore, Owings & Merrill LLP was selected as the winner, both for the nature of the development proposal and the quality of design. Our final concept was submitted with two towers at a height of 192 feet, 27 feet higher than the guidelines would allow. One of the conditions of our acceptance was a requirement to reduce the tower height to 165 feet. We agreed and proceeded to reform the Atlantic Avenue building into one integrated piece by taking the area from the two towers and placing it over the central view corridor and open space. This later developed into a public observatory under a large dome, which was supported by four arches, forming a major covered public space.

Many meetings were held with the developer, The Beacon Companies, led by Norm Leventhal, Ed Sidman, Alan Leventhal, Mark Leventhal, Jim Becker, and Carl Gladstone. Monthly in-progress reviews were held with the BRA (Bob Kroin) and a design committee from the Boston

Society of Architects, The Beacon Companies, and SOM during all phases of development. Periodic meetings were held with the Boston Preservation Alliance, the excursion boat operators (Bill Spence), and other organizations that had an input into the process.

The meetings with the BRA were of critical importance to the development of the final scheme; it was in this forum that trade-offs were made allowing for more area above grade in return for higher quality architectural development. Through this mechanism we were able to define gross building area to the glass line instead of the face of the outside wall, thus allowing for a deeper window setback and greater exterior wall thickness. This led to the development of the exterior fabrication of precast window units (for depth) and brick infill at most columns and spandrels. Using precast allowed for an inexpensive integration of detail and ornament.

There was a great deal of research on this subject, since cast ornament had not been used in buildings since the 1920s and the level and scale of detail using precast was unknown. But by using vibrating tables for the fine-scale ornament, we were able to form extremely fine details at very little cost premium.

Within the composition of the project, the ends of the finger piers and the tops of the towers facing each other became very important elements. These elements were designed as curtain wall construction in white framework to allow for more contrast and more visibility from afar, in order to punctuate the silhouette of the complex and to identify the complex as belonging to the late 20th century, not the late 19th century. Much like the white painted church spires and bay windows that permeate old

Boston, these features add contrast and complexity to the composition. They also open up key points of view from highly desirable spaces within the development. This vocabulary of framework was also integrated into the ground floor of the project in the form of storefront windows and entrances to office, residential, commercial, and hotel functions.

Throughout the design, the ferry terminal pavilion went through the most expansive series of modifications on the project, with the possible exception of the central space. At one time it was a two-storied, stepped and layered piece with a skylight dome. (A similar dome was used by Norman Foster on the Reichstag Dome in the 1990s). It was connected to the main complex by a series of open lattice colonnades that also formed Rowes Walk. These elements, along with the two-story pavilion concept, were later abandoned as inappropriate to the essence of the concept. Monumental, custom columnar light fixtures were used to give definition and reduce the scale of the walkway.

The walkway was conceived from the start as a public space that would connect the building sites to the north and south and allow the public to have full access to the water's edge. This project was conceived as a 100 percent accessible facility and to emphasize this feature, a grand ramp connects the upper walkway (Rowes Walk) with the lower waterfront walkway that circulates around each finger pier building.

When considering the Rowes Wharf site, the most notable characteristic of Boston's central area was the way the city seemed to have a red glow in the sunlight. It's a very red city, perhaps more so than any other. The red brick seems to engulf its occupants. A further consideration was the street pattern of Boston. The central Boston circulation pattern has evolved over a considerable period of time into a radial system. The use of landfill in the harbor over the years has enlarged the city into a loosely organized series of rings with roads coming out from its center. What is particularly interesting is how buildings have maintained a zero lot line, where the shapes of the buildings have conformed to the roads that they front. This creates a special character where the building elevations are the walls of the public space, creating a stone maze as the building façades change with differing road configurations.

Where Boston's central area meets the harbor, the spokes of the road pattern turn into linear buildings that protrude into the harbor. Many of these structures were wharf buildings used for the storage of goods and have since been modified into housing, offices, and retail spaces. They create a very distinctive edge to the city with buildings and water alternating to form a fringe where the city meets the water.

Boston's skyline is like a tent with the tallest buildings in the center, and adjacent buildings stepping down. The city's form was a major determinant in establishing the massing of Rowes Wharf with the taller buildings at Atlantic Avenue, and the shorter wharf buildings stepping down toward the harbor. Rowes Wharf accommodates a complex program of offices, condominium residences, a hotel, health club, restaurants, below-grade parking, retail spaces, and facilities for private and commuter boats. The buildings comprise 665,000 square feet on a 5.38-acre land and water site, two-thirds of which is devoted to open space.

By continuing the urban façade established by the two buildings immediately to the south of the site, the building connects with the traditional texture of the city. The private domain of hotel, residential, and commercial uses is enclosed by a continuous habitable wall. By following the curve of Atlantic Avenue, this wall reinforces the street edge and further defines the street as the primary element of the public domain. Unlike the free-standing apartment towers next door, which disrupt the continuity, Rowes Wharf reinforces it. It restores the urban fabric, shares in the public realm, and establishes continuity with the traditional city. On the waterfront, the tradition of finger piers is also continued with the wharf buildings. The ferry pavilion enhances public use and prolongs the viability of the waterfront as a public amenity.

The BRA, the primary agency responsible for review and oversight of this project, mandated a 50-foot-wide, three-story-high visual corridor through the site to provide views of the harbor from Broad Street. This led to the design of Foster's Court, the centerpiece of the composition. Framed by four monumental arches, Foster's Court punctuates the habitable wall, making a gateway from the water to the city. This has been developed into a major public space, both a passage and a gathering place. The importance of Foster's Court as part of the public realm is signified by its monumental scale and its interpretative use of classical elements: the dome, pilasters, and the arch.

The intention was to make the somewhat self-effacing urban façade a background to the public domain of the street and the harbor: a wall enclosing the public room of the city and the waterfront. The twin towers, whose height was limited to 15 stories by BRA guidelines, are therefore rendered in a traditional, almost vernacular manner to symbolically represent and literally enclose the private realm.

Like the traditional wharf buildings, which have served Boston Harbor for more than two hundred years, the wharf buildings at Rowes are very straightforward—almost industrial in their appearance. They extend a welcome to those approaching the city by boat, and frame the arched centerpiece that is the gateway to the city. The ferry terminal pavilion is placed on axis with the Broad Street vista, establishing its importance as a public symbol, and a point of arrival, reinforcing its connection to the larger urban context.

An innovative construction technique involving up-down construction was implemented for the main building site of Rowes Wharf. This allowed the structural steel superstructure above grade to be erected immediately upon completion of the caisson foundations. The multi-level, reinforced concrete substructure was simultaneously constructed as excavation extended downward below the ongoing superstructure construction.

Specially encased highly durable steel pilings support a precast concrete raft just above the harbor water level to form the bases of the office, residential, and terminal structures that extend out over the harbor. Structural steel construction was used for these buildings, minimizing foundation loads. A precast concrete dome system was used for the main pier terminal building. Floating pile restrained docks are adjacent to the piers for easy boat accessibility under all tidal conditions.

Washington University Psychology/Biology Laboratory

Location: St. Louis, Missouri, USA
Client: Washington University (Dick Roloff, Vice Chancellor)
Year: 1993–1995

When I first met Dick Roloff, he was a developer of shopping centers in Clayton, Missouri. In 1994 I contacted Dick, who at that time was the Vice Chancellor of Washington University in charge of the expansion, design, and construction of the campus. Dick was a traditionalist and believed that the main campus, a product of a master plan by Cope and Stewardson in the Campus Gothic style, should be maintained.

Washington University is a magnificent campus, constructed almost entirely of Missouri red granite blocks with limestone trim, slate roofs, many brick chimneys, and metal windows. The existing buildings are positioned to form small, intimate courtyards where students can gather and sit.

The site, on top of a hill and overlooking St. Louis, was the setting for the 1904 World's Fair. The Brookings building, the main administration building for the campus, was built for the fair. Dick asked me if I would

be interested in designing a new building for the psychology department; I said yes, and he put me on the list of architects to be interviewed for this project. During the interview I talked about the context, the traditional use of materials, the importance of detail and human scale, and the importance of durability and longevity of the building. Also discussed were the state-of-the-art laboratory facilities that would have to be flexible enough for either wet or dry laboratories, since psychology can be either a wet or a dry science, depending on the point of view of the department head. The interview went well and we got the job. I knew nothing about labs but we hired Josh Meyer, a principal at laboratory experts GPR, to become our team's lab consultant.

The project is located on the south side of the campus next to the existing biology building and in front of the 1960s Monsanto building. One of the goals of this project was to establish a gateway or entrance from the south side of the campus where the president's residence is located. In doing so, it was important to mask the view and presence of the Monsanto building, since it is incongruous with the architecture of the rest of the campus. This was achieved by creating a pass-through at the ground floor of the tower and marking this entry with a tower that would identify this campus point of entry from afar.

The ground floor of the psychology building is used as administration offices and the animal storage entrance point. The four floors above grade are all laboratory spaces with a central circulation and services spine. These floors are unique as lab floors since they have all services needed for laboratory functions on the perimeter as well as the central spine to provide ultimate long-term flexibility.

Banco de Occidente Headquarters

Location: Guatemala City, Guatemala
Client: Banco de Occidente
Year: 1978–1981

In 1964, Hurculano Aguirre, a wonderfully polite and gentle man who was the owner and chairman of a small bank in Guatemala City, visited Nina, Wisconsin to view the opening of the Nina Bank Building, a wonderful piece of architecture by Bruce Graham. Many years later, as a result of that meeting, Mr Aguirre came to us for the design of this facility.

Three buildings were constructed in Guatemala City for one of the oldest banking institutions in Guatemala. The largest of these is in the center of the city's oldest section, Zone 1. The others are suburban branch banks.

The goal of the bank was to establish a new image and identity in Guatemala City, with the branch banks having a common but varied relationship to each other, so their identities and services could be customized to meet their customers' needs. To that end, a common palette was developed where materials, furniture, fabrics, teller counters, and logo identification would be similar from zone to zone, but each would be used in different ways.

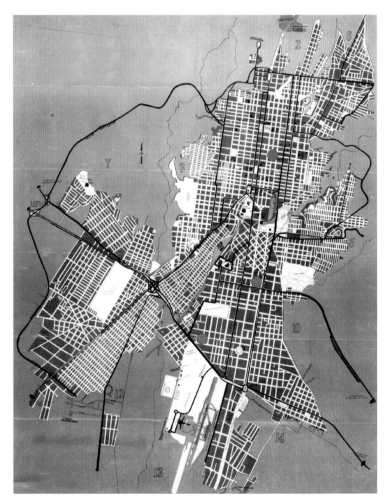

Programming for the Zone 1 regional headquarters required maximum teller and public contact areas on level 1, executive offices, boardrooms, and semi-public contact on level 2, and an employee lounge and non-public space on level 3.

The design solution incorporated an interior and exterior courtyard, a two-story banking room, and predominantly opaque stucco walls at the exterior to minimize the amount of street noise entering the building.

A local volcanic stone base at street level minimizes vandalism and provides a more durable surface in this area of high pedestrian traffic.

Terrace openings to the north and setback openings on the west control light. Operable wood louvers modulate ventilation, while the courtyard is covered with a translucent fabric roof to allow soft light to enter the interior.

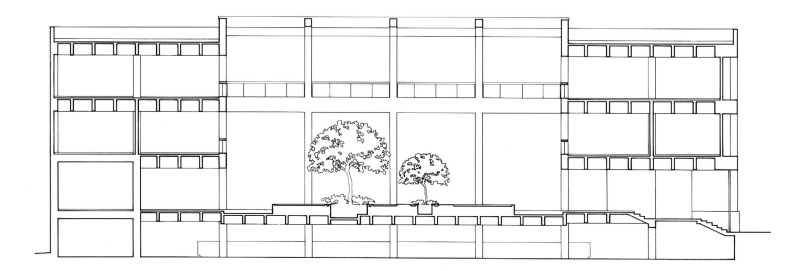

Architectural continuity was sought through the use of indigenous colors, textures, materials, light, and shadow. Local architectural concepts of open courtyards, terraces, gardens, fountains, and trellises were integrated into each design to reinforce the building's relationship to the Guatemalan context. Patterns of light and shadow on wall surfaces, and the reflective properties of water and tile were included to impart a sense of openness and serenity.

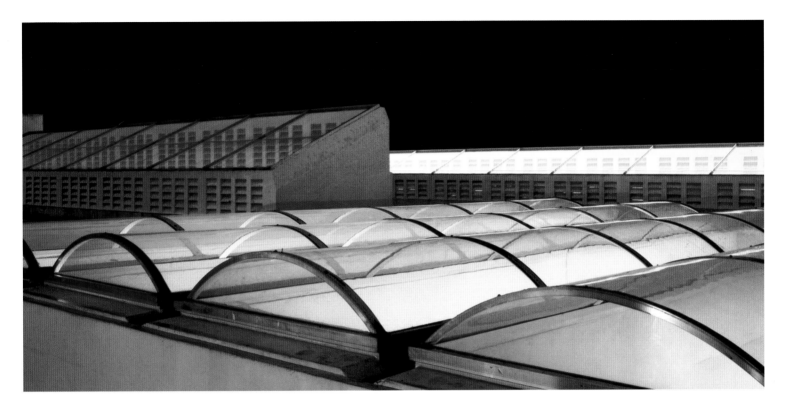

The goal was to achieve a functional and economic design for these projects through the studied adaptation of traditional concepts and materials within the context of contemporary architecture. This approach has been overlooked in most urban and rural reconstruction projects in Guatemala.

The predominant local materials used were concrete and concrete block faced with stucco, small volcanic stone pavers, mahogany wood, and locally available fabrics and glass. Construction involved labor-intensive, low-technology methods. The structures were all poured-in-place, reinforced concrete one-way joint systems with exterior shear walls to resist earthquake forces.

Located on a long narrow property fronting an arterial street, the 10,000-square-foot Zone 9 branch is bordered on both sides by continuous, low quality, commercial shopping. As the site is only accessible from the street, the program called for a drive-in banking facility.

The skylights placed along the bank teller wall are parallel to the long east–west axis of the facility. As the sun rises in the east it casts long horizontal shadows on the terrace wall. As the morning progresses toward noon, the shadows become vertical. The shadows continue to lengthen until the sun sets. This motion of light on the wall is like a sundial that animates the interior space.

The location of the reflecting pool in front of the main entry to the bank allows the visitor to look over the pool and see the activity of the main space. However, one must walk around the pool and the partial height wall before accessing the main room. This was done to compel the visitor to view the space from a different vantage point. The use of color in this branch is intended to add to the illusion of exterior space, particularly since this facility has no exterior exposure.

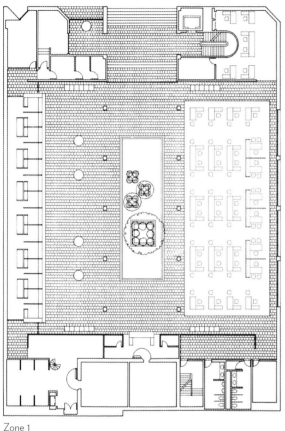

Zone 1

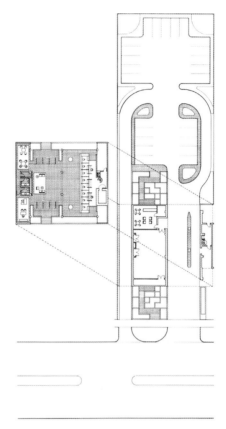

Zone 9

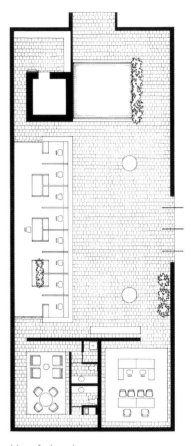

Montufar branch

Other components of the program included eight teller stations, and after-hours banking. The solution was to elevate the typical banking area above grade, depressing the drive-in to allow for automobile circulation under the banking space. The bank is accessed from the street and parking areas through symmetrically terraced and landscaped platforms. Eight large mahogany doors pivot at each entry to allow air circulation.

The Montufar branch is a small, eight-teller facility located on a property with existing party walls on all sides, and is accessible from two points through existing shopping centers. Skylights were designed to provide natural light and ventilation with minimal direct sunlight on work surfaces. Each skylight uses concrete block louvers for ventilation. In addition, a small open courtyard with a reflecting pool is used to increase the sense of openness, strengthening the illusion of the interior as exterior space.

Color is a pervasive essential ingredient to vernacular architecture in Guatemala, and my contextual approach to the design of these buildings would have been void without it.

Olympia Center

Location: Chicago, Illinois, USA
Client: Olympia & York, Chicago Superior & Associates, Equity Financial & Management Company
Year: 1978–1982

This project began with a meeting in the Los Angeles offices of Carter Hawley Hale, the owner of the land and the owner of Neiman Marcus. Also present were Michael Prentiss from Cadillac Fairview; Sam Zell, who was with us by telephone from the Golden Gate Bridge; Harold Walker, and me. The assembled team realized that this was a very valuable piece of land and that it could support a very large structure; however the office market was soft in this part of the city. It was decided at this meeting that the project should be a mixed use of retail, office, and condominium residential and thus we proceeded with the design work. Midway through the project the work stopped because of the failure of Carter Hawley Hale and Cadillac Fairview to come to terms on a development agreement; Sam Zell brought in Paul and Albert Reichmann from Olympia & York to continue the project. It should be noted that Fazler Kahn, the great structural engineering partner at SOM, was working with me on the development of the structural concept and it was his foresight that allowed the structural expression to be distinctive and unique.

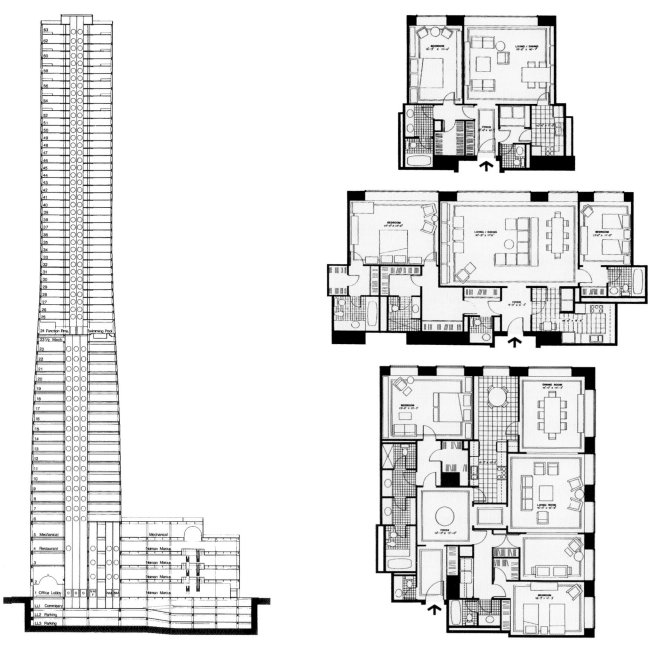

Section

Olympia Center is a major multi-use landmark on Chicago's Magnificent Mile. Sixty-three stories and 720 feet high, the 1.42-million-square-foot building incorporates 204 luxury condominiums, 327,000 square feet of office space, and a four-level basement parking garage. SOM provided architectural and engineering services for the development, as well as condominium and public space interior design.

The site is located on the east side of Michigan Avenue, between Superior Street and Chicago Avenue, and wraps around the 777 Michigan Avenue Building, fronting onto Chicago Avenue. Neiman Marcus occupies most of the grade level and all of levels two, three, and four.

Condominiums make up the top 39 floors of the tower. Level 24 is the Club level, providing condominium amenities including a lounge, party rooms and catering kitchen, swimming pool, locker rooms, exercise room, and a racquetball court. The 430-car self-park garage occupies three levels

beneath the tower and four levels beneath the south low-rise portion. A commissary and valet are located below the tower at lower level one.

The condominiums were designed to recall the graciousness and elegance of the turn-of-the-century Chicago apartments designed by Benjamin Marshall. A sequence of individually defined rooms is linked by a formally articulated circulation corridor. Bathrooms and dressing rooms are elaborate.

The building's massing combines low-rise and high-rise portions with the tower located on Chicago Avenue. By adopting this solution, the building's design preserves the low-to-middle-rise character of Michigan Avenue and Superior Street, reinforces the open space edge already existing along Chicago Avenue, provides better views for the condominiums located in the upper half of the tower, and allows the department store more freedom in structure and in layout.

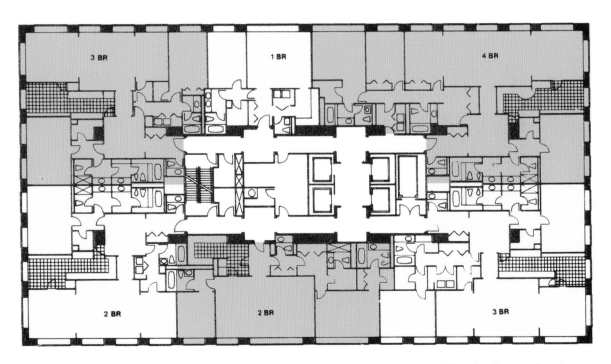

Typical condominium floor plan

A major feature of the tower design is the integration of clear span office space with an economical condominium structure. This is accomplished by maintaining a constant width of core structure while reducing the lease spans as the tower ascends, thus making a transition from the larger lease spans needed in the office space to the shallower lease spans at the condominium floors. This was done with the exterior concrete "tube" structure taking on a gentle curve at both the north and south sides of the building to give the building its distinctive form.

The tower structure combines a reinforced concrete exterior tube with conventionally reinforced concrete flat-slab floors in the condominiums, and a one-way joist slab floor system in the office, department store, and parking garage portions.

The exterior "tube" structure is conceived as a basket that expresses its horizontal and vertical forces. It is most dense at its base, where the department store is located, and as it rises through the office space.

At the first condominium floor the center of the tower is opened up to convey fewer forces and to provide a special feature in the center of the building useful for condominiums, thus providing corner units and center units with unique characteristics. This continues throughout the condominium floors until the tower begins to open up both vertically and horizontally where the "tube" action of the structure becomes minimal. This allows the top 12 floors to be open to views and provides double-height spaces, duplex living units, and very special units within.

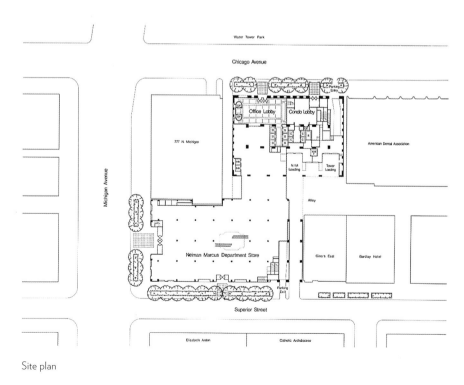

Site plan

Olympia Center   57

United Gulf Bank

Location: Manama, Bahrain
Client: United Gulf Bank
Year: 1982–1987

This 12-story, 100,000-square-foot office building located in the diplomatic quarter of Manama, Bahrain is responsive to its physical, climatic, and cultural context.

The three-story arcade at ground level creates an additional mediating layer, shielding pedestrians from the harsh sun, and from the dust, noise and heat of the street, continuing the tradition of arcades and shaded streets commonly found in the region. The large openings in the arcade occur opposite the entrances to the bank and the retail spaces. Smaller square openings, which also contain concealed lamps for night lighting, occur near the ground and at the mezzanine level. These openings are angled and flared in plan to modulate the daylight in the arcade. Projecting light shelves help illuminate the ceiling of the arcade using bounced daylight during the day and artificial light in the evening. Entering the building lobby, one is immediately aware of the lines from which the building geometry is derived. All lines converge at the semicircular glass mosaic fountain around which a spiral stair establishes the connection to the atrium floor one level up. Around this atrium is the cafeteria.

On typical floors a semicircular reception area recalls the spiral stair and fountain at the ground floor. These link the typical elevator lobby to the atrium while resolving the axial shift of the building. The typical floor plan is organized with the core elements located against the alley wall. There are two primary office zones: a private office zone along the exterior wall with views to the outside, and an open office zone around the atrium with views into the courtyard. An arcade composed of shelving and storage units, art display cases, and shutter doors separates these two zones. Ambient lighting can be provided artificially through lights installed in the private office coves and by means of indirect light bounced off the fabric ceilings in the open office areas. Task lighting is built into the typical, custom-designed workstations.

Recognizing the street as a figural space, the curved façade acts as a mediator between the public realm of the street and the private realm of the bank, while also evoking images of local fishing boats.

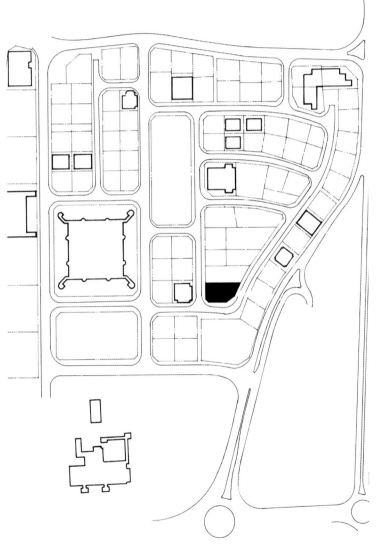

Site plan

The precast concrete exterior wall is responsive to issues of climate, context, and solar orientation. All windows are deeply recessed, blocking out high midday sun, while vertical green glass fins, oriented north–south, effectively intercept lower east and west sunlight while maintaining transparency. A very special feature of the typical wall, as seen from the interior of the private offices, is the way natural light is reflected onto the ceiling. This is accomplished with the use of a translucent glass panel above each vision glass, which emits a diffused light into the office space.

The light is then reflected onto the ceiling with an internal light scoop or reflector. This reflector blocks the view of the translucent glass from inside the office space in order to reduce the intensity of light coming from the panel and into the eyes of the occupants. If the light source was visible, it would shut down the pupils of the occupants and the rest of the room would appear dark.

The resulting effect is that natural light can be directed to the surfaces where it is needed most. Open office areas surround a 12-story atrium, bridged by glass block terraces that allow daylight to penetrate into all interior spaces, and which subdivide the atrium into four 40-foot cubes, breaking down the scale to that of a traditional Middle Eastern courtyard. External light is admitted to the atrium through a pattern of narrow slots in the thick northeast wall. At night, the terraces glow as hanging fixtures cast light both up through the glass block, and down to the atrium floor. The square at the center of each terrace contains a small pool that recalls the fountains in traditional courtyards.

Variations on a theme are seen in the progression from the typical floor levels through the management floor to the executive floor that contains the boardroom and the chairman's office and apartment. Ornament is used sparingly, in key locations such as mosaic fountains, wood ceiling elements in executive offices, and atrium air grilles, and is based on tight geometric patterns reminiscent of regional arts and crafts with contemporary and original interpretations.

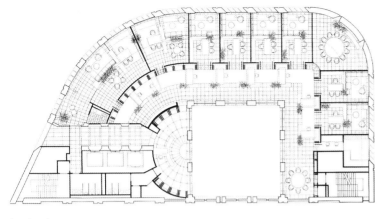

Level 9 plan

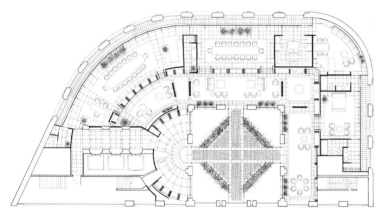

Level 5 plan

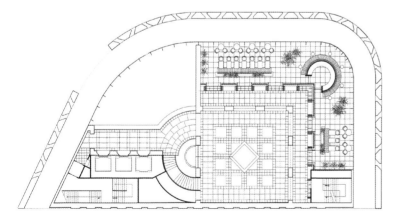

Ground floor plan

Each of the bank's façades responds uniquely to the orientation of the sun and the shape of the site, forming a sculptural whole that changes from every approach. The screen-like expression of the various exterior elevations is evocative of the moucharabie—the traditional latticed sunscreen, which provides daylight without heat and glare and affords views without sacrificing privacy—while reinterpreting the concept in an abstract way at a new scale. Both inside and out, ornamental motifs are abstracted from traditional patterns and are intrinsic to the overall concept and structure; they are not applied decoration. To paraphrase Louis I. Kahn, "ornament is the celebration of the joint."

Although the fishing and pearl industries have declined in Bahrain, the people still have boats—dhow—that they pull up on the beaches and live in. These boats have a distinctive shape. Our site, with its curved corners, has the same shape as the back of those boats. By holding the edge of the site, the building recalls a shape that is very much a part of the local context. The colors of the Bahrain landscape are incorporated into the building. The green Solex glass in the vertical fins, for instance, is the color of the Gulf and the color of the local sand was matched in the concrete to reflect the color of the desert and the indigenous architecture.

Concept development

The site is in the diplomatic district, a new section of Manama. Although many of the buildings in the area have been designed by local architects, the United Gulf Bank came to us, not seeking a typically American building of glass and steel, but wanting something that was rooted in indigenous Islamic architecture. We looked at several alternatives as we usually do during the early design stages. One alternative had a symmetrically curved form with an atrium and the core along the back, but the client said that it looked like a perfume bottle and it was rejected. Other schemes had the courtyard spaces along the outside wall of the building, but were eventually also rejected because it made more sense to use the atrium to bring light into the core of the building rather than use it where we already had light. We ended up using the placement of the core and atrium in the "perfume bottle" scheme but with an asymmetrically curved front that more closely followed the site.

We also studied various fenestration ideas, including a Corbusian scheme with precast brise soleil and schemes that packaged windows into double- and triple-story frames. We finally arrived at the idea of creating a wrapper wall with recessed windows.

We developed the light scoop fairly quickly. Since the flush glass at the front of the light scoop would have been the brightest surface in the room, we soon determined the shape and depth of the scoop by ensuring that the glass could not be seen from any point in the room. On the interior, the cove ceiling was originally shorter to provide plenum space for ductwork, but we eventually moved the cove back to bring daylight deeper into the space.

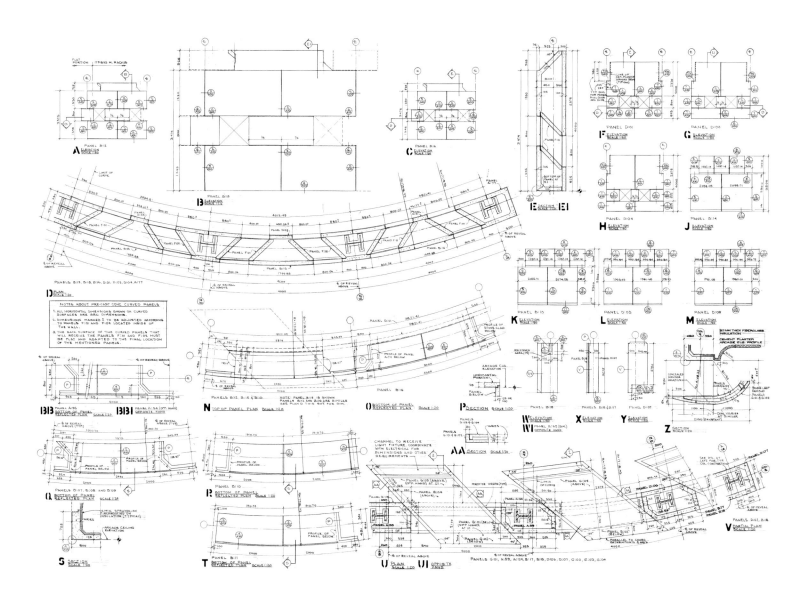

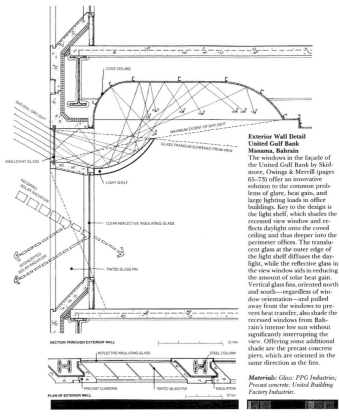

**Exterior Wall Detail
United Gulf Bank
Manama, Bahrain**
The windows in the façade of the United Gulf Bank by Skidmore, Owings & Merrill (pages 65–73) offer an innovative solution to the common problems of glare, heat gain, and large lighting loads in office buildings. Key to the design is the light shelf, which shades the recessed view window and reflects daylight onto the coved ceiling and thus deeper into the perimeter offices. The translucent glass at the outer edge of the light shelf diffuses the daylight, while the reflective glass in the view window aids in reducing the amount of solar heat gain. Vertical glass fins, oriented north and south—regardless of window orientation—and pulled away from the windows to prevent heat transfer, also shade the recessed windows from Bahrain's intense low sun without significantly interrupting the view. Offering some additional shade are the precast concrete piers, which are oriented in the same direction as the fins.

Materials: Glass: PPG Industries; Precast concrete: United Building Factory Industries.

Although we gave the recessed view windows a silver reflective insulating glass, they still had to be shaded from the intense western sun. We first looked at horizontal sunshades, but didn't feel that was right, and then went to thin vertical fins, but the client did not like that because they would block the view. The concern with the view led us to the heat-absorbing glass fins that did not touch the glass wall, thus eliminating heat transfer. Only about 11 percent of the heat from the sun now actually makes it into the building. We built a large model of a typical office and tested it under various lighting conditions because we were not absolutely sure that the day lighting scheme would work. These tests verified that the reflected light would reach the work surface of the desk.

Construction and technology

The superstructure system consists of a structural steel frame with composite metal deck and concrete floor slabs. Composite steel beams span between the exterior column line beam and column members are moment-connected to provide the required resistance to lateral loadings. A central atrium has interlinking crosswalks of structural steel beams infilled with architectural glass block slabs.

The foundation system is a combination of individual reinforced concrete spread footings and continuous strip footings. A reinforced concrete basement wall is at the perimeter of the lower level.

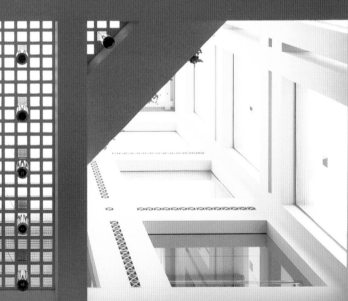

Saudi Aramco Corporate Headquarters Complex

Location: Dhahran, Saudi Arabia
Client: Saudi Aramco
Year: 1991–1993

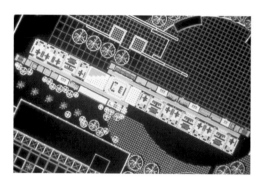 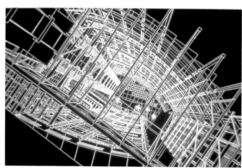 

Saudi Aramco is the world's largest producer of oil. Its world headquarters are on the outskirts of Dhahran, a medium-sized city on the east coast of Saudi Arabia. The headquarters is a compound where up to 50,000 expatriates from the USA and Britain live and work. The residential component of the complex appears as if it was lifted from a scene from a 1960s movie set in Southern California—indeed the housing was prefabricated and shipped to the Dhahran site from California.

The office component of the complex is composed of two 1950s SOM (Gordon Bunshaft) courtyard buildings of unremarkable quality and three 1980s horizontal banded office buildings by Caudill Rowlett Scott. Saudi Aramco came to SOM in 1992, a time of need for SOM, and commissioned the redevelopment of Saudi Aramco's requirements for the next century. The project lasted for about two years; SOM had completed the construction documents but the project was halted when the price of oil reached a low of $13 per barrel. We had a wonderful relationship with all involved at the headquarters and it is one of the projects that we were sorry to see stopped.

This 3.7-million-square-foot corporate office complex was planned in three phases to provide a vision for the area and a framework from which to evaluate and guide future change. The overall plan incorporates new office and mixed-use buildings within an existing campus of technical, research and administrative buildings.

The new corporate headquarters tower serves as the focal point of the campus. At 20 stories, the tower is twice as high as the buildings that surround it, clearly marking the center of the complex. The primary programmatic elements of the tower are two curvilinear pieces, 10 and 20 stories high that enclose a 10-story central atrium. The resulting narrow 10-meter spans provide natural light for each office while offering complete planning flexibility. The exterior wall is a collection of expressed components, materials, and shapes.

The broad east façade is broken by a set of stacked three-story atria. These atria are set against a 12-story black granite shear wall that ties the soft curving forms to the rectilinear geometry of the existing buildings.

The entire campus is linked by a new two-level galleria. This 150-meter covered galleria terminates in the main arrival atrium of the new corporate building. Within the galleria, a 60-meter exhibition wall with a permanent installation displays satellite-photographed aerial views of the geographic region. The galleria also houses a new auditorium, conference center, and employee dining facilities. There will also be a major exhibition facility displaying the history and science of oil exploration, discovery, and uses.

The proposed Phase II and Phase III office buildings to the west of the tower will accommodate the growth of Saudi Aramco into the future. The second phase is envisioned as a low-rise of six stories that connects the new tower to the facilities to the north and acts as an east–west link to the complex. The third phase will consist of a 15-story slab tower with punched masonry openings of varying sizes and compositions to complete the image of the complex.

The harsh desert sun is regulated through the use of vertical glass fins, stainless steel trusses, and horizontal sun shades that allow uncompromised vistas without solar heat gain.

Commerzbank Headquarters Competition

Location: Frankfurt, Germany
Client: Commerzbank
Year: 1991

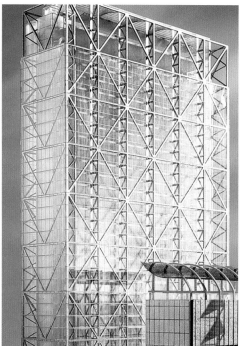

This project began as a competition for a major building in the center of Frankfurt, Germany. The competition was very intense with Norman Foster and I.M. Pei among the competitors. Norman Foster eventually won the project, based on a scheme that is reminiscent of the National Commercial Bank in Jedda by Gordon Bunshaft of SOM. His scheme, like mine, was heavily influenced by sustainability features and he eliminated the existing building, which I tried to save.

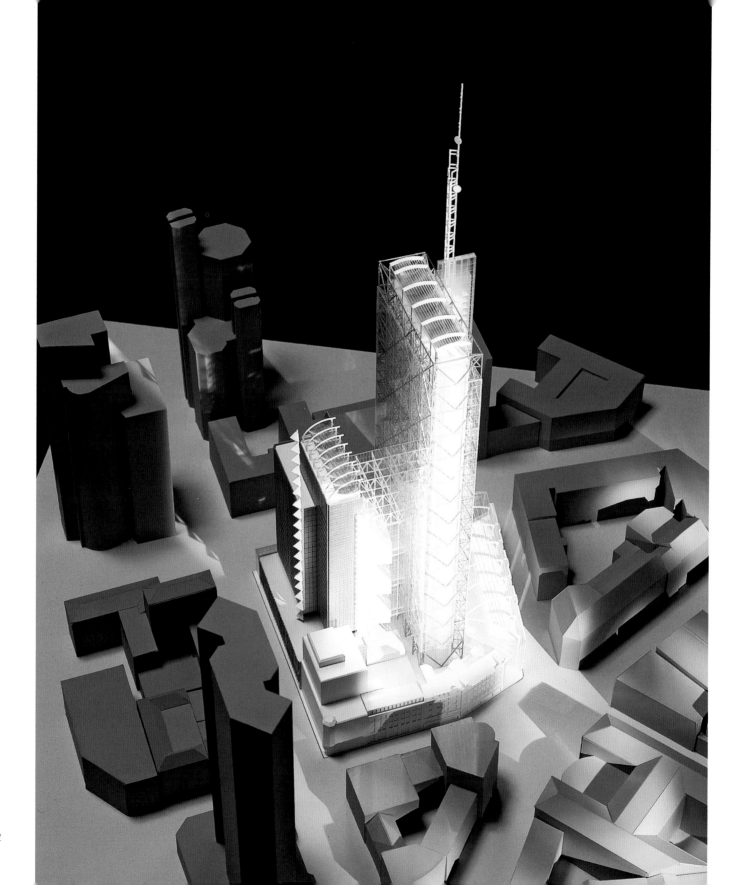

In an effort to consolidate all currently dispersed offices into a single facility, Commerzbank requested an addition to the 30-story tower that housed its corporate staff. The design of the new addition envisioned a dynamic, modern expression, balanced with environmental awareness. The resulting design consists of a 50-story high-rise connected to the existing tower by a series of hanging gardens and surrounded by a six-story office component that relates the complex to the low-rise scale of the surrounding neighborhood. The vertical circulation system and core elements for this tower were envisioned to be located to one side of the occupied space in order to free up the usable zone of the tower floors and ensure complete flexibility of layout.

Constructed as clear spans, free of columns or other fixed elements, the tower floors allow for great planning flexibility and create exterior views for each work station, as required by German labor regulations. An exposed steel frame structure is contained between two glass envelopes to eliminate cold air infiltration and act as the return air plenum.

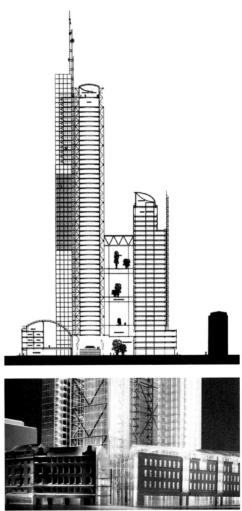

Jin Mao Tower

Location: Shanghai, China
Client: China Jin Mao Group Co.
Year: 1992–1999

On March 24, 1993 we were visited by Chairman Zhang, Mr Zu, and Mr Ruan at the offices of Skidmore, Owings & Merrill in Chicago. The purpose of their visit was to introduce the project competition to us and ask if we had any questions. They also asked us (and all other competitors) to suggest three potential jurors. The first question I asked was why they wanted an 88-story building. Why not two buildings on the site, say a 50-story office and a 38-story hotel instead of a tall mixed-use building? After all, it would be cheaper and would be constructed much faster.

Their response was that it had to be 88 stories because Deng Xiaoping was 88 when he stood on the site and declared that it would be the new financial center of China and that "to be rich was glorious." It was also stated that this happened in August, 1988, so the number 8 became very important as well as a symbol of good luck and prosperity. Later, at lunch at the Blue Moon restaurant in Chinatown, after we had eaten and the fortune cookies were handed out, Mr Zhang opened his and found the numbers 8, 16, 24, 32, and 40 on his fortune and was very excited. He showed it to all of us and quickly put it in his wallet. I then looked around and said that there were 8 of us and that this was March 24: 3 x 8 = 24. I knew right there that I would design this building around the number 8.

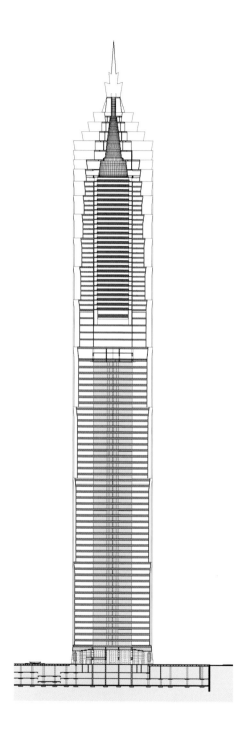

Jin Mao Tower

The concept for Jin Mao was a modern soaring tower that would become the central focal point of the Pudong District, welcoming all who approach it. In a symbolic way, it is reminiscent of the ancient Chinese pagoda.

The biaxial symmetry of its form responds to views from all directions. Its gently stepping and undulating form ascends in a progressively rhythmic way, increasing the sense of height through the use of a forced perspective.

This also acts as a wind damper to diffuse the lateral wind forces on the mass, and creates a horizontal datum for the location of night lighting features. It was important to relate the Jin Mao Tower to the culture and indigenous character of China and its people. The ancient pagoda, one of the precursors of the manmade skyscraper, was the basis for the memory of this tower. It is not a copy of a pagoda, but rather an analogy to the profile, in much the same way as the 1950s simple rectangular International style glass box forms were evocative of the towers at San Gimignano, Italy.

The pagoda symbolized the center of gathering within villages and cities throughout ancient China, and as such, the analogy is fitting to a tower in Shanghai intended to be the center of the new Pudong Financial District. In this sense, it is uniquely Chinese in character and symbol. However, in its use of materials, building systems, the technology used to construct it, and the nature of its spaces and functions, it is a state-of-the-art, international building of the highest quality.

The building top is a culmination of the stepping system, clustered and transformed into a profile and surface composition that can be identified from several kilometers away. Its metallic form glistens in the sunlight and changes as the sun moves across its surfaces.

The exterior wall is comprised of granite, stainless steel, aluminum, and glass. Its primary emphasis is vertical. At its center and throughout the two-level sloped sections of the façade, the vertical mullions are spaced at .75 meters in order to create a surface density that emphasizes the special components of the composition. This provides a mediating scale element between the fine-grained texture of the surface, and the large-scale symbol of the tower. All other surfaces are on a 1.5-meter module. The primary color of this tower is silver. This palette has a harmonious relationship with the sky, and it reflects the adjacent context at lower levels.

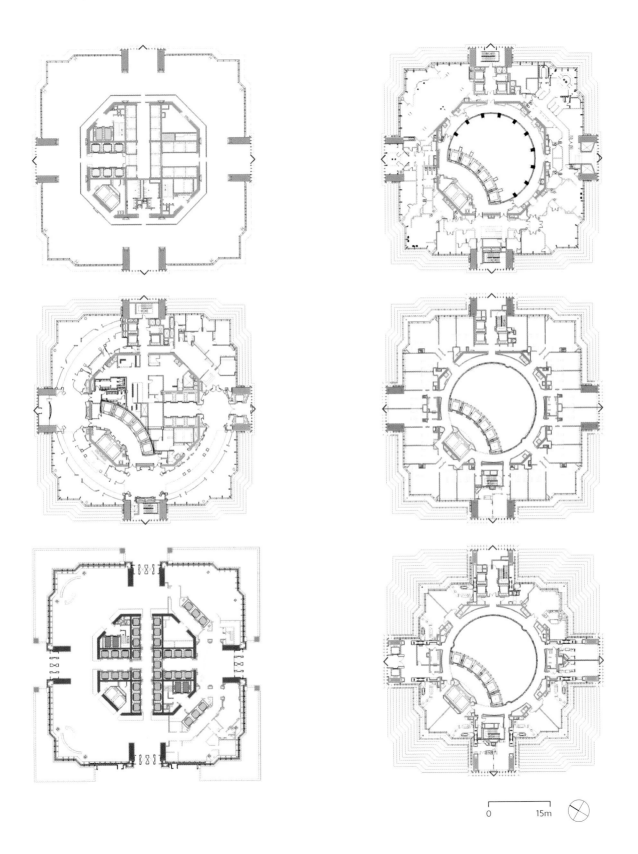

0   15m

An Ode to the Jin Mao Building
By Wang Xi
August 18, 1998 (from the Jin Mao Tong Xin)

Translation by Vadim Menstell Hsu

The year is 1998. The country is at peace and the times are prosperous. In this auspicious atmosphere the 88-story Jin Mao Building has been constructed. It stands by the East China Sea on the bank of the Huang Pu River, and symbolizes China's 5000-year-old tradition of building pagodas. After five years devoted to incorporating the world's latest high technology, at the cost of $500 million, this tallest building in China is now complete. For the people, this building represents the rise of Pu Dong as well as the rise of China. Ascending the tower, and looking afar, we see the Huang Pu River flowing eastward. Beyond the great bridges arching high and the Pearl Tower soaring skyward, the Bund (Wai Tan) emerges through the mist. All the beauty of the city meets the eye. In the light fog of late spring, the tower can be seen through the clouds; it wins the hearts of all the people. In late winter when snow falls, the tower is wrapped in a bewitching silver cloak. On a clear day in the morning and at dusk, gentle breezes form ever changing images—this is the grand view of the Jin Mao. When night falls, thousands of lights shine on the building and the glass walls glisten, evoking the impression of a city that never sleeps. No one passes the building without stopping. All who stand there proudly praise the tower and long to ascend its heights. Truly it may be said that eminent people and foreign merchants will gather here as if in a great courtyard of commerce—a source of great wealth. This is the happy result of the reform policy and the opening of China.

"I drew inspiration from the famous old poem, 'The House of the Yellow Crane' (Huang He Lou), by Tang Zhui Hao, which immortalized that most eminent of historical houses. I believe that a great building must not be without literary tribute."

The Jin Mao Tower design is not strictly based upon the number eight. However, upon learning the importance of that number, it became intriguing to weave elements of it into the design. It was never a constraint, as we did not let it govern any design decisions. The elements of the building that worked best in conjunction with eight came very naturally, such as the octagonal core, the eight main super-frame columns and the eight-sided exterior at the top. The setbacks of the building were also examined with eight-floor increments in mind, and very early in the design of the tower we looked at the setbacks as mathematical increments of eight by doubling it as in the form of the first setback (2 x 8 = 16 floors).

We reduced the number of floors in each setback zone by one-eighth until we reached the hotel (16, 14, 12 and 10). At each eight-floor zone, the pace of setbacks was changed to single-floor increments at the hotel, or one-eighth of eight (8, 7, 6, 5, 4, 3, 2, and 1). The final combination of floors totalled 88.

The client's goal was to create a landmark for the Pudong District: a fitting tower to be placed in the center of the master plan for this new financial and commercial center, and to represent the collective agencies of the Shanghai China Foreign Trade Centre Company, the occupiers of the office component of the tower.

The Jin Mao Tower is a 3-million-square-foot (278,000-square-meter) multi-use development. It houses a 555-room Grand Hyatt Hotel in the top 38 stories, affording impressive views of the city and the surrounding region. Office floors are in the lower 50 stories. Jin Mao's six-story podium houses hotel function areas, a conference and exhibition center, a cinema auditorium, and a 226,000-square-foot (21,000-square-meter) retail galleria. The base of the tower is surrounded by a landscaped courtyard with a reflecting pool and seating, offering visitors a peaceful retreat from Shanghai's busy street activity.

Jin Mao Tower

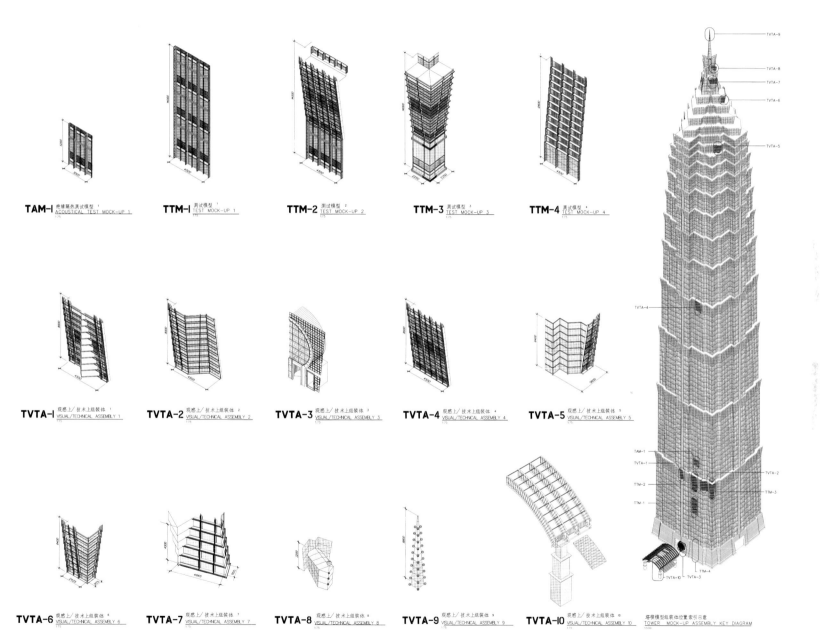

TAM-1 绝缘隔热测试模型 ¹
ACOUSTICAL TEST MOCK-UP 1
1:75

TTM-1 测试模型 ¹
TEST MOCK-UP 1
1:75

TTM-2 测试模型 ²
TEST MOCK-UP 2
1:75

TTM-3 测试模型 ³
TEST MOCK-UP 3
1:75

TTM-4 测试模型 ⁴
TEST MOCK-UP 4
1:75

TVTA-1 观感上／技术上组装体 ¹
VISUAL/TECHNICAL ASSEMBLY 1
1:75

TVTA-2 观感上／技术上组装体 ²
VISUAL/TECHNICAL ASSEMBLY 2
1:75

TVTA-3 观感上／技术上组装体 ³
VISUAL/TECHNICAL ASSEMBLY 3
1:75

TVTA-4 观感上／技术上组装体 ⁴
VISUAL/TECHNICAL ASSEMBLY 4
1:75

TVTA-5 观感上／技术上组装体 ⁵
VISUAL/TECHNICAL ASSEMBLY 5
1:75

TVTA-6 观感上／技术上组装体 ⁶
VISUAL/TECHNICAL ASSEMBLY 6
1:75

TVTA-7 观感上／技术上组装体 ⁷
VISUAL/TECHNICAL ASSEMBLY 7
1:75

TVTA-8 观感上／技术上组装体 ⁸
VISUAL/TECHNICAL ASSEMBLY 8
1:75

TVTA-9 观感上／技术上组装体 ⁹
VISUAL/TECHNICAL ASSEMBLY 9
1:75

TVTA-10 观感上／技术上组装体 ¹⁰
VISUAL/TECHNICAL ASSEMBLY 10
1:75

塔楼模型组装体位置索引示意
TOWER MOCK-UP ASSEMBLY KEY DIAGRAM

In addition to the tower and podium, Jin Mao incorporates three below-grade levels with a total area of 615,000 square feet (57,000 square meters). These levels accommodate parking for 993 cars and 1000 bicycles, hotel service facilities, additional retail space, a food court, an observatory elevator lobby, and building systems equipment areas including electrical transformers and switchgear, a sewage treatment plant, a domestic water plant, a boiler room, and a chiller plant. Above the 88th-floor observatory are several floors for mechanical and maintenance equipment. The tower reaches 421 meters and is the tallest building in China.

The process of designing the first super-tall building in China involved a rigorous series of challenges. The Chinese are to be respected and admired for their depth of review and strict approval process. All aspects of the building were examined and discussed in great detail by Chinese and foreign experts retained by the client. With the absence of Chinese codes to govern some aspects of super high-rise buildings of this type in China, the Unites States' standardized Uniform Building Code (UBC) was applied. The Shanghai Institute of Architectural Design and Research was retained in the pre-construction phase as SOM's associate architect and engineer responsible for assisting with local codes and practices.

One example of SOM's use of both international and Chinese codes is the tower's fire protection. The universally recognized "defend in place" strategy for fire protection of high-rise buildings is used along with areas of refuge to comply with codes and standards of the People's Republic of China, which requires an empty safe refuge room every 15 floors. SOM designed these areas as conference centers to maximize use of the space. To supplement SOM's full-service architectural, engineering, and interiors capabilities, additional consultants were retained for acoustical, fire/life safety, building codes, geotechnical, lighting, security, sewage treatment, telecommunications, vertical transportation, wind engineering, and exterior and interior building maintenance equipment. The many state-of-the-art systems that are integral to this design make it one of the most intelligent and advanced buildings on the globe—such advances will lead China's building program well into the next century.

Advanced structural engineering concepts were used in the design of the tower, which is subjected to typhoon winds, earthquake events, and poor soil conditions. Open-ended structural steel pipe piles, extending 270 feet (82 meters) below grade, support the tower, providing high-load carrying capacity and small settlement characteristics. A 4-meter-thick reinforced concrete mat is used as an interface between the superstructure and the piles. A 1-meter-thick slurry wall extends 36 meters below grade. Used around the perimeter of the site, this acts as a temporary retaining wall, a permanent water cut-off wall, and a permanent foundation wall.

Composite materials of reinforced concrete and structural steel are used for the primary building functions and are interconnected with the exterior composite (reinforced concrete and structural steel) mega-columns by two-story-deep composite outrigger trusses at three levels within the building. Outrigger trusses, between levels 24–26, 51–53, and 85–87 use large-diameter structural steel pins in circular and slotted holes to allow for relative movement between the central core and exterior composite mega-columns due to creep, shrinkage, elastic shortening,

and variations in temperature during construction. Pin connections allow the outrigger truss members to move and maintain alignment until final bolted connections for a permanent structural system can be made. Wide column spacing at the exterior and the lack of any interior columns provide great flexibility for the office and hotel spaces, allowing for dramatic, uninterrupted views of Shanghai.

The use and placement of structural steel and reinforced concrete provides optimum structural efficiency for this super-tall structure with very few material premiums required for lateral wind and earthquake loads. The combined use of structural steel and reinforced concrete provides excellent mass, stiffness, and damping properties, giving the structure optimal dynamic characteristics.

When designing the base of the tower and podium, a stately strong and monumental character was needed. I felt that it was important to set up the tower as a classical piece, formal and deliberate, with axial entries and gardens on the plaza. I used blue Orissa granite, stainless steel grilles, and horizontal stainless steel shelves to integrate the ground plane to the vertical surfaces, and to link the metallic tower to the building's base. The strength and power of the terraced walls used on Beijing monuments was very influential and it felt appropriate to reference this memory in the base of the Jin Mao Tower.

The tower is separated from the plaza by a moat, a polished black granite reflecting pool filled with water that is broken only at the building entrances. This imparts a feeling of transition from one world to another as one walks across this zone into the building. Each entry is designed as a moongate. Each moongate consists of two glass layers that enhance the entry sequence and give it a timeframe, a zone of through movement, not an instant threshold of crossing, from outside to inside. The intent was to add mystery to each individual's entry experience.

The sloping granite and stainless steel walls have a power and serenity reminiscent of the temple structures at the Ming Tombs near Beijing.

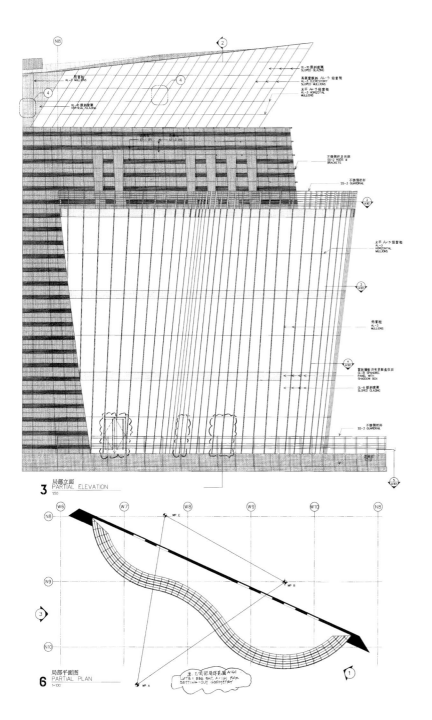

3 局部立面
PARTIAL ELEVATION
1:50

6 局部平面图
PARTIAL PLAN
1:100

The glass roof structure curves upward at its edge in much the same way as the roof overhang in traditional Chinese construction. The dragon metaphor is seen in the undulating glass canopy at the main entrance to the ballroom on the ground floor. The vaulted skylights of the main atrium evoke a spatial quality perceived in the grand spaces of the temple structures.

The atrium of the hotel extends from the 54th floor through the spire of the Jin Mao Tower. Formed by cantilevered walkways, it projects into the void from the core wall that surrounds the office building elevators, mechanical equipment, telephone and communication equipment, and electric closets. These cantilevered walkways access each hotel room from a set of glass-enclosed elevators that rise through the atrium.

The podium forms the western boundary of the Jin Mao site and is intended to house all hotel functions that are independent of the hotel rooms, such as the ballrooms, large conference and exhibition spaces, truck dock, storage, and servicing needs. It also contains the cooling towers for the entire complex as well as a four-level retail and entertainment complex. The retail complex is accessed both by a set of elevators contained in a glass shaft located between the tower and the podium, and by escalators located on axis with the building link that connects the tower to the podium.

The overall building form of the podium was originally designed to be two dragons around a pearl, but it was thought to be too powerful a symbol. As a result, the podium was conceived as a massive horizontal cocoon about to open its wings for flight. The curved and sloped glass wall at the north elevation provides views out to the Pearl Observatory and the Cultural Park of the Pudong Commercial District. Vertical circulation elements, whether elevators, escalators, or stairways, are constructed of stainless steel and glass, and the moving mechanical elements of each system are open to view. Visitors arriving at the third floor at the base of the atrium are engulfed in a space full of light from the skylights, and the backlit media wall. Above is a suspended bridge of modulated grids that forms a diagonal walkway of translucent glass through the space on level four. Light fixtures mounted below the surface of the glass light both the bridge itself and the spaces below.

Projecting out from the walkway on each floor, two crescent-shaped balconies provide hotel guests with a clear view of the atrium void. These balconies are placed sequentially to one side of each lower balcony so as not to block the view when looking up at the atrium. This creates a spiral within the surface of the atrium, adding a dynamic sense of motion.

Jin Mao Tower

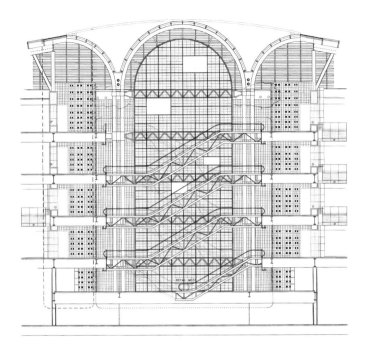

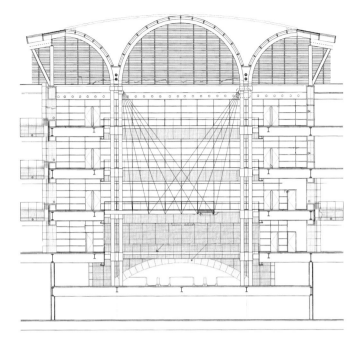

Section through atrium

The building's intelligence is nested in several components that employ a vertical and horizontal cable highway. This cable highway consists of both single- and multi-mode fiber optic cable and Unshielded Twisted Pair (UTP) Category 5 cable. The highway is optimized to accommodate an extensive range of tenants, building services, and future technological interconnections for data, voice, and video, including ATM and FDDI. Tenants are offered both Direct Tenant Services (DTS) and Shared Tenant Services (STS) for voice through the fiber and UTP highway, and a building Private Branch Exchange (PBX). STS for data is offered as well as the cable plant for intra-tenant Local Area Networks (LAN).

The cable highway supports connection of a complete PC-based Direct Digital Control (DDC) system controlling and monitoring all mechanical, electrical, elevator, lighting, and building operation components. The building's amenities include fax and copy centers, high-speed print centers with user PCs and CD ROM recording, document manufacturing, training, audio visual and teleconference centers, and private convention facilities. The cable highway serves the office, retail, and hotel spaces allowing for shared amenities and integrated systems for each function, providing enhanced ease of operation and maintenance.

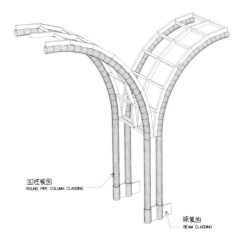

圆柱覆面
ROUND PIPE COLUMN CLADDING

梁覆面
BEAM CLADDING

Pidemco Tower Competition

Location: Singapore
Client: Pidemco Land Limited
Year: 1995

The primary reference for the aesthetic nature of this proposal is embodied in the character of flora and fauna found in the rich tropical environment of Singapore. The building is polychromatic and intense, and referential to tropical plant material with strong flower and pod forms anchored to sturdy stems and branches.

The aesthetic is in complete contrast to the character of the adjacent urban context, which is ironically uniquely western and international in character. The development of this site offers an architectural opportunity that mediates the cultural traditions of Singapore, those of time and place, with the evolving technological frontier of tomorrow.

The design attempts to physically reinforce and expand the urban registry of the central business district with a distinctly identifiable architecture responsive to both the client and the city. The creation of a world-class place is sought through the scaled flexible working spaces that are defined by the qualities of light, color, form, and garden.

This conceptual design for the building's site explores a modulation between the celebrated cultural traditions of Singapore, as a port city of commerce and trade, and a visionary edifice for the future. Architecturally, this vision begins with the delineation of a series of scale readings of the urban pattern that inform the building massing and orientation. Internally, the formal building organization develops a plan that maximizes leasing flexibility, panoramic views, and atria. Externally, the street's geometry shift creates opportunities for three-dimensional shaping and a memorable paired silhouette.

The resulting family of new buildings draws inspiration from a rich indigenous palette of color, materials, and form. The resulting expression attempts to complement existing gateway views to the city by dynamically extending the skyline southward, establishing a sense of place that will galvanize perimeter site value and growth.

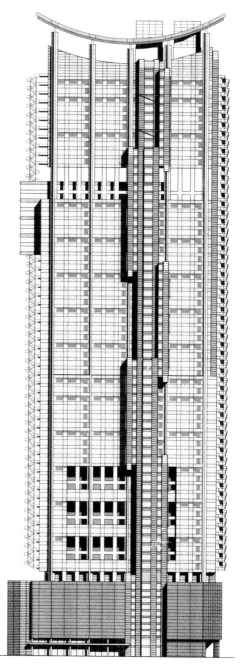

East elevation

10 Ludgate Place

Location: London, UK
Client: Rosehaugh Stanhope Properties, Stewart Lipton
Year: 1988–1992

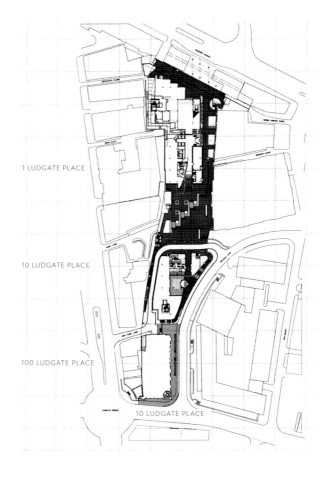

1 LUDGATE PLACE

10 LUDGATE PLACE

100 LUDGATE PLACE

10 LUDGATE PLACE

The genesis for the design of this building arose from a number of issues. First, the site is located between a traditional limestone building to the south, and a modernist building with exposed structural steel and glass to its north. To the east and west are various mid-1970s stock curtain wall structures of questionable construction and proportion with few redeeming qualities. To the northeast is a poorly conceived and detailed postmodern edifice.

It was clear that 10 Ludgate must distinguish itself from its neighbors and make a statement in its own right. The opportunity existed to create a piece that both resonated with, and had a sympathetic relationship to, 1 Ludgate to the north, viewing all other structures as fabric background buildings that draw little attention. Second, the city planning officials

required a stone façade, and desired that the building be a "London" building. The third consideration was the physical nature of the site itself, which consists of a raft structure spanning the British Rail lines that run below the entire building.

The depth required for this structure necessitated that the ground floor be lifted up higher, at its midpoint, than the adjacent Seacoal Lane. Seacoal Lane, which borders the site to the east, is a sloped and curved public one-way street that creates dynamic movement adjacent to this wall. The primary public vistas are from the northeast and south entry points to Seacoal Lane. The northeast corner of the building is at the convergence of two view corridors, and it denotes the entrance to the arcade from Seacoal Lane to the east. The corner on the southeast signals

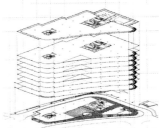

the southern entrance to the arcade. The segments of these corners are set back by 1.5 meters and meet the surface of the top floor, which is also set back 1.5 meters, connecting the two corner elements with the top. This helps to emphasize the delicate quality of the extended column elements that are not set back. These vistas allow the east wall to be perceived as a compact curved surface.

Another important view of this building is from the pedestrian-only plaza to the north. The figure of the building from the other elevations is an orthogonal configuration that responds more sympathetically to the nature of the space created by its insertion. For example, the north façade presents an elevation of a more formal character to the newly created plaza. The arcade is used as a porte-cochère for guests arriving by vehicle during inclement weather.

It was critical to synthesize the important aspects to derive an image that was unique, but deferential, to the existing context. The key to the expressive nature of a building on this site was how it addressed Seacoal Lane. The building must read as a massive form from the entry points to Seacoal Lane, employing vertical elements that stack up against each other in a layered manner. It must be open and glassy when viewed from the inside looking out in order to provide optimal views for tenants. It should contrast in tone from the adjacent buildings—themselves ranging in tone from light beige to medium bronze anodized glass. It must have a fine grain texture in contrast to the generally larger scale put forward by the adjacent context. And, it should be a truthful expression, a sympathetic resonance to 1 Ludgate in regard to its exposed structural steel frame, not replicating or mimicking its vocabulary.

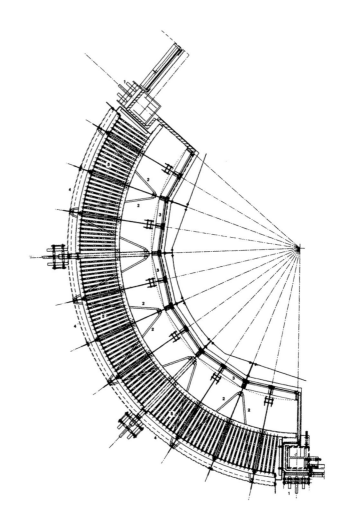

Although not literal, the exterior image of 10 Ludgate was informed by the memory of the British Rail yards previously located on the site. The tracks and their auxiliary systems of truss and cable structures are traced metaphorically in the façade. The blackness of the skin helps reinforce this relationship.

The idea of hanging the granite components perpendicular to the wall, versus in-plane with the enclosure, satisfied all of these requirements. It produced a truthful expression of the use of stone on an exterior wall without pretending that the building was built entirely of granite. By placing it perpendicularly, its true thickness is expressed, and by hanging it, its intrinsic strength and purpose can be seen.

The building's dark polished stone and frame contrasts with the surrounding environment. The exterior wall of 10 Ludgate is composed of a unitized aluminum panel system for the window and spandrel area, and an aluminum-clad steel system for the column covers. Added to this system was a series of 50-millimeter polished granite "fins" or slabs supported by 40-millimeter stainless steel support pins. These pins penetrate the vertical mullion elements of the wall and cantilever the granite slabs from the mullions at mid-span. The column cover is a U-shaped steel channel with stainless steel fins spanning from flange to flange and penetrating through each of three rows of granite slabs, in effect hanging the granite off these channel column covers. The aluminum spandrel panels are bent horizontally and braced vertically with aluminum braces, or stiffeners, exposed on the exterior to increase the density and detail seen on the exterior wall. Stainless steel horizontal elements have been added to accentuate the verticality of the stiffeners when seen at an oblique angle, reducing the apparent bulk of the spandrel and identifying the floor slab location.

What is it that makes this a typical London building? In studying London architecture, a number of observations were made. Most London buildings, regardless of style, are built to the lot line, defining the public realm from that of the private. Many buildings celebrate their corners. Most have depth, texture, and detail in their walls; the type and scale of detail relates to the workman who built the structure, or carved its ornament. Most indigenous architecture in London is classically composed, that is, it has a base, middle, and top. This building has a base defined by its arcade, a middle that has the texture of the typical wall, and a top defined by its extended columns and setback penthouse façade.

10 Ludgate Place

Chemsunny Plaza

Location: Beijing, China
Client: Beijing Chemsunny Property Co. Ltd.
Year: 2002–2006

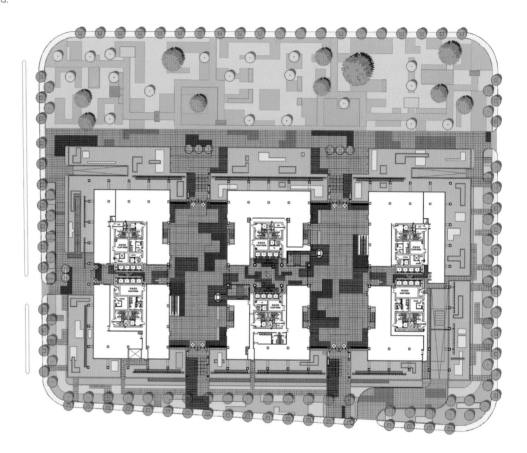

Chemsunny Plaza is located 2.4 kilometers west of the Forbidden City. The project site is an integral part of the Beijing financial district and the Xidan commercial district. Chemsunny is a 15-story office building with two major atria and an approximate gross above-grade area of 132,000 square meters. Three basement levels have a gross below-grade area of 43,084 square meters.

The ground floor contains the primary entrance lobbies. Individual lobbies to each elevator core are connected to the base level of each atrium. The ground floor also contains separate office space as well as the entry to the below-grade retail area.

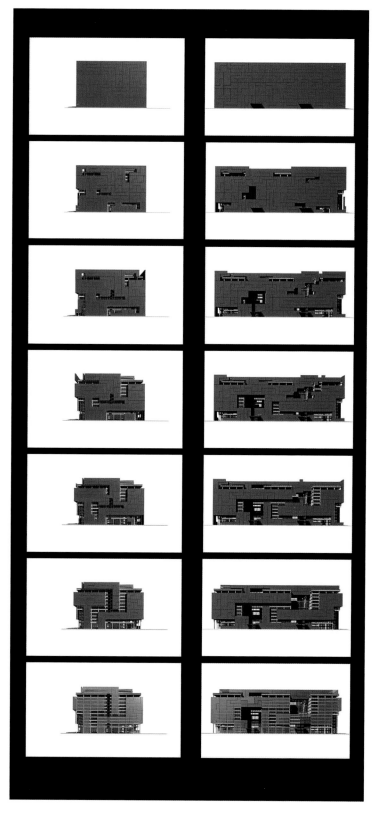

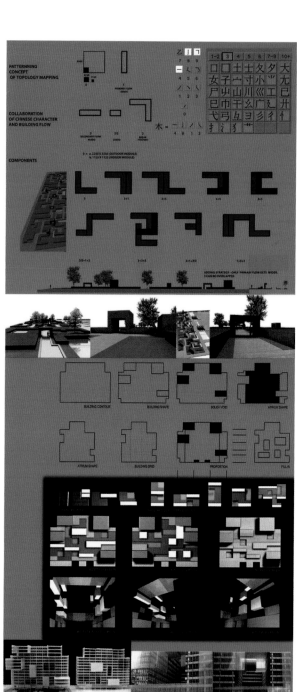

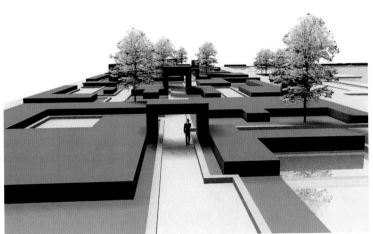

The calligraphy of the Chinese alphabet was employed to relate this building to the Chinese culture and ethos. We distilled the alphabet into its simplest character figures:

a long dash, a short dash, a long vertical mark, and a short vertical mark. Combine these and one obtains various L figures; rotating these L figures results in a vocabulary that can be manipulated to form a sculptural element on the elevations of the block building that is Chemsunny.

At its most basic element, Chemsunny is three block buildings that are linked together by bridges that connect the blocks at low and high points. One low bridge and one high bridge on the north façade connect the

three walls together. One high bridge and one low bridge, alternating with the north bridges, connect the southern façades. Each atrium is expressed on the exterior with a seven-story cable-net-supported clear glass exterior wall that almost disappears when viewed from a distance, giving the illusion of an open hole in the wall. The L forms that are extracted from the elevations leave a void that is partially filled with a cantilevered sun screen. The surfaces that are left as flush walls are double walls of clear glass with sun shading blinds in the interstitial space for sun protection.

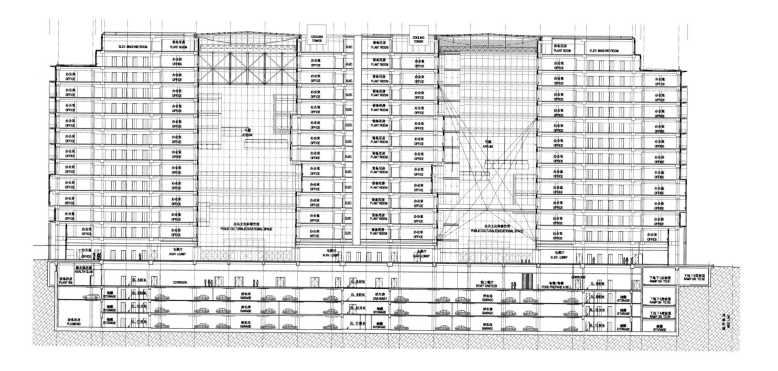

Longitudinal section

North elevation

Elements of the exterior wall are also operable to allow tenants to enjoy fresh air that has been tempered by the double wall system. The double wall is externally ventilated with heated air in the cavity rising to the top and venting from a reveal. All double wall areas are cantilevered out from the exterior columns by approximately 1.5 meters to minimize any reading of the structure on the face of the building, except when the erosion of the wall leaves the column and beam system of the building exposed, which is the case on the corners and at the base of the building. The structure at these points is clad in stainless steel.

The building's two atria are huge spaces, scaled as enclosed streets between buildings. Skylights bring as much light into this space as possible, since tenants of the adjacent buildings have a view into these spaces. The bridges that connect the building components add a strong sense of enclosure to these spaces and the use of the cable net window support system adds an intricate layer of detail to the views from within the atria.

The side walls of the atria are modulated by "drawer-like" elements that push out into the void and allow the tenant spaces views up, down, and across the atria.

Chemsunny Plaza 129

These drawers are clad in wood, stainless steel, and back-lit glass to add interest and variety to the space. Spanning between the two buildings in the middle of each atrium are suspension bridges, supported by cables that connect to the atria walls at various points. This feature, in addition to connecting these floors together, helps to animate the space with the motion of people walking through it. The cables also catch the direct sunlight coming through the skylight and glisten from time to time. At other times they will be in shadow and become dark lines that weave through the space. They will always vary in appearance, depending on where the observer is positioned, and they will be very dynamic from the point of view of the person walking on the bridge itself.

The strategy of L-shaped elements is continued on the paving surfaces both in the atrium and on the plazas and driveways on the exterior. L-shaped and bar-shaped planters also appear to float in the water features that are adjacent to and under the body of the building. The water at this location is treated like a reflecting pool to extend the features of the above-grade building downward. The landscape at the north of the complex between the driveway and Chen An Avenue has a three-dimensional design that links with the context of the Chemsunny building. It remains to be seen if this feature will be carried out, since this land belongs to the City of Beijing.

At the top of the building are three floors that are stepped back from the roof parapet, which is at a maximum height of 49 meters. These floors set back in order to maintain a constant cornice line along the parade route of Chen An Avenue. The roofscape at this level will be treated as a patio for the executive floor to enjoy in good weather. The mechanical floor occupies the top of this setback.

The structural system for this complex is composed of conventionally reinforced concrete columns on 9-meter centers and a concrete core for lateral bracing. The large floor bridges are supported by steel Vierendeel trusses that are two stories deep and very rigid in order to withstand earthquake forces. The truss that spans the 27-meter atrium is also used to support the top section of the cable net structure for the atrium exterior wall.

Xiamen Post and Telecommunications Center Competition

Location: Xiamen, China
Client: Xiamen Post and Telecommunications
Year: 1995

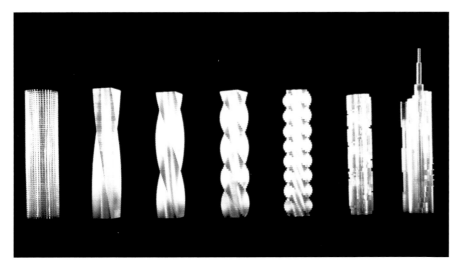

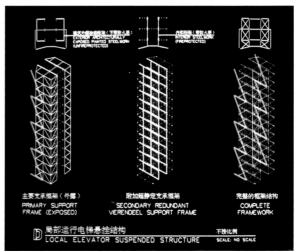

The city of Xiamen is on the east coast of China, directly across from the island of Taiwan. It is viewed as a second-tier city in China and is known for its lush garden atmosphere. The competition was held to select an architect to design the new headquarters facilities for this region's postal system. Participants in the competition included Michael Graves, SOM, SIADR, Callison Architects, and others. SOM won the competition and formed an association with SIADR, the institute responsible for the construction documents.

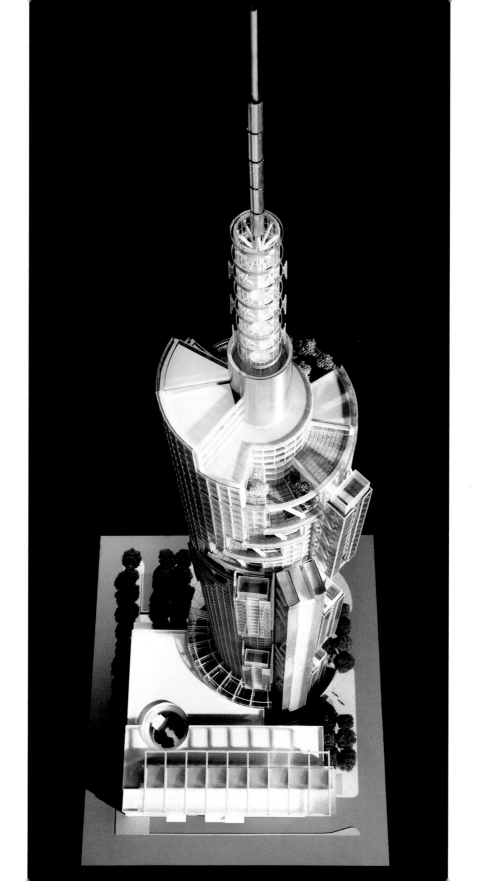

The Xiamen Post and Telecommunications Center is a 1.3-million-square-foot (120,000-square-meter) mixed-use development. The facility's main components are a 968,000-square-foot (90,000-square-meter), 63-story office tower and a 322,000-square-foot (30,000-square-meter), 6-story postal building.

This combination is accomplished through the introduction of multi-story sky gardens that spiral from the top to the bottom of the building. Each floor has an identical plan and rotates a notch as the building rises. However, the only indication of the rotation is the visual spiral created by the placement of the gardens.

The building's vertical circulation system is on full display here. Five elevator zones serve the 63 stories. Zone one is accessed through the lobby at the base of the building and serves floors 2 through 11. Zones two to five are accessed by sky-lobbies at floors 24 and 48. The sky-lobbies are accessed by an expressed stainless steel shaft on the exterior of the building. At each sky-lobby, occupants exit and transfer to local elevators, which rise both up to the zone above the sky-lobby and down to the zone below. These elevator banks are anchored on the side of the cylindrical building in clear glass shafts, thus highlighting all vertical movement taking place in the facility. This elevator system creates the maximum efficiency of space utilization by reducing the shaft space required for elevators to a minimum. The top of the building is celebrated with a functional spire rising above the central concrete core. The spiraling gardens transform into a continuous rooftop garden for executive offices and meeting areas.

At the time of writing, construction has been completed on the basements of both the high- and low-rise components, along with the six-story low-rise component. Construction has not yet proceeded on the high-rise although all foundations necessary for the support of the tower are installed.

Frequency waves, the basis of telecommunication, inspired the design of the tower. The essence of the design is to physically merge the curve of frequency waves with the celebrated tradition of Xiamen as a garden city of arts and commerce.

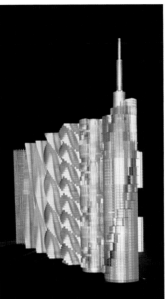

General Motors at Renaissance Center

Location: Detroit, Michigan, USA
Client: General Motors
Year: 1996–2005

We were first approached by General Motors and the Hines organization in 1996 to present our qualifications for the renovation of the Renaissance Center (originally designed by John Portman in 1972). GM had recently purchased the entire complex from Ford Motor Company and had plans to move its offices from the Fisher Building (designed by Albert Kahn in 1920) to the Renaissance Center. We were hired two days later to help to formulate a master plan for GM. This required a complete assessment of the Renaissance Center facility and recommendations on how to convert this building, or series of buildings, into a Class A facility.

In assessing the building, we found many problems:

- Many elements of the building were out of date and not up to current code compliance.

- The entire facility was disconnected from the rest of the city, blocked off from Jefferson Avenue and the rest of Detroit by two very large berm structures in front of the building that contained the mechanical plant for the facility, and a light rail station that sat on top of the east berm.

- Light rail lines traversing in front of the automobile entry, near the center of the facility on Jefferson Avenue, further obscured the sense of entry to the facility.

- The interior of the podium building had no sense of orientation. Because the major atrium space was completely circular and symmetrical with no clues as to where one was within the space, it was very easy to get lost.

- The perimeters of the facility on the east, west, and south were cut off from grade by elevated roads ringing the facility.

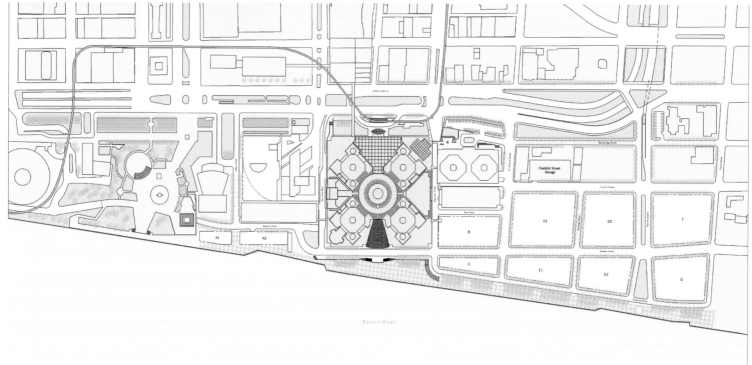

General Motors at Renaissance Center

- The elevated roadway to Tower 500 and Tower 600 to the south created an unsightly and inappropriate ramp in front of the retail space at grade.

- There was no connection to the Detroit River to the south of the complex even though the complex was within 200 feet of the river's edge.

- There was no security.

- The hotel, retail and office functions were completely connected; the four office structures and the central hotel had no separate entrance identity.

- Circulation to each office tower was through a shopping mall. The entry points were very hard to find and not visible to most visitors.

- The office towers had no interconnection and this posed a problem for GM since it planned to eventually occupy all the office space.

- The entrance to the complex off Jefferson was a 1991 redo of the original Portman entrance and was in a style and character unsympathetic to the modernism of the original facility.

- The original exterior wall of glass fiber reinforced concrete (GFRC) was failing at some locations and the 1991 alteration was fastened to the GFRC. The polished granite alterations were not compatible with the character of the original architecture.

- The original podium façade was solid and blocked the view to the Detroit River to the south.

- All office building related finishes were sub-standard and in need of upgrade.

Our approach to solving these problems was very comprehensive and complicated because GM wanted to move in and occupy the entire building as soon as possible and much of the construction work would have to be staged around occupied space. This added a tremendous cost and logistics burden to the process but was offset by the savings that would be achieved in rent for GM. The project from start to finish took nine years to design, construct and fit out. It was a monumental task given the size of the project, as the Renaissance Center contains more than 5 million square feet of space.

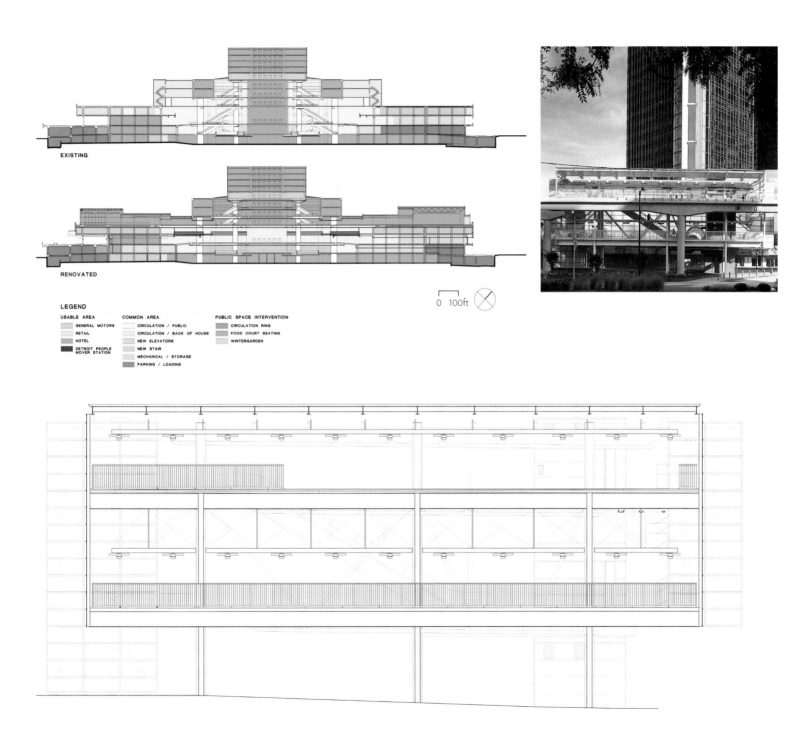

EXISTING

RENOVATED

0 100ft

LEGEND

USABLE AREA
GENERAL MOTORS
RETAIL
HOTEL
DETROIT PEOPLE
MOVER STATION

COMMON AREA
CIRCULATION / PUBLIC
CIRCULATION / BACK OF HOUSE
NEW ELEVATORS
NEW STAIR
MECHANICAL / STORAGE
PARKING / LOADING

PUBLIC SPACE INTERVENTION
CIRCULATION RING
FOOD COURT SEATING
WINTERGARDEN

Thirteen major projects were incorporated in the renovation of this facility:

- The berms were removed from the front of the building and the mechanical plant was reconnected to the city's central system.

- The light rail station was removed and replaced as far to the east as possible in order to free up the entrance.

- The raised roadway that barricades the south side of the facility from the Detroit River was removed and the entrance was relocated at grade.

- A winter garden was created on the south side of the podium to allow natural light to enter the atrium space and to give this space an orientation point.

- A circulation ring was created to connect the four office towers together and to connect the new north entry to the new winter garden and south entry.

- The retail, hotel, and office functions were separated for clarity of entrance, identity, and wayfinding.

- Redundant escalators were removed for ease of circulation.

- A new entrance feature worthy of Class A international standards was   created.

- The Jefferson Avenue lobby was removed and replaced with materials and features befitting a world-class headquarters facility.

- All retail window walls were renovated.

- The south podium exterior wall was removed and replaced with window wall to take advantage of the views to the river.

- The raw parking lot on the river was converted to a landscaped and paved plaza.

- The front entrance was organized to provide vehicular access to the hotel, retail, and office lobbies and to provide an enhanced pedestrian way to the main entrance. The front yard setback space was landscaped.

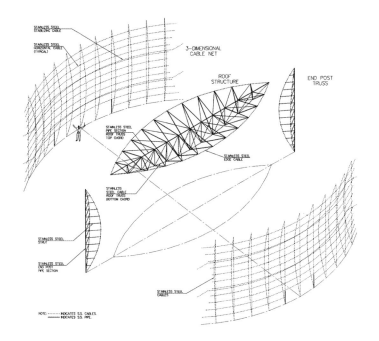

The pavilion

The main entrance to the GM facility is reached by automobile through a circular driveway drop off. Bollards and custom light fixtures define the driveway edge and the pedestrian walkway. The entrance pavilion is an almond-shaped, all-glass, free-standing piece with a unique cable and post suspension system to support the all-glass walls. It has been designed for the display of new products from General Motors and can be seen from several blocks east and west of the site. The structure is all stainless steel and the cable structure is supported by two columns, one at each end, that are connected by a bow truss that spans between them and supports the all-glass ceiling.

Lighting for the pavilion comes from the floor and washes the structure with white light at night, in much the same way as trees are uplit for theatrical effect. The floor is white Carrara marble with a polished black border. The pavilion is approximately 30 feet high, 30 feet wide and 90 feet long. The special aspect of this structure is the kinetic way in which the structure responds to the natural light. When there is no direct sunlight on the structure there is a soft glow and the glass takes on a more solid appearance.

The landscape adjacent to the pavilion is formal and ceremonial with flag poles used for announcing foreign guests and a double row of trees providing a continuation of the green belt landscaping on either side of the site along Jefferson Avenue.

The transit station

The new transit station for the Detroit light rail system has been designed to meet the needs of transit passengers who are entering or leaving the General Motors facility. This is a three-story facility with passengers embarking and disembarking trains at the highest level and connecting to a pedestrian bridge system at the intermediate level and entering or departing from the city at grade level. Each level is connected by a set of escalators and an elevator in addition to two sets of enclosed stairs. The structure is a basic steel construction, painted white and glazed on the south wall with translucent glass that allows natural light into the three levels and glows when lit by the sun. In the evening when this wall is lit from within, light gently washes the landscape. The east and west façades are glazed in clear glass to facilitate viewing of oncoming trains.

In the early morning or late afternoon when the sun is coming in from the sides and is low, the stainless steel struts glisten and shimmer with reflective light and the glass seems to disappear.

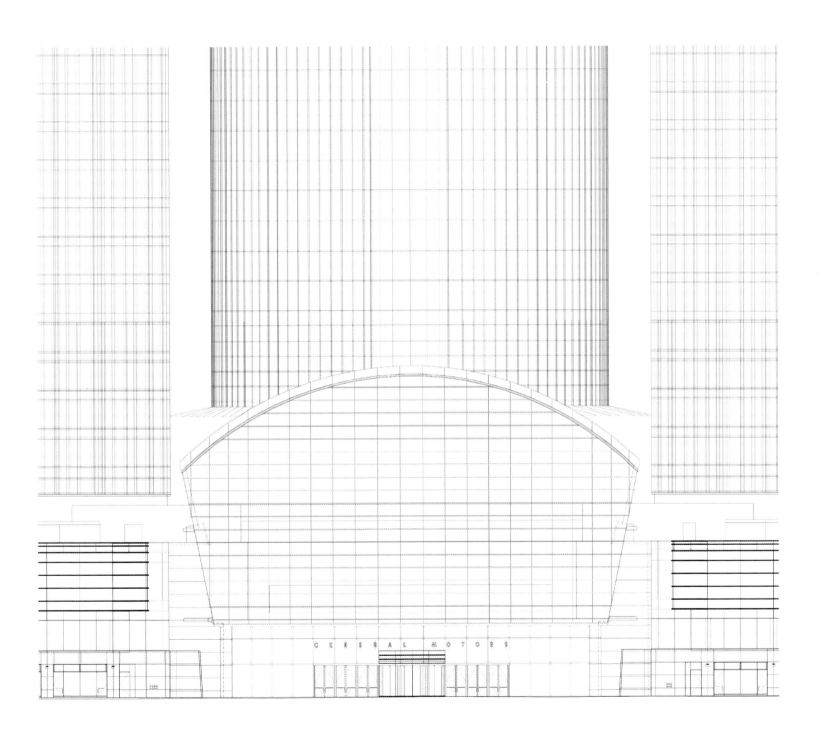

General Motors at Renaissance Center

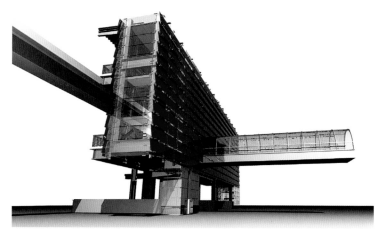

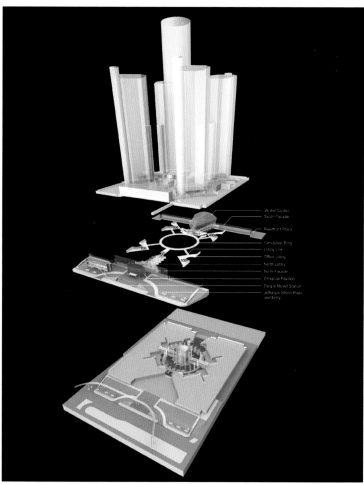

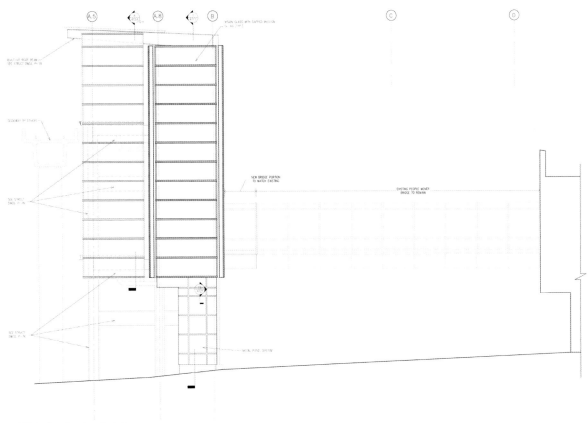

West elevation transit station

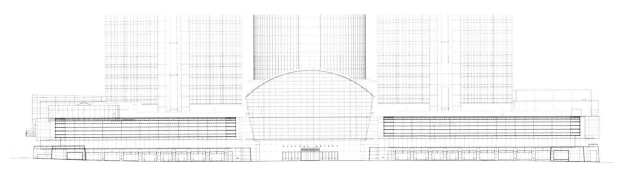

South elevation podium

The lobby

The building's main lobby is accessed at two levels—at grade through the pavilion and at the mezzanine level by bridges that connect to the Millinder Center across the street and the bridge from the transit station. The primary features of this lobby are two undulating 4-inch-thick glass walls by British artist Danny Lane. This sculpture, named *Borealis*, is 26 feet high and 45 feet long on each side of the lobby. It consists of approximately 2000 clear polished glass pieces, laid on end and supported by a base wall beam at the floor to spread the weight of the structure across the floor and to the building's existing columns. It is laterally braced by a solid stainless steel shaft at one end of the wall and individual hangers off a trussed structure that is cantilevered off the slab of the mezzanine. The piece was experimental and took five series of erection procedures over a five-month period to perfect the sequence and refine the design. The lighting for this sculpture is mostly behind the glass at the mezzanine level, casting light up to the ceiling and through the glass, giving the ceiling a dramatic pattern of undulating light with red and white light tones. A gallery space for the display of GM messages and projected imagery is envisioned for the area behind the glass sculpture. The movement of light and images through the glass wall has the effect of objects appearing and disappearing as they move through this space.

Connecting the lobby to the circulation ring is a link space, designed with wood panels set at 45 degrees from pedestrian movement into the facility. Window wall storefronts are behind a series of stainless steel-clad columns that lead the visitor to a pair of escalators that in turn lead to the circulation ring at the second level. This point in the path is also where the mezzanine circulation connects to the circulation ring. Here, the atrium comes into full view and the visitor is able to see the interaction between the retail circulation one level below, the GM World display two levels below, and the hotel amenities and meeting room circulation one level above. At this point, one steps onto the circulation ring.

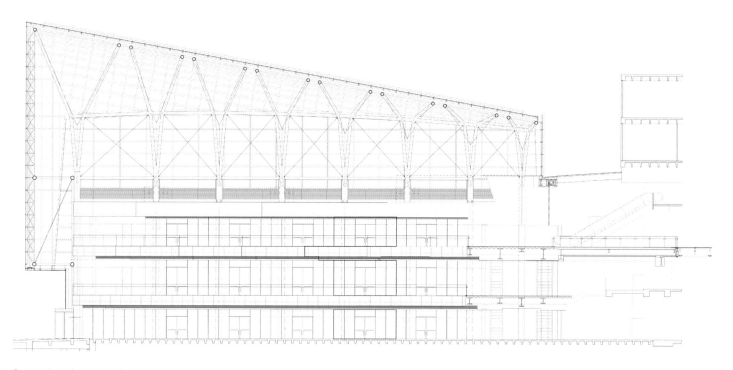

Section through wintergarden

General Motors at Renaissance Center

The circulation ring

The circulation ring is an all-glass floor made of three layers of tempered glass laminated together with the top layer acid-etched to a custom grid pattern. The glass floor is lit from below and gives the floor a lantern-like quality. The added benefit of this system is that it provides a much-needed light source to the atrium with light flowing both up to the ceiling and down to the first floor. The structure of the ring is painted steel suspended from above by twin cables and approximately 20 feet on center. The railings are clear laminated glass with cherry wood handrails connected by machined stainless steel brackets. The ring has become so popular that employees will walk the ring for fun during their breaks and at lunchtime. It has eight points of exit, four serving the four tower lobbies, two serving GM University, one serving the main lobby, and one serving the winter garden. Each office lobby is color coded and numbered for easy identification.

The wintergarden

The wintergarden is entered from the circulation ring and from the south entrance to the GM facility. It is a five-story skylit space that lets in natural light for most of the day and gives the atrium a strong point of orientation. It is a fan-shaped space that opens up to the south with a large curved window allowing panoramic views of the Detroit River and the Canadian border beyond. The structure consists of a lightweight steel top cord and a form of bicycle truss tying cables to a floating ring. The structure is painted yellow ochre in order to project warmth into the space. The sides of the wintergarden are formed by cantilevered walkways in a sawtooth configuration, clad in eucalyptus veneer, impervious to sunlight. These walkways access all glass storefronts that are seen from the floor of the wintergarden and help animate the space with shopping activity. The base of this space is filled with tables and chairs for casual dining and the space is planted with palm trees. There is an audiovisual equipment setup for special functions and GM hires out this space for black-tie functions on a regular basis. From this space one can look up and see the central hotel tower and two of the four office towers soaring into the air. Outside the curved glass wall, where the curved wall meets the straight wall, a spectacular view into the structure that supports the curved five-story glass wall is revealed.

The exterior wall

The existing exterior wall at the south elevation was changed from the original solid wall to an all-glass enclosure to take advantage of the view of the Detroit River and to allow light into this retail-oriented space. At grade, this exterior condition was previously a basement space since the roadway was above grade in the original design. The wall at this level was clad in precast concrete, with large framed windows on both sides of the wintergarden entrance to help frame the entry and to provide framed openings for street-level retail. At the east and west elevations of the podium the existing polished granite was flamed to give a softer finish that would better contrast with the glazed surfaces it frames. Overlaid onto the stone are a series of stainless steel tubes that provide shadow and connection to the window wall, which contains the same detail at its mullion line. At the main entrance, a grand scaled linen-textured stainless steel wall provides a differentiating element to both set off the delicate pavilion structure and contain General Motors signage. Behind this wall surface is the hotel's grand ballroom.

The retail storefronts

The typical stick system retail storefronts within the facility have all been removed and replaced with a mullion-less butt glazed clear glass system with a wood horizontal plain. This solution brings warmth to the tough board-formed concrete environment of the Renaissance Center and helps provide continuity of materials throughout all retail areas. This condition also provides adequate space for ceiling-recessed down-lighting in front of the retail. All signage in this wall is behind the clear glass in neon or store logo identification.

The level-two office lobbies

The four office lobbies on the second floor are color coded for orientation and identification. Each lobby is identified with a full-height, revealed colored lacquer wall, framing a curved glass element that is used to identify GM employees. Within each lobby is a front desk that issues security passes to visitors doing business with GM within the office space. (Floor treatment in these spaces is provided by GM's tenant architect.)

Burj Khalifa

Location: Dubai, United Arab Emirates
Client: EMAAR
Year: 2003–2008

The competition

Mark Amirault and Robert Booth contacted us in spring, 2002 to arrange an interview with them to discuss the possibility of designing the Burj Khalifa. They had seen the Jin Mao Tower in China, which I had designed several years earlier. Bill Baker, George Efstathiou, and I met them in New York and showed them several super tall buildings that we had designed, both residential and mixed-use. We talked about the importance of architectural and structural integration to achieve an efficient and affordable design. At the end of the interview they asked me how they should decide which architect to choose, since they had interviewed several that they thought were capable of doing the project. I suggested they should have a two-week ideas competition, at the end of which they could select the scheme that would best meet their needs.

A few weeks later they pursued that direction, we developed our concept, submitted it and we were selected. My understanding is that the competitors' submitted material was displayed and then each concept was presented to Mohamed Alabbar and the directors of EMAAR, who judged the submissions on criteria including initial visual impact, buildability, and cost. Our competitors were KPF from New York, Cesar Pelli from New Haven, Connecticut, Carlos Ott from Canada, and NORR Architecture from Dubai. SOM was the only firm that contained all disciplines including architectural, structural, mechanical, interior design, and urban planning.

The concept

In developing the initial concept for Burj Khalifa, I searched for elements within the existing context and culture of the area to reflect on and draw inspiration from. Within the Middle East and in Dubai, there are strong influences of onion domes and pointed arches, and patterns that are indigenous to the region, some of which are flower-like with three elements, some with six, and so on. Other influences include spiral imagery, and the philosophy embedded in Middle Eastern iconographic architecture and motifs. These motifs have their origin in organic growth structures and plant materials.

The form is geometric in plan, starting with three branches and three pods. The specific shape of these branches is modular in nature and in function, and organic and biomorphic in form. The form can be found in flower petals, leaves, and seeds, in animals such as birds, and sea creatures including crustaceans. The overall composition is a vertical object reduced and transformed by spiral reduction of branch lengths until it reaches its central shaft, at which point the shaft peels away to reveal a triptych configuration that erodes in a spiral manner until a single spire remains. The resulting impression is organic and plant-like. This typology is indeterminate in its size and can be expanded vertically by adding modules to its base or continuing to divide the spire element.

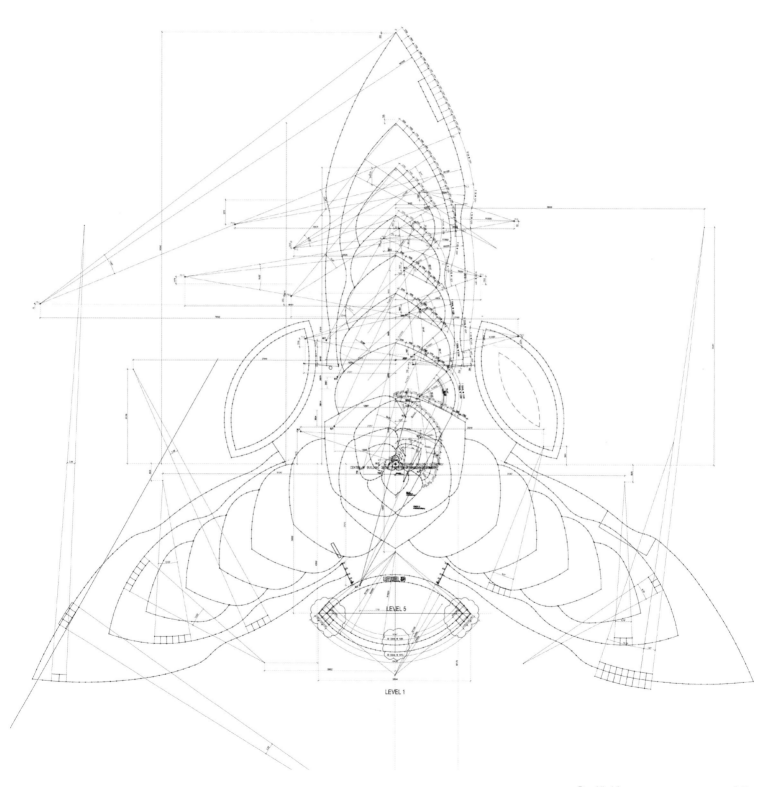

CENTER OF BUILDING / CENTER OF ROTATION OF MOVEMENT

LEVEL 5

LEVEL 1

Burj Khalifa   161

Observed in silhouette, the setbacks connect the Burj Khalifa to the surrounding city, both now and in the future. At the lower floors, the setbacks relate to the existing low- and mid-rise buildings that characterize the current landscape. As the region grows and taller high-rise buildings are constructed, setbacks at the higher floors will ensure that the tower always remains connected to its context. As the building rises from the ground I feel it wants to appear as if sculpted from the earth and crystallized into a vertical stalagmite of glass and steel. Its base should be very dense and solid, reaching out to connect to the contours that ascend to its base and expressing the enormous weight it is carrying above.

To me, "organic" means that it is a form that looks as though it is emerging from the ground and ascending vertically. The flower image comes from looking at the building in plan, or from the air, looking down at the building. The reference to the Islamic dome structures can be seen when looking up at the legs or branches of the tower and looking at the plan of each section of the three legs of the building. The pointed dome form in plan became an ideal form for the development of bay-like windows from individual units to provide a more panoramic view of the city and the Gulf. This form also provided a surface at each bay that would reflect light without the use of large flat surfaces that can sometimes be disturbing to the viewer when the sun is reflected by them.

The developer's objectives

EMAAR had just finished developing the Marina project, a massive venture on the Gulf. Six towers in the range of 40 stories had been built, and from this experience the demands from people in Dubai to live and work in high rise-structures were understood. After the Marina project, EMAAR embarked on a monumental project of more than 500 acres, with plans to build many millions of square feet on this piece of land. It felt that a landmark structure in the form of a super tall building was needed in order to give the entire project an identity and a critical mass. A tall tower would not only give the master plan an identity, but would also become the identity for EMAAR and the country of Dubai. The image of Burj Khalifa was later used in a highly successful advertising campaign in a select number of high-quality magazines on a worldwide basis to help establish a brand name for the project.

I felt that a tower of the height expected from EMAAR, to be the world's tallest tower, should somehow embody these indigenous forms and should also be organic in nature.

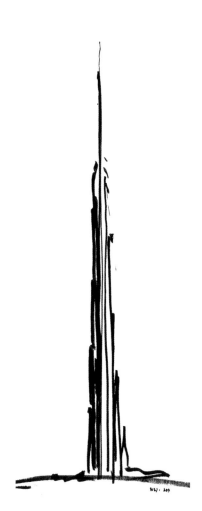

May 2003

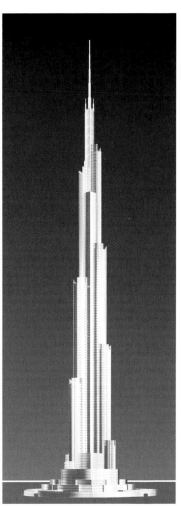

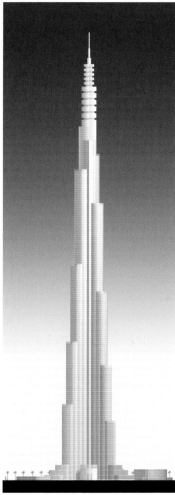

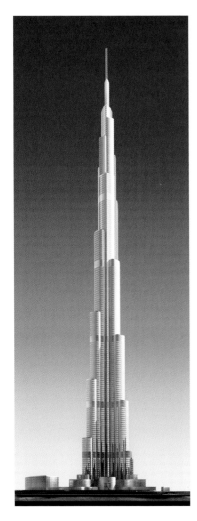
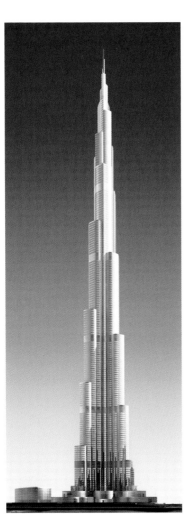
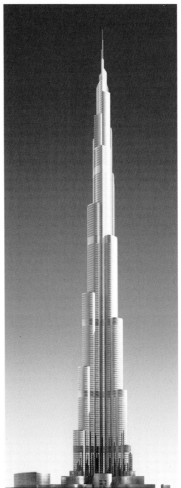

Final scheme

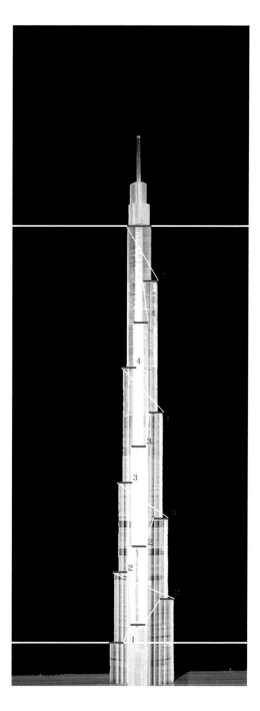

It is very difficult for a developer to make money on a super tall building—that's why there are so few of them around. They are usually built for some other purpose, such as a national symbol or landmark, or as a catalyst for a much larger project where the tower itself may not make money but the sites around it will become more valuable. There are exceptional cases, like Burj Khalifa, where the building will justify a high premium for its space.

Even so, the building fundamentally must be designed to optimize all of its systems to become affordable. The primary difference between a super tall tower and two towers half the size is not the cost per square foot, although a super tall building will be more expensive on a square foot basis. Factors including the time it takes to build one tall building versus two shorter ones, the cost of the money during that time, and the loss of revenue through lost rent for the time difference, make most super tall buildings financially unfeasible.

Structural integration

The integration of architectural and structural concepts is essential in the design of super tall structures.

For a project to be viable, the building needs to be well suited for the functions it contains, the structure must be able to respond to the function it supports, and it must be cost effective. The structure of the Burj Khalifa is modular, with a central hexagonal shaft or core and three branches that spread out at 120 degrees from each other. Attached to these branches are wall-like columns at 9-meter spacing that simply drop off as each leg sets back, avoiding complex and costly structural transfers. One of the key issues in the structural design of super tall buildings is that the building has the shape necessary to shed negative forces imposed on it by the wind

moving around the building. Commonly known as vortices, these are the forces that move a building from side to side. This is not the movement that one expects from the wind trying to blow the tower over, it is a wind force that if not designed for will create a sideways movement that is rapid in its frequency and thus of high acceleration; the kind of movement that makes the water in your sink move or the chandelier hanging from the ceiling swing. This is the kind of movement that if felt inside the building, makes the occupants very uncomfortable.

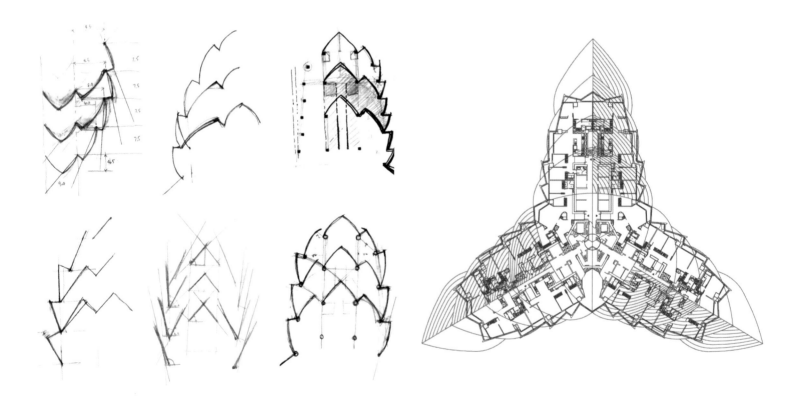

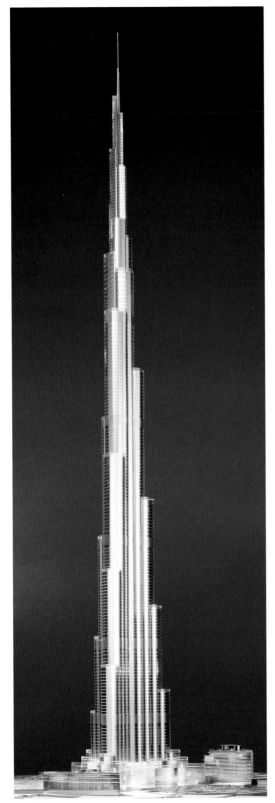
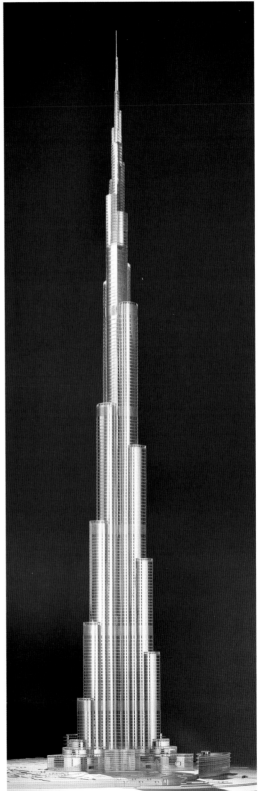

The shape of the building is very important in the mitigation of these forces and we tested, by wind tunnel test, several variations of the concept until we got the orientation and stepping system to optimum performance and verified that the building shape responded properly to the maximum winds expected on the site.

Other structural issues include design for overturning, torsional movement, and foundation stability.

Environmental awareness

The building will feature an innovative condensate collection system. Hot and humid outside air, combined with the cooling requirements of the building, will result in a significant amount of condensation of moisture from the air. This condensed water will be collected and used for irrigation of the tower's landscape plantings. This system will provide about 15 million gallons of supplemental water per year, equivalent to nearly 20 Olympic-sized swimming pools.

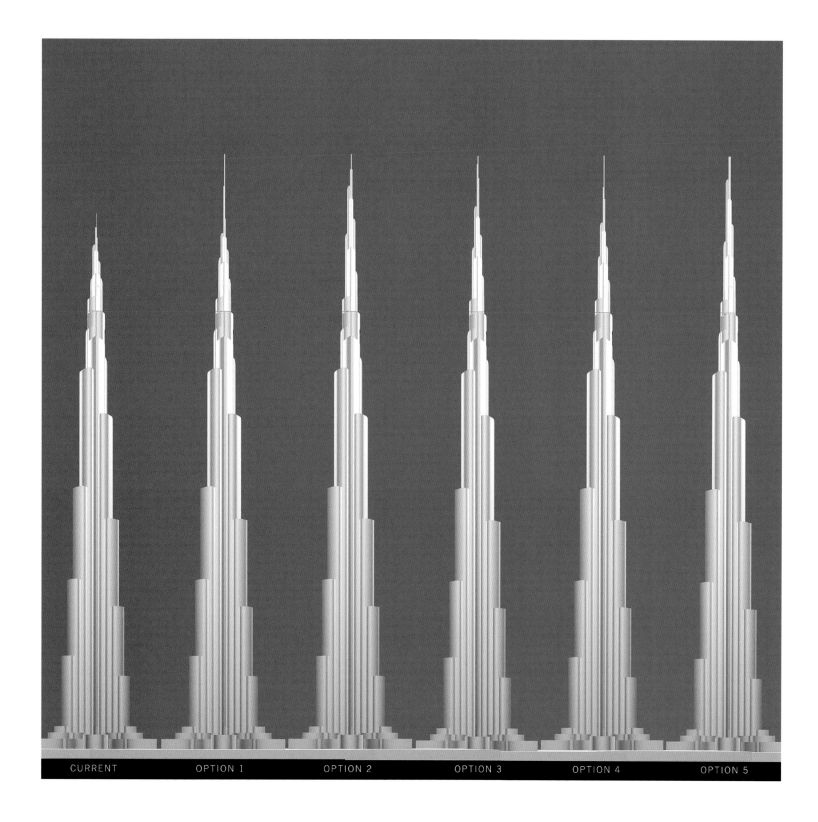

CURRENT   OPTION 1   OPTION 2   OPTION 3   OPTION 4   OPTION 5

TOP

G

F

F

F

E

D

C

B

A

A
A
A
A
A
A
A
A
A
A
A
A
A
A
B
B
A

C

B

A

C

B

A

C

B

B

TIER 24
TIER 23
TIER 22
TIER NEW-3

TIER 21

TIER 20

TIER 19

TIER NEW-2

TIER NEW-1

TIER 18

TIER 17

TIER 16

TIER 15

TIER 14

TIER 13

TIER 12

TIER 11

TIER 10

TIER 9

TIER 8

TIER 7

TIER 6

TIER 5

TIER 4

TIER 3

TIER 2

Tower tiers

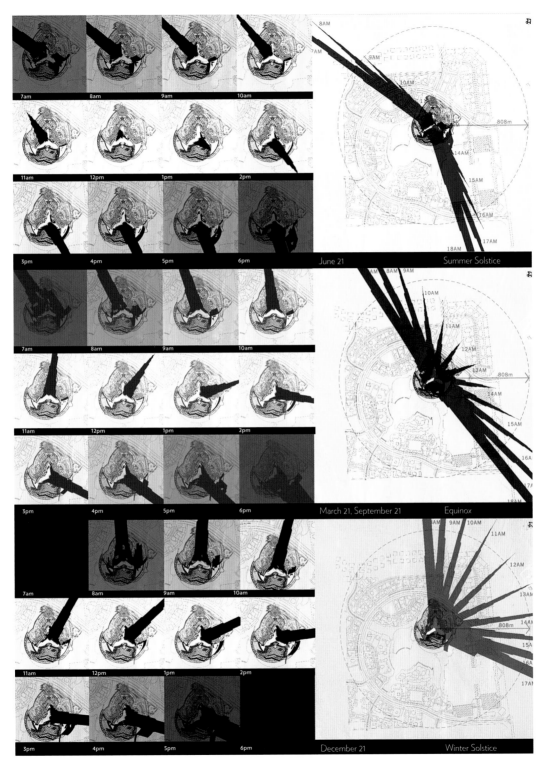

7am 8am 9am 10am
11am 12pm 1pm 2pm
3pm 4pm 5pm 6pm

8AM 7AM 9AM 10AM 808m 14AM 15AM 16AM 17AM 18AM

June 21   Summer Solstice

7am 8am 9am 10am
11am 12pm 1pm 2pm
3pm 4pm 5pm 6pm

7AM 8AM 9AM 10AM 11AM 12AM 13AM 808m 14AM 15AM 16A 17A 18AM

March 21, September 21   Equinox

7am 8am 9am 10am
11am 12pm 1pm 2pm
3pm 4pm 5pm 6pm

8AM 9AM 10AM 11AM 12AM 13AM 808m 14AM 15A 16A 17AM

December 21   Winter Solstice

Sun studies

Tower exterior wall, typical detail

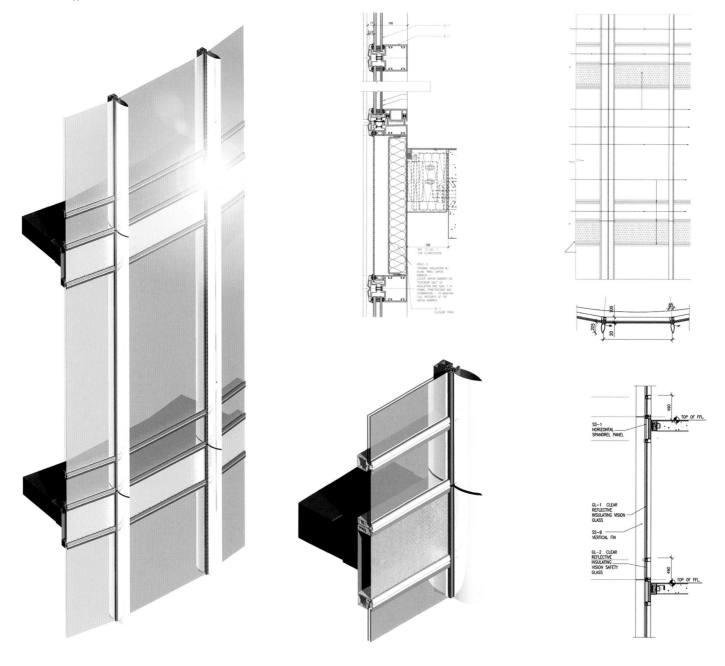

Burj Khalifa

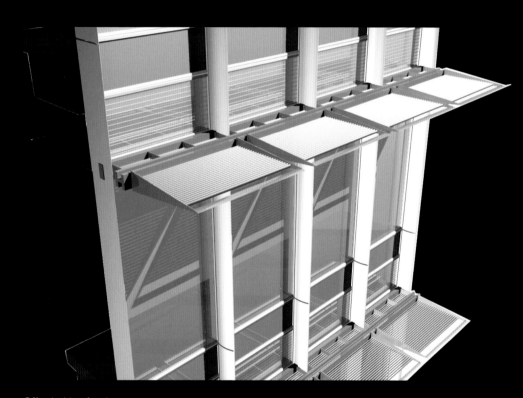
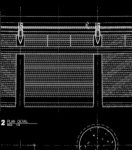
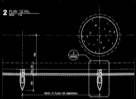
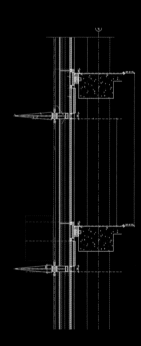

Office building façade

Stack effect mitigation

Also known as chimney effect, it occurs when the temperature difference between exterior and interior air induces air movement.

In a cold climate, warmer inside air rises through the building; colder outside air rushes in at the base.

The process is reversed in a hot climate like Dubai: colder air inside falls, drawing in the hot outside air at the top of the building.

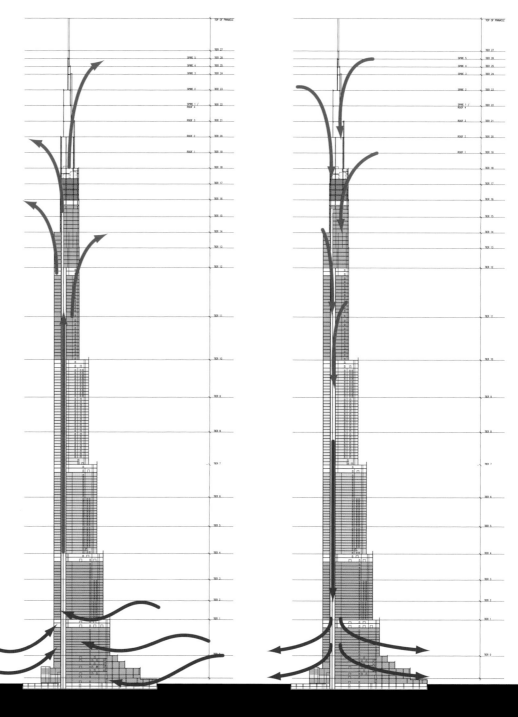

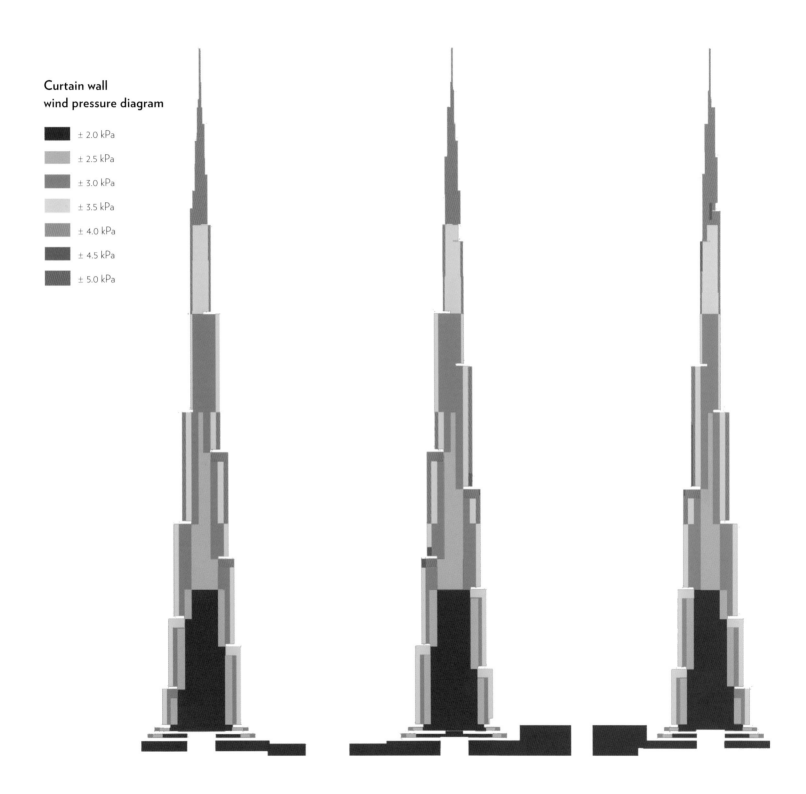

Curtain wall
wind pressure diagram

± 2.0 kPa
± 2.5 kPa
± 3.0 kPa
± 3.5 kPa
± 4.0 kPa
± 4.5 kPa
± 5.0 kPa

Directional distribution of winds

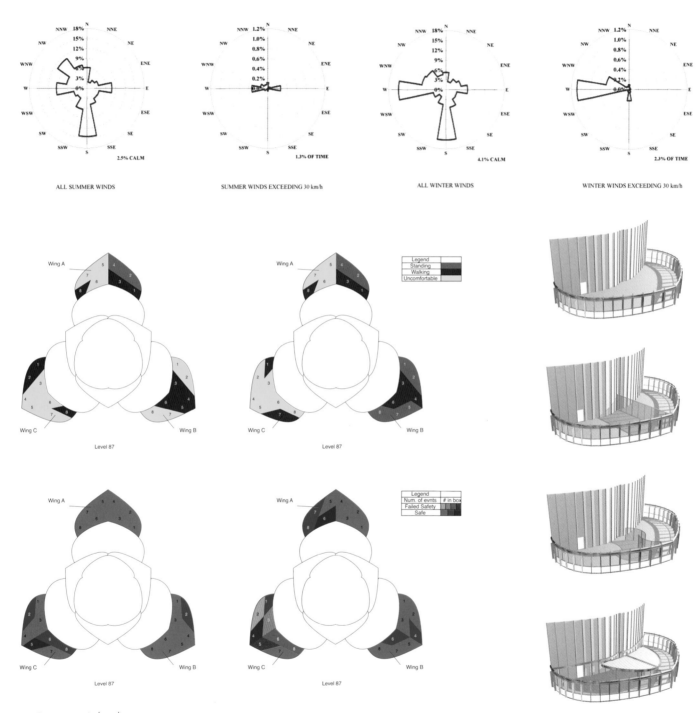

ALL SUMMER WINDS

2.5% CALM

SUMMER WINDS EXCEEDING 30 km/h

1.3% OF TIME

ALL WINTER WINDS

4.1% CALM

WINTER WINDS EXCEEDING 30 km/h

2.3% OF TIME

Legend
Standing
Walking
Uncomfortable

Wing A

Wing C

Wing B

Level 87

Legend
Num. of evnts | # in box
Failed Safety
Safe

Tower exterior terrace wind studies

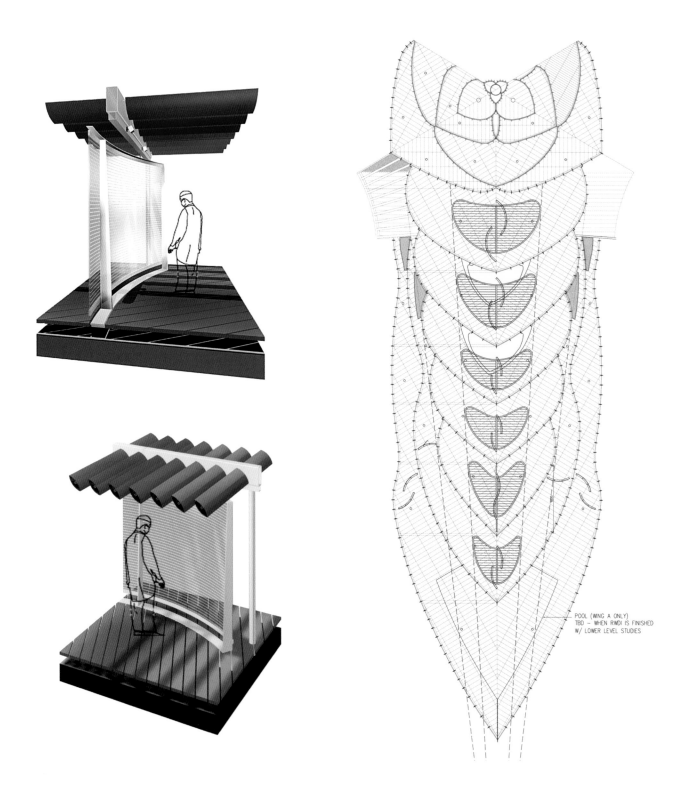

POOL (WING A ONLY)
TBD – WHEN RWDI IS FINISHED
W/ LOWER LEVEL STUDIES

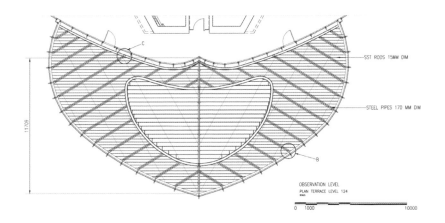

SST RODS 15MM DIM

STEEL PIPES 170 MM DIM

OBSERVATION LEVEL
PLAN TERRACE LEVEL 124

0   1000   10000

PURLIN TYPE I 150 mm

PURLIN TYPE II 200 mm

PURLIN TYPE III 250 mm

R=85 MM

A PROTOTYPE VERT. MULLION   **B** PROTOTYPE TRELLIS SYSTEM   **C** PROTOTYPE TRELLIS SYSTEM

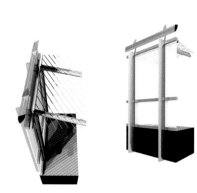

Details of observatory

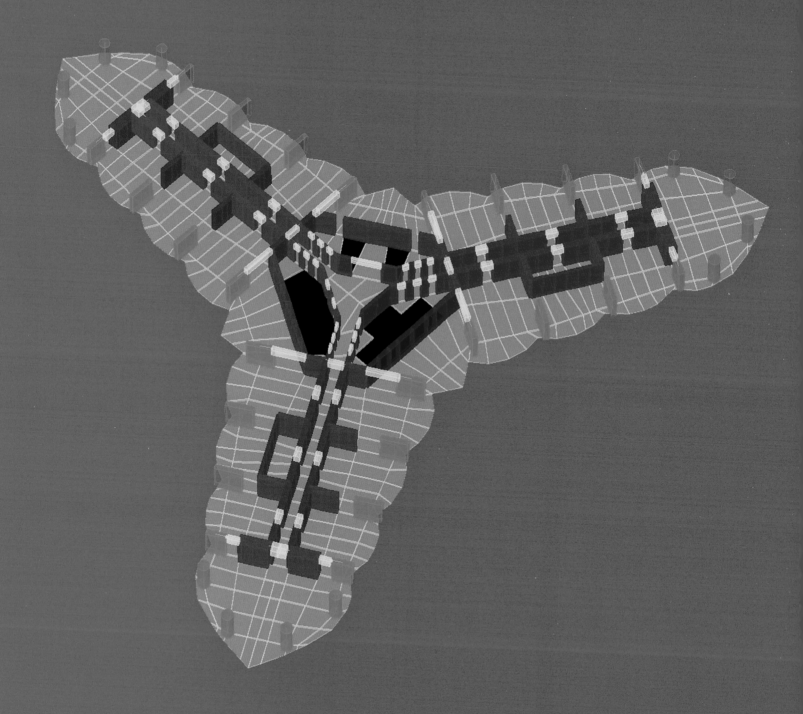

Burj Khalifa

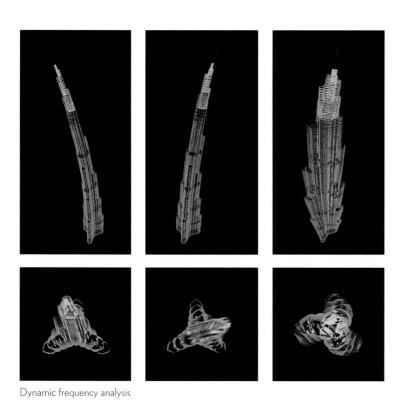

Dynamic frequency analysis

The pavilions

The focal point of each entry is the pavilion structure. These buildings are consistent with the geometry of the tower but very different in all other respects. The tower is reflective while the pavilions are transparent and crystalline. The pavilion structure is cable-supported using the lightest structural system possible while the tower is concrete: solid and robust.

The pavilions will take in light, manipulate it and tame its effect on the interior environment. At night, the pavilions will become lanterns that glow and shimmer from reflected light off water features in and around the structure, and will emit inviting warmth from sculptural features within.

There will be serenity and a theatrical quality to these spaces, befitting their role as entries to the world's tallest structure.

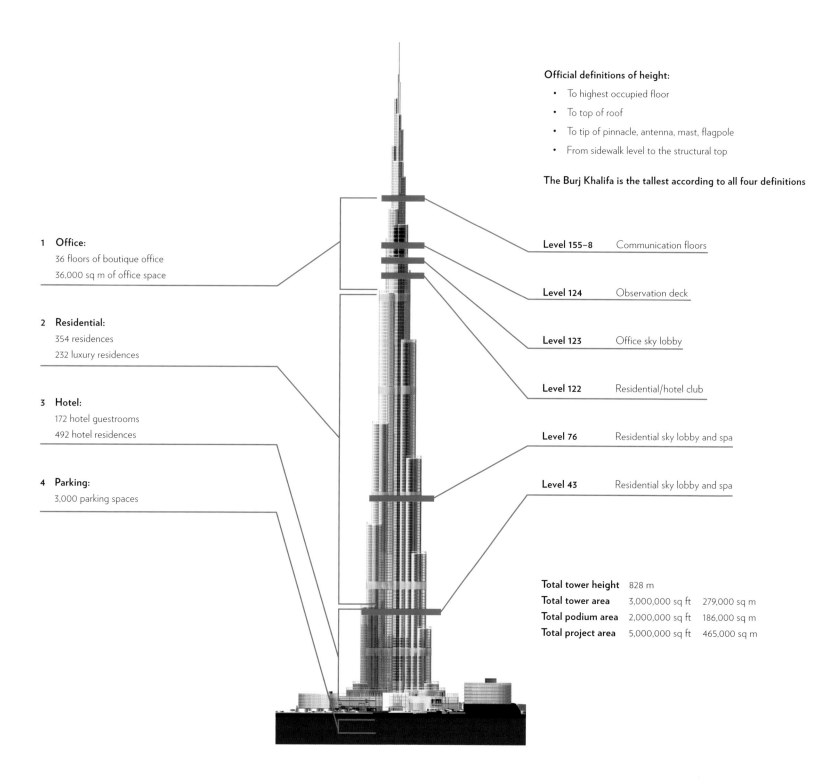

Official definitions of height:

- To highest occupied floor
- To top of roof
- To tip of pinnacle, antenna, mast, flagpole
- From sidewalk level to the structural top

The Burj Khalifa is the tallest according to all four definitions

1 Office:
36 floors of boutique office
36,000 sq m of office space

2 Residential:
354 residences
232 luxury residences

3 Hotel:
172 hotel guestrooms
492 hotel residences

4 Parking:
3,000 parking spaces

Level 155–8   Communication floors

Level 124   Observation deck

Level 123   Office sky lobby

Level 122   Residential/hotel club

Level 76   Residential sky lobby and spa

Level 43   Residential sky lobby and spa

Total tower height	828 m	
Total tower area	3,000,000 sq ft	279,000 sq m
Total podium area	2,000,000 sq ft	186,000 sq m
Total project area	5,000,000 sq ft	465,000 sq m

1 Main entrance

2 Security gates

3 Hotel entrance + 16 DMD parking egress

4 Residential entrance + 10 DMD parking egress

5 Office entrance + 6 DMD parking egress

6 Office entrance road parking

7 Office annex 16,000 sq m entrance

8 Spa building

9 New mall

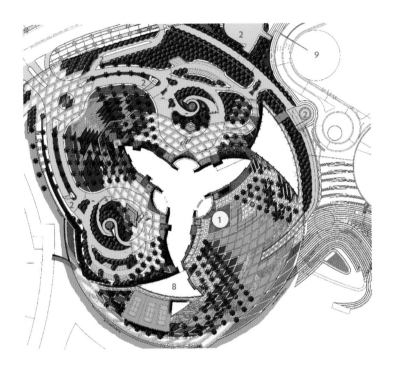

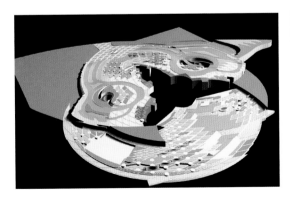

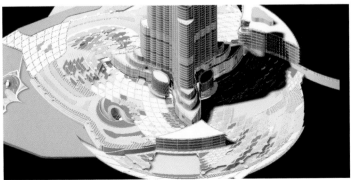

The exterior of the pavilion will be a full double wall. Heat from the sun will be contained within the two glazed surfaces by sun-shading devices that operate to provide optimum shade to the interior when sun is hitting the pavilion and optimum transparency when no sun is present. Using a glazing system without mullions, the glass panels are silicone glazed on four sides with pressure plates at each intersection on both internal and external glazing systems. The plates are supported by stainless steel rods that connect to the cable net system running both vertically and horizontally through the interstitial space.

The pavilions are designed as instruments of light.

Tower exterior wall

By contrast, the tower's exterior wall is solid and reflective, shielding sunlight from its interior spaces. It will be a kinetic visual experience reflecting the color of the sky as the sun moves over the building. The design of the façade went through a series of studies, although it was initially presented as a stainless steel, high efficiency, low-e, double-glazed façade with floor-to-ceiling glass to take maximum advantage of its views from great heights. The details of the mullion system were studied using extruded tubes attached by brackets at approximately 450 millimeters from the glass surface and later developed into wing-shaped mullions of polished stainless steel projecting from the glass wall by 225 millimeters at every 1.2 to 1.5 meters on center throughout the body of the tower.

The polished stainless steel vertical fins are shaped to reflect the elements within the tower façade. At the tower's base the fins are deeper and the glazing elements are more horizontal in proportion, and are fritted with gray line work that will reflect in the polished fins, creating a pattern of curved lines when seen obliquely. In the tower the vertical fins also serve to separate adjacent panels of glass and help give the impression that the faceted glass is curved. At the terraces created by the setbacks, the fins become the structure for the handrails and the light fixtures that will illuminate the tower at night. They will provide a sense of secondary enclosure for units with terraces. The spandrel panels of the tower skin will be stainless steel with a linen texture. This texture is helpful in reducing any distortion in the metallic surface of the flat stainless steel panel.

The reflective glass is designed with a thicker outer light of glass and a thinner interior light in order to reduce what is known as a "pillowing" effect when the pressure of the air in the interstitial space is greater or lesser than the outside air pressure. By using a thicker exterior layer of glass, the interior light will deflect before the exterior light, thus maintaining a flatter appearance from the exterior.

Near the outer points of the three wings of the tower the modules of the mullions modify and increase in distance until they reach the maximum width of 2.2 meters, thus enhancing the panoramic view from the tip of the tower. This move also establishes a greater density of activity and materiality near the central spine of the tower that dissipates as it moves out toward the end of the tower.

At the mechanical levels the use of stainless steel is increased to 70 percent stainless, 20 percent glass, and 10 percent open, composed in horizontal ribbons. Added to this texture are 200-millimeter polished stainless steel tubes that become the structure for the window-washing equipment. These tubes wrap around the entire mechanical floor and come into the enclosure at the central spine where the window-washing rigs are stored.

The exterior skin is typical on all surfaces of the tower above the third floor until it becomes the spire, at which point the density of the verticals increases as the radius of the surfaces decreases, in order to reduce the size of each individual piece of glass.

At the very top, the spire is solid steel, clad in stainless. The primary focus of the design for the exterior wall was to eliminate any horizontal surfaces that could collect the fine-grained desert dust and sand, to reduce the staining that would result from light rains.

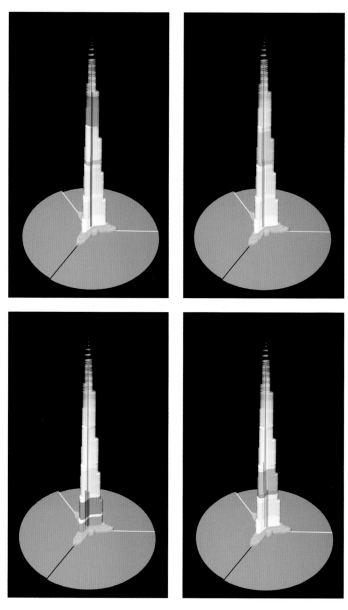

Clockwise from top left: Custom luxury office, luxury residential, residential, hotel

Concourse Level

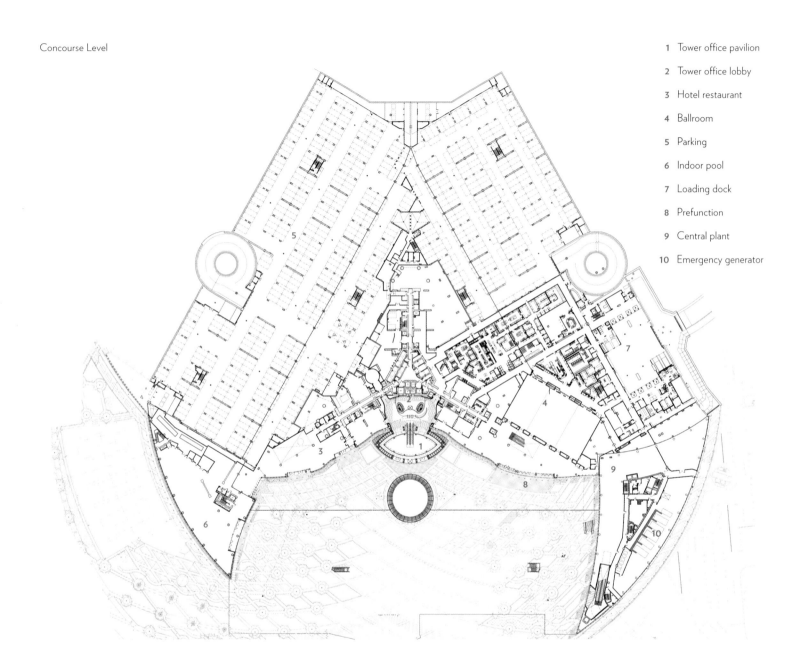

1 Tower office pavilion

2 Tower office lobby

3 Hotel restaurant

4 Ballroom

5 Parking

6 Indoor pool

7 Loading dock

8 Prefunction

9 Central plant

10 Emergency generator

Ground level

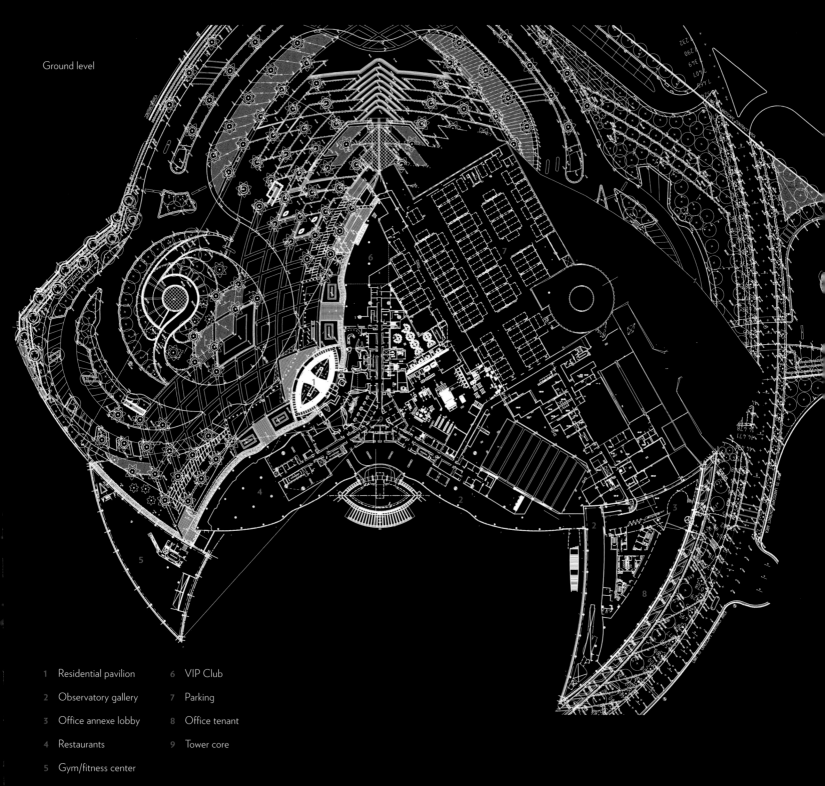

1 Residential pavilion

2 Observatory gallery

3 Office annexe lobby

4 Restaurants

5 Gym/fitness center

6 VIP Club

7 Parking

8 Office tenant

9 Tower core

Level 1

1 Hotel pavilion

2 Spa

3 Hotel prefunction

4 Hotel restaurant

5 Ballroom drop off

6 Office annexe entry

7 Office tenant

8 Hotel

9 Lobby bar

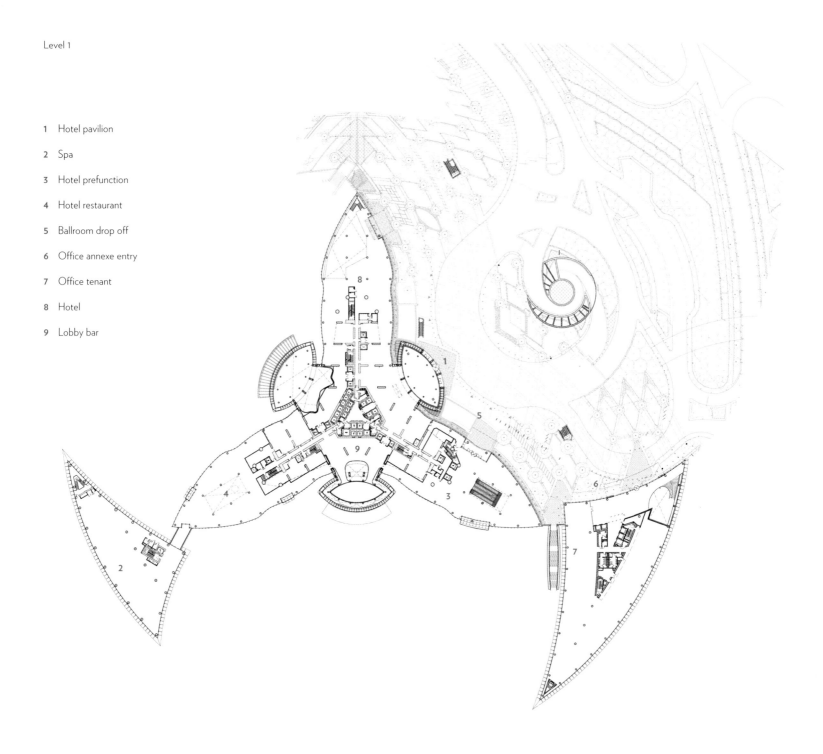

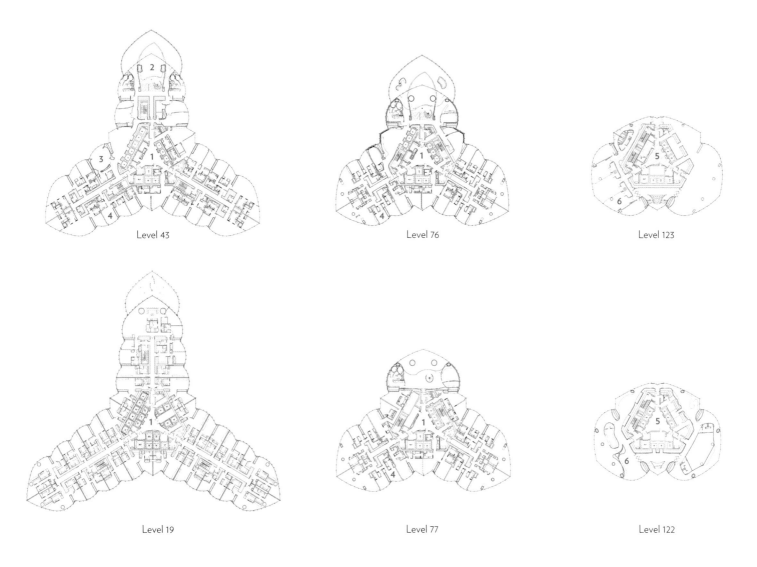

Level 43

Level 76

Level 123

Level 19

Level 77

Level 122

1 Tower residential core   5 Sky lobby transfer

2 Residential spa   6 Meeting room

3 Residential lounge   7 Food service

4 Residential units

Tower top

The top of the Burj Khalifa has been the subject of continuous discussion and development. The reason for this is that the initial concept scheme had a greater aspect ratio than the early massing developments after the competition. Compounding this was the desire of some members of the development team to keep the height of the tower down to something in the 550-meter range. They felt this height would still achieve the desired goal of the world's tallest building when completed. The problem I had with this was that I couldn't get the tower to look or feel like the competition scheme, and the massing schemes that we developed were also not satisfying to Mohamed Alabbar. Throughout the months as we continued to develop the floor plans, the exterior wall, the structure, the life safety systems, the elevator systems and mechanical plant, we were working on the massing and the top. At each meeting with the client during this phase, we would produce another massing model. Each time we would inch it higher and there would be pressure to reduce it. Finally, after the developer of the Palms in Dubai surfaced a concept by I.M. Pei that was significantly taller that the 550-meter limit we were up against, EMAAR allowed us to pursue taller schemes. This was the breakthrough that we needed to get the massing right and to develop a top that was of sufficient mass to feel like it belonged to the base and middle of the tower, and that could almost complete the stepping system that was developed at the lower levels.

We lived with this scheme for about a year but I was still not satisfied that we had it right; we kept studying it and as time went on we had what I felt was the top. The next step was to convince Mohamed that this was right. It was no easy task, since it meant going back to the wind tunnel test and revising the structural calculations both for acceleration of movement and for foundation strength. We were in the middle of testing piles that had been driven on site at the time. During the last design development meeting for the tower and the first schematic design presentation of the interior design for the residential public spaces and office public spaces, we commissioned a 1:500 scale model in stainless steel with a removable top piece and presented the then-current scheme and the new proposed final scheme to Mohamed. He loved the higher and final scheme and directed that it be pursued. That was all we needed to finish the testing and re-engineering of the tower. As it turned out, the additional mass actually had a dampening effect on the tower, so Bill Baker was happy, I was happy, and so was the rest of the design team.

Residential pavilion

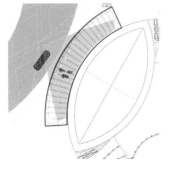

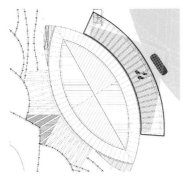

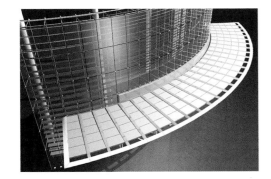

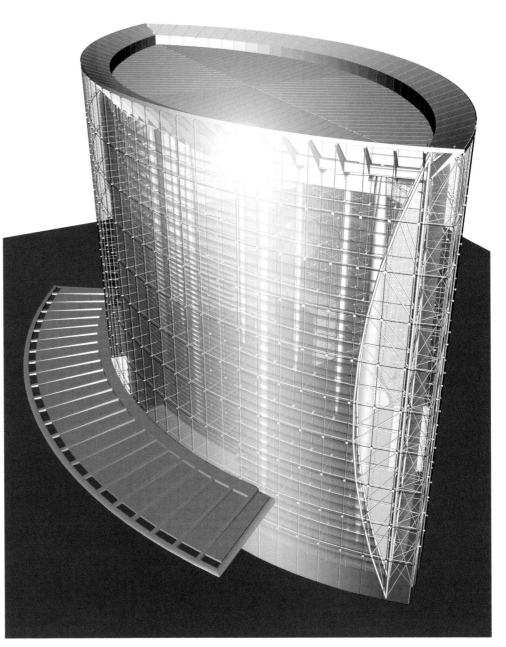

Burj Khalifa

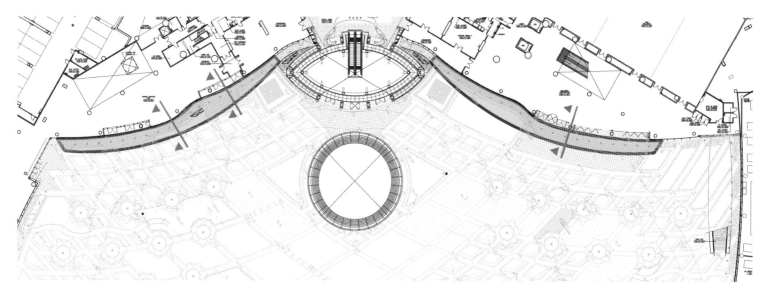

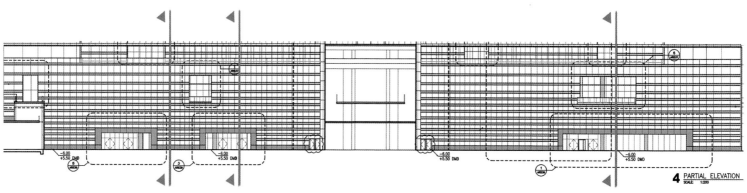

4 PARTIAL ELEVATION
SCALE: 1:200

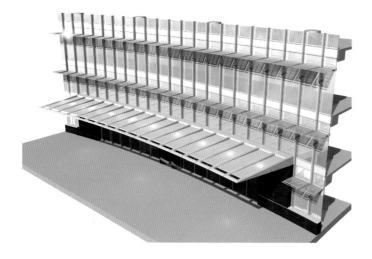

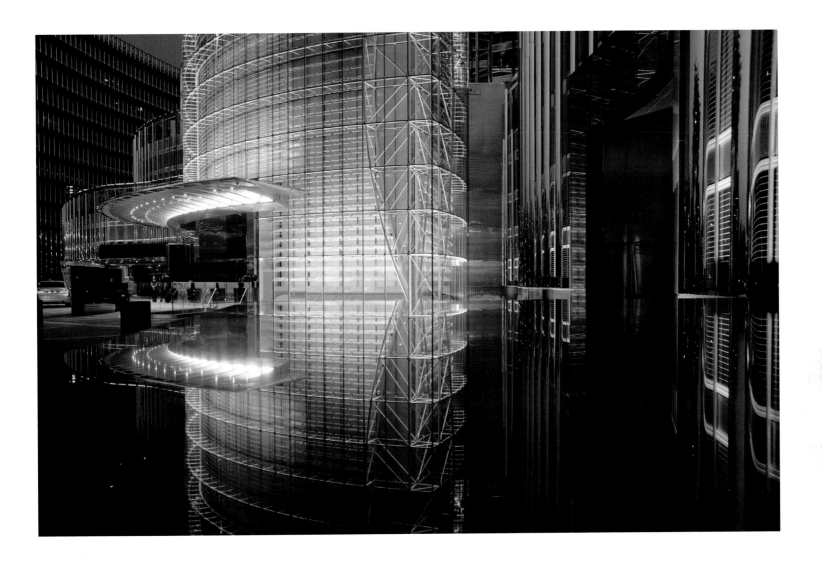

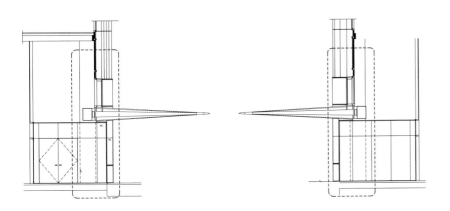

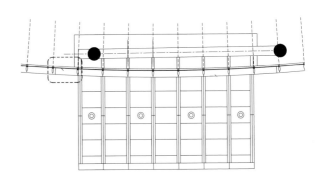

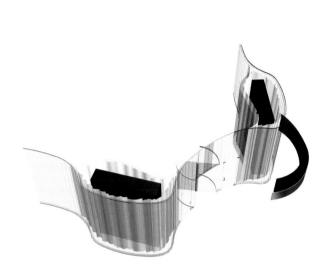

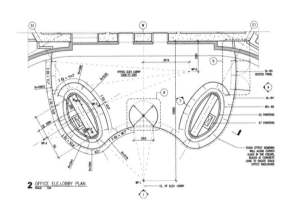

2 OFFICE ELE. LOBBY PLAN
SCALE 1:50

Burj Khalifa

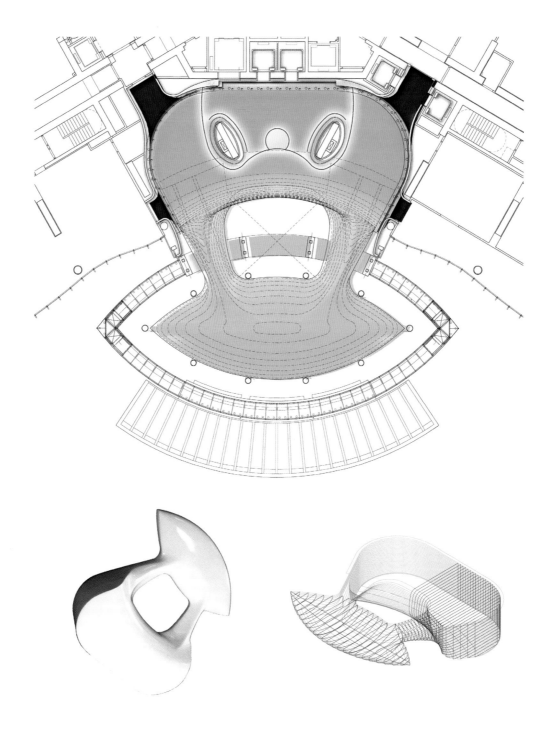

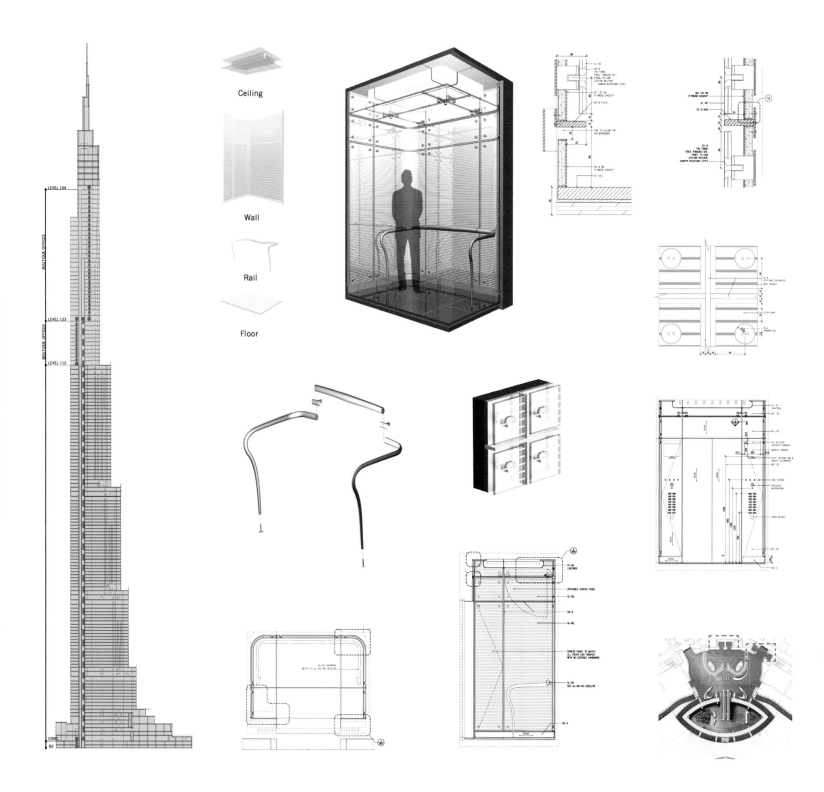

Ceiling

Wall

Rail

Floor

LEVEL 154

LEVEL 123

LEVEL 112

CONC.

B2

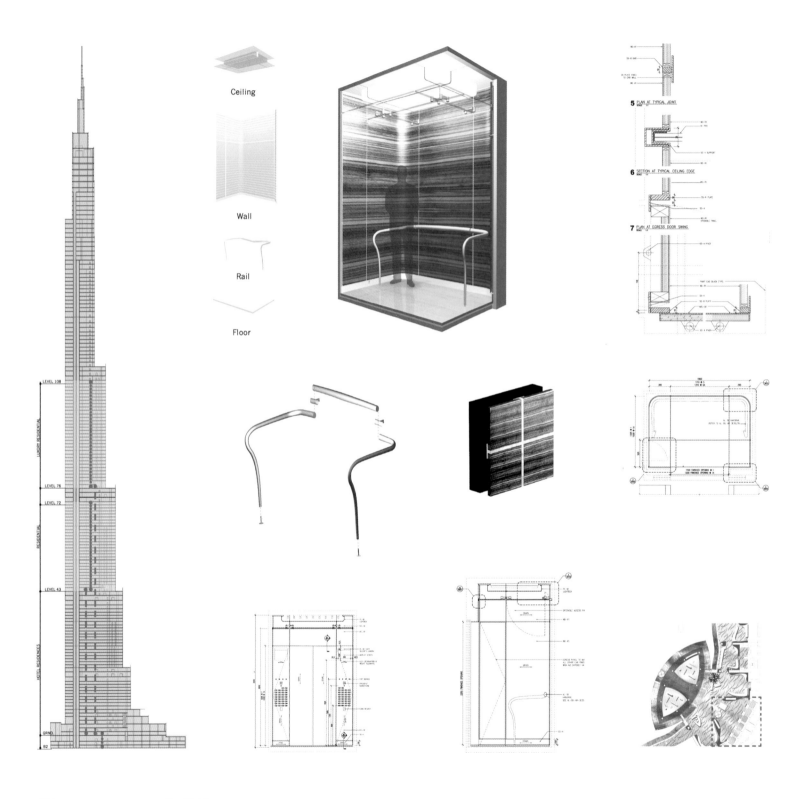

Ceiling

Wall

Rail

Floor

The interior

The interiors of this project were just as important to the success of the project as the massing. We were finally selected and released to develop a concept for the interior spaces for the residential and office components of the building. Georgio Armani was to personally direct the interior work for the hotel. The interiors for the observatory and passageways to it were given to an exhibit designer. Nada Andric led the interiors effort for the residential public spaces, and Marshall Strabala, the Burj Khalifa studio head for the later phases, led the effort for the office lobby. Nada felt, as did I, that the interiors should be an extension of the wavy exterior character of the exterior and proposed a series of spaces that were freeform in nature and of varying heights as one moves through the spaces of the public areas. She also discovered that these forms were embodied in the Arabic alphabet and studied their relationship to find a philosophic response that would connect the two. She enlisted the help of Lonny Israel, a graphic designer from our San Francisco office, to develop some pattern ideas for the floors, based on the Arabic script. We liked the connection and it gave the interior development a solid connection with the context of Dubai and the tower design. She developed each space with and without the strong use of this idea and we presented both to Mohamed Alabbar in his home.

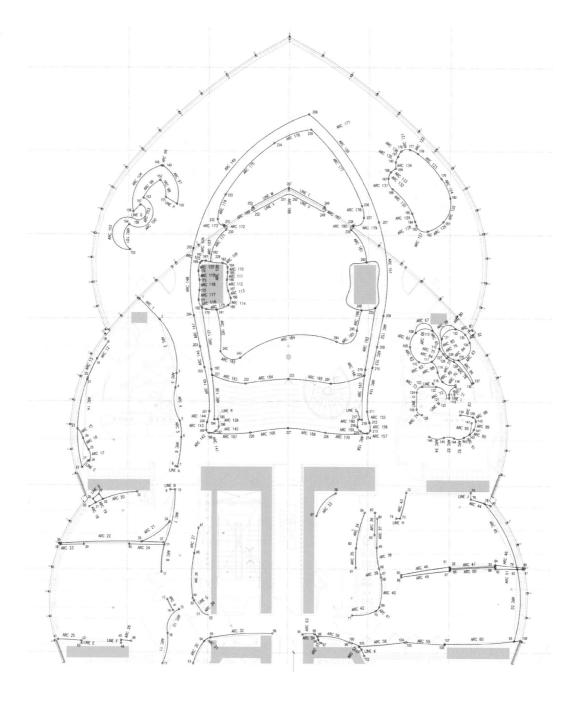

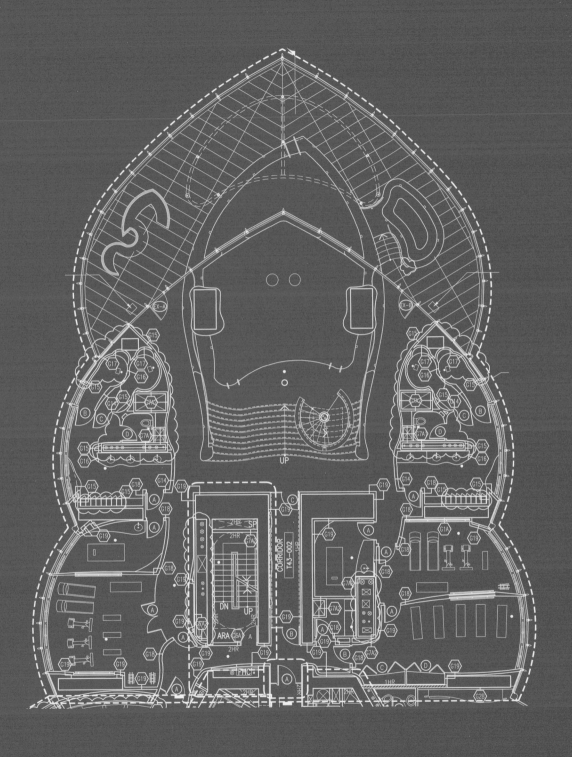

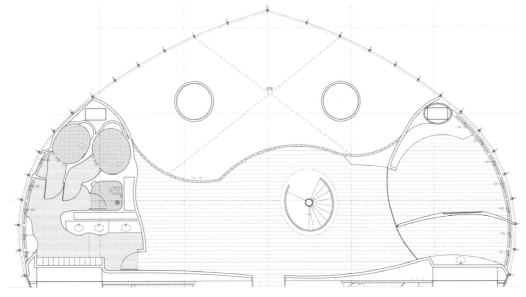

Mezzanine plan

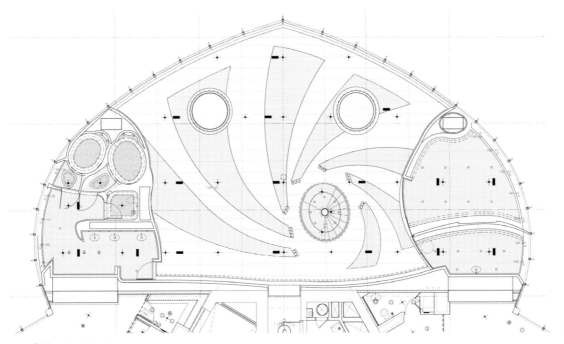

Reflected ceiling plan

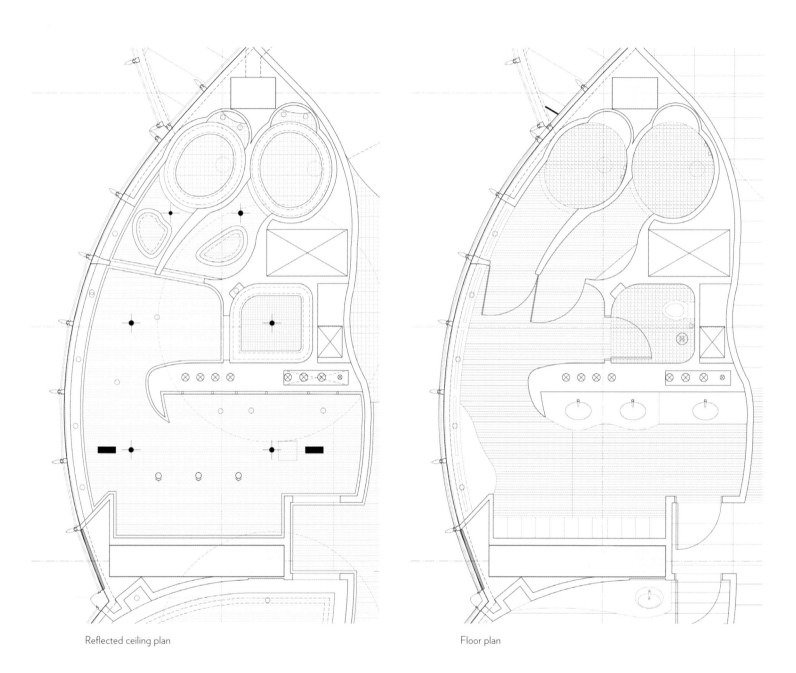

Reflected ceiling plan

Floor plan

Burj Khalifa

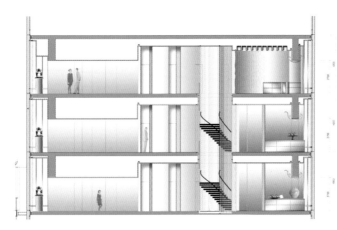

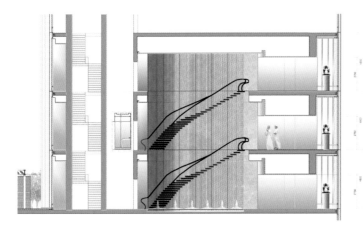

The office lobby design was a somewhat different challenge since most people coming to this entry would be driving and parking in the adjacent underground garage. EMAAR also did not want to drive directly on the level of the water court features that were just outside the office pavilion and so we proposed bringing the automobile traffic to the front door below grade in a skylit driveway. The drop-off area is open to above with a large circular opening to let light into this space and the office lobby at this level. The development of the lowest level consisted of back-lit glass walls, landscaping, and an escalator system that conveyed occupants to the level at which they would access the elevators to shuttle to the 123rd floor sky lobby. At this point there is a concierge/security desk and an undulating glass wall with a card reader system that controls access to the elevator system. An important feature of the office lobby space is the free-form ceiling made of wood, and bridge system that connects the hotel space above to the upper level of the pavilion structure. This feature continues the organic nature of the project into the office environment much the same way as the curved walls do for the residential entrance and public spaces. This highly sculpted feature becomes a landmark that differentiates this pavilion from all others.

Building statistics

The Burj Khalifa is a large-scale mixed-use project consisting of approximately 600 luxury condominiums including two spas and meeting facilities, 200 hotel rooms with ballroom and support amenities, 350 hotel condominiums, 50,000 square meters of luxury office space, a grand spa and health club, 7 restaurants, the world's highest public observatory, 3 floors for communications, 6 mechanical floors and 3000 parking spaces. The tower's gross area is more than 300,000 square meters above grade with a total of 450,000 square meters including below grade levels.

Reflected ceiling

Chairman's suite – level 154

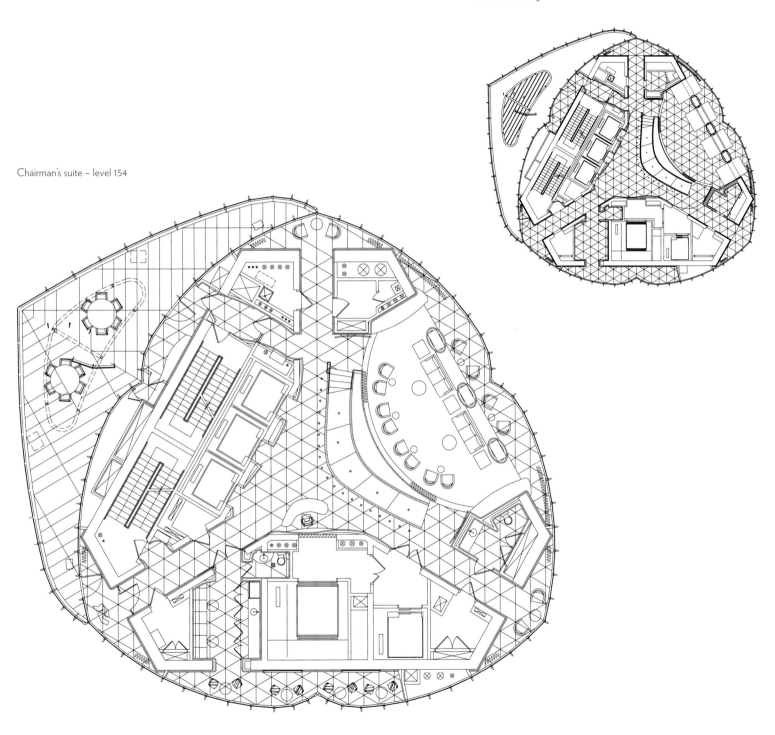

Zifeng Tower (The Nanjing Greenland Financial Complex)

Location: Nanjing, China
Client: Greenland Development
Year: 2003–2008

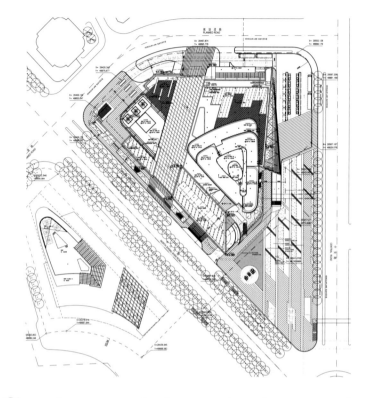

During the period of heavy construction activity in China (1993–2005), the mandated manner of selecting an architect for most of the significant new projects was through the competition process. Even though Greenland is a private developer, it was required to stage a competition to award this project. The competition for Nanjing Tower was a two-stage event, with a presentation of the concept to Greenland officials along with their selection of esteemed professionals and professors, and a second presentation to officials from the city of Nanjing, the city's planning director, the mayor, experts from the local universities and architects from the USA and Europe.

The competitors for this project were Philip Johnson and Alan Ritchie, HOK, ECADI, and HPP from Frankfurt. The first jury awarded our scheme first place by a unanimous vote of four to zero while the second jury selected us as the winner by a vote of twelve for our scheme to eleven for the HPP scheme. After an extensive period of negotiation we were awarded the contract.

The Nanjing tower form has been derived from three elements of life in Nanjing: the Yangtze River flowing through the city; the lush green landscape environment and garden city atmosphere; and the dragon and column iconography so prevalent in Chinese culture.

The tower is shaped in a triangular form, to relate to the shape and size of the building's site and to take maximum advantage of the views of the mountains, lake, and historic buildings in Nanjing.

The stepping of the tower relates to the functions within the tower and the desire to shape the floor plates to achieve maximum efficiency.

The curved corners of the tower present a soft, continuous surface to the exterior of the building. The tower is comprised of office, hotel, and retail above grade, with retail and parking below grade. The top of the tower houses restaurants and a public observatory.

Zifeng Tower (The Nanjing Greenland Financial Complex)

Within the clear glass walls are a series of landscaped atria that will further differentiate this zone from the typical wall features of the building. This zone uses clear glass and a minimal mullion support system to maximize the transparency. At these three- and four-level atria, the floor increments will be used for executive concierge reception lounges, gathering spaces, and meeting rooms for the 500-room Intercontinental hotel. At the office zone these setback areas create the potential for two additional corner offices per floor.

Occupying the first seven floors of the site is a vertically organized shopping complex with a skylit atrium that runs diagonally through from street to street, allowing for interior circulation to the retail floors and pedestrian passage through the site. This atrium is positioned to provide a continuous sight line to the ancient Drum Tower on the nearby hill from the residential district to the north. The project is also serviced by a subway station on the apex of the triangle. The concourse level, containing a restaurant and the lobby for the observation level, is opened up to allow light and air to reach its interior. At the observation level, a garden with water features is accessed by a ramp and stairs. Three lower levels provide parking and service access to the retail, hotel, and office functions. The grade level is punctuated by entrances to the office building, and the atrium lobby to the residential tower. The entrance and ground floor lobby to the hotel and entrance to the ballrooms are located in the seven-story podium. Because of the city mandate, only three entrance points are allowed for drop-off and pick-up activities, necessitating a perimeter driveway running around a third of the site.

A significant spire element at the top of the building soars to 458 meters and is one of China's tallest structures. This feature is seen as a major identifying element that will culminate the expression of the tower atrium feature and will reinforce the dominance of this tower as a landmark in the city. At night, the spire will be lit and will be a beacon in the Nanjing skyline. The intent is that the atria will also be lit in a similar manner to reinforce the connection between the spire and the stream of atria running down and around the building.

The vertical and horizontal clear glass seams separating the differentially textured glass surfaces of the tower are metaphorically analogous to the clear water of the Yangtze River separating two interlocking dragon forms.

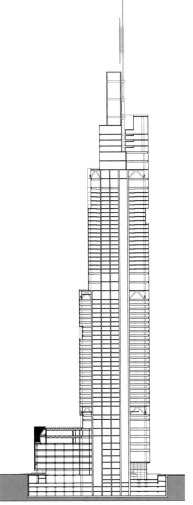

Longitudinal section

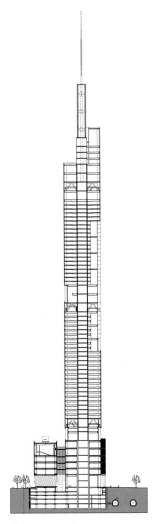

Transverse section

Zifeng Tower (The Nanjing Greenland Financial Complex)　　　231

Nanjing Greenland Tower A1

Nanjing Tower · Dancing Dragons

Interlocking
Forms

Mass/Voi

CONCEPT

ELEMENTS

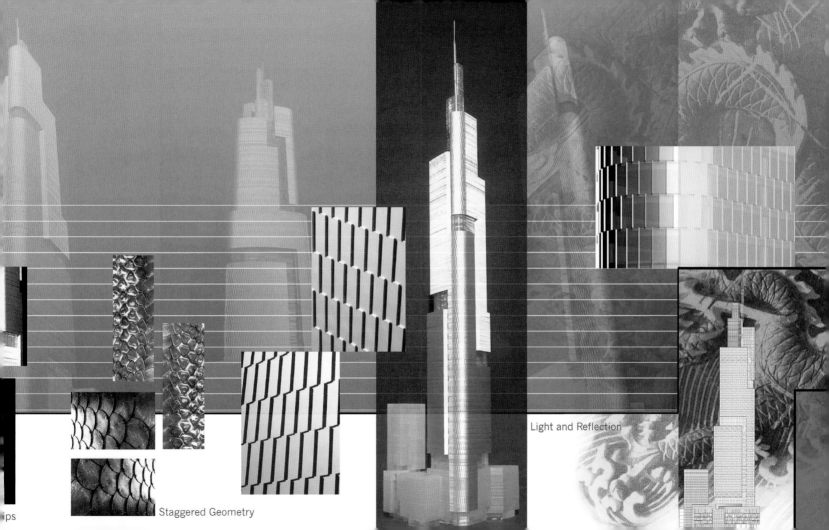

Staggered Geometry

Light and Reflection

This exterior treatment changes direction from one major component to the other in an effort to more clearly identify the two dragon forms interlocked around the central core of the building. The exterior wall of this tower has a distinctive directional feature. Each pane of glass is angled at 7 degrees from the occupied space and the module alternates or staggers by 0.75 meters from floor to floor to imbue the skin of the building with a scale-like quality that emphasizes the similarity of the building's components to that of a dragon layer.

238   Zifeng Tower (The Nanjing Greenland Financial Complex)

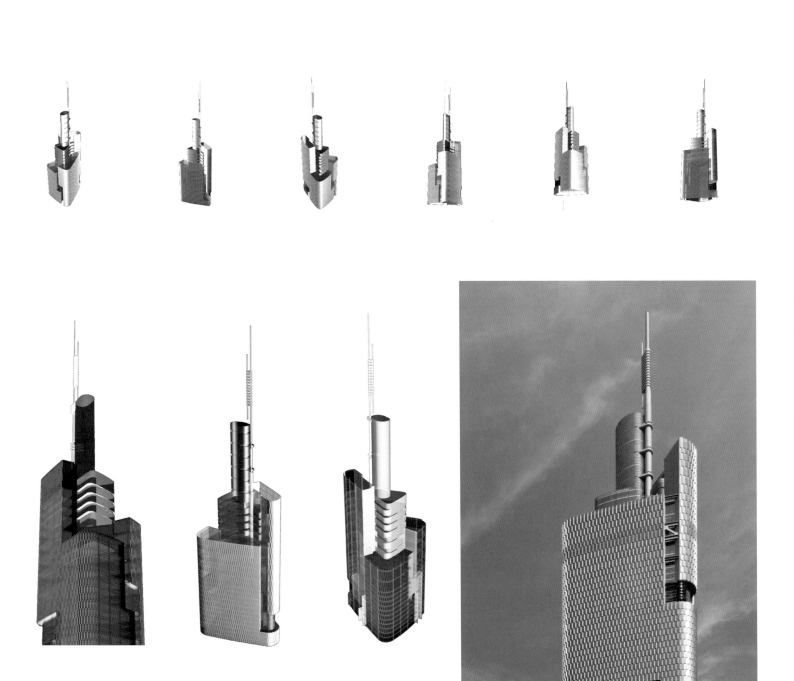

Zifeng Tower (The Nanjing Greenland Financial Complex) 239

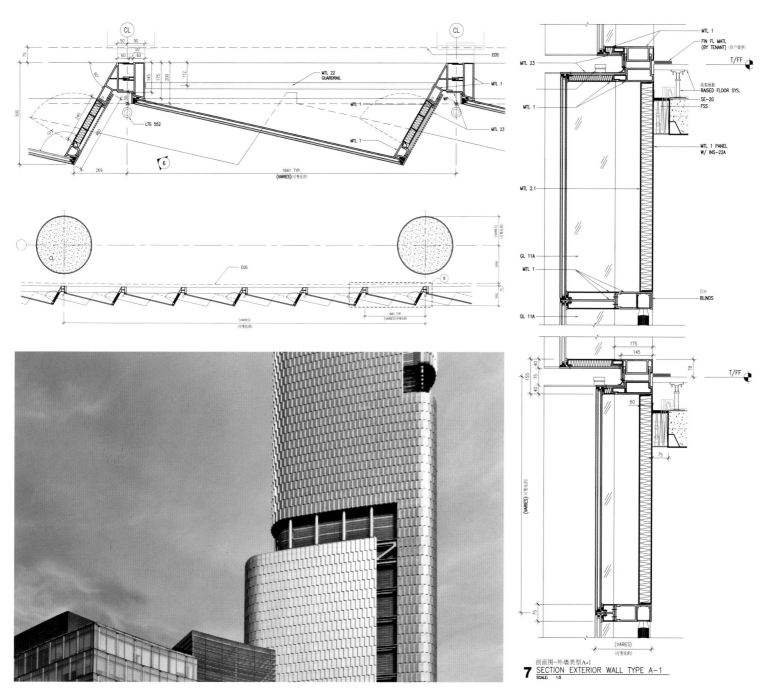

MTL 1

FIN FL MATL
(BY TENANT) (住户提供)

MTL 23

T/FF

高架地板
RAISED FLOOR SYS.

SE-20

FSS

MTL 1

MTL 1 PANEL
W/ INS-22A

MTL 2.1

GL 11A

MTL 1

百叶
BLINDS

GL 11A

CL

CL

EOS

75

50 90
20
60 60

MTL 22
GUARDRAIL

145
175
200
112

MTL 1

500

240
450

WP

MTL 23

10°

LTG 552

MTL 1

269

1661 TYP.
(VARIES) 可变化的

6

EOS

8

(VARIES)
可变化的

1661 TYP.
(VARIES) 可变化的

(VARIES)
(可变化的)

1250
500 75

175
145

T/FF

155
40
75
40 75

60

78

(VARIES) 可变化的

75

(VARIES)
(可变化的)

剖面图-外墙类型A-1
7 SECTION EXTERIOR WALL TYPE A-1
SCALE: 1:5

Tower exterior wall

Podium studies

Zifeng Tower (The Nanjing Greenland Financial Complex)

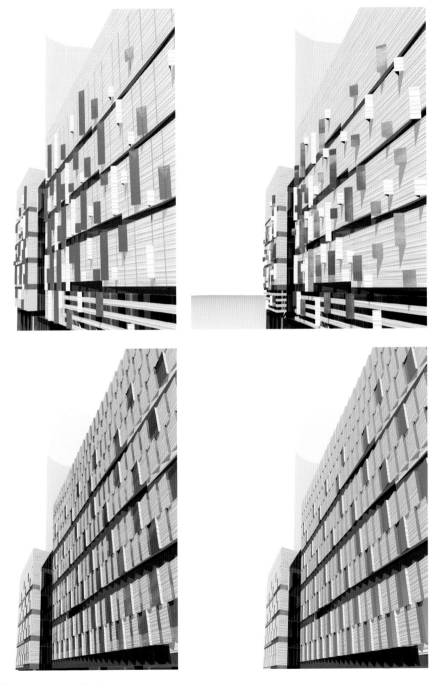

Podium exterior wall studies

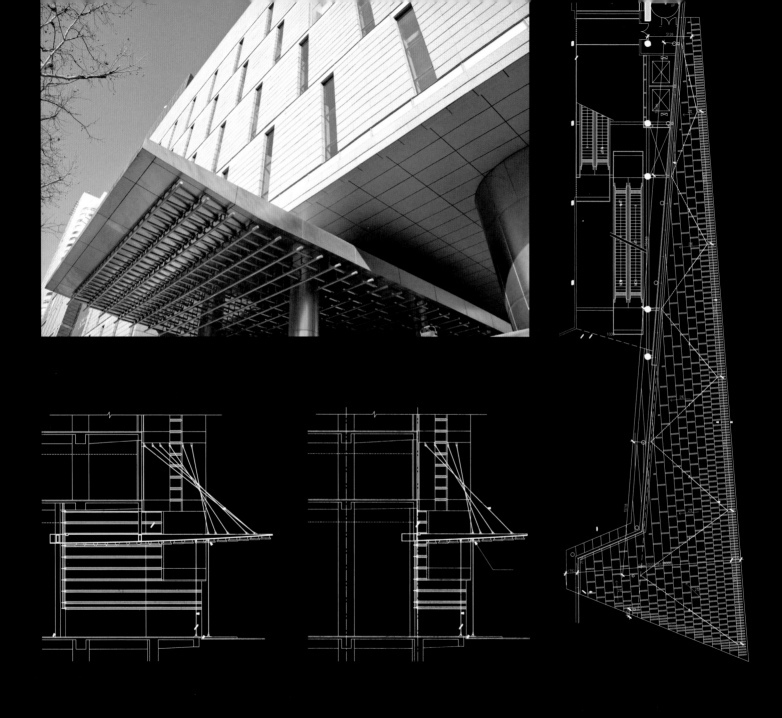

Zifeng Tower (The Nanjing Greenland Financial Complex)

Zifeng Tower (The Nanjing Greenland Financial Complex)

At the podium, in an effort to relate to, yet differentiate from, the tower's texture, the exterior is clad in a textured stone surface, punctuated by a series of directional slots, where the skin of the exterior is cut and peeled open to expose the interior of the retail area for use as advertising or viewing points. This feature is composed in a random manner to enrich the façade and give life and animation to what is basically a solid wall condition. The roof of the podium is landscaped and used by the residents and hotel guests as a recreational space. This is where the outdoor swimming pool is located.

The residential tower of the project is designed to both connect and be separate. It is the desire of the owner to be able to sell this section of the project, while identifying it as part of the complex. The exterior expression of the residential tower feature is clad in a double-glazed, low-e glass system that is flush with the exception of narrow vertical window slots that relate to the proportion of the slots in the podium and the ventilation slots in the tower. These slots shift on a 3-meter module to further relate this tower to the surrounding context of the complex. This tower is 100 meters high and has a relationship to the existing residential tower to the north, forming a gateway between the two residential districts.

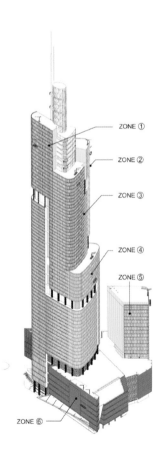

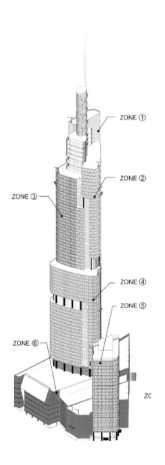

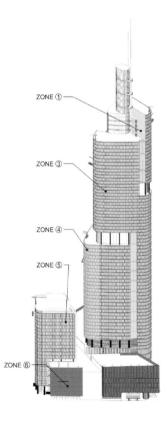

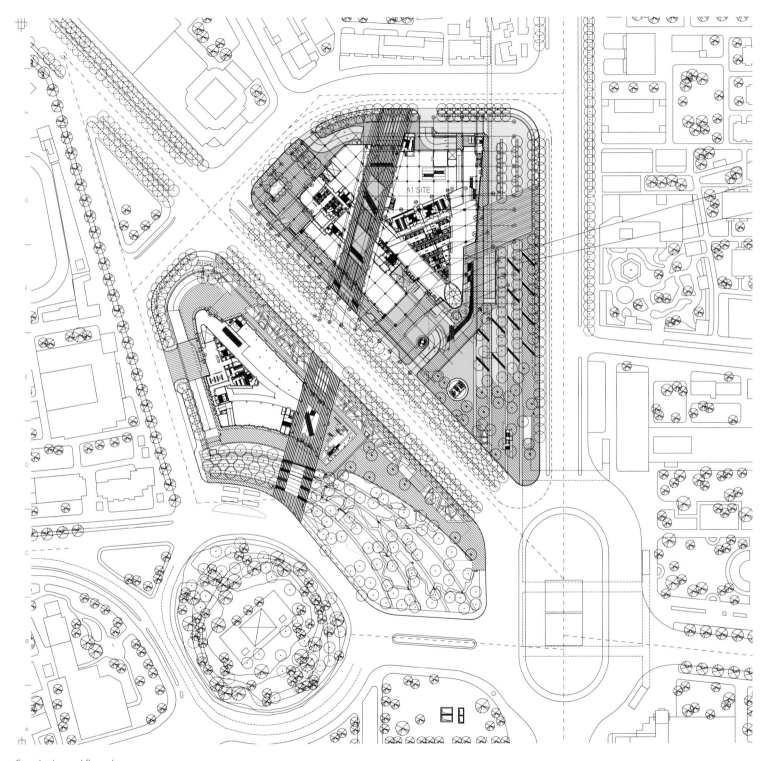

Site plan/ground floor plan

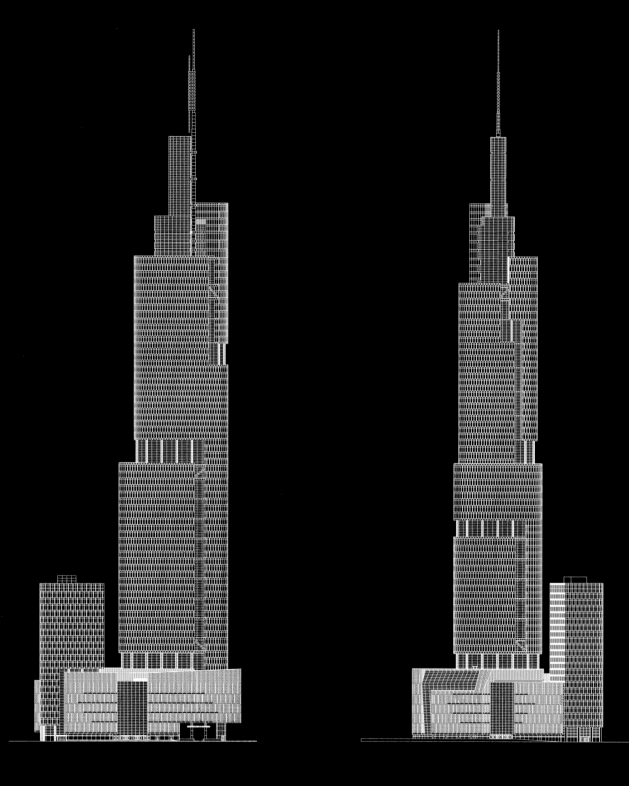

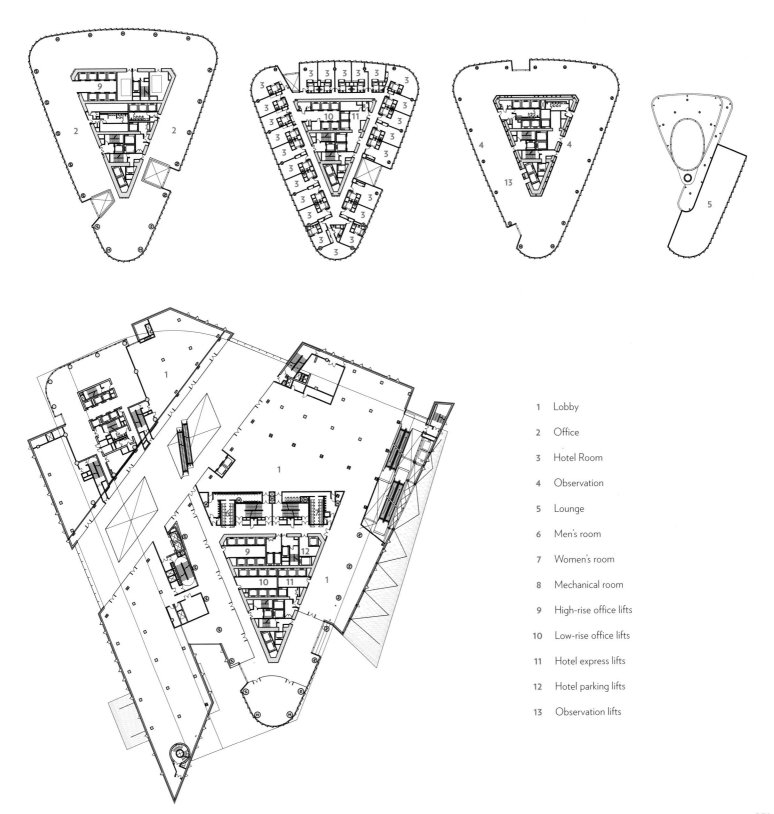

1   Lobby

2   Office

3   Hotel Room

4   Observation

5   Lounge

6   Men's room

7   Women's room

8   Mechanical room

9   High-rise office lifts

10   Low-rise office lifts

11   Hotel express lifts

12   Hotel parking lifts

13   Observation lifts

Zifeng Tower (The Nanjing Greenland Financial Complex)

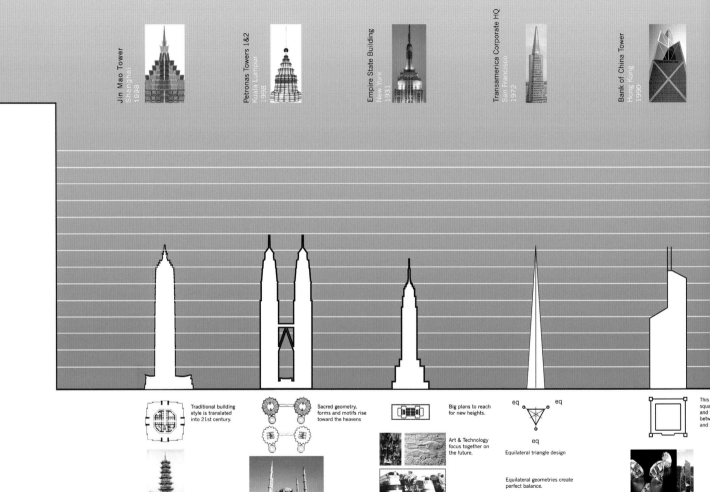

Jin Mao Tower
Shanghai
1998

Petronas Towers 1&2
Kuala Lumpur
1998

Empire State Building
New York
1931

Transamerica Corporate HQ
San Francisco
1972

Bank of China Tower
Hong Kong
1990

Traditional building style is translated into 21st century.

Chinese Pagoda

Sacred geometry, forms and motifs rise toward the heavens

Islamic Minarette

Art & Technology focus together on the future.

Art Deco Era

Big plans to reach for new heights.

eq   eq

eq

Equilateral triangle design

Equilateral geometries create perfect balance.

This
squa
and
betw
and

Crys
Supe

SYMMETRY

BALANCE

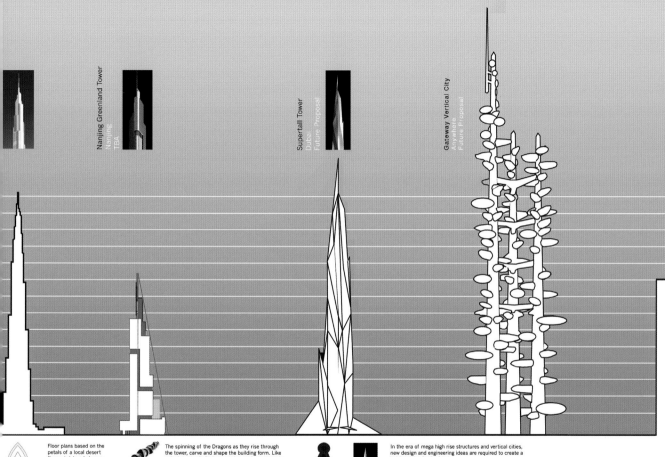

Nanjing Greenland Tower
Nanjing
TBA

Supertall Tower
Dubai
Future Proposal

Gateway Vertical City
Anywhere
Future Proposal

Floor plans based on the petals of a local desert flower, twist and change geometry as they rise up the majestic tower.

Beauty found within asymmetrical form

Flower of the Desert

The spinning of the Dragons as they rise through the tower, carve and shape the building form. Like spinning camshafts in an engine, such asymmetric designs harness, focus and balance energy.

The design of the building is driven by a desire to invigorate the city by gathering and fusing the energies of people, commerce and place. The plan design allows for dynamic flows into the site. The tower carries this energy upwards through the building to the iconic beacon.

Dancing Dragons

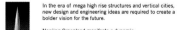

In the era of mega high rise structures and vertical cities, new design and engineering ideas are required to create a bolder vision for the future.

Nanjing Greenland manifests a dynamic shift away from singular monolithic ideas, towards a more freeform architecture which demonstrate a body composed of multiple ideals that signify a more advanced and sophisticated identity for its owners and users.

Future Architecture and Design

601 Congress Street

Location: Boston, Massachusetts, USA
Client: Manulife Financial
Year: 2000–2005

601 Congress Street is a 480,000-square-foot office building, located in South Boston near the Customs House district. Immediately to its south is the open-cut Ted Williams Tunnel that connects Logan International Airport to South Boston and the central business district to the west. D Street, which connects the Customs House District to South Boston's residential neighborhood, borders the building on the west; directly to the northwest is the newly established triangular park that will be the heart of this new district's development. Directly across Congress Street will be a new residential and hotel development and to the south is another office site, temporarily being used as at-grade parking.

The entrance, which faces the new park, is located on the corner of D Street and Congress. It is identified by a prow-like radiused tower piece that rises 15 floors. The mass curves gently to the south, forming the northern building façade and steps down to 11 stories to relate to the anticipated building across Congress Street in the master plan, designed by Alex Kreger. The mass then curves on the northeast corner in order to open views down Congress to the site east of this building. The curved form of this project is not a literal translation of the site boundaries, since it does not absolutely follow the property line; its curves are intended to provide a feature to viewers who come south on Congress Street, since this site is at the apex of Congress Street's curve to the east. Likewise, the curve on the northeast corner will provide a focal point of interest for those traveling west on Congress. The curved geometry also opens the site and views from neighboring building sites and thus increases the value of the surrounding context. The most unique feature of 601 Congress Street is the way that the façade references the historic fabric of the adjacent structures in the downtown Boston area with setbacks that peel away from the entrance prow, at the third level and at the 11th floor. This condition gives the building fluidity and plasticity and is a reminder of its proximity to the Boston Harbor, just one block away.

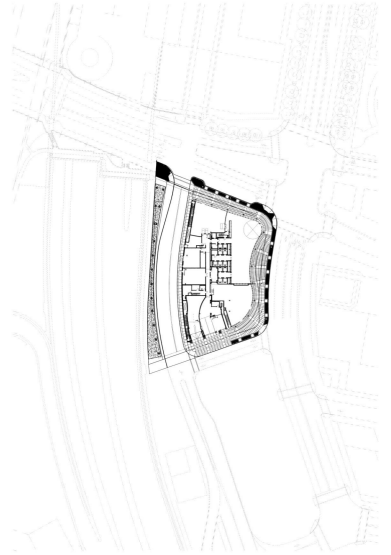

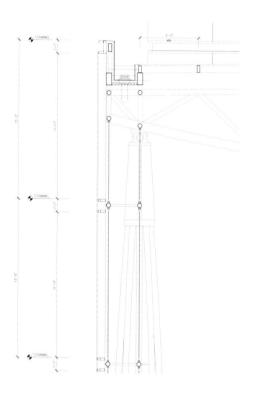

To the south, the building addresses South Boston with a six-story skylit atrium. Additionally, this atrium serves as the overall image of the building from the Ted Williams Expressway. The atrium provides office occupants and users of the conference center with a large meeting breakout space and is also used to host large dinners and other public functions. Landscaping within the atrium creates a green winter garden with pleasant views for the occupants whose offices front this space. The landscaping of the atrium relates back to the parkway landscape of adjacent D Street as it crosses over the Ted Williams Tunnel. The skylight roof of the atrium is supported by four super columns assembled from steel tubing that are uplit in the evening to provide a sculptural feature that is visible from inside the atrium and from the exterior view of the building from the south.

The exterior wall of 601 Congress is composed of a clear glass, floor-to-floor double wall with sun control devices and a ventilated interstitial cavity.

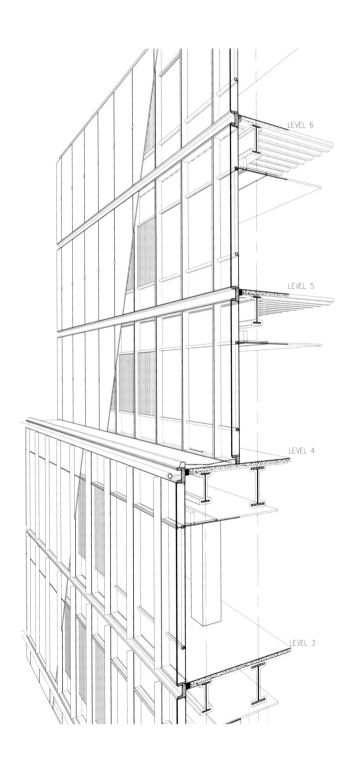

LEVEL 6

LEVEL 5

LEVEL 4

LEVEL 3

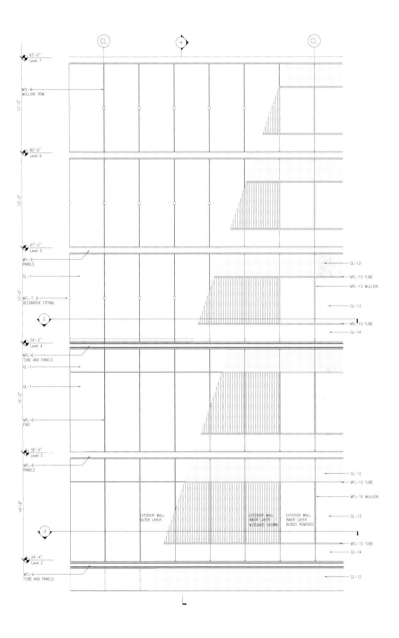

93'-0"
Level 7

MTL-6
MULLION TRIM

80'-0"
Level 6

67'-0"
Level 5

MTL-6
PANELS

GL-1

MTL-7, 8
DECORATIVE FITTING

2

54'-0"
Level 4

MTL-6
TUBE AND PANELS

GL-1

GL-1

MTL-6
FINS

39'-0"
Level 3

MTL-6
PANELS

3

24'-4"
Level 2

MTL-5
TUBE AND PANELS

GL-12
MTL-10 TUBE
MTL-10 MULLION

GL-13

MTL-10 TUBE
GL-14

GL-12
MTL-10 TUBE
MTL-10 MULLION

GL-13

MTL-10 TUBE
GL-14

GL-12

EXTERIOR WALL
OUTER LAYER

EXTERIOR WALL
INNER LAYER
W/BLINDS SHOWN

EXTERIOR WALL
INNER LAYER
BLINDS REMOVED

CL

4

CL

The double wall allows the exterior to be all glass and to be light and transparent. The double wall concept is new to North America with variations only occurring in two or three other small applications in the USA. The new cutting-edge technology was developed in Europe and has proven to be highly energy efficient.

The outer light of the double wall, spanning from the floor to underside of the stainless steel spandrel, is laminated and double-glazed with a low-e clear coating for increased U value, condensation control, and acoustic performance, and to shield its occupants from the noise of Logan Airport a short distance away. The inner light is a clear single $1/4$-inch pane of glass, on hinges that allow for cleaning the interior of the glass, forming the 8-inch interstitial space. At the base of this glass is a 1-inch opening to allow interior air to flow into and through the cavity, exhausting the heated air into the ceiling plenum and then back to the core where the mechanical return air system extracts it or reuses the heat as return air.

The incorporation of the double wall system helps to achieve the goals of the major tenant by establishing a new paradigm for the development of energy-efficient office buildings in the United States.

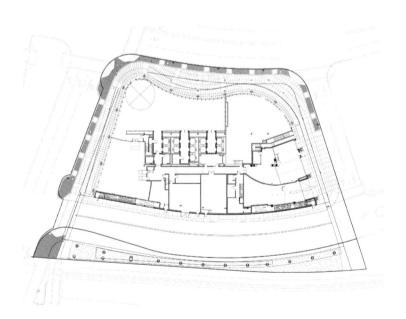

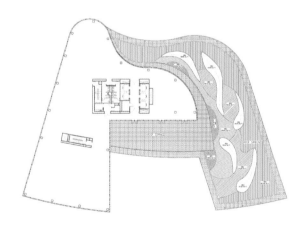

This system is the first of its kind to be used without introducing mechanical extraction at the window unit and marks a breakthrough in the engineering of double-wall systems.

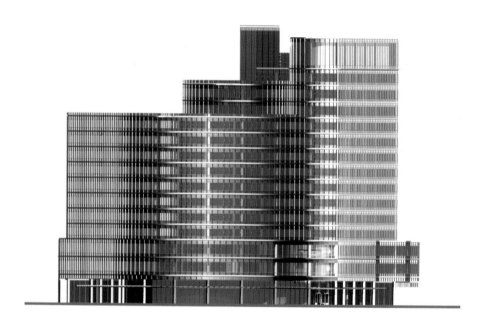

At the base of the building the clear glass wall is set back, exposing the building's perimeter columns, which are clad in linen-textured stainless steel. This provides additional sidewalk area, allowing coffee shops and food service venues to provide exterior seating areas during comfortable weather conditions. The sidewalk is covered by a clear glass canopy to mitigate negative wind effects at pedestrian circulation and sitting zones around the building.

All double-wall conditions contain 4-inch-wide vertical blinds in clear aluminum finish, which are used to shade the interior from unwanted direct sun when pulled and set. Vertical blinds were chosen to provide a texture to the façade that was random but controlled, enhancing the wall's visual character. The random pattern, horizontal in nature, complements the horizontal character of the building's spandrel expression. These blinds will appear to float within the double wall as they span from aluminum tubes located at the ceiling and at desk height. Above the blinds are textured glass panels with mirrors coating on their back surfaces that will enhance the metallic nature of the overall wall. Below the blinds, from floor to desk height, is a textured glass panel that diffuses light coming into the space and minimizes views into the workstation zones of the occupied space. This feature adds to the functional character of the wall and adds visual interest as well. At night the textured clear panels project a soft glow of light from within, enhancing the visual character during early evening hours.

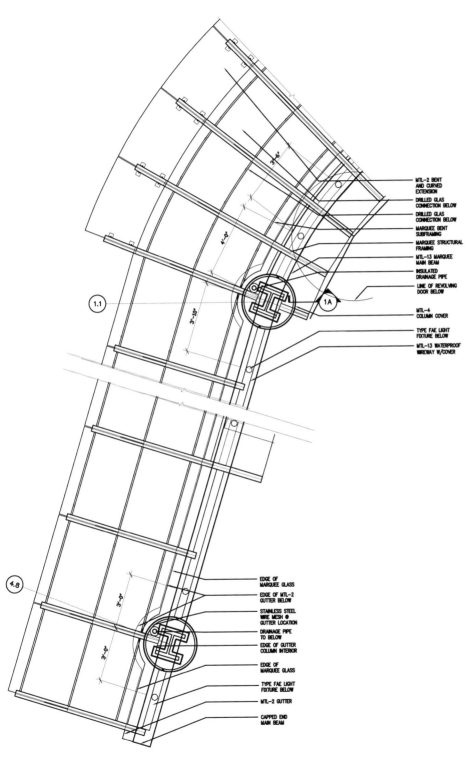

MTL-2 BENT
AND CURVED
EXTENSION
DRILLED GLASS
CONNECTION BELOW
DRILLED GLASS
CONNECTION BELOW
MARQUEE BENT
SUBFRAMING
MARQUEE STRUCTURAL
FRAMING
MTL-13 MARQUEE
MAIN BEAM
INSULATED
DRAINAGE PIPE
LINE OF REVOLVING
DOOR BELOW

MTL-4
COLUMN COVER

TYPE FAE LIGHT
FIXTURE BELOW
MTL-13 WATERPROOF
WIREWAY W/COVER

EDGE OF
MARQUEE GLASS
EDGE OF MTL-2
GUTTER BELOW
STAINLESS STEEL
WIRE MESH @
GUTTER LOCATION
DRAINAGE PIPE
TO BELOW
EDGE OF GUTTER
COLUMN INTERIOR
EDGE OF
MARQUEE GLASS
TYPE FAE LIGHT
FIXTURE BELOW
MTL-2 GUTTER

CAPPED END
MAIN BEAM

601 Congress Street

The all-glass building is a major departure from the brick, limestone, and red granite buildings in the immediate area. By making the building transparent, the aim is to dematerialize the building's bulk, making it appear less massive than its 480,000 square feet of space would appear if it were composed of more opaque traditional materials. The transparent skin helps to achieve this, and the double-wall technology was the only way to give transparency to 90 percent of its surface area without the use of highly reflective glass or a major reduction in the use of clear glazing. The new Massachusetts energy code was prescriptive in nature and would reduce the use of clear double-glazing to 30 percent of the surface area. However, this double wall was specifically tested for energy performance by the window wall fabricator, Permasteelisa, prior to official acceptance of this system.

The building's rooftop is planted with tall prairie grasses that are sympathetic to the winds of the Boston Harbor. These tall grasses require minimum maintenance. This planting provides a habitat for birds and insects and provides great insulation for the roof surfaces. The lower rooftops are accessible from the 11th floor and a terrace is provided to view the harbor and the rooftop plantings. From this terrace, it feels like the viewer is on a tall cliff overlooking the harbor and the South Boston community. The experience is both exhilarating and serene. The impression of the tall grasses waving in the wind is that of a moving sculpture surrounding the terrace.

One of the special requirements of the Massachusetts Bay Transit Authority (MBTA) is the incorporation of a passageway through the site of the MBTA cable transit system. On the west side of the ground floor, space has been provided for electric cable cars to run beneath the building, connecting the developments in this new area to the central business district to the north. Special consideration was given to the structural system and the first-floor ceiling height to accommodate this feature. There are also two levels below grade for on-site parking.

The mechanical plant is on the top floor of the tower piece and is shielded by a series of louvers that are set back from the building's clear glass system to minimize their impact on the all-glass expression of the building. This cavity between the louvers and the glazing system is lit at night, making the building glow. The elevator enclosure located in the middle of the building is exposed and expressed as a separate building element as the building's massing peels away from the main façade and from its larger floor plates to form the tower portion of the project. This exposed elevator enclosure is clad in clear glass and is also lit at night.

Trump International Hotel and Tower

Location: Chicago, Illinois, USA
Client: Donald Trump
Year: 2000–2008

We first met with the Trump Organization in the summer of 1999 when one of Donald Trump's development managers came to Chicago to look for sites on which to build a hotel and condominium building. He called our office to inquire about our interest in carrying out the architectural services and to get an idea as to our fees for performing this work. We were about to submit a proposal when all activity on Trump's part ceased.

In the spring of 2001, the *Sun-Times* announced that it had entered into a joint venture with Donald Trump for the development of the *Sun-Times* site and that the 1950's headquarters building and printing facility would be torn down to make way for a new building. Upon reading that news I picked up the phone and called Donald Trump and stated that I had some thoughts on what could go onto that site, that we still had the sketches that we did in 1999, and that I would like to meet him to discuss these and other ideas. He agreed to a meeting and within two weeks I was in his office with three schemes to show him.

These three tower schemes were all towers of 2000 feet in height, the tallest towers allowable by FAA regulations in the United States. I presented these to him and he recognized that they were very early ideas but there was one approach that he liked and asked me to pursue it. I then began to study that concept and developed three variations to it that I modeled. We set up a meeting with Charley Reese, Micha Koeppel, Russ Flicker and Donald Trump Jr. to be held in our offices on September 11, 2001 at 9 am.

We all arrived a little early and as I was going into the meeting, Ray Clark told me that an airplane had just crashed into the World Trade Center in New York. I entered the room and announced this; we went into a conference room with a television set, turned on the news and were stunned by the images that we saw on the screen. We continued watching and wondering how the fire was going to be put out when we saw the second plane head for, and crash into, the second tower. We sat there stunned for another two hours, watching the disaster in progress and viewing it in complete disbelief when the two buildings collapsed. We watched until the announcement that the Santa Fe Building, where our office was located, was being evacuated and that all historic buildings in the Loop were also being evacuated. The meeting moved to Trump's lawyer's office for another hour or so to discuss the contract issues and then adjourned.

Nothing occurred for the next two weeks until the Trump Organization called and asked us to pursue a new scheme with a revised program that would take the building to a height of between 900 and 1000 feet. We began studying the project with these new criteria and developed a scheme of stacked parallelograms that responded to the adjacent heights of the Wrigley Building, the IBM Building, and the residential building to the north. It was still early in the process when we went to see the City Planning Commissioner to get feedback on the still-preliminary idea. The Trump Organization felt that we should also discuss this concept with the *Sun-Times* since it was thought that word would get to the press either way. Trump had an agreement with the *Sun-Times* that since it was a partner in the venture, it would give any newsworthy information about the project exclusively to the *Sun-Times*. That evening, *Chicago Tonight*, a local television program, featured a panel on which I sat along with Lee Bay and others who were very complimentary about the concept.

A critic from the *Tribune* heard about our meeting with the city, and since we could not talk to him until after the *Sun-Times* published the material about the meeting, he was very upset; when he did write about the project, he criticized it heavily, in spite of the positive press it had received from other critics. I subsequently met with him and he gave me his reasons for the criticism, which I listened to, and as I refined the Trump Tower design in design development, I modified the building from a parallelogram form to a slab tower with its east and west walls radiused to allow the corner units to function. He thought this was a much better scheme and complimented it in his next article about the project. He has remained positive about the building.

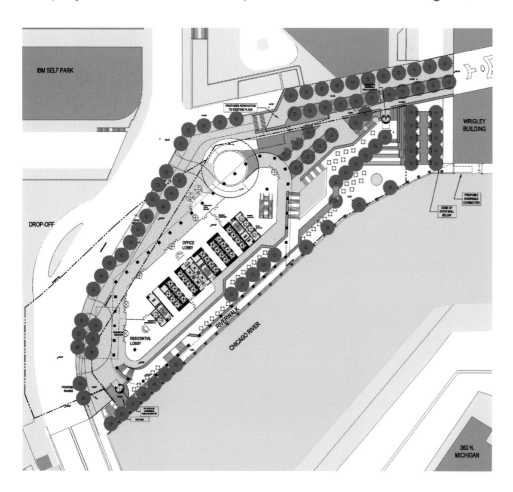

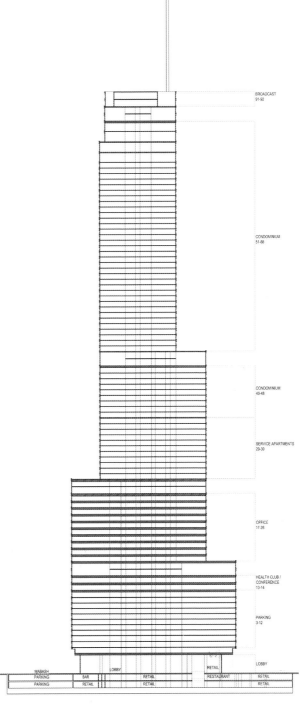

BROADCAST
91-92

CONDOMINIUM
51-86

CONDOMINIUM
40-48

SERVICE APARTMENTS
29-39

OFFICE
17-26

HEALTH CLUB /
CONFERENCE
13-14

PARKING
3-12

LOBBY

WABASH
PARKING | LOBBY | RETAIL | | RETAIL
| BAR | RETAIL | RESTAURANT | RETAIL
PARKING | RETAIL | RETAIL | | RETAIL

Trump International Hotel and Tower   273

Frederick Watermark Illustration by Brad Holland

Picture

The future had settled on Steve Kreder - good job, ...STEVE KREDER SETTLED INTO HIS 22ND SEAT IN A
a great job, and the perfect plan. Slow, steady...crowded business... he thought, it all just comes together.
In Tokyo (lands) between him and his future...Flight attend, he would be flying for 11 hours. And that
...was fine... hey, it was great. Today would be New York to
...San Francisco... from San Francisco to Tokyo. Sunday would
...be the rest of the days, and he'd be back at the international
...inquiry desk... Monday morning. ¶ Someone would ask,
..."Hey, Steve... how was your weekend? You got into trouble
...in...?" And everyone... was grinning, because Steve
Kreder wasn't kidding about his future. It was a matter made
on the I.E. desk: women and sometimes... were bring
¶ "Nothing to tell," he would answer, and there would be a
chorus of boos. "But Mindy's coming into town next weekend." And there would be cheers. "You'll get a full report."
¶ Then they'd all go back to their analysis data and the news
and numbers from the Asian markets: Zurich, Frankfurt,
and London. Later, they'd call the portfolio managers. ▶

Before construction

When completed, the Trump Tower Chicago will be the tallest building project in the United States since the Sears Tower was completed in 1974. The architectural design strategy for the Trump Tower Chicago is contextual. The south side of the tower is parallel to the bank of the Chicago River; this position enables the structure to vary from Chicago's north–south grid to create a special condition. The building is shaped to reflect its functions within the tower and the need to provide as many views up and down the river as possible.

The first setback occurs on the east side of the tower, at a height that is essentially the same as the cornice line of the Wrigley Building to the east. The next setback is on the west side of the tower and relates to both the height of the residential tower to the north, and Marina City to the west. The third and final setback is on the east side of the tower and relates to the height of the IBM Building immediately adjacent. Setbacks in the tower's massing provide additional connections to the surrounding context and integrate the tower into the overall composition of its riverfront setting.

The façade treatment of this tower relates to the Wrigley Building through the use of clear, low-e coated glass. A very light palette of materials will enhance the detail and whiteness of the Wrigley Building. It relates to the Mies van der Rohe-designed IBM Building to the west with the spacing and articulation of the steel mullion system and the tall columnar base at grade. The Trump Tower will stand alone as a shimmering tall tower on the Chicago River and will enjoy stunning views of Lake Michigan and the Chicago River.

Materials include a light silver palette of brushed stainless steel spandrel panels and clear anodized aluminum that reflects and refracts light from the surrounding context. The polished stainless steel mullions are wing-shaped, with curved surfaces on both sides that project out 9 inches from the glass line. They are curved in order to eliminate any visual reflective distortion and to provide a metallic quality.

Through the contemporary synthesis of adjacent building fabrics and modulations, the Trump Tower Chicago expresses a truly modern architecture, consistent with Chicago's architectural heritage.

Trump International Hotel and Tower

At the base, the body of the building is raised 30 feet above the entrance on Wabash Avenue and nearly 70 feet above the Chicago River, opening up an extensive, landscaped promenade that steps down like terraces on a hillside for three levels, until it meets the river. This promenade provides a pedestrian connection between Michigan Avenue and State Street and will be a sunny area where retail shops will open up to terraces and walkways. Tables and chairs for relaxing and enjoying the beautiful views of the river and river traffic will animate the space. It will also provide public assembly spaces and some entertainment activity at the river's edge and will connect to the river taxi system that brings commuters from the west train stations to North Michigan Avenue. There will be excursion boat launching facilities from the lowest level fronting the river. All levels will be accessible by elevators and stairs, and the circulation systems will be treated in a ceremonial way to heighten the experience for the visitor.

The terrace levels will be heavily landscaped with large trees, shrubs, ground cover, and flowers in large planting areas at the upper level; fountains, water plants, trees, flowers, and hedges at the intermediate level; and trees and flowers at the lowest (river) level. Storefronts will be clear glass set into a cut stone wall that frames each retail bay. Each bay will have a canopy for shade. Graphics for the retail will be controlled.

At the Wabash entry, a suspended and cantilevered clear glass canopy helps protect guests from wind and water at the automobile drop-off points. Connected to this on-site circulation system will be a circular ramp that connects the upper Wabash level to the parking levels in the tower. This double-helix ramp will be clad in a translucent laminated glass and will be backlit during the evening, adding lantern-like lighting to the adjacent plaza.

Trump Tower Chicago is a unique mixture of luxury condominiums, parking for 1100 cars, 130,000 square feet of retail space, and hotel/condominiums. Purchasers of the hotel condominiums will be able to rent out their units. Condominiums in the tower range in size from 750 square feet to more than 10,000 square feet at the penthouse level. Each unit will have floor-to-ceiling, double-glazed semi-reflective glazing with panoramic views of Chicago.

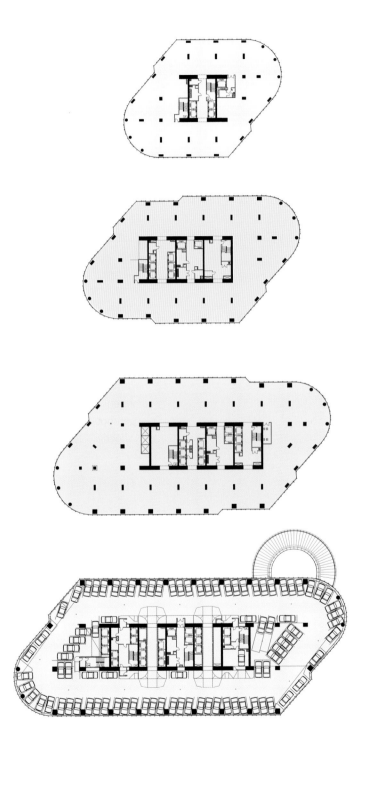

Trump International Hotel and Tower

Entrance canopy

Trump International Hotel and Tower

7 South Dearborn

Location: Chicago, Illinois, USA
Client: European American Realty, Ltd.
Year: 1999–2004

7 South Dearborn is designed as a 108-story, 1550-foot tower, the top 13 floors of which will be dedicated to communications facilities. Three primary antennae were designed to support digital TV, analog TV and other communications functions. With these antennae, 7 South Dearborn would achieve a total height of 2000 feet, making it the tallest structure in the United States.

The mixed-use complex will include 360 residential units on 40 floors, 765,000 square feet of office space on 36 floors, and 800 parking spaces on 12 floors in addition to the 13 floors of communication facilities. The 75,000 square feet of retail at the concourse and grade levels will include restaurants, shops, and amenities such as a food delivery service, a private fitness club, a dry cleaner, and a drugstore. If realized, the tower would continue the successful transformation of Chicago's central business district into a community enlivened by a full range of residential, retail, and commercial activity 24 hours a day, seven days a week.

The massing of 7 South Dearborn was conceived as a figural piece that would stand alone in the city of Chicago as its tallest structure and the symbolic center point of the downtown central business district.

The primary massing features are the stepped or telescoping massing, the curved corners and the distinctive notches separating the top three building segments. The massing of 7 South Dearborn fits with the Chicago tradition of structural expressionism.

Parking is located in the base of the tower, which is expressed as a massive wall. The next two sections are office floors supported by a central concrete core and perimeter concrete columns. Above the office floors, separated by a distinctive "notch" feature, are 20 floors of residential units that are cantilevered from the central core to a distance of 32 feet. Above a second notch are 20 additional floors of residential units with a depth of 22 feet, from the exterior wall to the central core, thus allowing more light

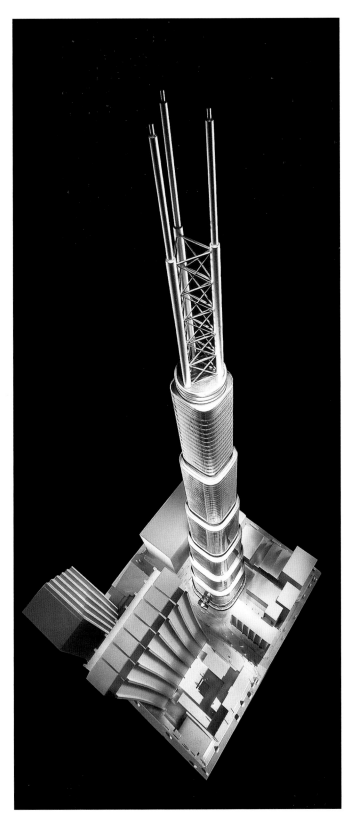

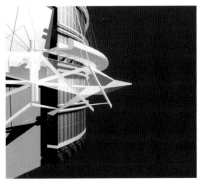

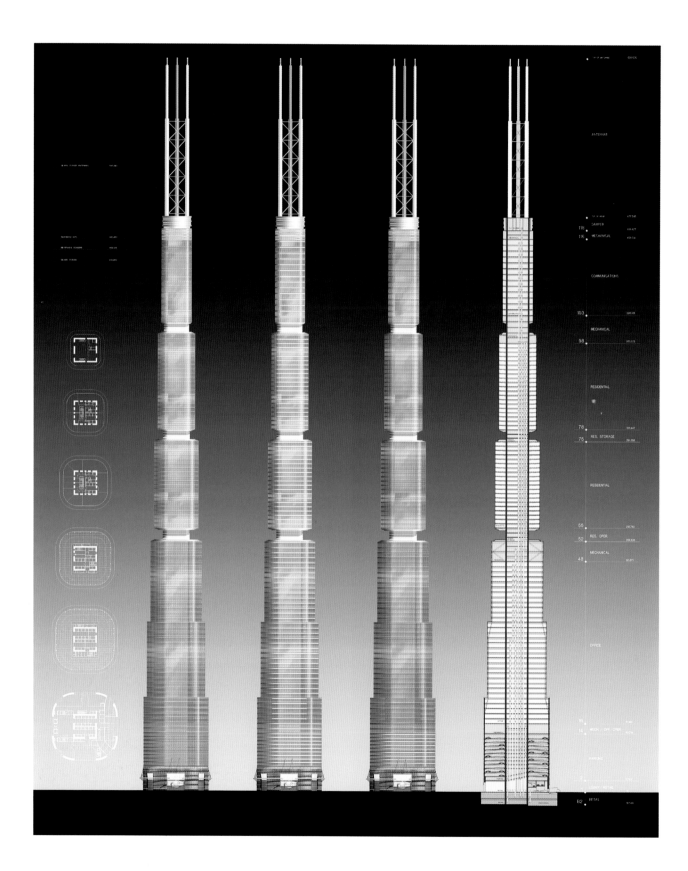

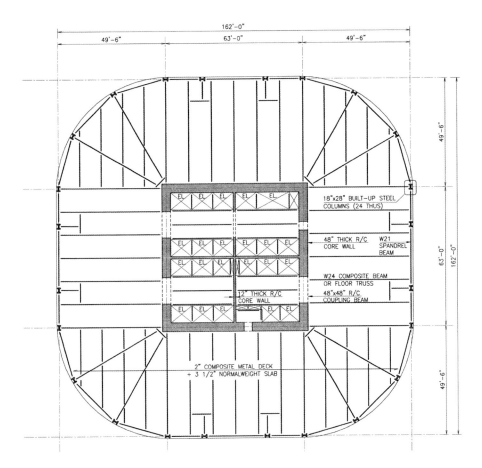

162'-0"

49'-6"   63'-0"   49'-6"

18"x28" BUILT-UP STEEL
COLUMNS (24 THUS)

48" THICK R/C   W21
CORE WALL   SPANDREL
BEAM

W24 COMPOSITE BEAM
OR FLOOR TRUSS

48"x48" R/C
COUPLING BEAM

12" THICK R/C
CORE WALL

2" COMPOSITE METAL DECK
+ 3 1/2" NORMALWEIGHT SLAB

49'-6"

63'-0"   162'-0"

49'-6"

per square foot of living area. At the third notch, the cantilever reduces to 12 feet and the function becomes communications-related facilities, including transformers, antennas, and microwave equipment for high-density TV broadcasting. These floors have non-metallic mullions and clear glass exterior walls to allow the microwave equipment to function without interference.

The notches on the tower have a number of distinctive uses. Primarily, the notches act as vents to the tower, relieving the wind pressure from the body of the building and reducing the forces imposed by vortices as the wind swirls around the building.

Secondly, the mechanical floors are located immediately below these notches that vent from the top through the notch rather than through the sides, thus eliminating the need for louvers on the façade. Additionally, each module of the tower can be maintained and cleaned independently from the others, utilizing the core as storage for window-washing equipment.

The curved corners are designed to relieve wind pressure on the building and equalize the lease-span depth on any one floor with the mid-span conditions. The stainless steel and aluminum exterior façade will be accented by light green, lightly tinted, low-e double-glazing. The tower will have six visibly distinct groups of floors.

This tower represents a major advancement in the engineering of tall buildings. Although taller than the Sears Tower, 7 South Dearborn's floor plates are substantially smaller. This is made possible by its stayed mast structural system, formed from a series of spaces that evolve from a reinforced concrete core. A limited number of widely spaced columns dot the perimeter of the office component, and the interior is column-free. The cantilevering of the upper 57 floors from a concrete core makes columns unnecessary on the exterior walls and provides 11-foot floor-to-ceiling uninterrupted views in all directions.

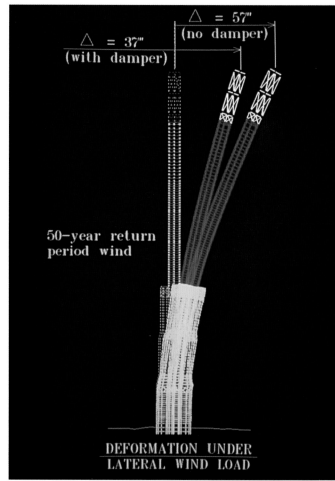

DEFORMATION UNDER
LATERAL WIND LOAD

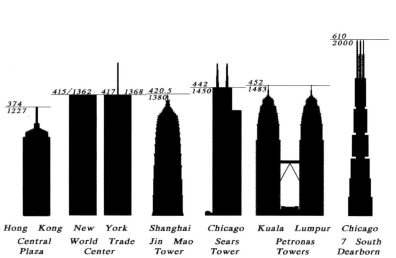

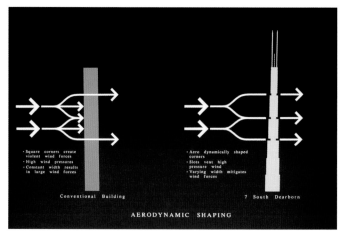

AERODYNAMIC SHAPING

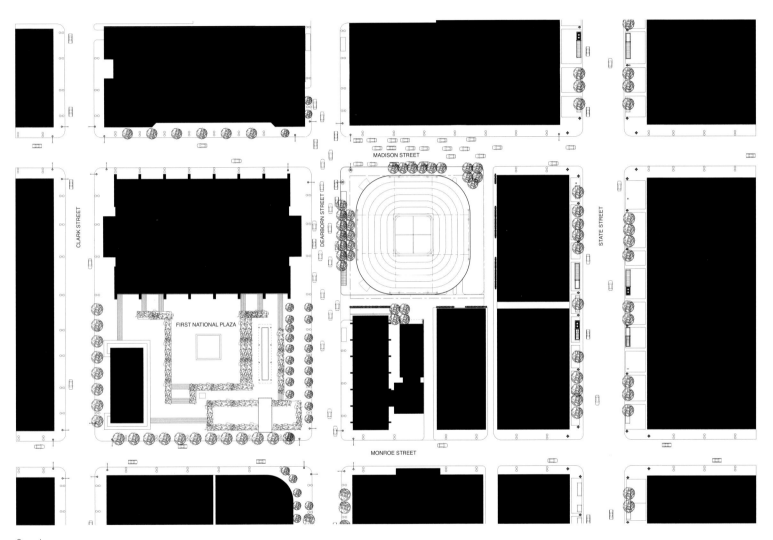

Site plan

Pearl River Tower

Location: Guangzhou, China
Client: China National Tobacco Guangdong Company
Year: Competition 2005

We first received a request to enter this competition in the summer of 2005. The Chairman of the China National Tobacco Guangdong Company was to head the search committee for an architect to design the company headquarters.

He was impressed by the Jin Mao Tower and wanted me to be involved in the competition, so invited SOM to be one of the participants, sending us a very thorough and enlightened competition brief. I emailed Gordon Gill, an associate partner and studio head at SOM, stating that this was the opportunity we had been waiting for—a chance to produce a zero-energy building potentially so innovative that it could help change the current direction of thinking about how we design buildings.

The next day, Gordon and I sat down and brainstormed the issues of harvesting natural forces to help create a zero-energy tower. We discussed an earlier solution I had developed for the Samsung Togok project in 1995 where wind turbines were proposed to capture the wind as it moved down the tower. We thought if the building could be shaped to more effectively capture the wind, then the turbine generators would be more effective. In fact, we could develop a scheme that we felt could change the current direction of architectural form-making from pure sculpture to form within a broader meaning, one that not only related to the ideals of structural expression but one that integrated the expression of harvesting the natural forces of wind and sun to help shape the form of the building. The use of a double wall with integral shading devices and photovoltaic panels was also discussed.

Gordon left the meeting exhilarated and ready to meet the challenge but what he produced in the next couple of days was startling. At first, I thought it was very bizarre-looking, somewhat like a three-sectioned automobile seat back. I was concerned that this form would be too strange to win the competition, but I waited until the development of the idea was demonstrated in the form of a Plexiglas stacked model. The model was magic. It was instantly expressive of the wind harvesting idea and it was a beautiful form. I knew then that this was a winning project. Gordon and his team continued to develop the science of the scheme, incorporating all the devices of wind turbine generation, photovoltaic systems and double wall as well as solar heating for hot water systems, radiant cooling within the structural slab and using the deep soil temperature to take heat from the cooling systems, an idea proposed by Roger Fruchette, director of our MEP group. I added the idea of shaping the ceiling slab to help reflect the daylight coming into the building to the work surfaces below.

Gordon proceeded to develop the scheme in model and presentation form and we found a metal worker in Arizona to model the concept in milled aluminum. The aluminum model was stunning and proved irresistible to the client. After the jury selected our scheme as one of the three finalists, the chairman came to Chicago to visit our offices and discuss the entry with us. One of the aspects of the project that he most identified with was the shape of the tower. He thought it looked like an index finger—like the President of China's index finger that he used to gesture to the west when making a point; he would make this gesture to us in an endearing way. We had a wonderful two-day meeting in Chicago and bonded with our new salute of finger to finger.

Form

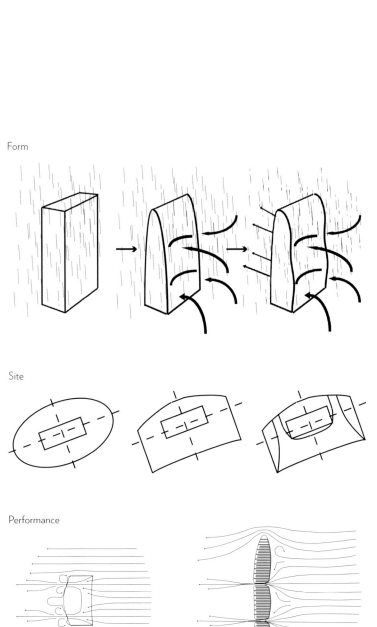

Site

Performance

Concept

The concept is of sky and man merged into one. The aim is a zero-energy tower, the embodiment of balance achieved through performance, function and beauty.

Philosophy

The design of the zero-energy tower demonstrates the principle of man harmonizing with his environment. The building is formed by the influences of its surrounding environment. It responds to and optimizes the natural forces of the environment with a goal of achieving balance and harmony with its site. The design exemplifies an understanding of the local environment and expresses it through new technologies in order to create an architectural expression and symbol for the 21st-century New Town development and the world beyond. The result of this concept is the zero-energy tower: a self-sustaining, high-performance example of environmentally intelligent architecture for the future.

Symbolism

The strategy for the project is to enhance the global profile of the China National Tobacco Guangdong Company as a responsible global citizen. The project advocates a progressive, environmental position that is intelligently planned and technologically advanced. The goals are to:

* provide the highest quality working environment for employees

* attract and retain the finest employees and thinkers for the company

* express a culture of global sophistication and progress

The design is modern, intelligent and advanced. The tower is designed to be expressive, symbolizing these characteristics; it will become the city of Guangzhou's greatest symbol of progress and importance for many years to come.

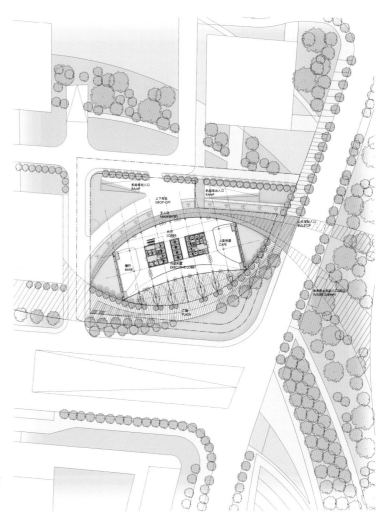

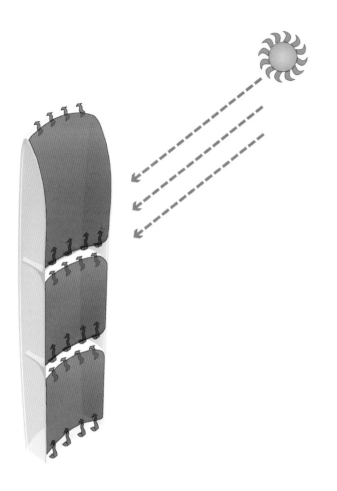

Form

The form was developed by a careful understanding of solar dynamics and wind patterns around the site. The fluid form of the tower is sleek, modern, and aerodynamic. It optimizes the solar path and uses the sun to its advantage. The smooth form presents a dynamic image, an impression reinforced by an elongated structural line. The form demonstrates the balance of performance with beauty.

Site

Building orientation is one of the most critical issues of the project. The plan is oriented to:

- Capture the solar path and minimize solar impact on the east and west façades.

- Harvest the prevailing winds from the south for energy generation.

- Orient the building in order to provide the best views for its inhabitants. The concave surface of the south wall captures the sun like a lens and focuses views to the park. This geometry also orients sightlines away from the face of the neighboring buildings to provide distant views of the park and city.

- Establish a lush, sustainable garden environment at grade That unites with the neighboring green spaces to interconnect pedestrian circulation through the site and to become a part of the larger urban fabric of the new city.

- Combine urban principles, environmental issues and programmatic requirements into a flowing expression of space and design that creates a special experience within the city.

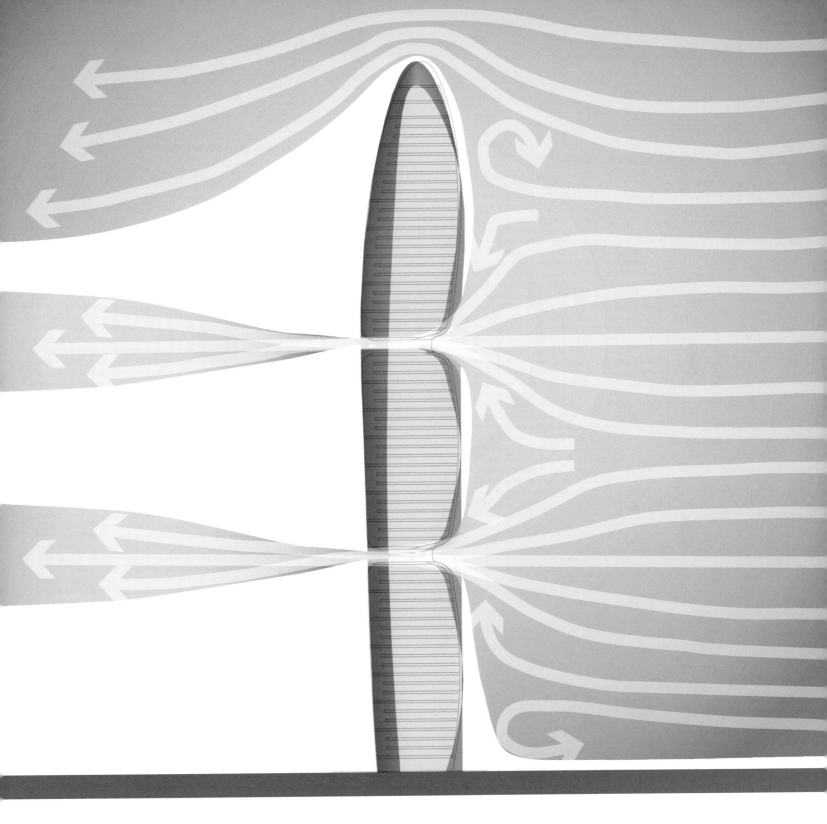

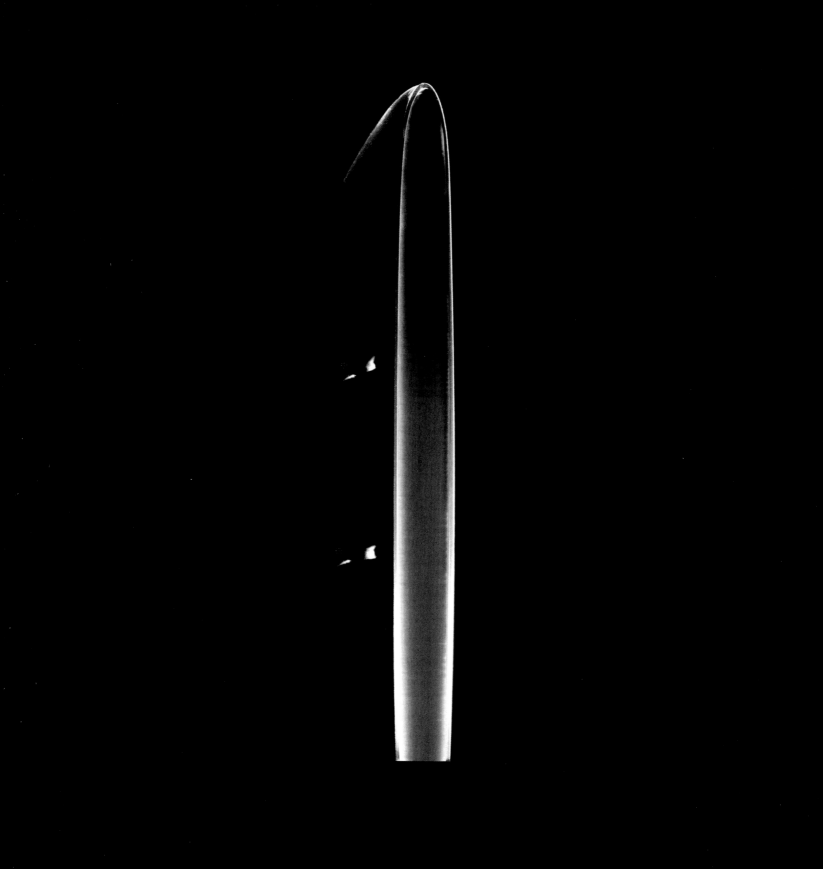

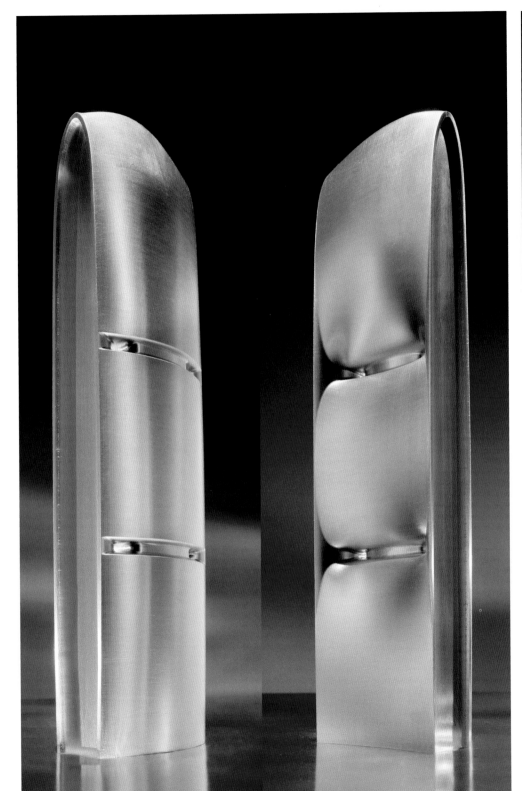
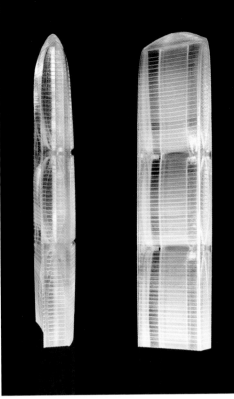

Pearl River Tower 299

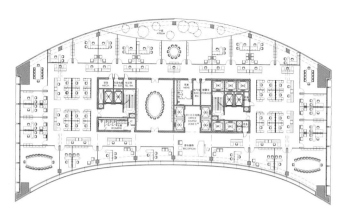

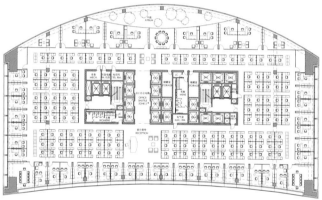

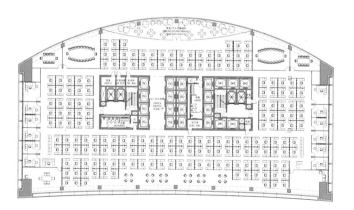

Pearl River Tower

Performance

The tower optimizes its site orientation, which is specifically attuned to solar energy and wind. The building minimizes wind force interference by using the airstream to stabilize itself. The fuselage, located at the mechanical floors, funnels the wind through turbine generators to create energy for the green atria on the north façade. The fuselage and the grey water collection system are representative of the technological features that position this building at the leading edge of technology. The goal of the building is to attain zero-energy consumption from public utilities and generate the required energy to sustain itself and possibly sell energy back to the grid.

Programming

The employee cafeteria, programmed for full-service food management, is located on level three. This location is appropriate for efficient delivery service and access from lower level parking.

Levels 4 through 51 are the typical office floors within the tower. These floor areas, of between 2300 and 2700 square meters, offer the latest in technology for single- or multi-tenant use. These office plans are organized on a 9-meter structural module. The exterior wall is based on a flexible 1.5-meter module for individual workstations, or can be doubled to a 3-meter module for private offices. For multi-tenant office configurations, each typical floor is capable of accommodating a circulation corridor around the core without compromising the efficiency of the workspace.

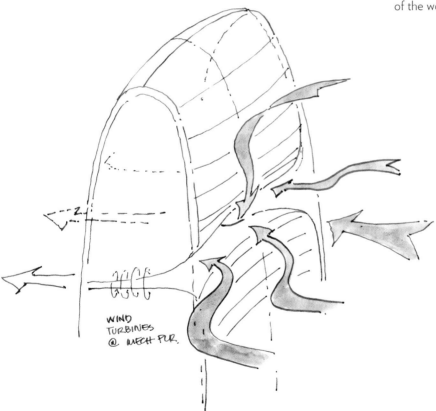

WIND TURBINES @ MECH FLR.

FACADE- FUSELAGE- DIRECTS/FUNNES -WIND.

The conference center is located above the executive floors at levels 67 and 68. The lower-level conference floor is designed as a 600-seat (540-square-meter) congress-style hall. The conference hall occupies one full floor and features ample pre-function and support space. The design of the hall allows it to be subdivided into two 300-seat halls for seating program flexibility. Each conference center will offer the latest in multimedia technology and dedicated food preparation areas, with break-out space for casual meetings.

The executive levels are located at floors 52 through 68 within the upper portion of the tower, to maximize views and privacy. The executive floors function as open-plan space, which can be subdivided as desired.

Above these floors are the restaurant and the executive club. The executive club occupies the sky dome at the pinnacle of the tower and features spectacular 360-degree panoramic views of the surrounding parks and city. This space is programmed for multifunction use such as small conferences, business lounges, dining, and receptions. The sky dome features a retractable glass roof located at the center of the dome, offering open-air functions when desired.

Double-deck elevator groups

Double-deck elevators have one car frame containing two vertically stacked decks. These elevators require a two-story main lobby. During building in-rush the lower deck stops, for example, at all uneven numbered floors and the upper deck stops at all even-numbered floors. Double-deck elevators offer a much greater handling capacity during filling and emptying of a building in comparison with normal elevators. Double-deck elevators are suitable both as express elevators for trips between the main lobby and sky lobby, and as normal elevator groups for buildings with large floor areas.

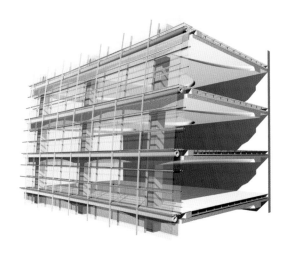

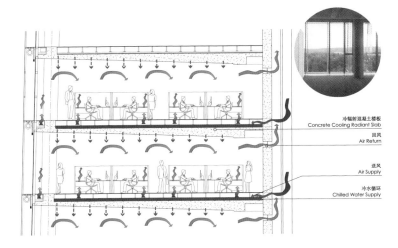

冷辐射混凝土楼板
Concrete Cooling Radiant Slab

回风
Air Return

送风
Air Supply

冷水循环
Chilled Water Supply

Intelligent building management

The quantity of outside air introduced into the building will be monitored by sensors that can identify 14 different indoor contaminants, including carbon dioxide. Computer fluid dynamic modeling will be applied where appropriate to predict environmental characteristics in performance critical areas.

Under floor air distribution (UFAD) system with radiant cooling

This air displacement system is chosen as an excellent complement both to the building's usage and to the ensemble of sustainable systems in place. The displacement system will rely on a raised floor that will serve as a pressurized plenum, and as space for routing electrical and data cabling. By supplying the required ventilation air at the lower zone of the room, heat given off by occupants and equipment helps push the air upwards via natural convection where it comes in contact with the chilled ceiling. As the air follows the natural contour of the vaulted ceiling it begins to cool and fall, until the process begins again. The result is that the air effectively tumbles toward the core of the building where it is ultimately exhausted from the space. The advantage of incorporating this thermal stratification within the ventilation scheme is that improved air quality is obtained by increasing the number of air changes, at a lower cost than a standard displacement ventilation system. Further, the system will provide superior temperature control, more flexibility for usable space, and will require less plant space and minimal fan energy for air distribution.

Plumbing/fire protection

The fire protection systems will consist of zoned automatic sprinkler systems throughout, with wet risers, hose reels, and combined fire water storage tanks and fire pumps, in accordance with Chinese code and NFPA standards requirements. The building will utilize a gravity feed system to minimize the pump energy cost incurred throughout the day in conjunction with low-flow plumbing fixtures and wastewater reduction systems.

A rainwater reclamation system is proposed to provide irrigation to the external site and potentially the internal atrium spaces with provisions for water treatment. A venetian blind with horizontal louvers is applied, which can be adjusted to deflect light in the upper window area and to shade the lower area. It is effective for glare-free light deflection.

HVAC

Stepped constant volume supply systems or variable air volume systems will be utilized in the building to provide superb comfort and improved ventilation effectiveness and temperature control. Modular air handling units are used to facilitate operation during the subdivision of the halls. As a large part of the energy consumed annually for the HVAC system will be for the dehumidification of the outside air, a system including sensible recovery units for exhaust heat recovery and desiccant dehumidification is proposed.

Pearl River Tower

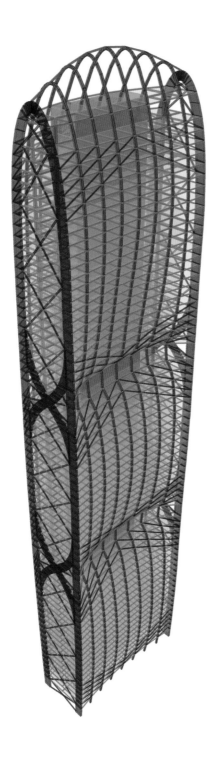

Integrated wind turbines

Two sets of wind turbines will be integrated within the building, located at each mechanical floor. These turbines will generate power that can be directly fed to the mechanical equipment with minimal losses. By adding curvature to the double wall façade, the entire building will serve as an air intake to the turbine locations, maximizing the velocity and thus the potential energy rendered from the system. The energy created by the turbines can be used directly or stored in batteries for later use.

As the relationship between the building and its environment evolved, a twofold strategy was developed to target a net-zero-energy building. Firstly, the energy required in sustaining a building of this size and nature within the site's climate was analyzed in an effort to minimize the baseline energy consumption. This was accomplished by a number of technologies such as building orientation, a dynamic high-performance building envelope, a day-lighting strategy, an intelligent building management system, partial active double wall, fully glazed low-e glass, internal shading for solar screening, integrated photovoltaics, solar collection for hot water usage, and an optimized building central plant. While following these strategies results in a vastly more economical structure, incorporation of innovative environmental strategies and renewable energies is essential to targeting a net-zero-energy building, and serves to distinguish this building from any of its class. These systems were chosen as being powerful in practice and in their simplicity in construction and operation.

A dynamic, high-performance building envelope will be incorporated into the design. The façade system will be optimized for the use of daylight while controlling solar loads to the interior zone and glare. The internal skin of the southern face will comprise a fully glazed, low-e glass, while the outer skin will feature an integrated photovoltaic system. A unique proposed feature is the routing of exhaust air through the interstitial space of the two membranes. Driven by convection currents, the cool dry air will provide thermal barrier heating as it travels upward until being ducted into the next mechanical floor. This hot dry air will be used as the energy source to passively recharge the desiccant dehumidification system.

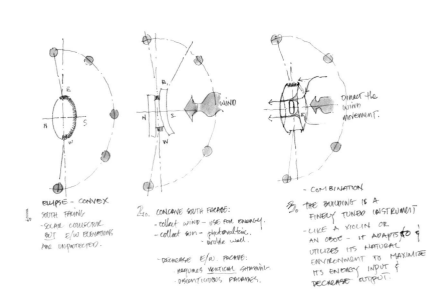

1. ELLIPSE - CONVEX
SOUTH FACING
- SOLAR COLLECTOR
BUT E/W ELEVATIONS
AND UNPROTECTED.

2. CONCAVE SOUTH FACADE:
- collect wind - use for energy.
- collect sun - photovoltaic.
- double wall.

- DECREASE E/W FACADE:
- requires vertical setback.
- discontiguous facades.

3. - COMBINATION
THE BUILDING IS A
FINELY TUNED INSTRUMENT
- LIKE A VIOLIN OR
AN OBOE - IT ADAPTS TO &
UTILIZES ITS NATURAL
ENVIRONMENT TO MAXIMIZE
ITS ENERGY INPUT &
DECREASE OUTPUT.

Direct the wind movement.

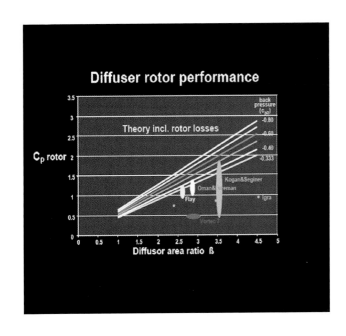

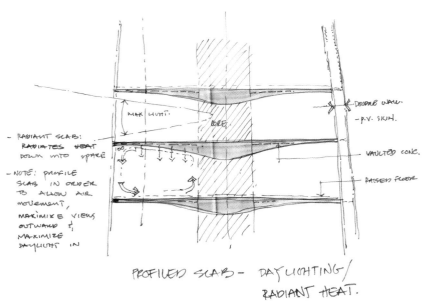

- RADIANT SLAB:
RADIATES HEAT
DOWN INTO SPACE

- NOTE: PROFILE
SLAB IN ORDER
TO ALLOW AIR
MOVEMENT,
MAXIMIZE VIEWS
OUTWARD &
MAXIMIZE
DAYLIGHT IN

MAX LIGHT.
BORE.

- DOUBLE WALL.
- P.V. SKIN.

VAULTED CONC.

RAISED FLOOR

PROFILED SLAB - DAYLIGHTING /
RADIANT HEAT.

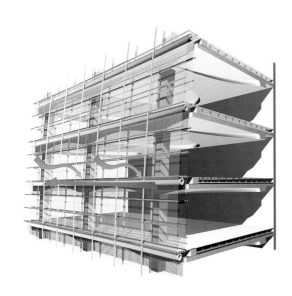

Gateway XYZ

Location: Chicago, Illinois, USA
Client: Chicago Central Area Committee
Year: 2005

The design of a gateway is dependent on the method of travel to and from a place. For the settlers, gateways were often discovered on foot or by boat and later, by train, by car, and by airplane. In the future, 25, 50 or perhaps 100 years from now, a gateway will be defined as a three-dimensional point in space; a series of x, y, and z coordinates and by a system of navigation that is controlled not by the passenger or driver but by an interactive series of coordinates in space that inform the vehicle of the safest path to his destination and direct the on-board navigator to comply with its directions.

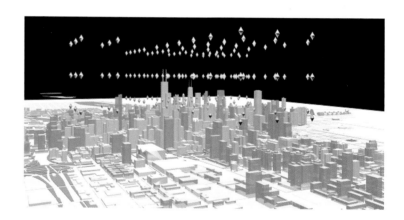

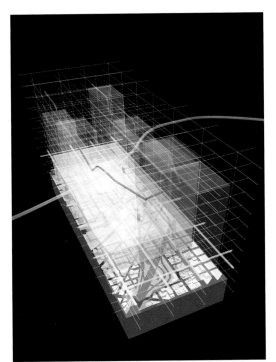

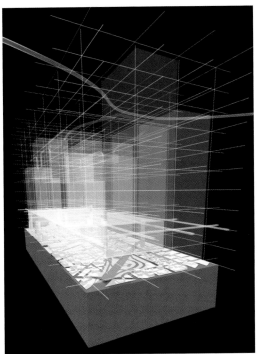

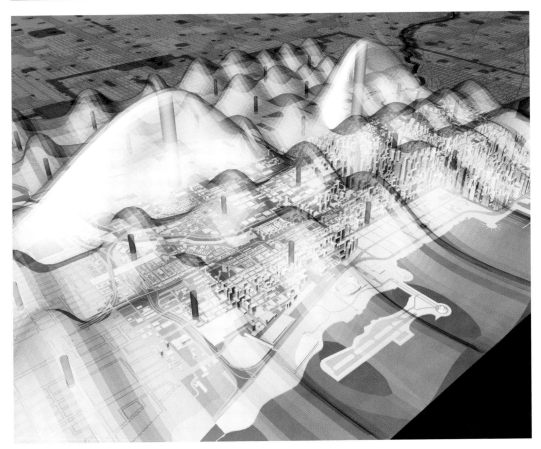

What is a gateway? A gateway is a threshold, portal, symbol, entry and/or transition.

Gateways change. Once physical places, gateways are now defined by a point in space. The definition of a gateway changes over time. Boundaries adjust depending on the mode of access and technology involved. A gateway is an ever-changing boundary that adjusts because the city is permeable and ever-changing. A gateway may be defined as a node in three-dimensional space, an intersection defined by a crossover of systems. The gateway of the future may be identified as a point of transfer.

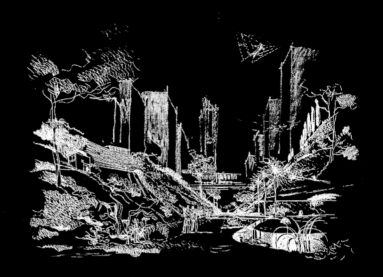

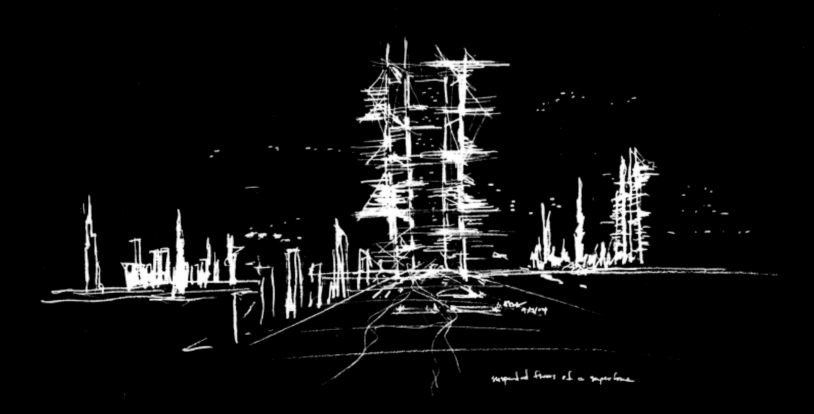

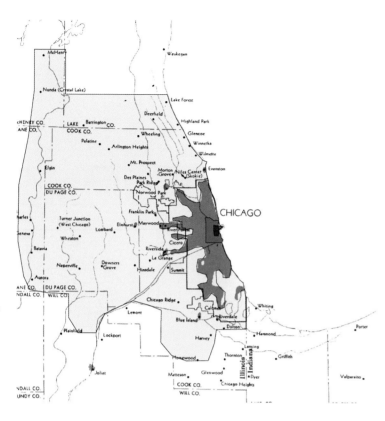

The gateway is a three-dimensional connector of intersections stratified across space. The virtual network generates new zoning parameters within cities. The connections across strata allow gateway access at multiple elevations. As access changes over time from surface to air, the existing grid goes green. As technology advances and develops new modes of transportation and materials, the possibility to go vertical increases and with this change comes a fundamental change in where we congregate, shop, and socialize. Vertical cities will emerge with lateral social spaces, gardens, entry points, and work venues in the structures occupied by residents in special zones or platforms that replace grade.

Paths, fields, and structures will be managed by navigation systems to allow maximum efficiency and occupancy of given points in space. Individual control will be reduced by controllers who will determine optimum routes.

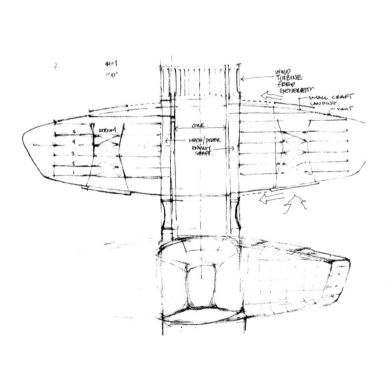

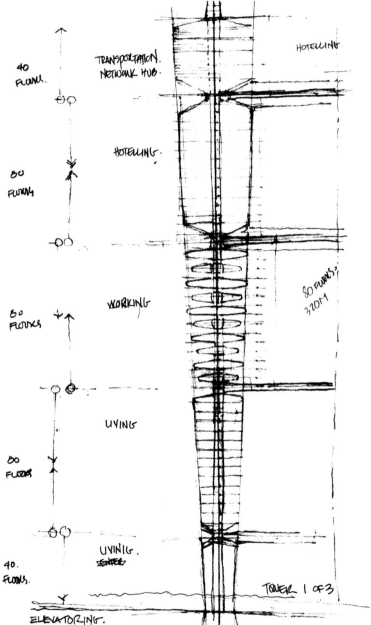

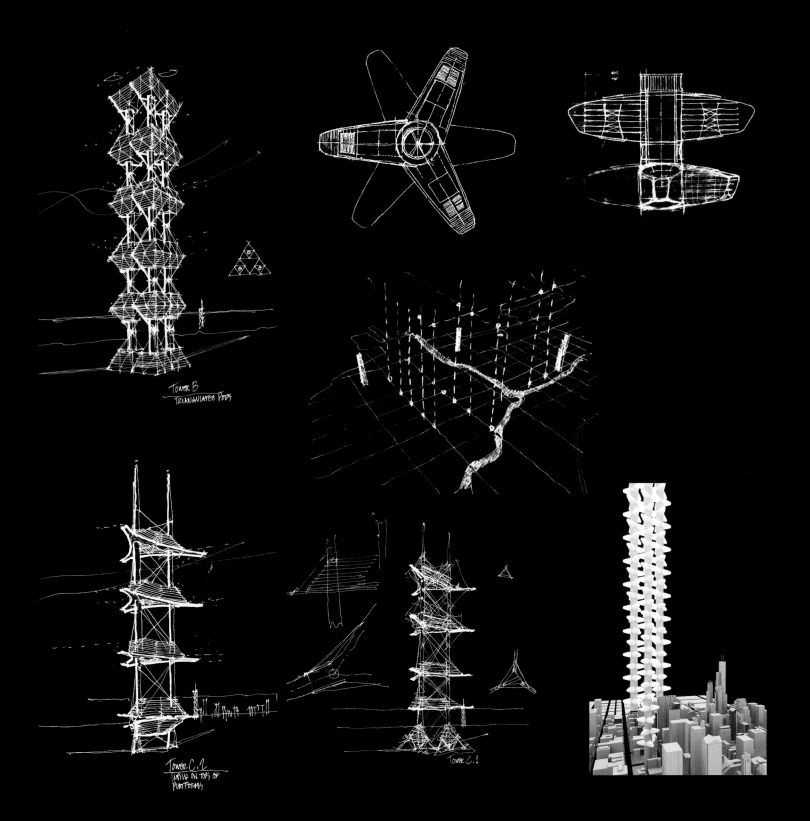

TOWER B
TRIANGULATED PODS

TOWER C.2
LINTELS ON TOPS OF
PLATFORMS

TOWER C.1

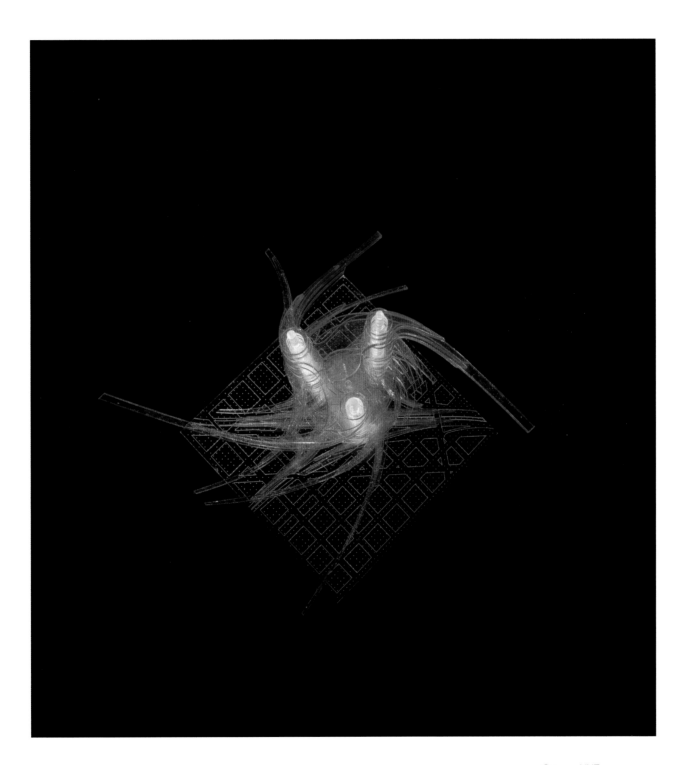

Jubilee Park Pavilion

Location: Canary Wharf, London, UK
Client: Canary Wharf Contractors, Ltd.
Year: 2004

The plan for this site included the development of an entrance to the below-grade retail and the provision of light into the below-grade environment. The entrance pavilion was to contain a pass-through from the street and surrounding structures to the Wertz-designed park over the Jubilee station, therefore creating two entrances into the pavilion.

Another issue was to design an entrance that was distinct and different from the two Norman Foster-designed pavilions that enter Jubilee station. It was important that our entrance contrast with Foster's, in order to signal a separate functional purpose. The design approach, therefore, was to contrast form while maintaining transparency for functional reasons. The form chosen was crystalline in character, directly contrasting with the soft, curved forms of the station entry.

The slope and form in plan derive from the constraints of the site and the desire to minimize the vertical figure of the piece. The total height was determined by the minimum clearance for the enclosed elevator. The biaxial symmetry of the building in plan is derived from the circulation access through the center and the regularization of the structure and skylight system and their relationship to the symmetrical composition of the Cesar Pelli-designed winter garden on axis to the south of this pavilion.

The structure for the pavilion is composed of round structural steel tubes welded and ground smooth to form a web-like figure. The structure is painted a Detroit Graphic matte black to allow maximum visibility for occupants of the retail space. The window frames are minimized in size to accommodate the connection and support of the double-glazed and laminated high-efficiency glazing to the steel frame below. The glazing system is four-sided silicone with mechanical constraints hidden from the interior and exterior by a unique and innovative clip system that connects the glass to the frame at the spacer between the two pieces of double glazing.

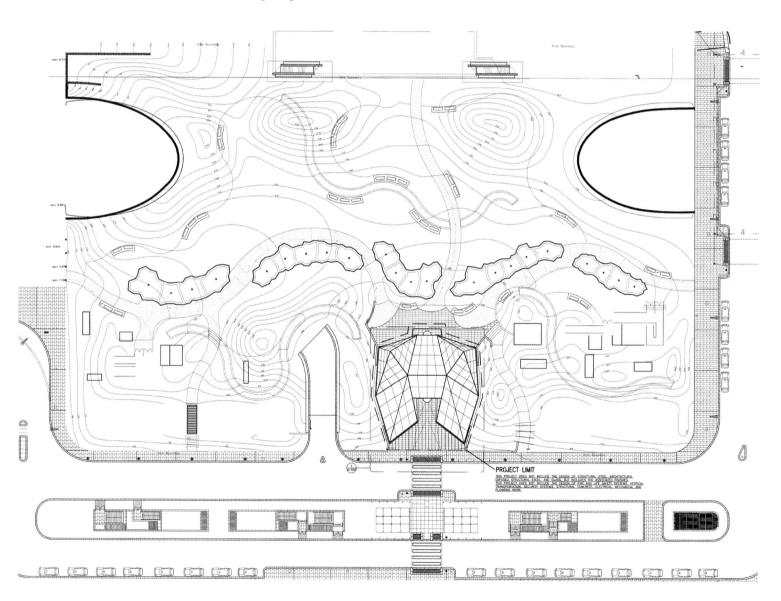

PROJECT LIMIT

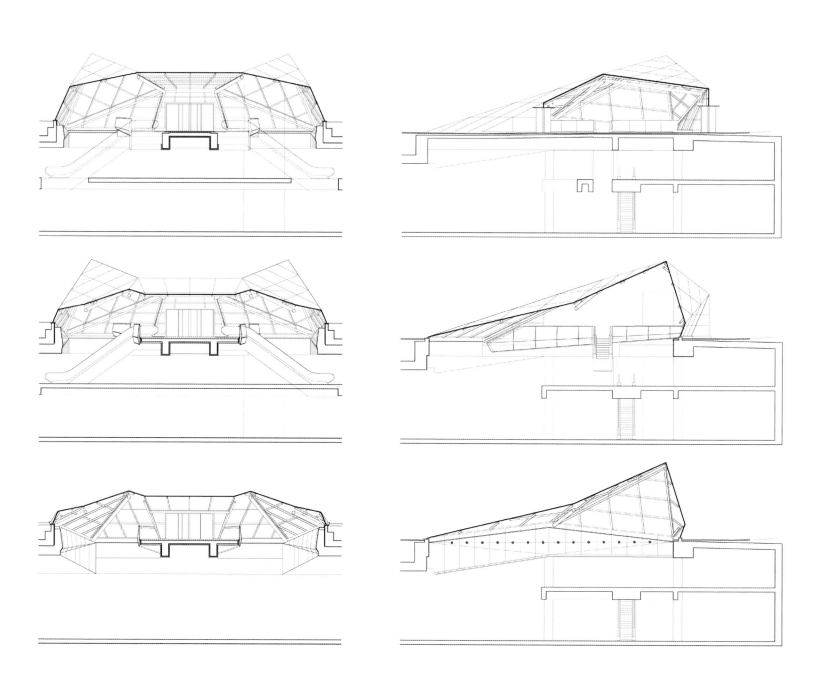

Jubilee Park Pavilion

Jubilee Park Pavilion

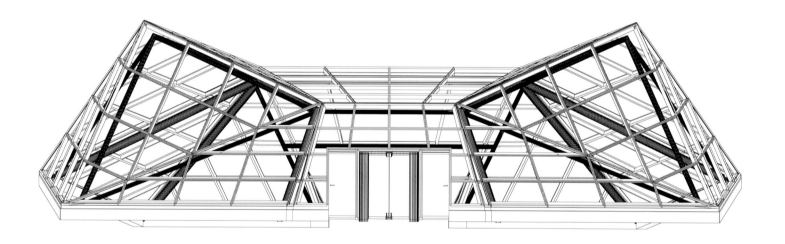

Jubilee Park Pavilion

Jubilee Park Pavilion

Jubilee Park Pavilion

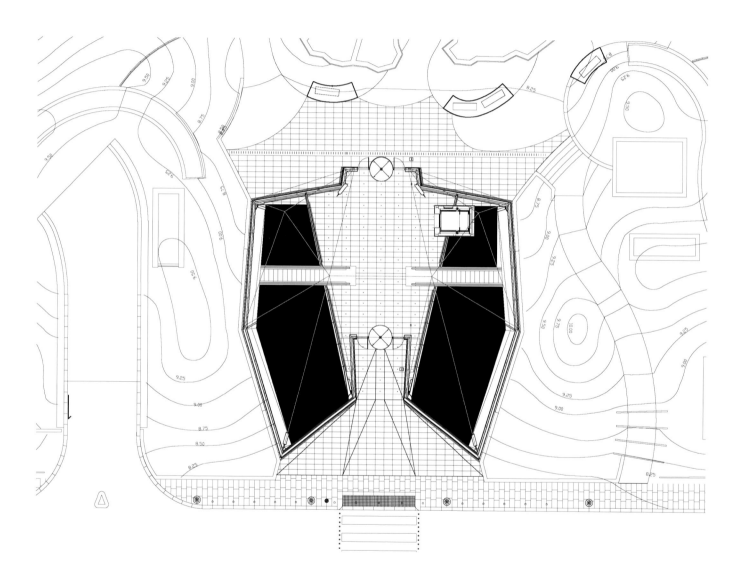

Kowloon Tower (Feasibility)

Location: Hong Kong, China
Client: Mass Transit Railway Corporation
Year: 1997–2000

For a tall tower to be truly meaningful, it should express the ethos not only of its owner, but of the city and culture within which it is placed, and it should speak to its context and reinforce the city's culture, and the character of its people. It should evoke emotions, and inspire and lift the human spirit.

For a tall building to be both a landmark in a city, and a structure with the power required to give the city an identity, its architecture needs to be unique, not only with regard to the other buildings in the city, but also within the context of world architecture.

The site of the Landmark Tower in Kowloon is at the edge of Victoria Harbour and directly across from the planned Central Station Tower. This required a dialog and creative tension between these two dominating structures. Together, if the proper resonance is created, these two structures can become a unique and unparalleled new gateway for the city, while maintaining their own individual identities.

The proposed Landmark Tower design is intended to be a kinetic structure with a series of subtly folding crystalline planes, each catching light at different angles, ascending in a sloped vertical shaft, and culminating in a tall spire that unifies and centers the composition. The resultant effect is an image that is constantly changing with the sunlight and direction of view. The composition is multi-directional, addressing all views toward the site. The uniqueness of this structure is fully appreciated upon entering the hotel lobby and discovering the 22-story atrium at the center of the tower, with views through the tower base to Hong Kong across the harbor. This atrium is created in part by the need to transfer the load of the central core out to eight super-columns located at the building's perimeter. Luxury hotel rooms and amenities are placed around this atrium with unparalleled views to the harbor, the island, and the station park.

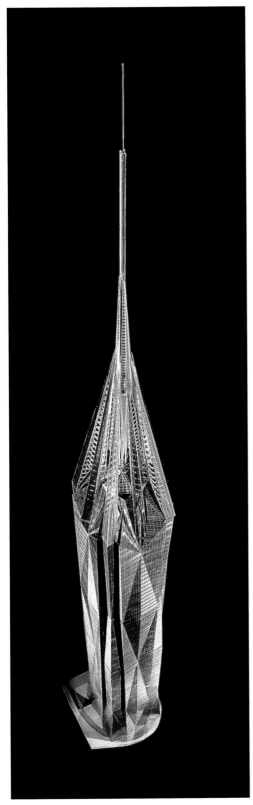

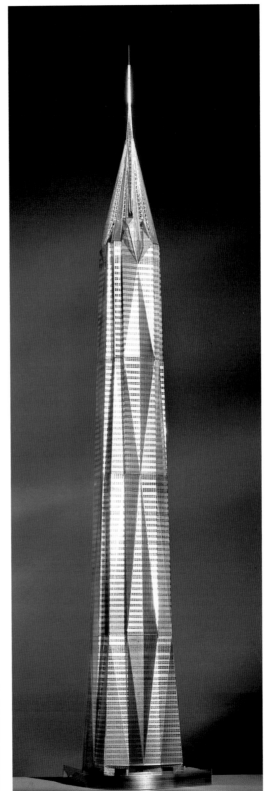

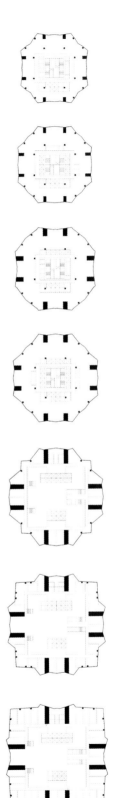

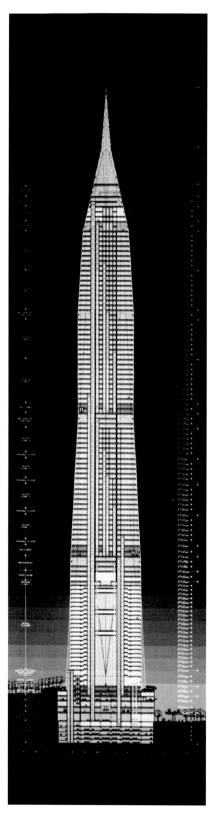

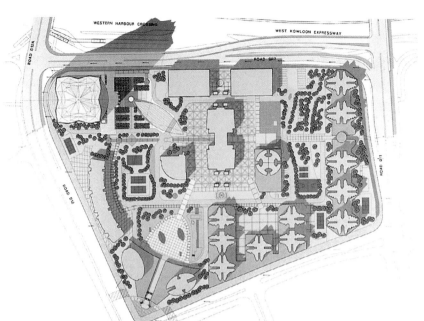

The feasibility and concept design is for a 1883-foot-tall (574-meter), 3.9-million-square-foot (360,000-square-meter) tower, which could be located at the MTRC land reclamation development site in Kowloon Bay. The multi-use building would be constructed on a podium over the new railway station and consists of a hotel, commercial office building, retail areas, assembly components, and a car park.

Located at the top of the tower are two multi-level fine dining restaurants and a public observatory, providing stunning views. Office space occupies the upper portion of the tower while a 5-star hotel with a 23-story atrium comprises the lower portion. A glass-enclosed circulation corridor on each floor overlooks the atrium space, providing access to guest rooms located on the building perimeter.

The podium portion of the project includes executive parking, retail shops and public spaces, the observatory entry, and loading dock facilities. Public access bridges to adjacent southern and western areas are connected to the retail space of the tower. Five additional levels of parking, serving approximately 740 cars, are located in the basement below the podium.

Samsung Togok Tower Feasibility Concept

Location: Seoul, South Korea
Client: Samsung Corporation
Year: 1995

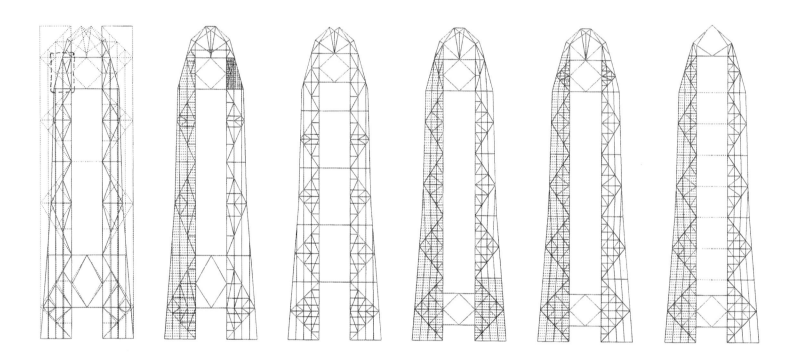

In fall 1994, we were contacted by Samsung to master plan a large tract of land in the Togok district of Seoul, South Korea and to subdivide this parcel into a series of developable plots that could either be sold off or developed over time by Samsung's development division. The Chairman of Samsung, Mr Kim, was interested in the development of a vertical city that could house all the office space for Samsung as well as many other functions.

The 111-story Samsung Tower is a multi-use building containing office space, residential housing, a hotel and conference center, a cultural center, a microelectronics showroom and an entertainment, sports, and retail facility. Planned for the Togok district of Seoul, the building's program is quite expansive with 6,674,000 square feet (620,000 square meters) of space above grade and 4,952,000 square feet (460,000 square meters) below grade.

It is truly a 21st-century building. Every facet of the Samsung Tower has been designed from a basis in rationality toward the primary goal of improving the quality of lives of both occupants and observers.

The tower structure will be composed of a combination of structural steel and reinforced concrete. When considering the design of this very tall building in Seoul, Korea, a city that has grown from a population of 100,000 people just 20 years ago to more than seven million people today, the context of the site was found to be relatively new and austere, void of history and culture but infused with an extremely high work ethic and national pride. Existing conditions for most residential structures in Seoul were 15- to 20-story block apartment buildings; many of these residential building types surrounded our site, which was at the intersection of two primary subway lines. Vertical expansion and mixed use was called for and a cultural renaissance was mandated.

The tower is envisioned to be state-of-the-art in ecological sensitivity through its use of the earth's natural forces to minimize waste and maximize efficiency of the building's systems.

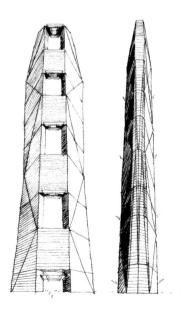

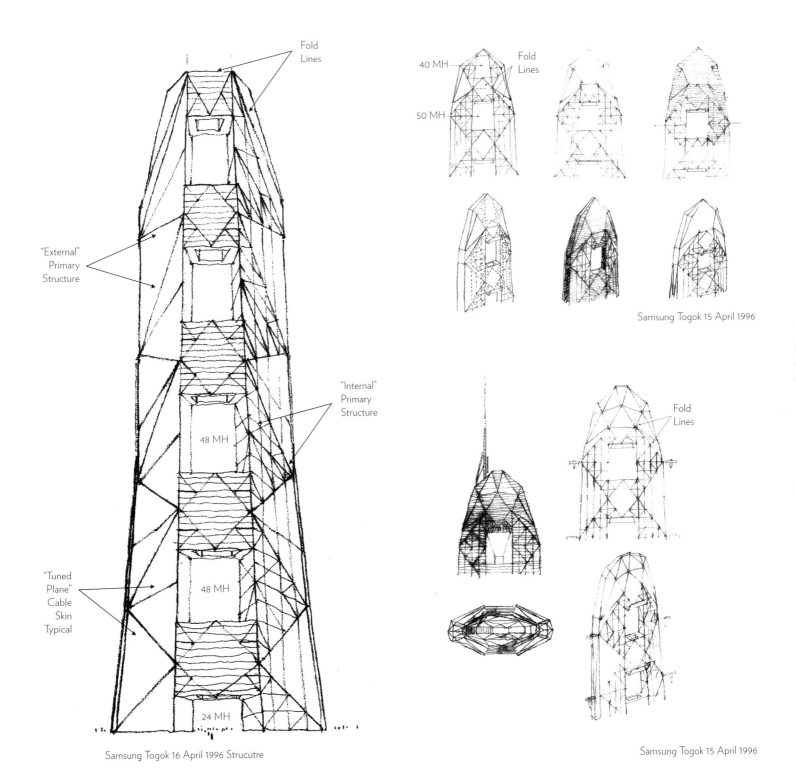

Fold
Lines

"External"
Primary
Structure

"Internal"
Primary
Structure

48 MH

48 MH

"Tuned
Plane"
Cable
Skin
Typical

24 MH

Samsung Togok 16 April 1996 Strucutre

40 MH

50 MH

Fold
Lines

Samsung Togok 15 April 1996

Fold
Lines

Samsung Togok 15 April 1996

Samsung Togok Tower Feasibility Concept   343

The use of technology to harness the forces of nature to create sustainability, the use of efficient systems, and the use of height to generate energy, were the focus of our process. Intended for a large conglomerate whose primary business is technology, this building was designed to be a working laboratory for sustainability. It features an accessible double wall system to house the latest photovoltaic systems and wind-driven turbo generators to capture air movements through the building's sky atria and within the double wall cavity.

The form of the building took the shape of a vertical slab of stone that had been weathered by many years of exposure to wind and rain. Its aerodynamic efficiency was maximized with a tapered form and building openings to disrupt the basic driving force of cross-wind oscillations and to shed the vortices that can build up around tall objects. The building was originally skinned in a smooth wall of glass that was later triangulated and folded in a series of flat plains to accommodate constructability. The diagonally braced structure was located at the perimeter of the building, occupying the interstitial space between the exterior and interior skins, increasing its ability to carry lateral wind forces. With 111 stories, this building accommodates 350,000 square meters of office, hotel, housing, retail, and entertainment facilities, vertically stacked for efficient transit by elevator systems zoned in a series of banks accessed by sky lobbies.

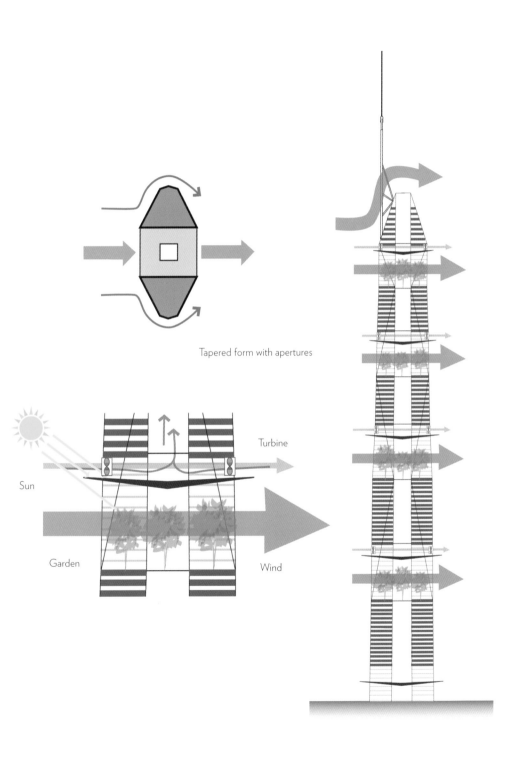

Tapered form with apertures

Sun

Garden

Turbine

Wind

Tower Palace III

Location: Seoul, South Korea
Client: Samsung Corporation
Year: 2000–2004

Tower Palace III is the last building to be built in the Togok district master plan developed by Samsung. The design competition process was used to select an architect for this statement building. Samsung shortlisted the competition entries to those of SOM, KPF, and Cesar Pelli and also visited each firm on several occasions during the design process to give critical and programmatic input. The scheme I proposed—a tripartite plan that maximizes the perimeter ratio to interior floor area, with each leg extending in a spiral stair step manner to a height of 92 floors—was deemed the winner and we were awarded the contract. The overall height of the tower was later reduced to 73 stories in the planning approval process due to neighborhood objections and shadowing of adjacent buildings.

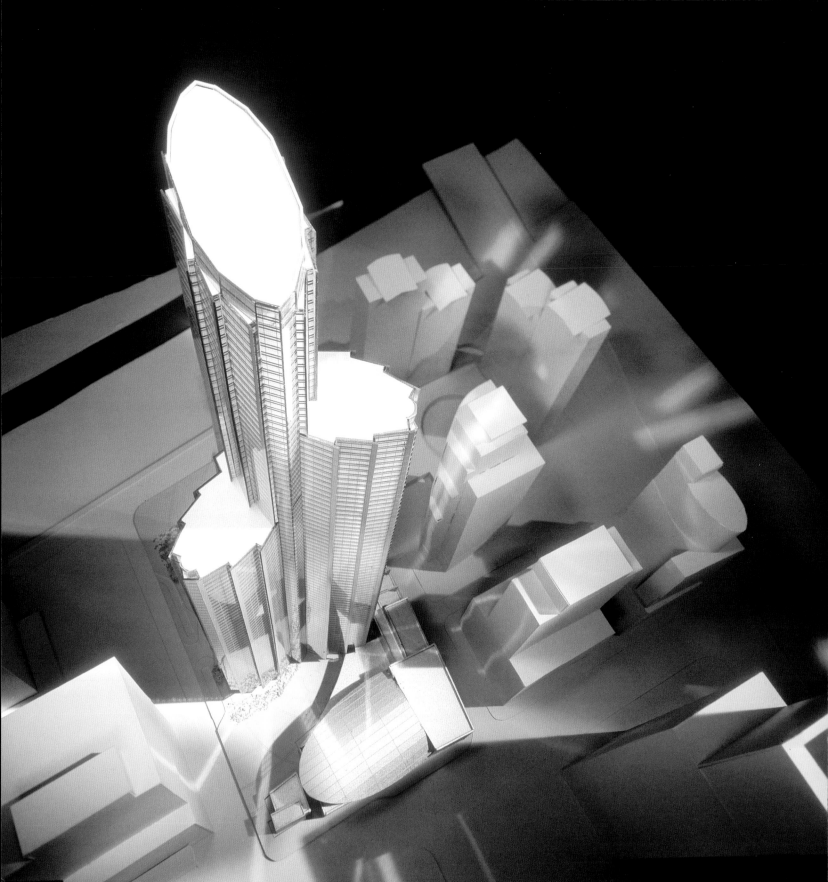

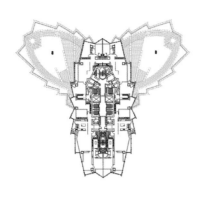

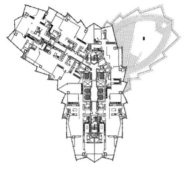

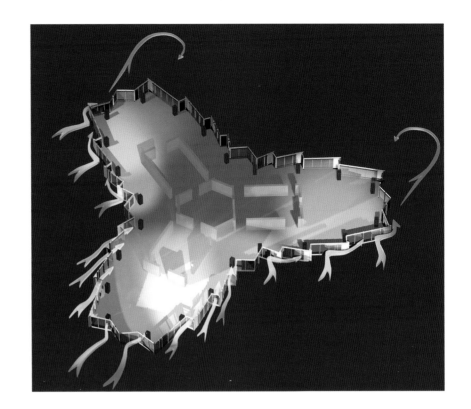

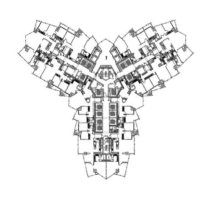

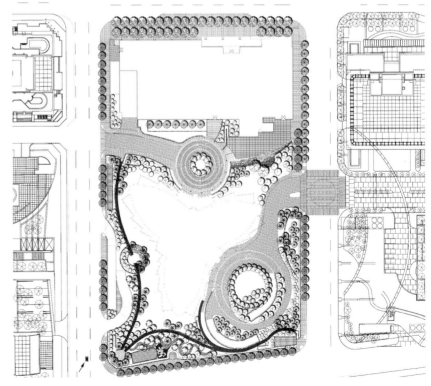

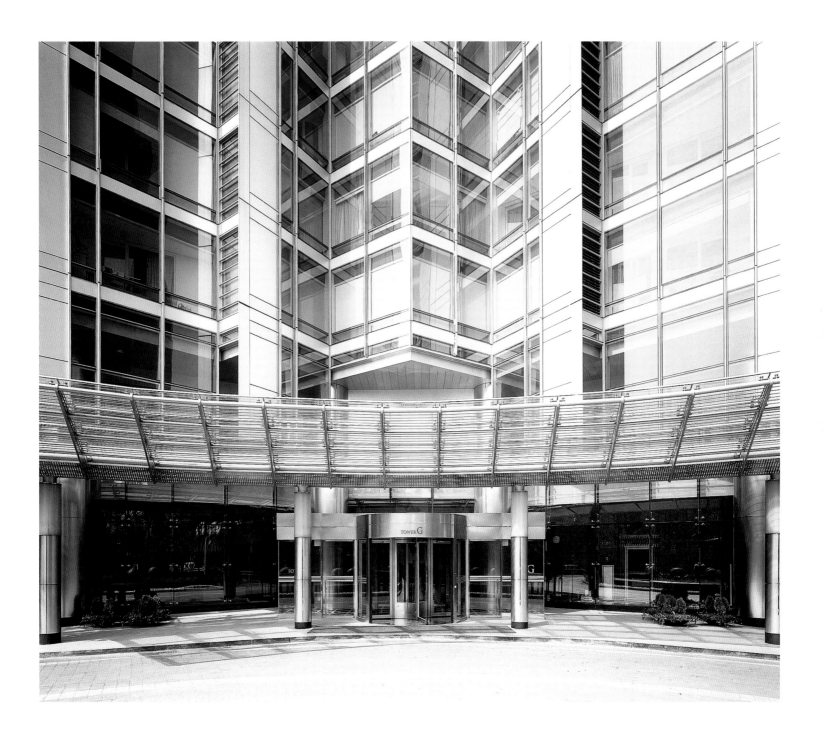

Tower Palace III   351

Tower Palace III is intended to promote a new standard of high-rise living for the people of Seoul, South Korea. The tower's design is derived from natural forms, and influences and integrates state-of-the-art building technology to provide a landmark structure for the city. This building also owes much of its conceptual image to a 1920's scheme for a tower on the Fredrichstrasse in Berlin by Mies van der Rohe. However, this tower is highly evolved from its original precedent and a subsequent prototype called Lake Point Tower in Chicago, designed by John Heinrich and George Schipporeit, both students of Mies.

The project includes a large southern park for the residents, a sports club, restaurants, retail shops by the associate architect Sam Woo, a gallery, a banquet room, a business center, and a sky garden.

The tower's tripartite form and plan arrangement provides for maximum view corridors at the lower floors and as the tower drops legs near the top, increased views for the penthouse units. It presents a tall slender face to the city while allowing residents views of both the dynamic northern cityscape and the tranquil natural landscape to the south. Since this was to be a 92-story tower, the tallest all-residential tower in the world, the structural concept was of paramount importance. We conceived a central core with three walls that form a tripod-like structure. These walls are the corridor walls to the units on each leg of the tower. Both the core and the walls were designed to take as much gravity load and lateral load as possible, reducing the need for massive columns at the exterior wall. The exterior columns were thus limited to gravity loads that are tied together at the third points of the tower by massive belt-like walls to help transfer the lateral forces to the core and corridor wall structure. The mechanical floors and refuge areas are placed at these two levels. The columns at the perimeter and the floor framing within the units are constructed of steel, due to the market's mistrust of all-concrete construction in Seoul, where several buildings and bridges have had catastrophic collapses in the recent past. The tower shape is very efficient in shedding the vortex forces and reducing the negative forces on the wall, thus reducing the horizontal acceleration on the building. In part, this is enhanced by the ribbed texture of the tower's surface and the differential heights of the tower's wings. The structure behaves exceptionally well against torsional forces, bending, and overturning. The tower's form is intended to add a truly unique shape to the skyline.

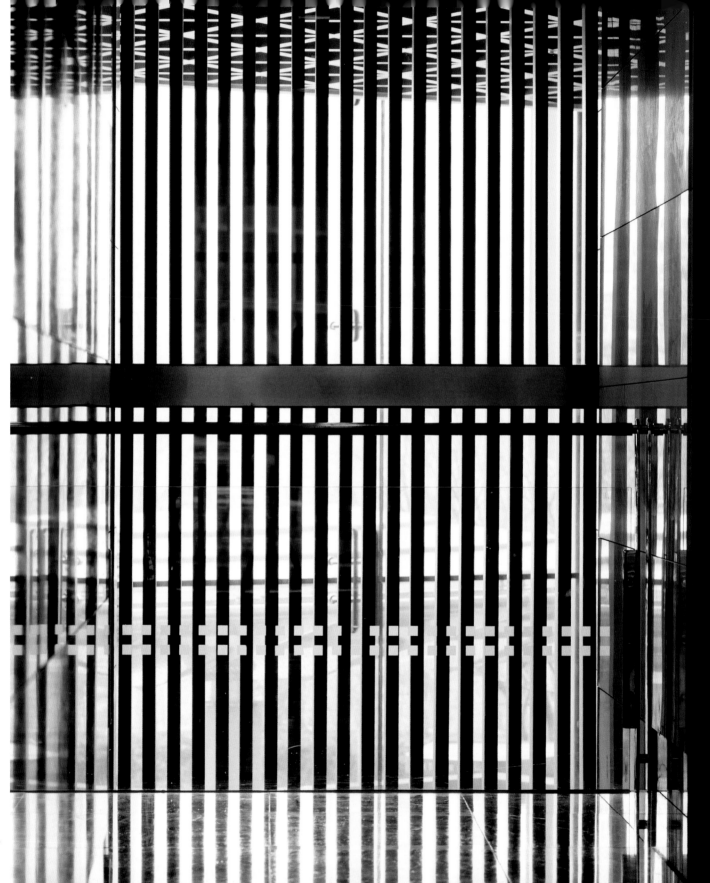

This form is characterized by a series of radiating planes, which provide a dynamic and ever-changing appearance as the sun moves across the faces.

These planes provide a strong sense of verticality to the tower and allow for the discreet movement of air through the units. The tower is clad in a light blue-green tinted high-performance glass to allow for maximum light transmission and bright views. Natural anodized panels provide a metallic quality to the solid surfaces and polished stainless steel rods that function as window-washing tiebacks and add brilliance to the exterior surface. Behind each solid panel sits a vertical fan coil unit. Each condominium unit has at least one enclosed balcony that opens to the adjacent living space and to the exterior, thus providing a form of "double skin" for the building where air is tempered and used to heat and cool the units within. The modulation of the wall planes provides for small surface openings where louvers are placed perpendicular to the glazed walls, thus minimizing their visual impact and organizing the louvered area in discrete zones.

The condominium units are organized around a layered concept that places the utility spaces along a central spine at the rear of the unit with living spaces along the exterior wall. This organization allows for an economy of service distribution with maximum flexibility of living space accommodations. Apartments available for purchase are served by three distinct elevator zones, while furnished rental apartments are served by one central zone of elevators.

Where the tower meets the ground, the skin stops and the column structure is exposed to reveal the lobby and core wall. The exterior wall at this level is glass and the core is clad in a green Verde antique marble. The exterior columns are clad in textured stainless steel. The main features at grade level are the drop-off and a glass canopy structure that protects visitors from wind and rain. The circular drop-off provides a quick and convenient ramp to and from the basement level below-grade parking.

Throughout the process, the Samsung Development and Construction group proved to be an excellent client and contractor and it was this project that led us to recommend it for the Burj Khalifa project, a much more demanding construction venture, but one we felt the firm was uniquely qualified for.

201 Bishopsgate, The Broadgate Tower, and The Galleria

Location: London, UK
Client: British Land
Year: 1998–2008

The 201 Bishopsgate/The Broadgate Tower project represents a significant continuation of the practice of constructing buildings that utilize the air rights above railway tracks within the City of London. Its concept is informed by the constraints imposed by the placement of the foundations and by the resultant robustness of its structural expression.

The project consists of two primary buildings: a low-rise, 13-story horizontal structure facing Norton Folgate and Primrose Street, and a 35-story tower on the western boundary of the site, accessed by an open public plaza.

These two structures significantly enhance the opportunities for tenants to select the type of space that best suits their needs, and increase the range of tenant types that will share the considerable amenities that already exist in the Broadgate complex. A covered skylit galleria space between these two structures will provide a protected public open space for retail activity. This space will also act as a pedestrian passageway connecting the Broadgate complex and Liverpool Street Station to the south with future development planned for the north. Directly adjacent to the galleria to the south will be a public plaza with additional retail space. This space will be landscaped with trees and vine-covered walls and will continue the tradition established throughout the Broadgate complex of providing important public urban spaces and amenities for tenants and citizens. The development of this phase will expand the public realm of the Broadgate Campus and will improve the character of the City's infrastructure that is adjacent to, or contained by, its boundaries.

361

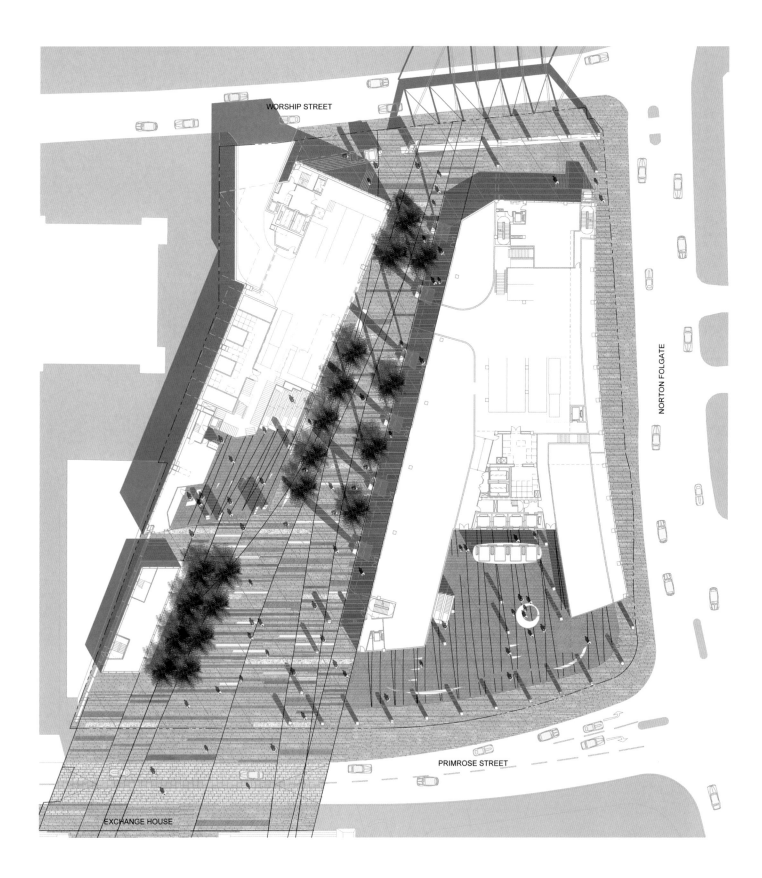

WORSHIP STREET

NORTON FOLGATE

PRIMROSE STREET

EXCHANGE HOUSE

The proposed 2.3-acre development has three primary components: The Broadgate Tower, 201 Bishopsgate, and The Galleria. The Broadgate Tower has 35 levels (including ground and roof plant) with a height of 178.4 meters AOD. Thirty-two of the floors house approximately 400,000 square feet of office space while the bottom three floors are primarily dedicated to a triple-height entrance lobby that serves ten double-deck elevators. The north half of the ground floor is given over to service functions and is approached from a vehicular ramp off Worship Street; the lobby, with its double-height entrance hall, occupies the southern part of the ground floor. The vertical cores are located along the tower's west façade, maximizing the views from the site to the south, east, and north. The low-rise, 13-level 201 Bishopsgate building has bicycle/motorbike parking and a retail mezzanine between the ground and first floors. Its roof parapet height is 74.46 meters AOD while its central atrium reaches 77.53 meters AOD. There are approximately 415,000 square feet of office space within levels 1–12. The ground floor and mezzanine provide close to 20,000 square feet of retail space along Norton Folgate Street and the Galleria. The floors are organized around a large central service core and a 13-level glass-enclosed atrium that bathes the interior offices with daylight. The site was created by building a raft over existing rail tracks and is bisected by a protected St. Paul's view corridor. The development passed through multiple iterations before this incarnation. The architectural expression and massing of this scheme reflect the current market and urban climate and the structural peculiarities of the site/raft.

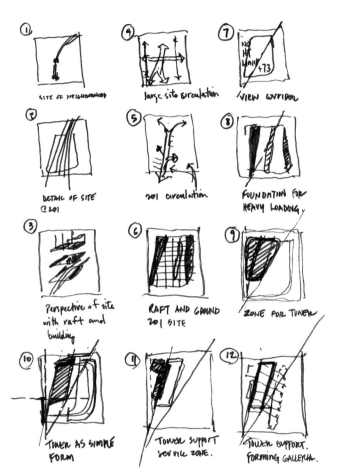

1. SITE OF NEIGHBORHOOD

4. large site circulation

7. VIEW CORRIDOR

2. DETAIL OF SITE @ 201

5. 201 circulation

8. FOUNDATION FOR HEAVY LOADING

3. Perspective of site with raft and building

6. RAFT AND GROUND 201 SITE

9. ZONE FOR TOWER

10. TOWER AS SIMPLE FORM

11. TOWER SUPPORT SERVICE ZONE.

12. TOWER SUPPORT. FORMING GALLERIA.

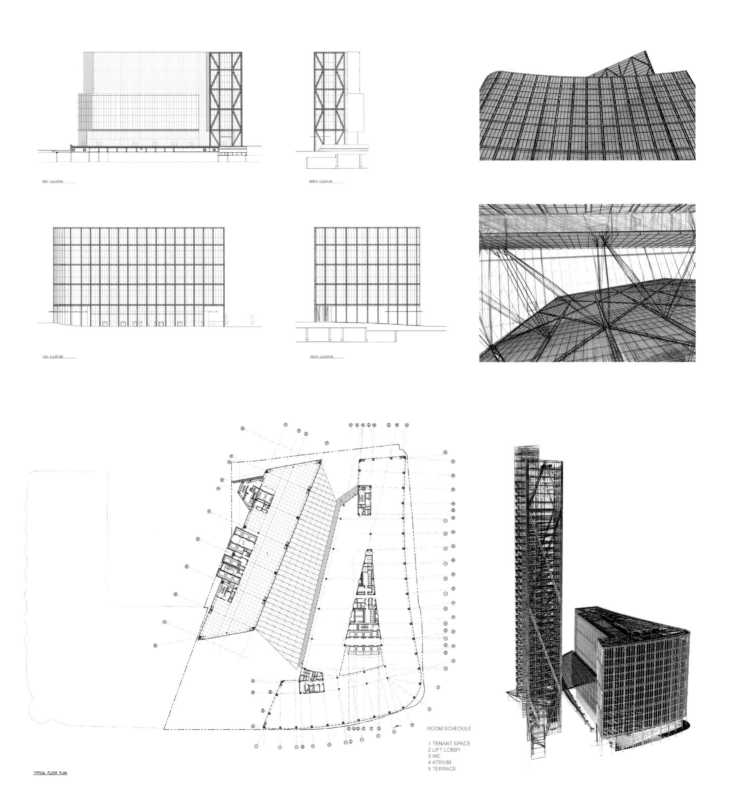

WEST ELEVATION

NORTH ELEVATION

EAST ELEVATION

SOUTH ELEVATION

TYPICAL FLOOR PLAN

ROOM SCHEDULE

1 TENANT SPACE
2 LIFT LOBBY
3 WC
4 ATRIUM
5 TERRACE

The Broadgate Tower is a gateway at the northern boundary of the City of London, creating a landmark for the Broadgate development while adding to the emerging cluster of tall buildings within the City of London. The tower also makes a significant contribution to the local townscape by increasing the diversity of tenant space in the area, opening the ground floor space for public uses, maximizing the potential of a site near a major transportation hub and outside the view corridors, and creating a new pedestrian route across the site.

The A-frame structure that spans the rail tracks and supports the tower creates a large public galleria space, which connects the developing neighborhoods to the north and northeast of the site with the major transport hub of Liverpool Street Station, while extending the network of public spaces within the Broadgate Estate. The height of the tower is based on a six-level module while the low-rise is organized on a three-level module. This sequence scales the two buildings appropriately while engaging in a dialogue with the industrial language of Worship Street Bridge and Exchange House. The material palette of stainless steel and glass enlivens the façades with an ever-changing interplay of reflections, light, and shadows. The exterior walls were designed to create a humane interior work environment with generous access to natural light and views.

800 meters

0 1875 m

201 BISHOPSGATE/BROADGATE TOWER PROPERTY LINE

BROADGATE ESTATES

Intersection of tower and galleria cover

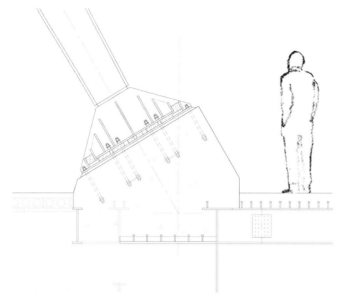

Base detail at tower strut

Canopy at tower entrance

201 Bishopsgate, The Broadgate Tower, and The Galleria

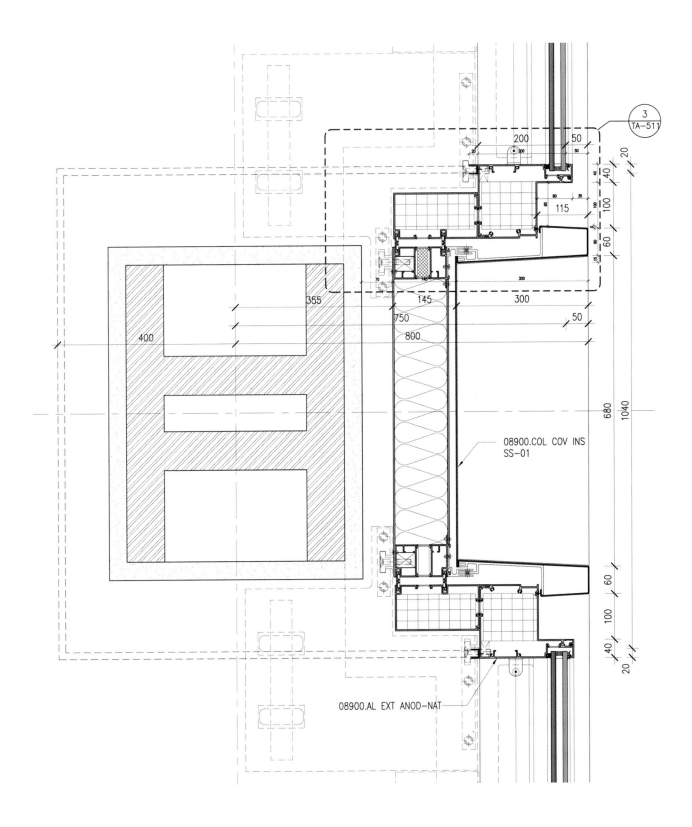

200
50
50
20
40
40
80
35
115
92
100
100
60
80
70
355
145
300
750
50
800
400
680
1040

08900.COL COV INS
SS-01

60
100
40
20

08900.AL EXT ANOD-NAT

3
TA-511

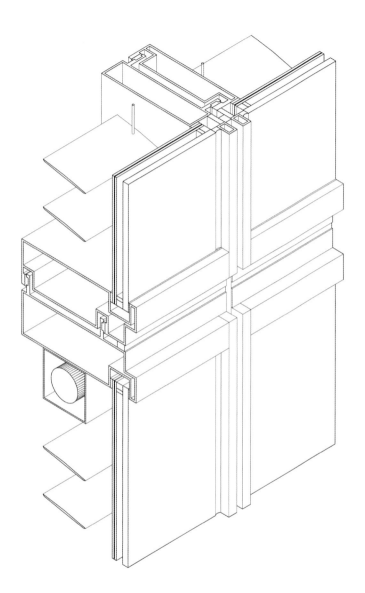

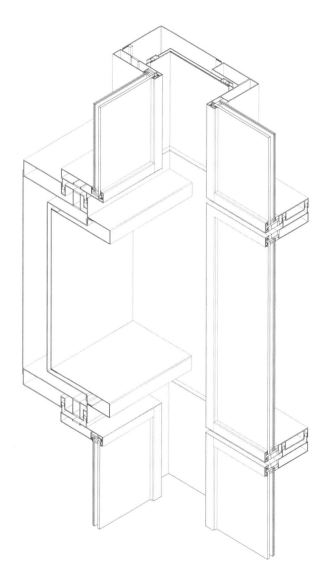

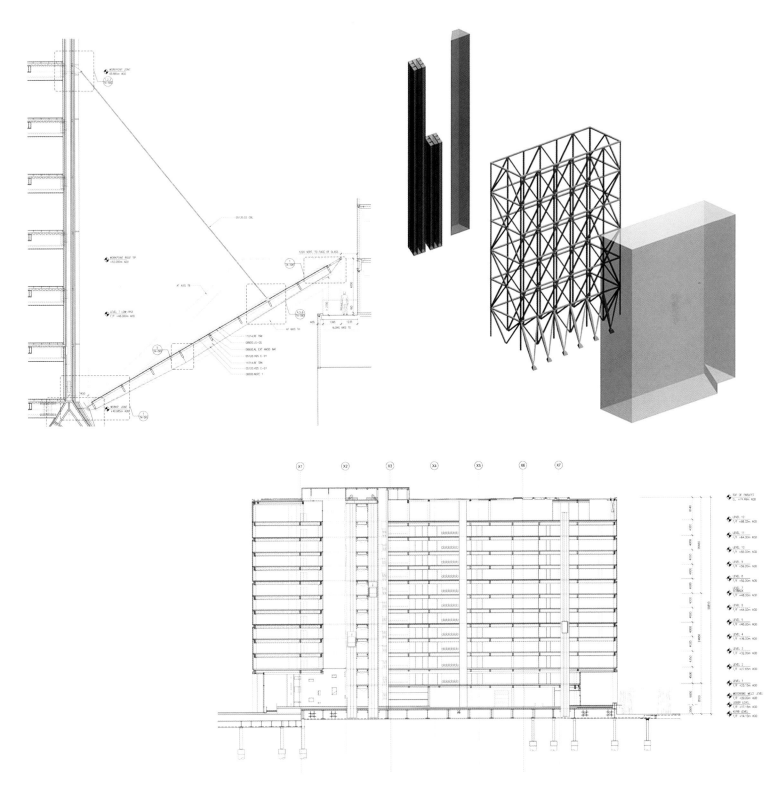

201 Bishopsgate, The Broadgate Tower, and The Galleria　　　371

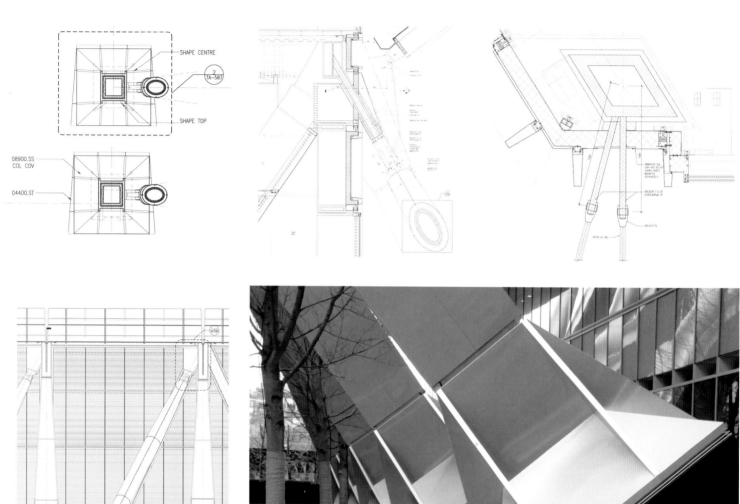

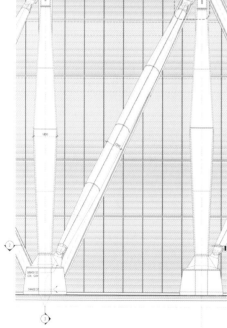

201 Bishopsgate, The Broadgate Tower and The Galleria

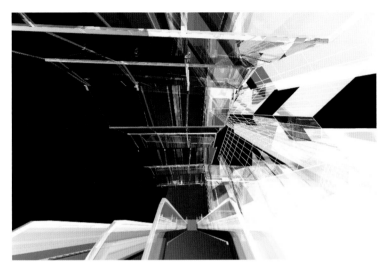

201 Bishopsgate, The Broadgate Tower, and The Galleria

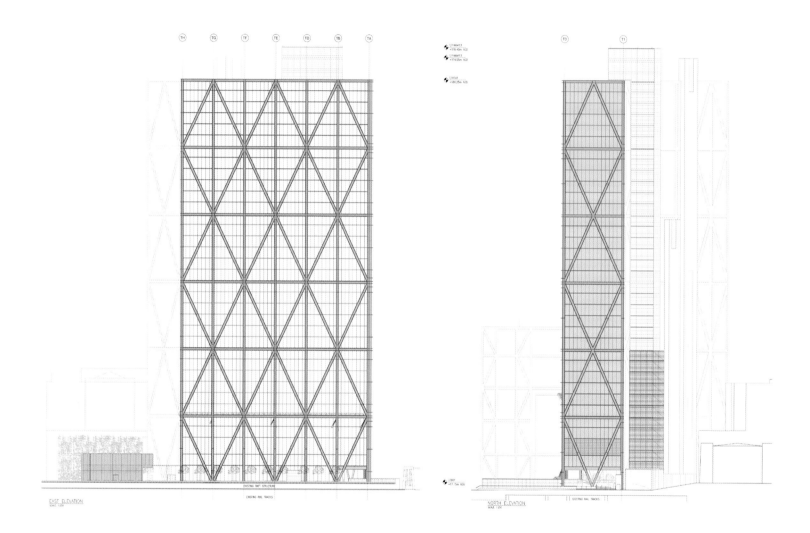

EAST ELEVATION
SCALE 1:250

EXISTING RAFT STRUCTURE

EXISTING RAIL TRACKS

NORTH ELEVATION
SCALE 1:250

EXISTING RAIL TRACKS

377

Palm Tower Dubai Competition

Location: Dubai, United Arab Emirates
Client: Palm Tower Development (Nakeel Development)
Location: 2003

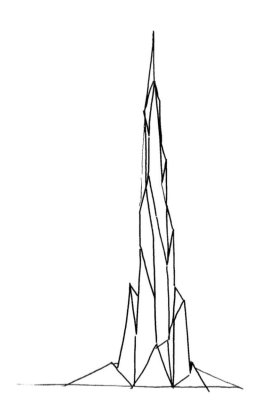

In February 2003, we were approached by Nakheel Development, the developer of the Palm Islands in the Arabian Gulf, to enter into a competition to design an 800-meter tower to be located near one of the Palm Islands. This was a very quick competition and we were only allowed a three-week period in which to enter. My first concept was a chillingly cool crystalline form rising out of the desert which I named the Crystal of Dubai.

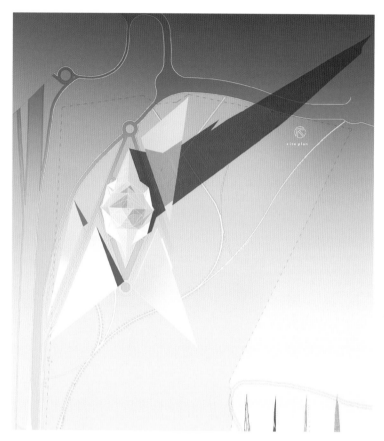

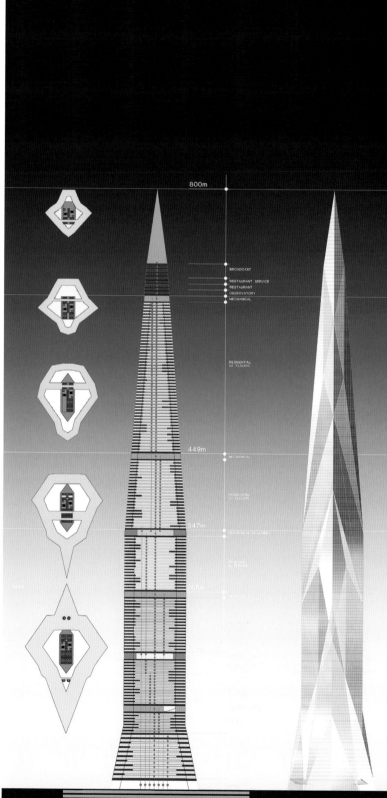

This mixed-use tower would consist of retail, office, hotel, and residential functions as well as support parking. In order to give a proper aspect ratio to the tower without providing a prohibitively deep lease span at the base of the tower, we developed an idea where there would be two supporting walls, one for the exterior and one on the interior, forming the edge of an atrium, much like the atrium in the Jin Mao Tower in Shanghai. However, this atrium would run the full length of the tower and all floors would be open to this atrium. There could be usable spaces within the atrium, such as meeting facilities or lounges, and full floors could be created at any level for functions that required large floor plates, such as trading floors, ballrooms, computer centers, meeting facilities, cafeterias, health clubs, tennis courts, and large restaurants.

The significance of this scheme is not in its style or sculptural nature but in the concept of unlimited atrium space that can be manipulated to suit the occupancy of the building and act as a paradigm for the next generation of super-tall structures that are more than one kilometer high.

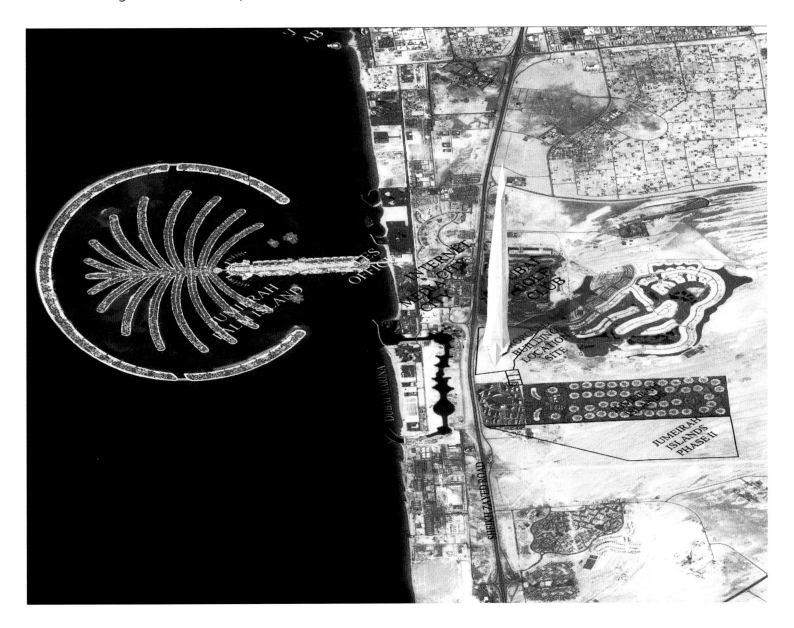

Central Bank Headquarters

Location: Jefferson City, Missouri, USA
Client: Central Bank, Sam Cook
Year: 2002–2004

In 1963 Bruce Graham designed the Central Motor Bank for Sam Cook, the owner of the bank. Sam, being an avid collector of Modern art, appreciated the simple, elegant design with its clear glass window wall and anodized aluminum façade. SOM later designed an addition of several drive-up teller stations; I was the studio head for that project. In 2001, Sam Cook came to SOM again to do another addition. He was frozen in Modernism and disliked immensely any aspect of post-modernism or historicism that had overtaken the country and requested that we design a modern piece to go along with his original headquarters.

Sam stated that he had a lot of difficulties with the first building in terms of climate comfort; given that the building was 100 percent clear single glazing it's no wonder why. I said that we could give him a building that was a 21st-century version of what he had and that he would be able to have climate comfort and clear vision out. I assigned Tim Poell, a studio head, to the project and Sam Cook immediately took to him. Tim proceeded to develop a concept, which I modified to feature all glass and shading canopy. Sam accepted the concept, which Tim further developed, making all the presentations and refining the details.

Existing Central Motor Bank

The Central Bank Headquarters is a two-level office facility with approximately 50,000 square feet of usable area connected by a simple open steel stair near the building's main entrance. The exterior expression is floor-to-ceiling glass with a narrow stainless steel spandrel panel at the floor line and a ceramic fritted pattern over the opaque areas where the ceiling occurs. The wall is exterior butt-glazed to eliminate any metal reading on the vertical glass joints.

The primary feature of this building is the expressive cantilevered roof trellis that shades the clear glass from the sun and covers the pedestrian circulation zones with an opaque element. This trellis is composed of cantilevered beams that support wing-shaped extruded aluminum tubes.

For the interior, we designed a space that looked and felt like it was completed in the Modern tradition of the 1960s. We used the bank's extensive abstract Modern art collection to infuse the work spaces with color and interest; mostly low height partitions were used to keep the space open. The basic services of the building are clustered in the center for easy access.

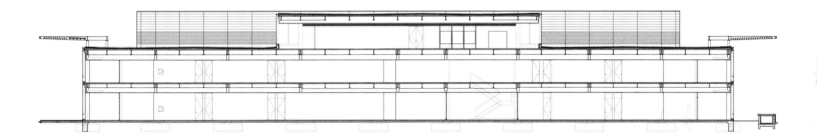

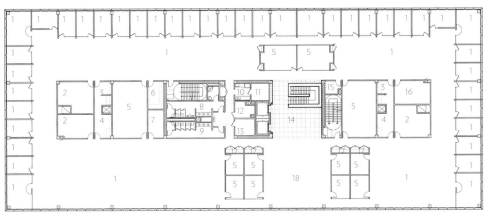

Upper level

1 Office
2 File/storage room
3 Coat room
4 Copy room
5 Conference
6 Support room
7 Equipment room
8 Men's room
9 Women's room
10 Pantry
11 LAN room
12 Storage
13 Electrical
14 Lobby
15 Telecom
16 Library
17 Closet
18 Reception

Ground level

1 Office
2 Support room
3 Coat room
4 Copy room
5 Receiving
6 PRV room
7 Manager's office
8 Assistant
9 Switchboard
10 Storage
11 ATM closet
12 Janitor's closet
13 Pantry
14 LAN room
15 Machine room
16 Electrical
17 Men's room
18 Women's room
19 Vestibule
20 Lobby
21 Conference room
22 File room

Lower level

1 Mechanical open to above
2 Storage
3 Electrical
4 Janitor's closet
5 Dry storage
6 Prep room
7 Mechanical
8 Vestibule
9 Pantry
10 Lobby
11 Kitchen
12 Men's room
13 Women's room
14 Lunch room

DS–1, Canary Wharf

Location: Canary Wharf, London, UK
Client: Phase 1 – Olympia & York; Phase 2 – Canary Wharf Ltd.
Year: 1998–2001

DS–1 at Canary Wharf is a 14-story office building located on the north side of the Canary Wharf Docklands complex, on a parcel with water to the west and north. To the east is the HSBC tower by Norman Foster and to the south is Canada Square, an open space surrounded by office buildings, designated for phase 2 of Canary Wharf.

The distinctive features of DS–1 are the two atria that face south; the glass corner column configurations that frame the body of the building and provide column-free corner office space; and the steel roof trellis that screens the mechanical systems on the roof and provides shade to the upper atrium skylight.

The lower atrium is seven stories high and has a glass wall inset to emphasize its depth. The top atrium is flush with the south wall and is sky lit through the trellis structure. The atria were designed to provide identity to tenants who occupy half of the building, and also to provide light and views to the U-shaped office space that surrounds them.

The atria were designed to be landscaped to provide a green connection between the building and the landscape at Canada Square. The two atria are separated by two full floors that are designed to contain large-space uses such as trading floors, assembly spaces, computer rooms or conference centers. The full floors are approximately 40,000 square feet while the U-shaped floors are 35,000 square feet.

The corner glass columns are cantilevered from the structure of the building to provide for an all-glass corner with floor-to-ceiling glass for maximum light into these corner spaces. In an effort to modulate the façade, these corner columns are visually tied to the body of the building by stainless steel straps that lace the column to the adjacent façades at every other floor.

The spacious ground floor lobby can be divided into two zones for separate control of major tenant lobbies and security screening stations. The primary feature of the lobby is a stainless steel ceiling trellis that echoes the roof trellis and draws visitors through the lobby to the elevator bank located to the north of the building. The rest of the ceiling is made of wood and the wall of the reception desk is paneled in light colored wood with a backlit onyx wall that provides visual interest and correlates with the backlit onyx columns that flank the entrances to the elevator core.

The free-standing building columns in the lobby are clad in brushed stainless steel. The lobby is connected to the concourse level via an ornamental stair. The concourse level provides connections to the extensive below-grade retail level that connects to the Jubilee transit line. Also located at this level is retail space that is accessible to the water's edge.

The exterior wall of DS–1 is comprised of brushed stainless steel spandrel panels, glass shadow box and clear low-e double-glazed vision glass. The exterior module is expressed with a 10-foot major rhythm and a minor rhythm every other 5 feet, with extended stainless steel tubes at every column line on 30-foot centers to provide a rich tapestry of metal and glass of varying dimensions and shapes. At the building's entry a large stainless steel canopy is suspended by cable supports.

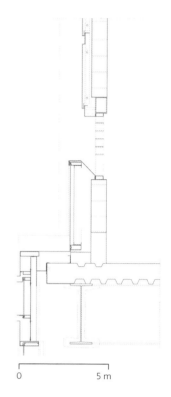

0   5 m

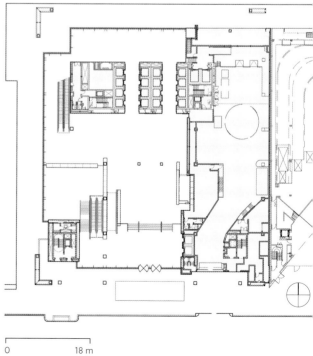

0   18 m

DS-1, Canary Wharf

Upper atrium

Reception

HQ–1, Morgan Stanley European Headquarters

Location: Canary Wharf, London, UK
Client: Canary Wharf Ltd.
Year: 2000–2004

This building for Morgan Stanley's European Headquarters began in 2000 as an expansion of its existing facilities at the Canary Wharf complex. The first building for Morgan Stanley was on Founders Court and was designed by Bruce Graham of SOM with Peter Ellis as the studio head. This first building was a transitional heritage style using red granite and Portland limestone with green mullions and clear glass. The ground floor arcade was arched and detailed in a rusticated fenestration. A limestone arcade at the top of the building contained the mechanical equipment. The objective of Morgan Stanley was to have HQ–1 relate to the first building so that the shared identity would create a more substantial corporate image.

HQ-1, Morgan Stanley European Headquarters   403

The site for HQ–1 was challenging because of its proximity to the DLR station directly to the east. The initial solution was to locate an expressed, glazed core on the east side and convey a sense of vertical movement and animation adjacent to the station. This was later revised to a solid core "party wall" configuration in order to receive an expansion building spanning over the station connected to HQ–2. Due to the lack of access to light and views to the east, the plan took on a U-shaped configuration at the third through ninth floors and a courtyard shape for the top floors.

The most unique feature of this project is the atrium that has access to both sky light and side light from the west through a grand atrium glass cable wall feature. The atrium floor plates terrace as they ascend upward through the void space, allowing for occupation of the void at various levels.

The exterior expresses its grid structure with 6-meter bays. Its reddish-brown granite cladding and precast concrete substructure connect the building symbolically to the original Founders Court project. The expression here is true to its nature without limestone trim or ornament. Instead, its structure as a grid is celebrated and enhanced by extending its frame at the corners and voiding usable floor space behind the frame to accentuate its skeletal nature. The mullion frame is painted a metallic copper with metallic copper gridded spandrel panels, to complement the granite color.

The lobby to this building is entered from the north and is announced by a reduction in the grid at the entry condition. Once into the lobby, a low first floor dimension created a challenge for articulating the entrance to the elevator zone. The solution was to create a backlit wall of onyx with a mirror polished stainless steel ceiling that would reflect the backlit wall and give the illusion of a double-height space. The remainder of the lobby was clad in a medium-tone Ana grey veneer, on both walls and ceiling, to convey a sense of warmth and reflect the simple materials.

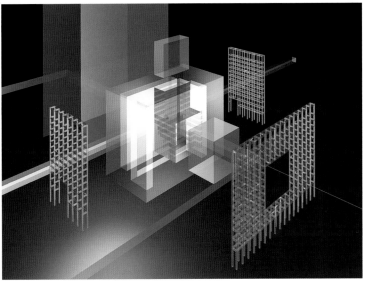

HQ–1, Morgan Stanley European Headquarters

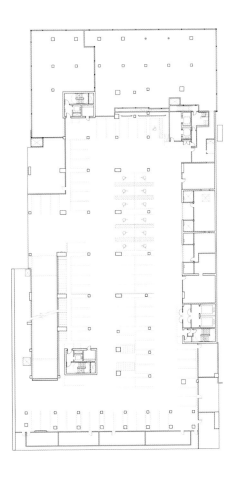
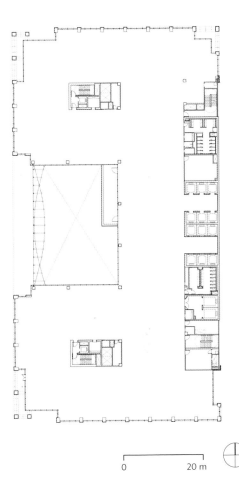

HQ–1, Morgan Stanley European Headquarters

DS–4, McGraw-Hill European Headquarters

Location: Canary Wharf, London, UK
Client: Canary Wharf Ltd.
Year: 2000–2004

The site for the McGraw-Hill European Headquarters is on DS–4 and is paired with DS–3 to form the eastern corners of Canada Square. The building has two major entrances: one from the south that connects the building lobby to the new Jubilee Underground station and Jubilee Square, and one from the north for auto and taxi drop-off. In addition, the northwest corner plays a unique role in the formation of the public square central to the second phase of Canary Wharf. At this point a round bay and rotunda feature accentuates a pedestrian entry point and provides a means of building identification at the top floor for McGraw-Hill.

Because of the large size of the building footprint, this building contains two stacked atria that face south and front on another public space called Jubilee Park. These atria are at the center of the southern façade and are located in plan to form a U-shaped floor plan. The two atria are expressed in different ways, giving the top atrium primacy and emphasizing the McGraw-Hill occupancy at the top of the building. The McGraw-Hill atrium is glazed with a large vertically supported glass wall with a full skylight. The exterior glass wall is curved in section and projects outward past the typical exterior wall of the building's south façade to emphasize this feature element on the composition of the south-facing façade. The atrium for the lower floors is four stories high and is subservient to the upper atrium in its exterior expression. The flush glazing of the lower atrium is noticeable in its transparency and its disassociation from the typical exterior wall.

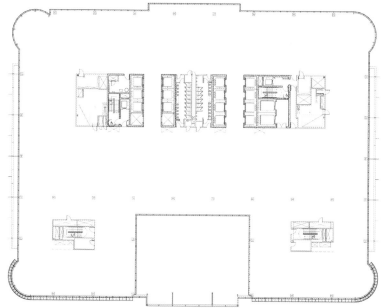

The exterior wall of DS–4 is designed to be sensitive to the orientation of the building and to reduce the solar loading on the building, especially on the east, south, and west elevations.

On the east and west elevations a series of vertical sun shade ladders are incorporated to reduce solar impact, while the south wall incorporates horizontal sun shading devices to minimize the heat from the midday sun.

The north face is flush, without shading devices since sun is not an issue on the north surface of this building. Two curved corner conditions on the southeast and southwest corners help the transition from the horizontal to the vertical expression. These corner elements create unique corner office locations to take maximum advantage of the park views to the west and canal views to the east. The exterior wall comprises double-glazed low-e tinted glass with stainless steel mullion caps and textured stainless steel spandrel panels. The entry condition on the south, facing the Jubilee plaza, is reinforced with a step-down arcade that directs focus toward the central entry. Here, the steel structure is exposed and is clad with a satin finished stainless steel cladding.

This building is connected below grade to an extensive lower-level network of shops, restaurants, service zones, and other buildings around the square and is also connected to the Jubilee station. DS–4 has three lower levels: two for parking and one for service and truck docks.

The lobby for this building is dramatic in size and finish. It occupies approximately 20,000 square feet and is 15 feet high. The paving is in a serpentine wave pattern that continues out into the Jubilee Square. The walls are clad in wide bands of cherry wood veneer alternating with bands of brushed stainless steel.

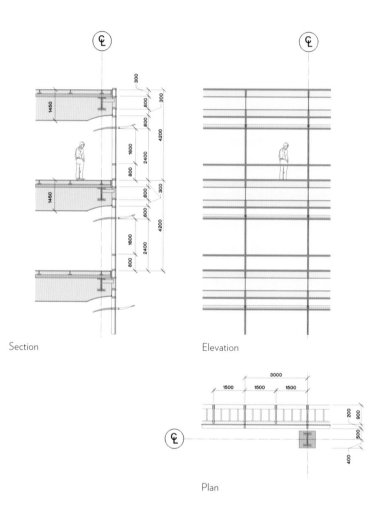

Section

Elevation

Plan

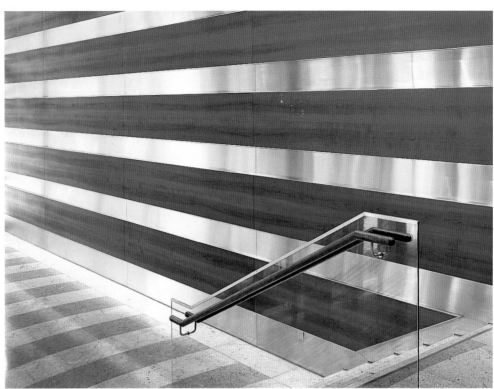

The core is clad in brushed stainless steel and the walkway between the two elevator cores is adorned with a glass sculpture by Danny Lane, a British sculptor who works in clear glass planks. This is his first installation using vertical glass planks, which created a sensuous wave of glass on each side of the pass-through. The ceiling is composed of a beam expression clad in metal panels with down lights and perforated metal ceiling panels to provide acoustic comfort. At the information and security station the ceiling changes to a luminous condition to provide a focal point for the large space. The elevator system is divided into two zones: a low-rise zone serves levels one through seven and a high-rise zone serves the remaining floors. Access at the lobby floor can be controlled to be tenant-specific.

Mitsui Headquarters Competition

Location: Tokyo, Japan
Client: Mitsui Bank
Year: 1998

This competition entry for the Mitsui Group's headquarters was a design for a symbolic tower for the company and a new landmark for Tokyo. The 40-story, glass curtain wall design provides a modern interpretation of the adjacent historic Mitsui main building. It is progressive enough to herald a new era for the financial institution, while retaining historical harmony with the area. The double curtain wall provides an interstitial air space to minimize thermal gains and losses. Native cypress trees stand at four-level increments, representing an environmental interpretation of classical columns.

The 116,500-square-meter tower includes offices, a 30,000-square-meter hotel with 250 rooms, and a small shopping mall on the lower floors. Special requirements of executive elevators, multiple entrances and circulation flow were met with unique solutions. Energy efficiency and low management costs were key considerations of the design.

The exterior wall of this double-wall concept is meant to be a cable net structure suspended from a main cantilevered truss at roof level. Suspended cables are attached to button-type anchors, which support the glass at each corner joint.

Catwalks at every four floors provide lateral bracing to transfer wind loads back to the building frame. These catwalks were also meant to support the cypress trees at each bay and provide a maintenance platform for the interior glass surfaces.

The platforms are also used as staging for the exterior lighting of the building and trees, which can be programmed to vary in color to meet special needs such as holidays and other events. They also act as a metaphor for the traditional Japanese overhangs on temple structures, thus linking them to established cultural references.

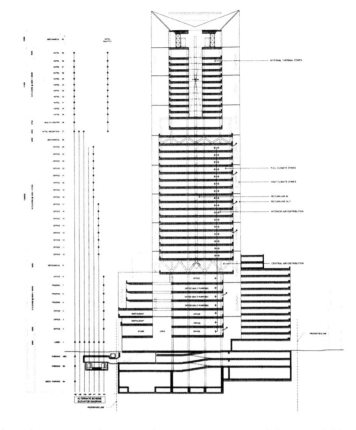

Near the interior glazing surface is an automated horizontal blind, activated by micro-motors to raise, lower, and tilt the blinds. A fan system, activated by photovoltaic panels, is envisioned for within the interstitial space. This system moves air around the building, taking advantage of heated winter air on the south by moving it to the north, thus creating a tempered environment and reducing heat loss from the occupied spaces. The surrounding district has been the heart of Japan's banking industry for decades, but is in need of urban renewal. The building design, with its luxury hotel and specialty shops, is meant to trigger revitalization of the area with its grandeur, dignity, and simplicity.

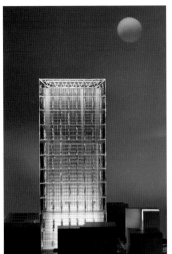
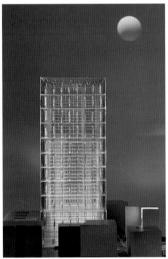
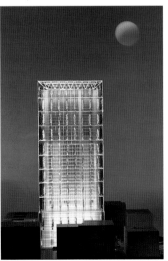

China National Offshore Oil Company Competition

Location: Beijing, China
Client: China National Offshore Oil Company
Year: 2003

Design

This design proposal seeks to reflect the business of the China National Offshore Oil Company by creating an architectural statement that represents its strength, economy, and purpose in today's rapidly advancing technological society. Its ecologically intelligent design provides meaningful and efficient corporate office spaces while upholding a strong corporate identity.

The forms take advantage of the public view at the corner by creating an opening that looks into the glass atrium joining the two buildings. Interior bridges provide views of the atrium, landscaping, and city, enhancing the horizontal circulation through the offices, and linking the two building forms.

Two major roadways bound the D1 site to the east and south. Site D2 is to the north and a secondary road is to the west. The D1 site is a prominent corner site. In response to this condition, the design proposal provides a public space at the corner using landscaping elements that include water features, trees, and outdoor terraces. The landscape design incorporates the same pattern established by the building plan and section of interlocking forms. The vehicular drop-off and entry to the building are located on the west side of the site. The entry is linked internally with lobby space, connecting the drop-off with the street corner.

The image of the building seeks to evoke a modern vocabulary of architecture that utilizes building forms appropriate to its function. The office spaces occupy efficient rectangular column-free spaces, providing maximum flexibility. The executive office spaces occupy the more prominent and distinguished upper levels of the taller form. These floors utilize efficient rectangular column-free spaces on expanded floor plates that surround the core. This arrangement provides larger offices, more

The concept is to create two interlocking forms that are integrated into the landscape and the surrounding city fabric, effectively creating a sense of place and identity at the street corner.

A bird does not sing because it has an answer ... it sings because it has a song.

— Chinese proverb

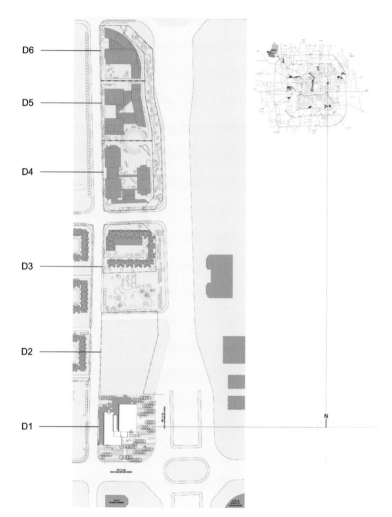

D6

D5

D4

D3

D2

D1

conference space, and more open areas. The executive floors also have two private elevators for comfort and security. These floors also have commanding views of the surrounding city and the street corner. The 500-seat auditorium, restaurants, meeting rooms, and business center spaces at the ground floor are more expressive forms, distinguishing their unique functions. The proposed careful use of color evokes the color-coded metal objects found on many offshore oil rigs, combined with a neutral (classic modern) material palette.

The curtain wall system incorporates glass and metal panels spaced 1.5 meters apart. As an identifying element, a sun-shading stainless steel mesh wall is held off the glass wall. The mesh allows visibility yet provides shade. Its design incorporates a unique pattern, emulating the building's interlocking forms, which will create a play of light and shadow on the façade.

There are three levels below grade. Two of the lower levels are for parking. The first level below grade contains the service docks for the building as well as mechanical space and the fitness center. The fitness center overlooks a sunken garden featuring a waterfall that connects to the landscaping at the ground level.

Vehicular traffic to the site is from the two secondary roads that form the west and north boundaries of the site. Vehicular access to the headquarters complex is from the western street. A central drop-off has access to the two-way parking ramp on the south side of the building, which takes vehicles to the below-grade parking.

Service traffic to and from the site is from the two-way parking/service ramp near the northwest corner of the site. This ramp gives service vehicles access to the service level, which is the first level below grade. A service ring road at that level connects the service docks of each building to the complex.

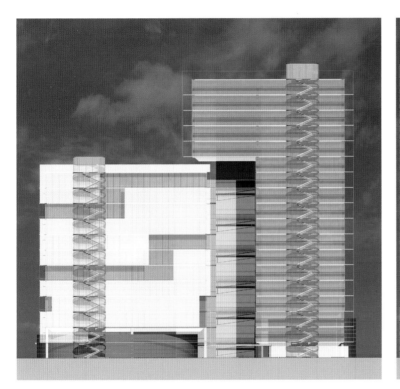
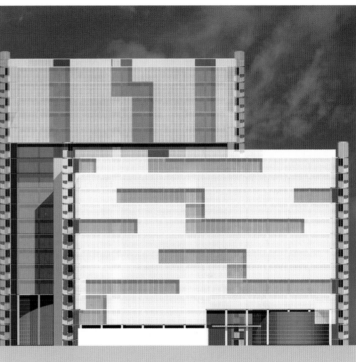

Bank Boston Headquarters

Location: São Paulo, Brazil
Client   Bank Boston
Year: 2000–2004

The client for this project comprised three entities: The Bank Boston in the USA, represented by Bob Champion; The Bank Boston Brazilian headquarters, represented by Alex Zera; and US Equities, as development manager, represented by Bob Wislow. Our first effort on this project was a five-day "tropicalization tour." We all gathered in Rio de Janeiro and spent a day touring Rio and a day visiting several parks and a fazenda near Rio, then off to Salvador to see the very interesting cultural mix of Portuguese and African origins and then onto the old summer capital. We finished up in São Paulo and toured museums, landscape features, and sites of interest. This was a terrific trip and impressed on us the festive nature and charter of the culture. Perhaps the most impressive aspects of the trip, other than the food, were the patterns in the landscape and paving. The colors of the buildings in São Paulo are predominantly white or light gray with black accents in the paving patterns. Because of its tropical climate, plant material grows at an alarming rate and the Bank Boston site was large enough to contain a large park that would act as a barrier between the heavily trafficked streets and the entrance to the headquarters. We hired a local landscape architect named Isabel Duprat who was influenced by Burly Marx, as were we after our trip, and together we planned the entranceway to the bank.

Bank Boston Headquarters   429

Site plan

All glass is set flush with the interior of the column in order to maximize the usability of the net square footage in the building.

The concept for the Bank Boston Brazil headquarters was to create an image that expresses the tropical nature of the Brazilian culture, but in a dignified manner befitting one of its leading financial institutions. The building consists of two stepped and landscaped slab elements connected by a freeform, two-tone stainless steel and glass link that wraps the low-rise component and extends to and becomes the top of the tall component.

Solidifying its 60-year presence in Brazil, Bank Boston has established its Latin American headquarters in São Paulo. SOM provided architectural design, engineering, and interior design services for the new 30-story office building. The 600,000-square-foot building includes 300,000 square feet of office space with an occupancy capacity of 3000 people. The headquarters will incorporate all banking functions with typical office space, a trading floor, private banking facilities, and an executive floor.

The interior lobby and ground floor amenities followed through with the strategy of incorporating organic forms into the orthogonal geometry of the bank's workspaces. The contrast between hard-edged and soft, curved surfaces helped relieve the tensions that can build up in the workplace and provide more calming areas for breaks, so important in the banking industry. Building materials consisted primarily of white granite for the column cladding with black granite accents every two stories. The spandrels are stainless steel panels above and below windows.

The floor-to-ceiling vision glass is a double-glazed, high-efficiency, low-e reflective glass system for maximum daylighting into the offices with minimum heat gain or loss. The exterior is accented with 3-inch polished stainless steel tubes that act as window-washing tie backs and provide highlights to the wall throughout the day. At the ends of the orthogonal L-shaped plan the exterior expresses its clear span structure and the spandrel panel is shaped to express the path of the post tensioning within each beam. The clear span structure provides ideal efficiency and flexibility for the bank carrels and workspaces.

Bank Boston Headquarters

Bank Boston Headquarters

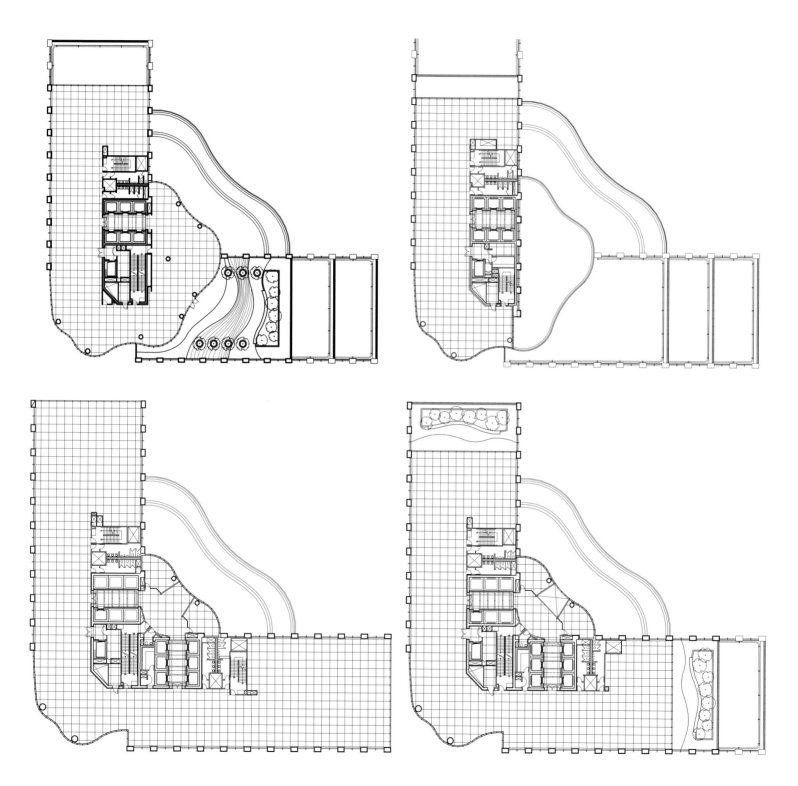

Bank Boston Headquarters

Bank Boston Headquarters

CCTV Headquarters Competition

Location: Beijing, China
Client: CCTV
Year: 2004

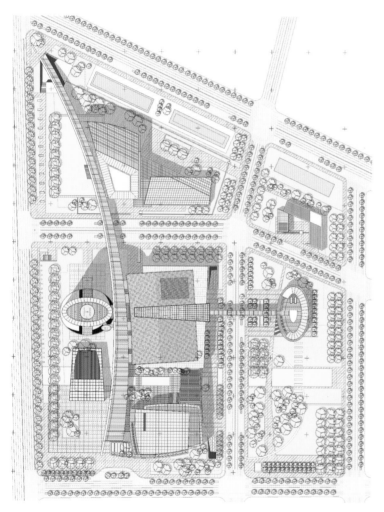

The programmatic functions of this design are divided into nine simple forms. These shapes create a dynamic interaction between buildings, and opportunities for different types of public open space.

Circulation and service spine

This element's primary role is to organize all the circulation, which includes all public and private internal pedestrian circulation, all data and technical cable runs and all the below-grade truck and service routes. This single element provided an all-weather connection to each component of the project, and is the defining feature of the project, unifying the entire composition of buildings.

The "solid" nature of the spine depicts strength and provides protection from traffic noises along the Third Ring Road and from solar heat gain from the setting sun.

The main building

This is the vertical landmark that controls the entire site, and addresses the major north–south axis of the CBD. All the office functions, as well as the research and training center, are contained within this 230-meter-tall elliptical shape. It is a shape unique to Beijing in its simplicity and clarity of expression.

Production facility

The production facility occupies the center of the site, and is the heart of the complex. The building is composed of two volumes linked by a tall atrium space for the studio audiences.

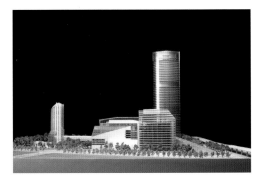
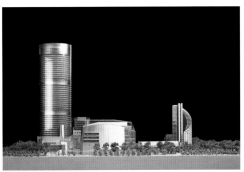

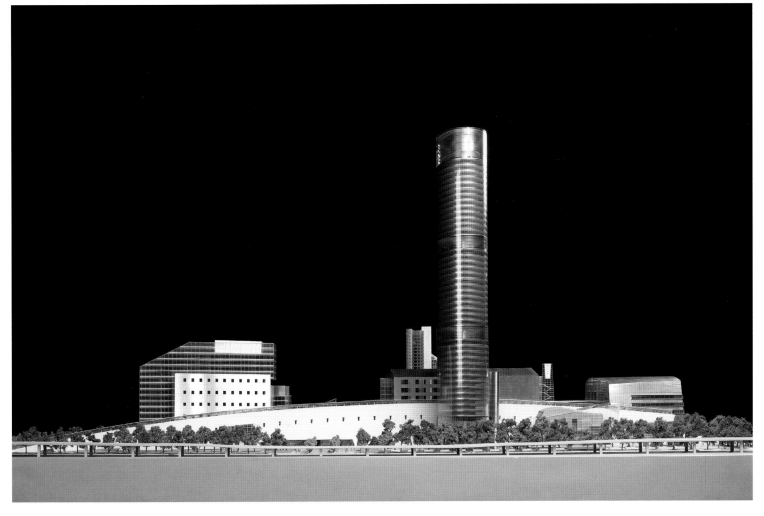

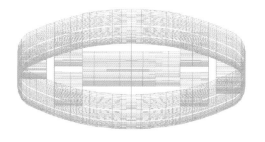

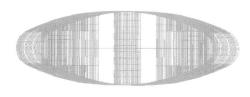

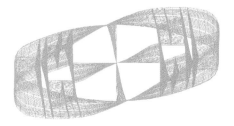

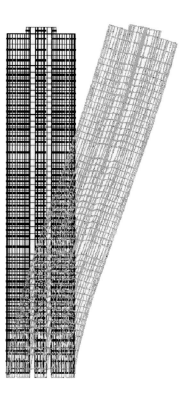

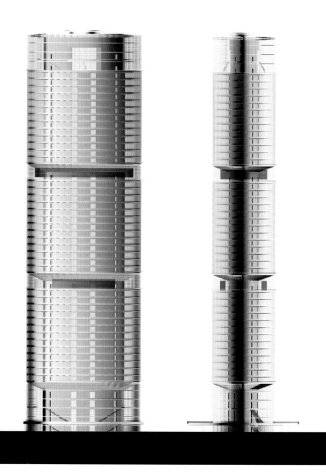

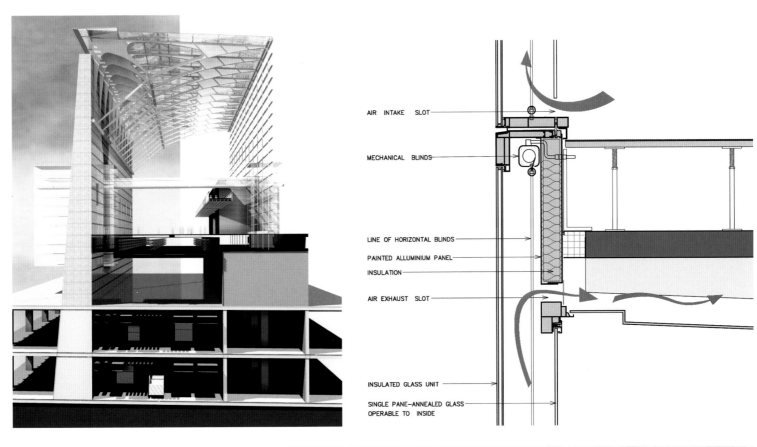

AIR INTAKE SLOT

MECHANICAL BLINDS

LINE OF HORIZONTAL BLINDS

PAINTED ALLUMINIUM PANEL

INSULATION

AIR EXHAUST SLOT

INSULATED GLASS UNIT

SINGLE PANE–ANNEALED GLASS
OPERABLE TO INSIDE

News and broadcast facility

This is the communications hub for the country and requires the most security. We placed these functions on the north parcel to separate them from the more public function on the south. The guard building is placed adjacent to the news and broadcasting buildings to achieve the best security outcome.

The cultural facility

The cultural facility is the southern termination of the circulation spine, and becomes the most public and vital area of the site. The media plaza for outdoor filming and general usage is placed between the production building and the 1500-seat TV theater. The intermission lobbies of the TV theater rise out of the media plaza and overlook the large park to the east.

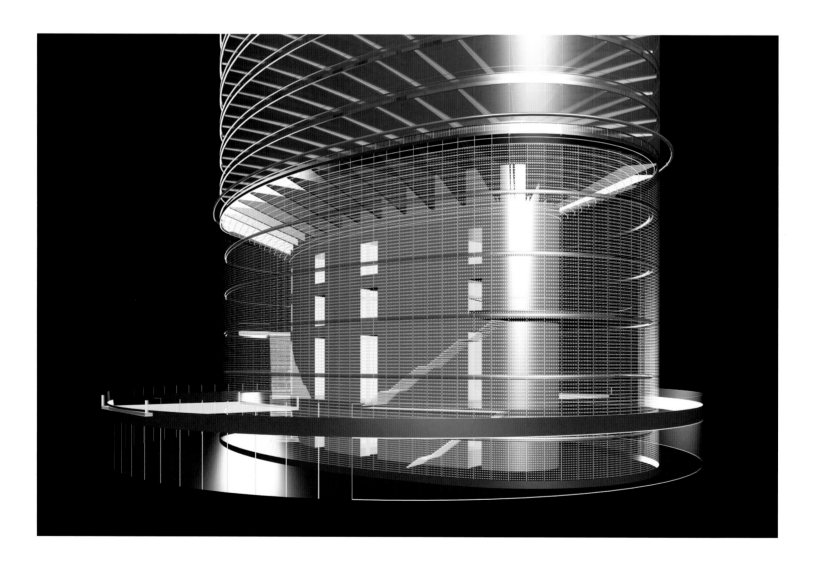

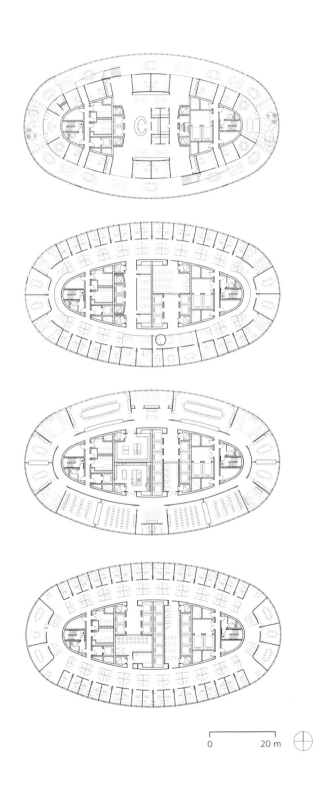

0　　　　20 m

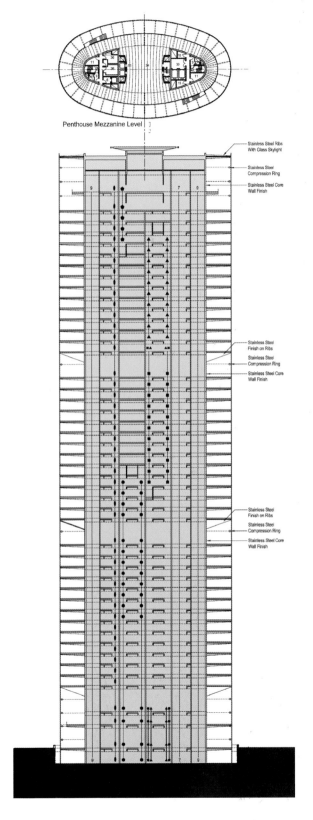

Penthouse Mezzanine Level

Stainless Steel Ribs
With Glass Skylight

Stainless Steel
Compression Ring

Stainless Steel Core
Wall Finish

Stainless Steel
Finish on Ribs

Stainless Steel
Compression Ring

Stainless Steel Core
Wall Finish

Stainless Steel
Finish on Ribs

Stainless Steel
Compression Ring

Stainless Steel Core
Wall Finish

449

The 800-seat concert hall is designed as a wooden musical instrument set in a simple glass box that becomes the jewel in the cultural plaza. The entire spine can be used for temporary exhibitions, in addition to large exhibition halls under the theater. Finally, the hotel is conceived as a terraced sculpture facing south over the landscape.

All of these elements are surrounded by large inviting open space that promotes clear interaction with the public. Integration of public open space throughout the site occurs in eight major spaces:

- The boulevard allée (along the western edge)
- The news reflecting pool
- The tower court or arrival point
- The cultural plaza
- The media terrace
- Audience plaza between the production building and the park
- The sunken garden, which becomes the connection to the new subway at the north
- The great park on the southeast corner that continues the green concept into the CBD

Structural innovations

The CCTV tower is envisioned with a structural concrete core rising the full height, with a 10-meter post-tensioned beam that tapers to the exterior wall. This will produce a column-free exterior wall for complete internal flexibility.

The studios in the production and new buildings are integrated with appropriate long-span construction to stack these large volumes and minimize site coverage.

The circulation spine is a long concrete wall clad in natural silver stone that cantilevers over the long glass wall to the east.

BTV Headquarters Competition

Location: Beijing, China
Client: BTV
Year: 2002

This proposal for a TV studio is about two different types of glass, which allow BTV to see the world, and the world to see BTV. The design is composed of two large, elegant glass components: a vertical transparent glass office tower, and a long, low-e, translucent glass podium containing studios and post-production facilities.

The building blends the urban excitement of the entertainment industry with the serenity of a quiet, contemplative garden. The podium contains a traditional flat roof garden that is surrounded by the "living functions" of the project, including the dining area and hotel rooms, while the tower contains a vertical garden within the double glass wall. Contextualism is a central theme of the project, which is designed as a modern abstraction of the strong horizontal banding found in many traditional Chinese screens.

The tower

This transparent volume, with floor-to-ceiling glass, is divided horizontally into eight groups of office floors by thin terraces that contain trees in stainless steel planters. The trees in the vertical garden are arranged in clustered groups within the façade. The top of the building is marked by a large truss that hovers above the roof garden, and holds both the helipad and the second glass skin. The 3-meter-wide space between the two glass walls (inner insulated glass and the single-glazed outer glass) is used to reduce energy costs.

Happiness is watching the show.

— Chinese proverb

The air space acts as an insulator, like a thermos flask. The temperature of this space can be controlled to insulate the inner office space from the extremes of heat and cold and therefore reduce total energy consumption.

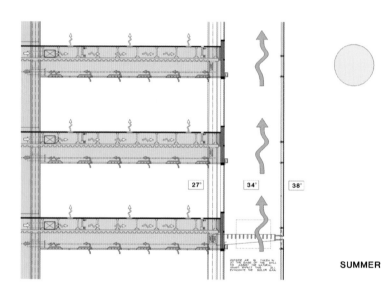

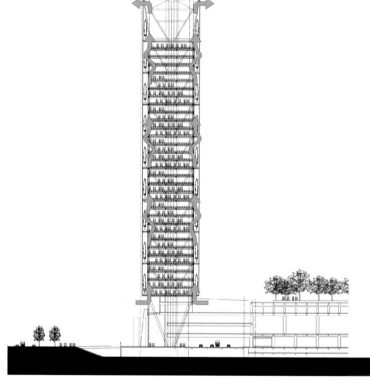

SUMMER

In summer mode, the solar gain will be collected in this air cavity by placing the blinds, operated by an automated building control system, on the outside of the inner layer. The collected heat will be evacuated at the top of the tower by exhaust fans, while a series vent will be opened on the lowest level to bring fresh air into the cavity. In winter the solar gain from the south side will be circulated horizontally to wrap the tower in a blanket of warm air.

The tower's active façade has lighting effects that can change the color of the building, and highlight the stainless steel detailing of the curtain wall and planters. Large translucent scrims for the projection of different types of moving images are also planned.

The podium

In contrast to the tower, a transparent glass box with the detail visible on the inside, the podium is a glowing volume with the details expressed on the outside. The podium is conceived as a battered wall divided into eight steps, which are clad with a backlit cast-glass skin that gives the building a soft glow.

On the lower levels, the studios, control rooms, and post-production rooms are aligned both vertically and horizontally along a common circulation spine. The common support functions—elevators, stairs, toilets, make-up, and waiting rooms—are also located adjacent to this circulation spine. Two large vertical atria on the east side of the podium bring natural

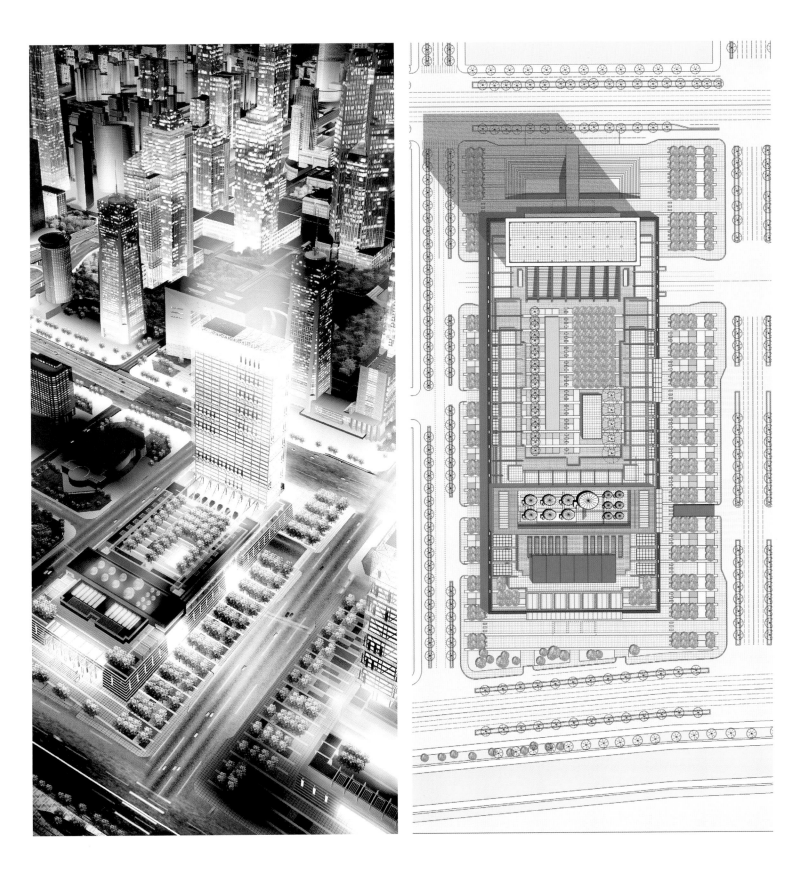

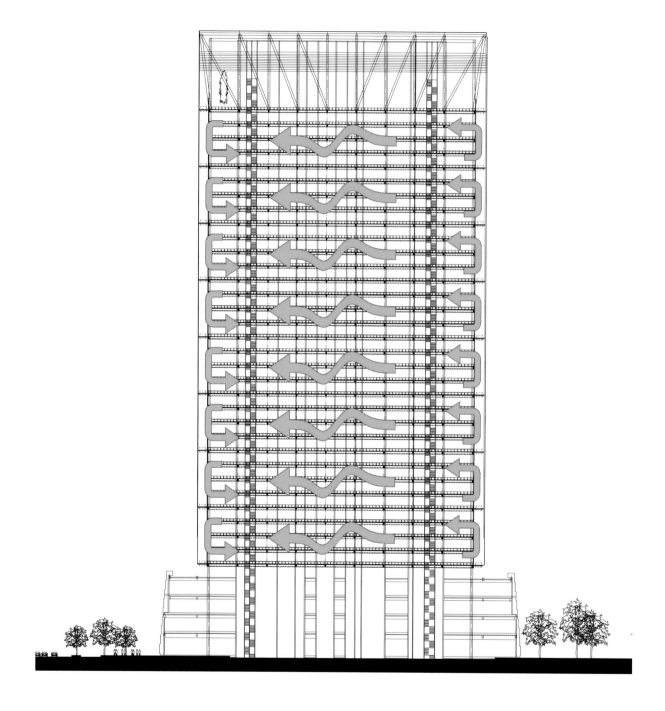

BTV Headquarters Competition

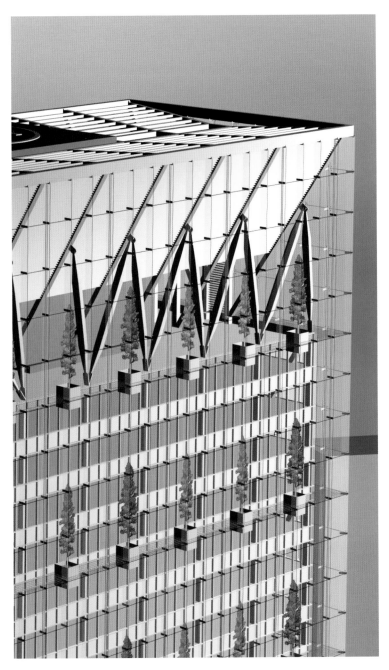

light into the podium. The large audience studio is located on the south side of the podium at level two behind the three-story transparent glass that creates the south lobby. This provides a separate, large, formal entry for this 1500-seat studio, which can be used for formal award ceremonies, banquets, or tours.

The podium spans north over Shengshi Jiayuan to connect into the office tower, and unify the base. This gives the tower a proper presence on Chang An Avenue, and allows for a large pedestrian plaza in front of the tower and for several drop-off areas for the studio complex. This area over the road is well lit by the placement of a large skylight overhead, and is landscaped with street trees. The east and west zones over the road are the production offices that "bridge" from the studio environment to the office space above.

Arrival sequence

The arrival court off Chang An Avenue is a generous landscaped plaza that becomes a public amphitheater for the TV news center. A long glass wall exposes the broadcast and production of the news.

The tower lobby is approached across an internally lit glass bridge that spans over the sunken garden. The arrival lobby is an impressively tall central space that orients the visitor to the project.

Landscape concepts—site organization

This is a continuation of the theme of horizontal banding found in the tower and the podium. The bands of paving that run east to west are an abstraction of TV's ability to connect the east and the west, and are used for pedestrian circulation between the planted areas. There are several areas for reflecting pools and places to sit and relax. Water is used as a counterpoint to the east–west lines. Three gardens on the podium roof are reserved for the use of BTV employees; the largest is the central garden with a dining pavilion in the center.

A large CBD public garden is located to the west of the site, so the largest landscaped space has been placed on the east side of the podium to create a similar feeling of space around the building. The studio's large circulation space overlooks this space. Once Phase Two is built, this area will create a central landscaped core for the project.

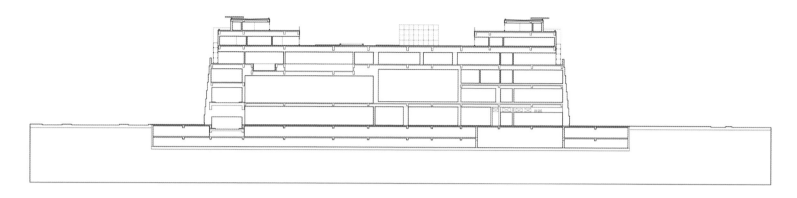

BTV Headquarters Competition

Shanghai Grand Project

Location: Shanghai, China
Client: Shanghai Grand Development Co.
Year: 2005–

The Shanghai Grand project draws its inspiration from the traditional Chinese box puzzle. The site for this project is at the east end of Century Boulevard, on the opposite end from Jin Mao. This area is partially residential, with a building height limitation of 180 meters. The zoning for this site will allow for 80,000 square meters of above-grade construction. The owner of the site, the Shanghai Grand Development Co., wanted an office building with character but without the detail and maintenance of the Jin Mao Tower. The height limit and allowable width of the façade along Century Boulevard restricted the mass to a rectangular box form and the right-to-light zoning for the residents across Century Boulevard mandated a stepped roof configuration.

The conceptual moves in the mass of the building relate to the pedestrian entrance on Century Boulevard, the automobile entrance off the courtyard on the south side of the building, and the views to the cultural park on the east. These features are either cantilevered out from the typical wall of the tower or are recessed in from the typical wall. In this manner, they

also aid in the expressive nature of the building's structure by showing the cantilevered floor configuration of the building. These zones of expression are developed in floor-to-floor clear glass with a double-wall configuration to satisfy the stringent energy codes. These zones will read as light and transparent, in contrast to the mildly reflective typical wall.

The typical exterior wall of the tower has a scale-like texture that incorporates operable panels on every floor to provide fresh air. The texture is achieved by sloping the vision and spandrel glass panel toward the sky by 5 degrees and expressing the vertical as a double clear glass layered series of fins at 3-meter centers on the short face and 4.5 meters on the long face of the building.

The structure for the tower is a 12-meter-wide concrete core shear wall to take the wind loads. The typical span from the core to exterior column is 10.5 meters and the typical cantilever is 1.5 meters from the face of the column to the exterior wall.

The Lakeshore East Master Plan

Location: Chicago, Illinois, USA
Client: Magellan Development, Joel Carlins
Year: 2001–2008

The Lakeshore East master plan completes an important residential neighborhood in downtown Chicago. This new neighborhood will be well connected to the lakefront park system and the Chicago Riverwalk through panoramic views and extensive pedestrian links.

The central feature of the plan is a new public park built at the natural grade level, where trees and native plants can flourish. The park will be an added amenity to nearby Chicago Park District facilities.

Within the park, a site will be reserved for a future elementary school. Paired with a potential new Chicago Park District field house, this neighborhood focal point creates a setting that will attract families to live downtown.

The master plan sets forth basic principles to guide the development of the approximately 25 acres into a vibrant urban neighborhood of new residential, hotel, office, and mixed-use development. Implementation of these principles will strengthen the areas adjacent to the site, by creating a comprehensive network of streets and open spaces that connect Lakeshore East to other developments and amenities within the city.

The master plan achieves City of Chicago goals by re-evaluating and improving on the development criteria previously set forth in the approved planned development of 1993. The master plan also incorporates the comments and goals of the Department of Planning and Development.

McCANN '08

463

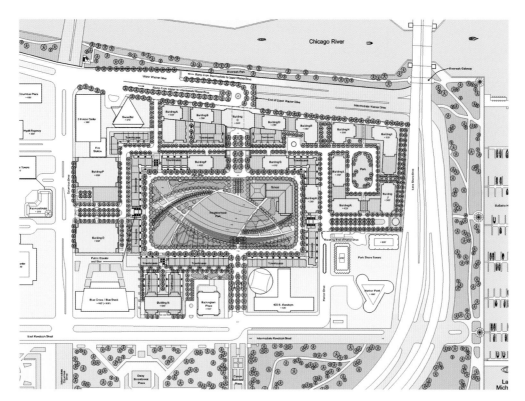

The Lakeshore East Master Plan

The Lakeshore East Master Plan   465

The following principles are key to ensuring the future success of Lakeshore East:

Urban framework

- Establish urban blocks that are similar in size to typical downtown Chicago blocks

- Develop urban streets in the character of a residential neighborhood

- Create a development that achieves diverse buildings on each block.

Access and connections

- Create a neighborhood that is easily accessible from all directions

- Develop clear pedestrian and bicycle links to the Chicago River and Lake Michigan

- Ensure convenient access between the upper and lower levels and maintain handicap access

- Provide convenient parking, drop-off, and service access without negative impact to the existing streets

- Extend upper Wacker Drive east to Harbor Drive to complete the local street system

- Ramp Field Drive down from upper Randolph Street, connecting to a new Park Drive ringing the public park at the natural grade level

- Create street standards that promote the pedestrian environment and efficient vehicular traffic.

Building height and massing

- Strengthen and complete the Wacker Drive street façade

- Step massing down toward the central park and the lake

- Frame the park with low-rise town homes

- Locate taller buildings with sensitivity toward neighboring uses.

Access & Circulation

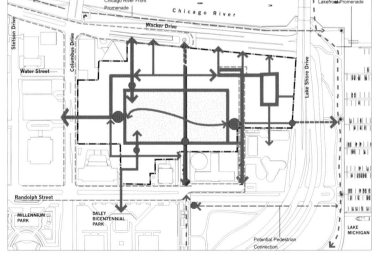

Maximize connectivity to surrounding development and create a permeable neighborhood

Level

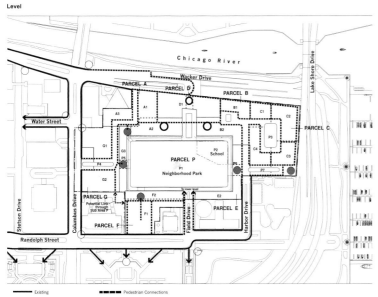

Open space

- Focus the majority of open space into a large, centralized public park at the natural grade level

- Connect Lakeshore East open space(s) to Grant Park, the Riverwalk and lakefront

- Provide new, shared green spaces between existing buildings and the proposed development.

Phasing

- Create flexibility in developing individual buildings/parcels, including associated parking

- Construct the park and buildings fronting the park in Phase I

Summary

The proposed master plan:

- Supports up to 10 million square feet, approximately two-thirds of the area previously approved by the 1993 planned development (14.6 million square feet)

- Achieves a lower overall density than the previously approved planned development due to an increased amount of open space, additional local streets and a lower density development

- Will create a new 6-acre public park in the center of the development, for a total of 8 acres of project green space.

The proposed development:

- Creates 5500 new condominiums and apartments, with an additional 240–270 new residential town homes. This is considerably fewer than approved by the 1993 planned development

- Introduces 2 million square feet of new office space

- Provides a new hotel with 900 to 1300 rooms

- Will meet parking requirements in 5–6 levels of below-grade parking podiums, which are screened from the park by town homes

- Will provide space within the public park for a future 45,000-square-foot elementary school.

Millennium Park

Location: Chicago, Illinois
Client: City of Chicago; Lakefront Millennium Managers
Year: 1998–2002

"Millennium Park is much more than just a park. It is a showplace for art, music, architecture and outdoor activities, and a tribute to the vitality and creativity of our city ... if anyone still has any doubt as to whether Chicago is a world class city, Millennium Park should convince them that it is."

Mayor Richard M. Daley, City of Chicago, 2004

In 1995, I traveled with Mayor Richard Daley on a sister-city visit to France. During the trip, I had a chance to talk with him about a project for the city's lakefront that, by completing Daniel Burnham's renowned 1909 Plan of Chicago, would be a great millennium project. I had brought along a copy of the Wacker Manual, the textbook used by all Chicago school children from 1911 to 1930 to educate them about the Burnham Plan, and showed him the arching breakwater envisioned by Burnham as the central element of the plan. Mayor Daley's response was immediate and positive. He liked the idea and said that I should talk it over with John Bryan, who was with us on the trip and was beginning to organize a group dedicated to a special project to bring Chicago into the new millennium.

Millennium Park   469

The 16.5-acre Millennium Park completes Chicago's 100-year vision of Grant Park. Daniel Burnham envisioned Grant Park as the front garden of the City of Chicago, formal in its composition yet accommodating in its functions. Numerous options and proposals for the site had been proposed over the decades, including a 1925 Grant Park guidelines call for decking over the rail lines; a 1970 proposal for a permanent band shell and lawns at Lakefront Gardens; and further proposed revisions in 1981.

The park is built over existing and expanded rail lines, bus lanes, two new parking levels, a multi-modal transit center, a new music band shell, Great Lawn, bridge, and performance facilities for music and dance.

Located between Michigan Avenue, Columbus Drive, Randolph, and Monroe Streets, the site for Millennium Park was an eyesore surrounded by offices, cultural institutions, stores, residences, and parkland, in the heart of one of the world's most beautiful, diverse, and vital cities. The park provides a new and exciting people-friendly destination for residents and visitors alike, a tribute to the City's motto *Urbs in Horto* (city in a garden) and a monument to Chicago's peerless civic leadership, generosity, and commitment.

The completion of Millennium Park represents not only a tremendous design and civic success, but also a significant technical and political achievement.

Plan one

My initial idea was to build the bulkhead arching into Lake Michigan, linking Chicago's Navy Pier to the museum complex and completing Burnham's vision of a grand lakeshore harbor. John Bryan suggested that a 400-foot-tall Brancusi sculpture could be the 21st-century centerpiece at the center of the arch, lining up with Buckingham Fountain. We developed preliminary drawings for the idea and had them priced by the Chicago Park District, but found that the $100-million-plus cost made the project difficult to justify.

Despite this initial setback, the idea for a millennium project for Chicago had been launched, and the concurrent renovation of the Soldier's Field football stadium eventually led to another, even more interesting scheme.

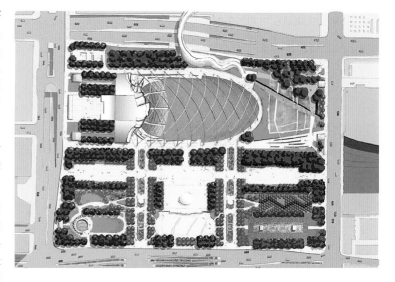

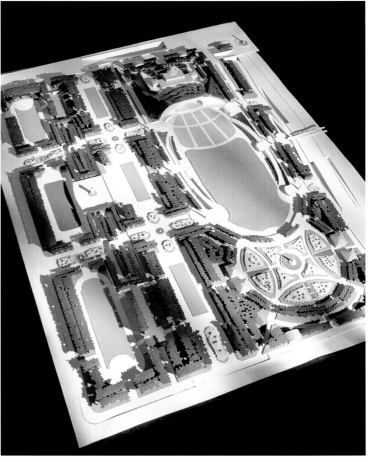

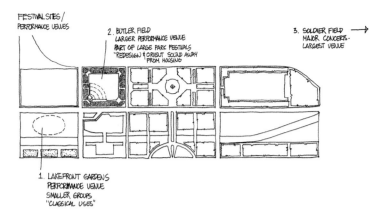

FESTIVAL SITES /
PERFORMANCE VENUES

2. BUTLER FIELD
LARGER PERFORMANCE VENUE
PART OF LARGE PARK FESTIVALS
"REDESIGN & ORIENT SOUND AWAY
FROM HOUSING"

3. SOLDIER FIELD
MAJOR CONCERTS -
LARGEST VENUE

1. LAKEFRONT GARDENS
PERFORMANCE VENUE
SMALLER GROUPS
"CLASSICAL USES"

FESTIVAL SITES — "ROOMS" WITHIN THE PARK THAT ARE
CONNECTED BY A FESTIVAL PATH -
A GRANT PARK VERSION OF A "MIDWAY."

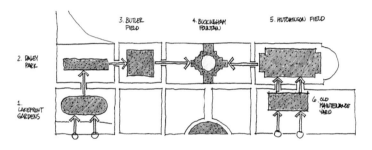

3. BUTLER FIELD
4. BUCKINGHAM FOUNTAIN
5. HUTCHINSON FIELD
2. DALEY PARK
1. LAKEFRONT GARDENS
6. OLD MAINTENANCE YARD

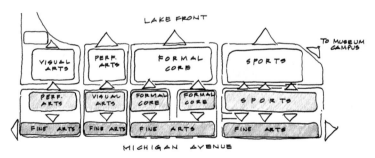

LAKE FRONT

TO MUSEUM CAMPUS

VISUAL ARTS | PERF. ARTS | FORMAL CORE | SPORTS

PERF. ARTS | VISUAL ARTS | FORMAL CORE | FORMAL CORE | SPORTS

FINE ARTS | FINE ARTS | FINE ARTS | FINE ARTS

MICHIGAN AVENUE

PROGRAM DIAGRAM

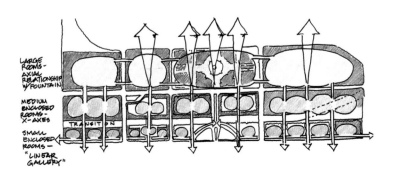

LARGE ROOMS -
AXIAL RELATIONSHIP
W/ FOUNTAIN

MEDIUM ENCLOSED ROOMS -
X-AXES

TRANSITION

SMALL ENCLOSED ROOMS -

"LINEAR GALLERY"

471

A "found" space

The shortage of parking at Soldier Field had led to a search for satellite lots that could be connected by transit. This logically led us to an abandoned rail yard adjacent to the Loop along the east side of Michigan Avenue, just north of the Chicago Art Institute, about two miles south of Soldier's Field.

For several decades the site had been used for downtown parking, but was little more than an ugly gash in the ground that separated Michigan Avenue from Grant Park and Lake Michigan. The mayor asked us to look at fitting a replacement for the Patrillo Band shell on the site, along with the parking garage to service the loop and Soldier Field.

We developed a plan that would contain 2400 car parking spaces and a band shell at the corner of Columbus Drive and Randolph Street. A park was also developed, to cover the structured parking garage and the still-operating train lines that separated the city from the rest of Grant Park. We designed a connecting infrastructure to the Burnham-designed elements at the Montgomery Ward Gardens, which would be the final piece of Burnham's Grant Park plan and an elegant way to create "found" public space for the City. The mayor liked the idea and we started developing the park using the name of "Lakefront Gardens."

A green bridge

Plans were begun for the underground parking garage and a stepped park serving as a "green bridge" between Michigan Avenue and Grant Park. Plans for the park included a band shell that could handle a seated audience of 4000 for outdoor music performance, an adjacent "great lawn" for informal seating of another 10,000 people, an ice-skating rink that in warm weather could double as an outdoor dining area, a restaurant, sculpture gardens, an indoor theater, and a pedestrian bridge to span Columbus Drive and connect the parks on either side of the drive.

Funding

Underpinning the design and planning of Millennium Park was the principle that the Park must eventually support itself financially. To meet this goal, two parking structures contributed to the park's operational costs in addition to extensive private contributors.

Cost of the new park topped out at $160 million. Although $140 million of this could be covered by bonds raised for the parking structure itself, a further $20–$40 million would need to be raised privately. Ultimately, more than $200 million was raised by the private sector, providing funds for spectacular elements of the plan and transforming the Lakefront Gardens project into Millennium Park.

Art: a key component

Throughout its conception and development, we sought the most significant artists and architects from around the world to create elements within the park. Truly international in reputation and experience, these designers have contributed daring and provocative artworks that have enhanced the initial conception.

At the first meeting of the Millennium Park Art Committee I suggested that the proposed band shell needed some special element—like a spectacular sculpture—and suggested that we get Frank Gehry involved. The committee agreed and I called Frank Gehry in Los Angeles; he agreed to take a look at some of our preliminary sketches for the band shell. Frank was initially cool about the idea. His initial response was "I'm an architect, not a sculptor!" The problem was solved when the Art Commission offered him the opportunity to design the entire band shell plus a pedestrian bridge that would span Columbus Drive and connect Millennium Park with the lakefront.

The Pritzker family came to the rescue with funding, contributing $15 million to the project. Thus Frank Gehry's extraordinary curved metal band shell began to take shape and would soon take its place as one of Chicago's landmark structures. In its execution, Gehry's band shell is both structure and sculpture, with its boldness controlled and mediated by the Park's Beaux Arts infrastructure and landscaping. Funding from BP Amoco was secured for the snake-like bridge, designed by Frank Gehry.

An instant destination

Two other important art works, Anish Kapoor's *Cloud Gate* and Spanish sculptor Jaime Plensa's *Crown Fountain*, have helped make Millennium Park one of Chicago's signature destinations. Both literally reflect and represent today's Chicago; Kapoor's piece through a highly polished surface that places a viewer at the center of a reflected view of the city, and Plensa's fountain through the video display of the faces of more than 1000 Chicagoans on screens at the top of two 50-foot towers, out of whose mouths pour a stream of water cascading into a pool below.

A place uniquely Chicago

Like the rest of Downtown Chicago, the Beaux Arts elements that define the infrastructure of the Millennium Park link this park to the 1909 Plan of Chicago. The "City that works" moves forward into the 21st century with spectacular new features but retains the elements of civility for which it is so well known.

Millennium Park

The Beijing Central Business District Master Plan Competition

Location: Beijing, China
Client: Beijing Central Business District Development Co. Ltd.
Year: 2004

Master plan design intent

The Beijing CBD master plan has been designed to take advantage of this remarkable site located at the core of the Beijing business district. The mixed-use program has been devised to offer an integrated and exciting environment that is forward looking, giving direction and vision to the future of urban life in the central business district. Its components have been organized to function together as an active 24-hour work and living environment. Each parcel and building has been designed to optimize location, orientation development, and identity. The individual parcels are linked physically and visually, with common amenity uses and a series of gateways, where circulation at and above grade connects buildings and parcels. This offers flexibility to the entire development and gives it a unique physical organization with distinctive urban spaces as well as a cohesive urban expression for the project. The gateways or "windows" can be considered as the driving concept for the design of the master plan. The CBD is seen as the "window to Beijing."

The window to Beijing

Metaphorically, the window can represent a view or gateway. In this case, the window is the gateway to Beijing, the threshold upon which one stands, acknowledging the past and moving into the future.

There are many great international cities that serve as windows to their cultures and countries. Typically, a great space and great buildings define each of these cities, which in turn symbolize the essence of the people and culture that they represent. The idea for the Beijing Central Business District stems from the understanding and appreciation of borrowed contexts. The idea is that within any framework, information, views, and experiences can be exchanged freely through clear means of access and communication. In the master plan, the framework is established through the existing grid of the city.

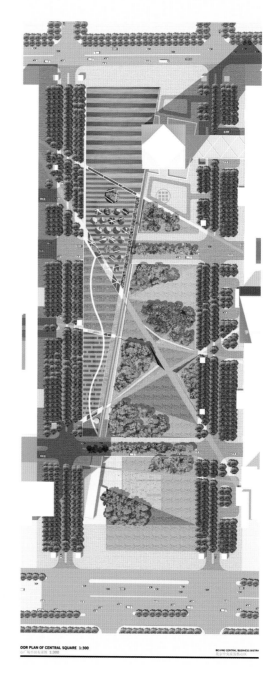

FLOOR PLAN OF CENTRAL SQUARE 1:300
广场平面布置图 1:300

BEIJING CENTRAL BUSINESS DISTRICT
北京中央商务区中心

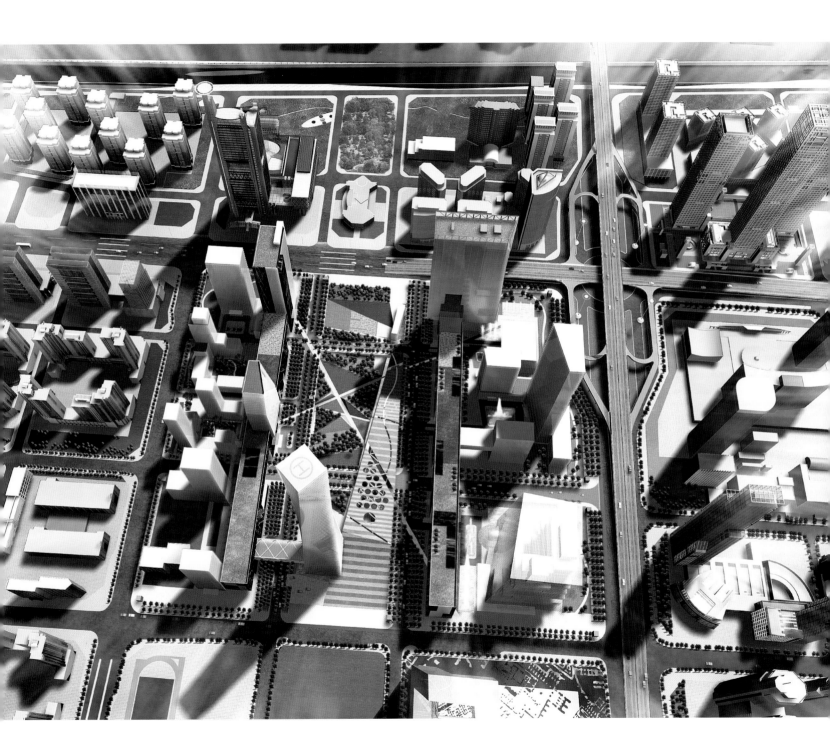

The Beijing Central Business District Master Plan Competition

This framework is layered by the free and intentional vistas of pathways and view corridors that connect existing and new places and objects together.

These corridors are connected through "windows" that are cut through the framework of the city in order to liberate and express events and spaces that are often unrealized within conventional design systems. In doing so, distant contexts are brought into view and distant spaces are immediately compressed into the occupant's space.

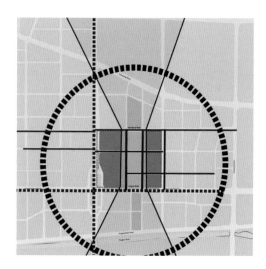
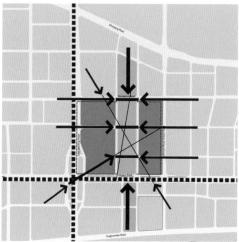

The project design is established on the premise that by opening views and connections through the city, this development will be clearly woven, not only into the immediate context, but the distant contexts surrounding the site as well.

Symbolism

The idea of the window symbolizes the open freedom of choice and communication critical to the success of business and culture.

The central park is the soul of the development. It is a social amenity and receives all contextual influences, physical and social.

The frames symbolize the social structure that holds the city together and makes Beijing strong.

The courtyards symbolize the expansion of the framework and the various types of development identities that can be accommodated with the plan. They are accessible through the windows in the frame and are addressed off the central space.

The central tower symbolizes the endlessness of time looking to the future while it turns its torso to recognize and honor the distant history that surrounds it. This is the manifestation of its borrowed context.

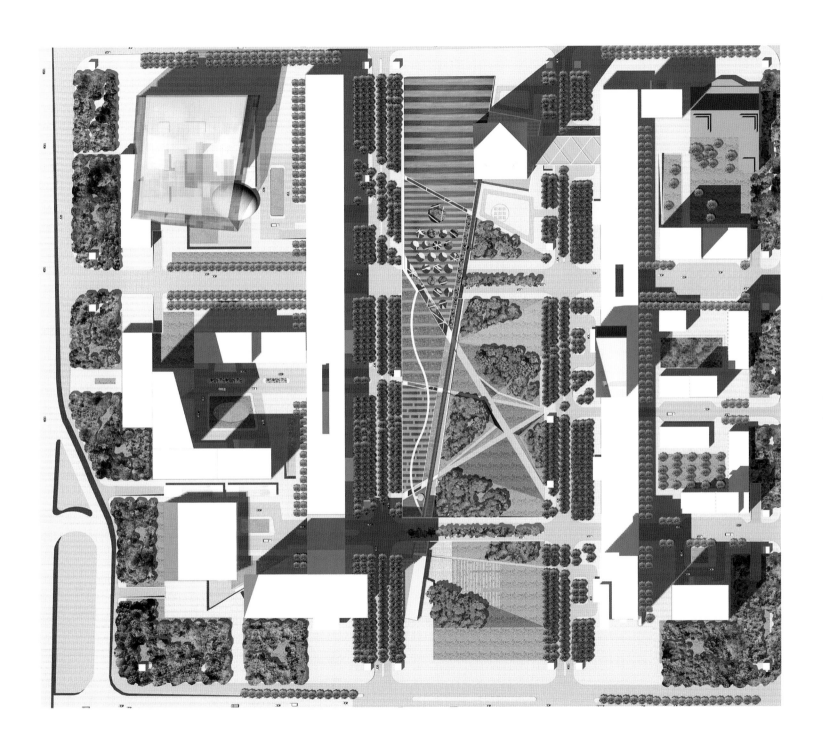

The Beijing Central Business District Master Plan Competition 479

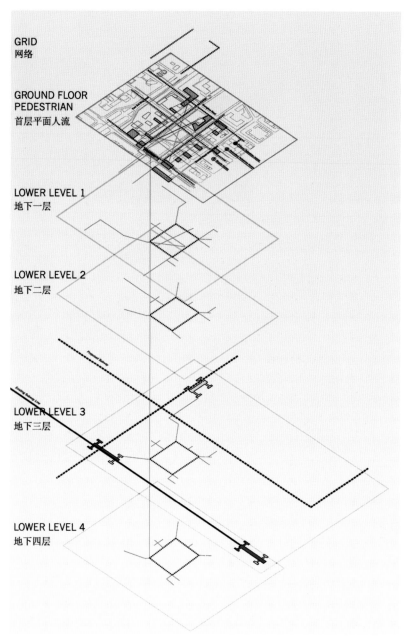

GRID
网络

GROUND FLOOR
PEDESTRIAN
首层平面人流

LOWER LEVEL 1
地下一层

LOWER LEVEL 2
地下二层

LOWER LEVEL 3
地下三层

LOWER LEVEL 4
地下四层

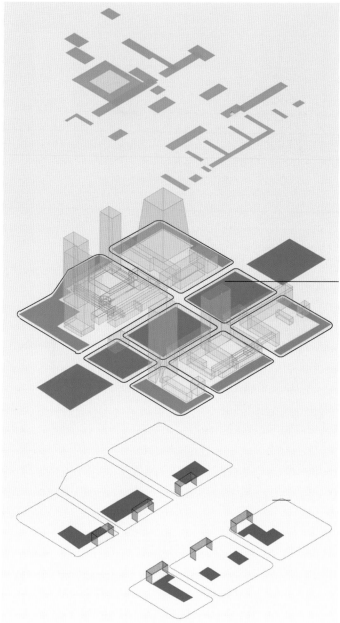

Master plan organization

The master plan is organized around a central space that is framed on either side. These frames are penetrated by the street grid and pathways, which create windows into the central space. From the public central space, these windows lead into courtyards. The courtyards provide opportunities for development identity and serve as the central space for each adjacent parcel.

Each parcel is organized to take advantage of a gateway or window into the CBD, a two-sided frame along the park, a courtyard that can be the identifiable space for building development, and a main tower.

Phasing

With all great developments, phasing is critical to long-term success. The recommended first phase of the development includes the central space, frames, and central tower. This establishes both the built and open space standards for the development and also allows development outside the frames to occur in any sequence. This approach offers ultimate flexibility to developers and investors. Since the sites are accessible from the periphery, this will also allow a flexible approach to construction with little or no interruption to the central area of the project.

The recommended second phase of the project would include the corner sites along Chang An Avenue and at Guanghua Road and the Third Ring Road. This would extend the connection below grade for retail and transportation systems.

The remaining residential and commercial parcels could then be the third phase. These parcels would be more centrally located. They are linked to transportation and service on both sides of the park and are physically and spatially connected to the great central space. All parcels are addressed off the central space and have tremendous equitable identification for corporate and private development.

Parcel design intent

The phasing of the towers, frame, and ancillary buildings of each parcel is developed in order to allow a flexible means of development construction and identity. In this way each parcel is capable of providing a variety of building types, scales, and organization, depending on client needs.

Landscape

The master plan is designed around a major social central space that is framed by landscape and surrounded by courtyards that provide an attractive environment for each type of user. The central space is a continuation of the park system that is proposed in the surrounding master plan of the central business district.

The e-garden

As specified in the competition brief, a major central space has been planned. This 12-hectare space is the social and commercial hub of the development. It is physically connected to the proposed city green space master plan that allows the green space to continue through the CBD. It becomes one of the proposed five great parks of the CBD: the science information park, the performance art square, the natural science park, the historic cultural park, and this commerce park.

The design concept for the park is that of layered systems of views and folded planes, which create a variety of programmable areas for the park. The folded planes allow light into the lower-level commercial development around the park and create a series of illuminated paths and windows through the park. To the west, the park slopes down to an elevation of 7 meters below grade, where it liberates the below-grade commercial use. Along this west edge is a major public plaza in the park that is covered by a garden canopy at street level. This area can be programmed and electronically wired to accommodate a variety of uses. It is an all-year venue and is partially protected by the canopy above. Concerts, outdoor exhibits, dining, and casual events are some of the urban activities that could occur here. This space is also connected to large grade-level plazas at the north and south end of the park. This "e-garden" allows 24-hour active uses with easy pedestrian connections from the lower-level trains at Chang An Avenue and Third Ring Road.

Court landscapes

The paths through the e-garden lead to development parcels that surround the space. Each parcel has a court. The concepts for the courts are specific to each development type and provide the spatial identity and organization for each development parcel.

In the commercial development, the court is predominantly hard and offers direct access to each building with clear and accessible addresses. The courts themselves provide great naming opportunities for corporations and, because they are connected to the main central space, these courts elevate the value of property along the periphery of the development by giving them a park address. In the residential development the courts are predominantly green. They are semi-private spaces designed to accommodate a variety of social uses. Typically, all courts allow direct vertical access from parking below. The courts give all parcels two-sided views, allowing vast amounts of natural light into the buildings.

Street landscapes

The major north–south boulevards that frame the park are layered in a sequence of spaces for pedestrian and vehicular movement. The spaces are heavily landscaped and create gardens at street level for spillover commercial activity, programmed activities for special events, vertical circulation from below-grade retail, bicycle traffic, and vehicular traffic.

Massing

The overall massing of the master plan takes into consideration the entire central business district context and has been designed to accommodate a practical sequence of phasing and construction and upon completion, to exhibit a unified composition with the greatest visual impact. The office towers are prominently located along Chang An Avenue and Third Ring Road while the residential buildings form intimately scaled courts to the east. The towers along Third Ring Road serve as the anchors to each of their development parcels. The organization of the massing to the east is more sympathetic to the existing context of residential buildings. Internally the frame of buildings that line the central space also recognize this shift in scale from west to east.

To the south, the massing along Chang An Avenue is of greater height in order to distinguish the physical entry to this site. These two gateway buildings frame the view to the central tower, which is the tallest in the project and complements the World Trade Center building directly to the west.

Traffic

The traffic system has been designed to allow efficient vehicular, pedestrian, and service movement through and around the site.

The main north–south central boulevards are designed as two-way, four-lane boulevards with bicycle lanes and public transportation. The design intent is to allow traffic access through the site to the main addresses along the boulevards. In order to ease traffic on the proposed boulevards, courtyard systems are designed so that dedicated visitors and traffic to specific buildings will leave the main streets and will not need to endure the general traffic as they drop off and visit specific buildings. Each parcel has its own private drop-off system.

Pedestrian traffic can traverse the site at grade, above grade and below grade and can take advantage of the building links or the central park to avoid vehicular traffic. This also increases traffic safety issues.

Service entries to the parcels are discreetly located along the east–west streets along the northern and southern edge of each parcel, allowing for direct access to below-grade parking for users as well as service. This also allows for dedicated service access routes that will never interfere with traffic in the center of the district.

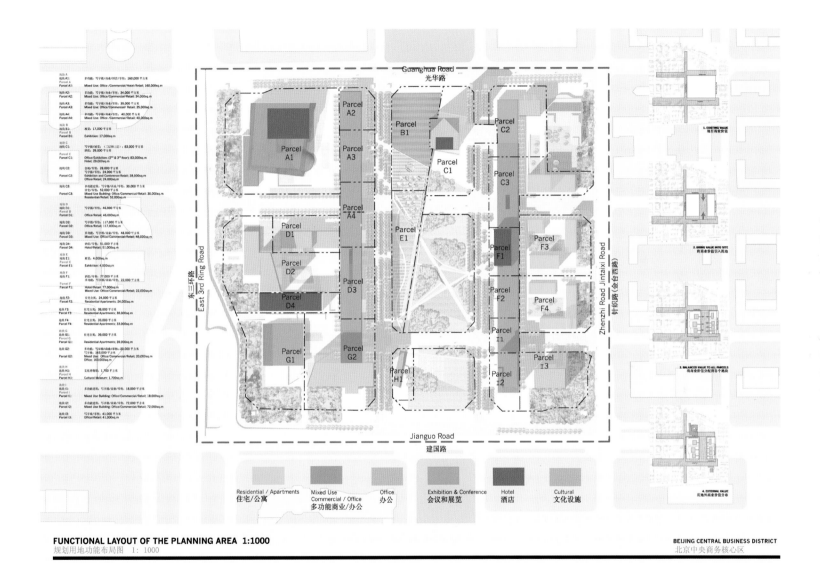

地块 A
Parcel A
多功能：写字楼/办公/酒店/零售：160,000 平方米
Parcel A1: Mixed Use: Office/Commercial/Hotel/Retail: 160,000sq.m
多功能：写字楼/商业/零售：34,000 平方米
Parcel A2: Mixed Use: Office/Commercial/Retail: 34,000sq.m
多功能：写字楼/商业/零售：35,000 平方米
Parcel A3: Mixed Use: Office/Commercial/Retail: 35,000sq.m
多功能：写字楼/商业/零售：40,000 平方米
Parcel A4: Mixed Use: Office /Commercial/Retail: 40,000sq.m

地块 B
Parcel B
展览：17,000 平方米
Parcel B1: Exhibition: 17,000sq.m

地块 C
Parcel C
写字楼/展览（二层和三层）：83,000 平方米
Parcel C1: Office/Exhibition: (2nd & 3rd floor): 83,000sq.m
消防：29,000 平方米
Hotel: 29,000sq.m
会议厅/零售：28,000 平方米
Parcel C2: Exhibition and Conference/Retail: 28,000sq.m
写字楼/零售：24,000 平方米
Parcel C2: Office/Retail: 24,000sq.m
多功能建筑：写字楼/商业/零售：30,000 平方米
Parcel C3: Mixed Use Building: Office/Commercial/Retail: 30,000sq.m
住宅/零售：52,000 平方米
Residential/Retail: 52,000sq.m

地块 D
Parcel D
写字楼/零售：46,000 平方米
Parcel D1: Office/Retail: 46,000sq.m
写字楼/零售：117,000 平方米
Parcel D2: Office/Retail: 117,000sq.m
多功能：写字楼/商业/零售：48,000 平方米
Parcel D3: Mixed Use: Office/Commercial/Retail: 48,000sq.m
酒店/零售：51,000 平方米
Parcel D4: Hotel/Retail: 51,000sq.m

地块 E
Parcel E
展览：4,000 平方米
Parcel E1: Exhibition: 4,000sq.m

地块 F
Parcel F
酒店/零售：77,000 平方米
Parcel F1: Hotel/Retail: 77,000sq.m
住宅/公寓：22,000 平方米
Parcel F2: Residential Apartments: 24,000sq.m
住宅/公寓：38,000 平方米
Parcel F3: Residential Apartments: 38,000sq.m
住宅/公寓：33,000 平方米
Parcel F4: Residential Apartments: 33,000sq.m

地块 G
Parcel G
住宅/公寓：39,000 平方米
Parcel G1: Residential Apartments: 39,000sq.m
多功能：写字楼/商业/零售：20,000 平方米
Parcel G2: Mixed Use: Office/Commercial/Retail: 20,000sq.m
写字楼：163,000 平方米
Office: 163,000sq.m

地块 H
Parcel H
文化博物馆：1,700 平方米
Parcel H1: Cultural Museum: 1,700sq.m

地块 I
Parcel I
多功能建筑：写字楼/商业/零售：18,000 平方米
Parcel I1: Mixed Use Building: Office/Commercial/Retail: 18,000sq.m
多功能建筑：写字楼/商业/零售：72,000 平方米
Parcel I2: Mixed Use Building: Office/Commercial/Retail: 72,000sq.m
写字楼/零售：41,000 平方米
Parcel I3: Office/Retail: 41,000sq.m

Guanghua Road
光华路

East 3rd Ring Road
东三环路

Zhenzhi Road Jintaixi Road
针织路 (金台西路)

Jianguo Road
建国路

Parcel A1 · Parcel A2 · Parcel A3 · Parcel A4 · Parcel B1 · Parcel C1 · Parcel C2 · Parcel C3 · Parcel D1 · Parcel D2 · Parcel D3 · Parcel D4 · Parcel E1 · Parcel F1 · Parcel F2 · Parcel F3 · Parcel F4 · Parcel G1 · Parcel G2 · Parcel H1 · Parcel I1 · Parcel I2 · Parcel I3

Residential / Apartments
住宅/公寓

Mixed Use
Commercial / Office
多功能商业/办公

Office
办公

Exhibition & Conference
会议和展览

Hotel
酒店

Cultural
文化设施

1. EXISTING VALUE
地行商业价值

2. BRING VALUE INTO SITE
将商业价值引入用地

3. BALANCED VALUE TO ALL PARCELS
将商业价值分配到各个地块

4. EXTERNAL VALUE
用地外商业价值分布

FUNCTIONAL LAYOUT OF THE PLANNING AREA 1:1000
规划用地功能布局图　1：1000

The Beijing Central Business District Master Plan Competition

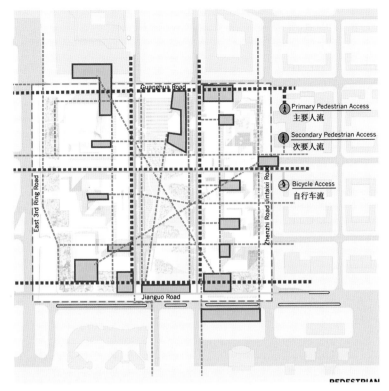

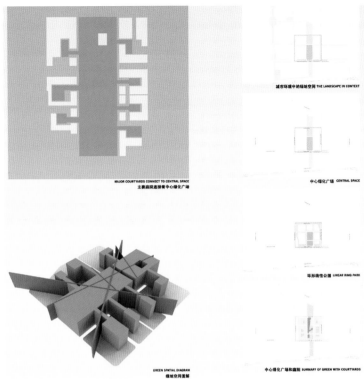

Safety

As building safety becomes more important, measures will be taken in order to ensure the latest precautions for user safety. Emergency safety components include:

- Concrete enclosed stairwells with pressurized smoke vestibules

- Dedicated fireman's lift linked to escape stair

- Helicopter evacuation from roof tops if possible. Linked high-rise floors allow for horizontal evacuation into adjacent buildings. Structure designed with redundancy of load paths to limit likelihood of progressive collapse

Environmental issues

In the master plan, the design will implement strategies that will result in an environmentally conscious and balanced development. These include:

- Building efficiency—natural daylighting and high-efficiency HVAC systems

- Water conservation—gray water treatment and rainwater collection and treatment

- Green energy production—photovoltaic cells and urban ecology to maximize green space

Building design intent

The buildings of the master plan will be designed to allow the maximum flexibility and efficiency in each floor plate and associated building systems. To attract and accommodate leading domestic and international corporations, the buildings will need to offer a variety of floor plate sizes as well as identity to each prospective tenant. The design intent offers an equitable identity to each parcel while allowing less prestigious tenants an opportunity to share in the prestigious address of the CBD central space. The master plan design exhibits numerous development solutions that display a variety of ways in which buildings could be developed. The parcels and buildings can be organized as large singular statements, as a group of towers, or as a singular expression of economic and social growth.

Steps Toward Sustainability

Sustainability to me means more than saving energy or the recycling of materials in and for the buildings we design. It is also about sustaining our world's unique cultures and about harvesting the world's natural and renewable forces. It is about thinking the way our ancestors thought when they built their homes, factories, and cities many years ago, before mechanical transportation and air conditioning, when man was forced to use the materials at hand to build the environment. Then, buildings had to relate to the context of the immediate climate for the provision of basic shelter, and the soil conditions and topography dictated certain responses to naturally occurring forces.

When one looks back at these sometimes-ancient structures, we see the roots of a culture and a diversity of culture that arises from these conditions. The way man lives is a reflection of these basic shelters and the environment that surrounds them. In many areas of the world these cultures of the past are diluted by the onslaught of modern civilization and a mechanized society, yet the richness of our culture still persists and is embedded in our memories and our heritage. It is this lingering association with the roots of our being that is fascinating to me and the subject is worthy of sustainability, just as the natural resources of the earth are sacred and must be preserved and sustained through inventive technical means.

Cultural sustainability

In relation to cultural sustainability, my work has concentrated on the subjects of memory and association with the uniqueness of a place. My first connection with this idea was when designing a headquarters building in Monterey, Mexico with Ricardo Legorreta and designing three bank buildings in Guatemala for Banco De Occidente. Here, the design philosophy was to embrace the immediate nature of the context, starting with the materiality of the place and the relationship it has with the sun and wind. The concept was to design a courtyard building that would allow light to enter into the center of the space. This courtyard was covered with a Teflon material that diffused the light and reduced shadows in the interior space. This is a very customary solution in Guatemala and one that is both functional and relates to the cultural heritage of the place.

The exterior wall of the bank was solid and extended to the property line, consistent with local custom. The materials used in the project were all harvested locally, including the concrete structure, stucco facing, mahogany windows, black volcanic stone floors and base, and the palette of colored paint used on the interior surfaces.

The orientation of the windows on the façade allowed light to enter, but the interior was also shaded from direct sunlight. These windows are also operable, to allow fresh air into the interior spaces. This building captures the public's imagination as something familiar, yet different. It fits into the context and the *memory* of the place, it retains the *customs* and *heritage* of the local architecture, it connects to the *traditions* of material and color usage and yet it retains a *uniqueness* that is of this place. All the fabric used in the building was woven locally by Guatemalan weavers and uses natural dyes found in local crafts and ceremonial dress. It embodies the art of the people who inhabit the place.

Cultural influences can be incorporated into highly evolved urban centers. These influences are usually very different from the more indigenous influences of a developing or third world environment but they express themselves in the environment in a way that reflects their makers. London is a good example of this, where the construction ideologies stem from the Industrial Revolution, where things are clearly "constructed" and put together, rather than made out of the earth as is the case in Guatemala. This difference is expressed in the design of 10 Ludgate, an office building built over rail tracks in the heart of London; the exterior wall is constructed using the fasteners as expressed features in the façade, thus exposing the technology of construction. This analogy of expressed components is embodied in much of the British industrial design and is an integral part of the culture.

Material sustainability

The use of materials that can be recycled is a long-term prospect for the practice of architecture since it looks to the nature of buildings' needs far into the future. The science of materials is changing rapidly and with the formation of nano-technology and its increasing popularity, the reuse of materials in the future is difficult to predict. New materials are being invented through molecular manipulation that will make the materials of today both cumbersome and inefficient. The prospect that a building will become functionally obsolete is a challenge for today's designers since it is with longevity of our building fabric that we achieve sustainability of our environment and our culture. It is far better to design for the long term in terms of durability, flexibility, and conservation now than it is to plan for the recycling of our materials for tomorrow's world. It is essential that we use materials that are *renewable* whenever possible, including materials that are farmed and found locally or readily accessible with minimal energy used in the transport or manufacture of the building materials. *Recycling* of materials for interior use, where the lifespan is much shorter, is a good idea and real benefits are achieved by such practices.

Energy harvesting from renewable sources

The practice of using locally available energy to operate the mechanical needs of our buildings has been largely ignored over the last century. We have become totally reliant on central systems and sources of energy for the running of our buildings' mechanical, electrical, and mechanized transportation systems and for the lighting of the spaces in which we work. Building design over the last 100 years has not advanced the integration of systems to harvest the earth's natural forces as potential sources of power to operate our buildings' systems.

Wind is a powerful force that has been used for centuries for pumping water and assisting in the manufacturing of goods. Its biggest drawback is that it is not always there; but with the use of batteries we can now harvest this source of power and reuse it when needed. Alternatively, the energy generated by the wind can be diverted to the energy grid to help reduce peak demands on the central system.

It is possible to design buildings to contain wind-driven turbines and it is possible to design these buildings in a shape and orientation that will gather or harvest the wind and funnel its force into wind farms that will generate enormous power.

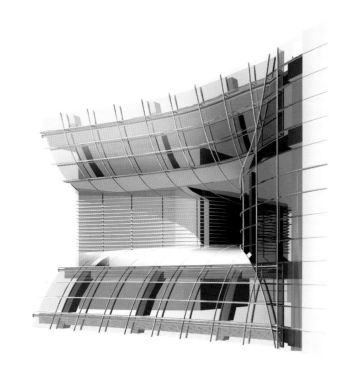

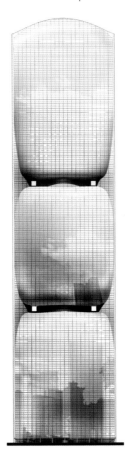

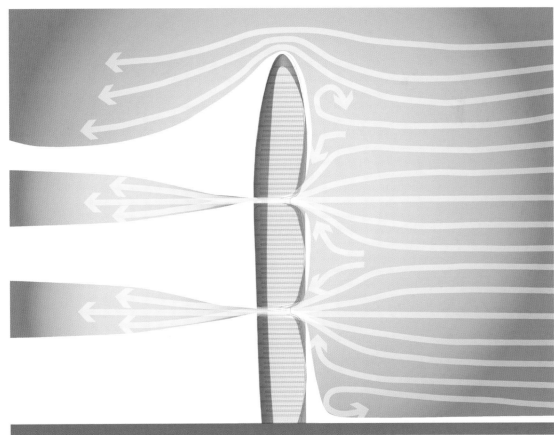

It is also possible to design wind gathering systems to take advantage of the wind's increased velocity as it moves around the corners of a structure. These opportunities are particularly viable when the building is a tall or super-tall structure, since the velocity of the wind increases the higher we go.

The energy from the *sun* has been used in architecture to a greater degree than that of the wind, though it is yet to be exploited to its fullest extent. Today's architecture is far more concerned with keeping the heat from the sun out of the building rather than finding ways to use the power from the sun to light our spaces, heat our water, and provide electricity for our air movement systems and power needs. *Sun shading* is a simple way to help alleviate the sun load on the building and there are many simple devices available to accomplish this, with varying degrees of vision control from within.

Sun shading is important in hot conditions, but it is possible to both shield the interior contained environment from the *heat* of the sun and to use the *light* from the sun to bring it into interior occupied areas so that it replaces artificial sources.

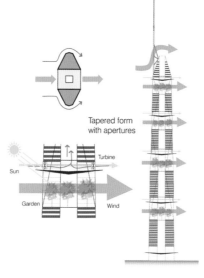

Tapered form with apertures

Sun

Garden

Turbine

Wind

Shenzhen

Samsung Togok

Sun shading of exterior walls

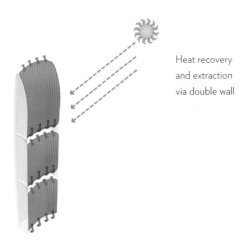

Heat recovery
and extraction
via double wall

Heat from the sun can also be used in a beneficial way to produce electric energy through the incorporation of *photovoltaics*. These devices have been growing in popularity and use since the 1990s but are yet to reach a competitive threshold. Photovoltaics are a viable way to generate power if used on rooftops or on façades where the orientation of the panel can be directed toward the sun. They are less effective on most overcast days and when there is no sun, and also not very successful when there is shade on part of the system. Photovoltaics can perform a dual purpose when integrated into the façade system of a building, shading the vision area from direct sunlight, while contributing to the energy needs of the building.

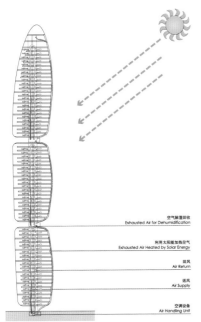

空气除湿回收
Exhausted Air for Dehumidification

利用太阳能加热空气
Exhausted Air Heated by Solar Energy

回风
Air Return

送风
Air Supply

空调设备
Air Handling Unit

Energy efficient equipment and daylighting

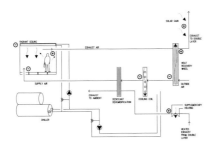

Solar collection for hot water

Building integrated photovoltaics

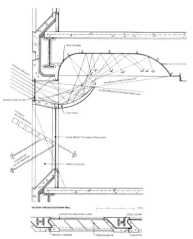

Natural daylighting in desert environments

The use of *double exterior wall systems* in the design of buildings in climates with high temperature variations, such as Chicago, Boston, or Denver, can be beneficial to the building's energy performance. Several types of double wall are available, tailored to different climatic conditions. In Germany, the double wall is most often used to temper the air and is usually externally ventilated. The tempered air, heated in the cavity between the two glass walls, is taken into the building through operable windows between the interstitial space and the occupied space, thus using the heated air as a form of heating for the building. This system is used in the Chemsunny building in Beijing.

Another type of double wall is used at 601 Congress Street building in Boston where the entire building is a closed double wall with the air from the interstitial space ventilated into the return air plenum and mixed with the building's return air system for extraction or reuse. This system reduces the radiant heat on the occupied space, since the sun shading devices that are placed in the interstitial space prevent the heat from entering the comfort zone.

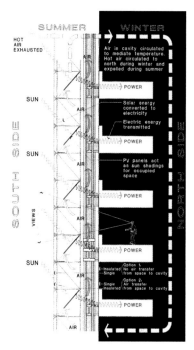

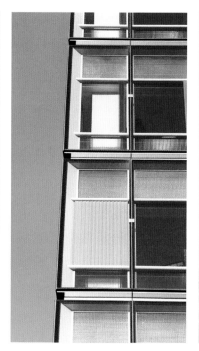

Double wall construction

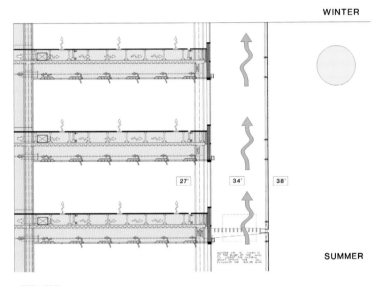

27°

20°

5°

WINTER

27°   34°   38°

SUMMER

This system could also be utilized for heating the pipes and water for hot water systems for buildings in climates that do not have freezing temperatures, such as Shenzhen.

When using a double wall to act as a *thermos bottle*, it is necessary to incorporate a double wall where the interstitial space is connected horizontally. In this way, the heated air in the interstitial space facing the sun can be moved to the cooler sides of the building where the air and wall are in the shade. The differential in temperature from the exterior to the interior is reduced, thus reducing the heating or cooling load significantly during the daytime. This system can be further enhanced by the use of a tempered source of air, such as from a subway or below-grade tunnel system, if this system can be connected to the interstitial cavity and can generate enough air to bathe the surface of the building with air at a temperature of ±55 degrees Fahrenheit. This would allow the temperature differential between the occupied space and the exterior (interstitial space) to be only 15 degrees, night or day. Further, this would significantly reduce the heating and cooling demand on the building and allow for relatively inexpensive heating and cooling systems to be installed, thus saving considerable initial and operating costs and resulting in substantial *energy conservation* through the use of thermal mass in the earth's *soil*.

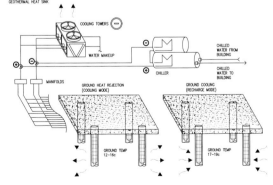

High efficiency chillers with geothermal heat sink

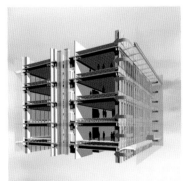

Thermos bottle concept, Summer

Thermos bottle concept, Winter

Water conservation is an increasing problem where untreated waste is polluting the earth's water sources. It is crucial that the construction of our environment practices water conservation and water purification. One way for our buildings to respond to demand is through water reclamation and on-site purification. *Rooftop planting* is an excellent way to help purify water sources while at the same time providing excellent roof insulation. It also adds to the habitat of birds and insects, which in turn add to the quality of life.

It is also possible in high-humidity environments (and highly desirable in high-humidity desert environments) to reclaim the *condensate water* from the building's cooling systems for use in the building, for landscape irrigation, or for conversion to potable water.

Building waste also has potential for energy generation through incineration and heat recapture but should be developed to ensure no adverse effect on the breathable air.

Conservation

Land conservation is a serious issue in a world where the population doubles every 50 years. Perhaps the most troublesome issue here is the erosion of the world's farmland through poor horticultural practices and through the use of low-density development and increasing urban sprawl. The long-term looming concerns of global warming are also factors in the earth's ability to grow enough food for its expanding population when soil conditions become too parched and unusable for farming.

One way to address this issue is through a comprehensive, global planning approach. Because current political conditions rule out the feasibility of a global approach, more local planning frameworks should be pursued. The planning framework developed in the United States in the late 1930s and early 1940s advocated the decentralization of the population base and the incorporation of a national highway transportation system. This policy has resulted in the greatest per capita pollution in history. It has also made it far too easy to develop farmland around the dense urban cores into suburban homes and has, in the United States, created a society where mass transit systems are secondary to the automobile and are increasingly unsustainable because of population decentralization. The economic resources involved in the construction and maintenance of infrastructure for automobile transportation are enormous when compared to the

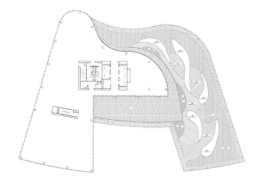

Rooftop garden

High-density, mixed-use

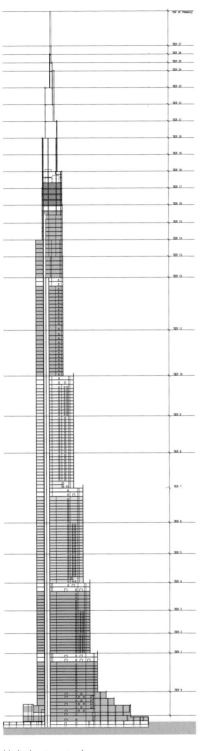

High-density, mixed-use

efficiency and convenience of mass transit. But for mass transit to be convenient, there must be a strong concentration of population in smaller areas than currently exists. In this context, *high-density* developments and high-density city cores could refocus our approach to how we conserve land as well as the vast amounts of *energy* consumed through our transportation systems.

An extension of this concept is through the incorporation of mixed uses within a single building or within walking distance from use to use. Over the last 50 years this experiment has been gaining ground. The first example of this typology was the John Hancock Tower, in Chicago.

The issue of *time* can also be a significant factor in the importance of sustainability. Through proper planning that takes advantage of density, energy efficiency, reduced travel times, and increased levels of comfort, we can have more time for the pursuit of those interests that contribute to our quality of life. We can prioritize our efforts to produce vehicles of delight and concentrate on the wellbeing, health, safety, and comfort of our civilization.

What we are all looking for is a plan for the pursuit of an increased *quality of life*, not just sustaining the life we started with.

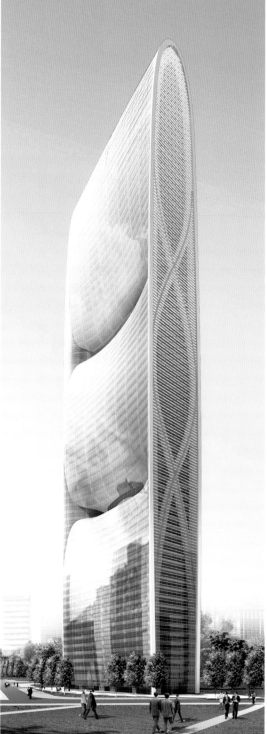

Windcatchers

Steps Toward Sustainability

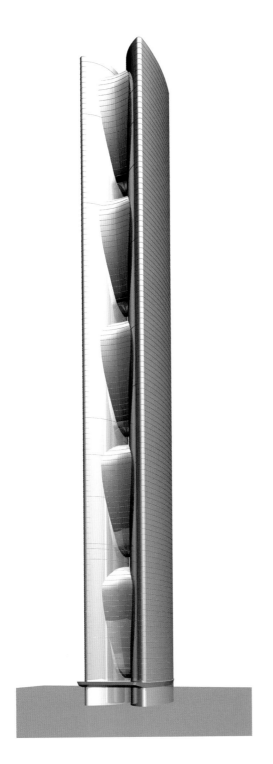
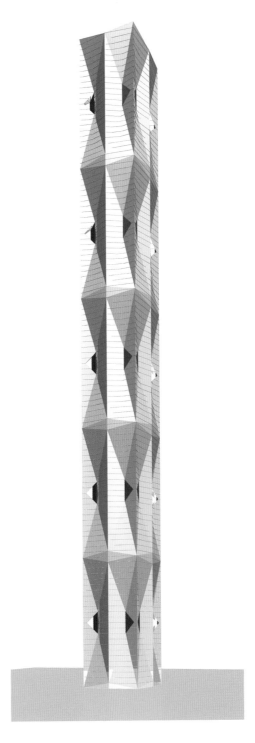

1944	Born in Chicago, Illinois, USA	1985	Elected to Fellow, American Institute of Architects
1962–1966	Studied architecture at Texas A&M University	1986	National AIA, Honor Award for United Gulf Bank
1967–1969	Bachelor of Architecture degree from University of Illinois	1987	Collaborated with Bruce Graham, Robert AM Stern, Jacquelin Robertson, Stanley Tigerman, Charles Moore, Tom Beeby on 1992 Chicago World's Fair
1966	Worked at offices of Perkins + Will, Chicago, Illinois	1987	Collaborated on 1987 Chicago Central Area Plan
1967	Began career at Chicago office of Skidmore, Owings & Merrill LLP, working under Walter Netsch, Bruce Graham, and Fazlur Khan	1988	Participated as group leader at Hamburg Bauforum, Hamburg, Germany
1972–1974	Site architect for WD & HO Wills Hartcliffe project, Bristol, UK	1990	Chairman, SOM Foundation (1990–1995)
1974	Elected to Associate at SOM	1992	Chicago World's Fair
1976	Collaborated with Ricardo Legorreta and Luis Barragan on Grupo Industrial Alfa Headquarters	1992	Participated in Berlin Zentrum for reunification of Berlin Won design
1977	Elected to Associate Partner at SOM	1993	Chairman/CEO of Skidmore, Owings & Merrill LLP (1993–1995)
1980	Elected to Design Partner at SOM	1993	Won design competition for Jin Mao Tower
1984	National AIA, Honor Award for Banco de Occidente, shared with Bruce Graham	1994	National AIA, Honor Award for Rowes Wharf, Boston
1984	Won competition to design Rowes Wharf, Boston		

1995	Recipient of Alumni Achievement Award, University of Illinois	2005	Recipient of Spirit of Life Award, City of Hope
1996	Authored SOM's submission for AIA Architecture Firm Award	2006	National AIA Honor Award for Millennium Park Master Plan
1997	National AIA, Honor Award for State Street Renovation	**2006**	Established ADRIAN SMITH + GORDON GILL ARCHITECTURE
1998	Won design competition for Samsung Tower Palace III	2008	ULI Award of Excellence for General Motors Renaissance Center
2001	National AIA, Honor Award for Jin Mao Tower, Interior Architecture	2010	CTBUH Global Icon Award, Burj Khalifa
2002	Published first monograph, *Pro Architect*, Issue 24	**2011**	CTBUH Lynn S. Beedle Lifetime Achievement Award
2003	Consulting Design Partner at SOM	**2011**	Co-author, "Toward Zero Carbon: The Chicago Central Area DeCarbonization Plan," published by Images Publishing
2003	National AIA Honor Award for Lakeshore East Master Plan	**2011**	National AIA Honor Award in Regional and Urban Design for the Chicago Central Area DeCarbonization Plan
2003	Won competition to design Burj Dubai (Burj Khalifa)	**2012**	Receives Texas A&M University School of Architecture Outstanding Alumni Award
2004	Won competition to design Nanjing Greenland Financial Complex	**2013**	Receives Honorary Doctorate of Letters Degree from Texas A & M University
2004	Chaired National AIA Jury for 2005 Architecture Awards		

Biography

Adrian D. Smith, FAIA, RIBA

Adrian Smith, FAIA, is an Architect of international renown, having designed many landmark buildings including the two world's tallest structures—Burj Khalifa, completed in 2010 in Dubai and Kingdom Tower, now under construction in Jeddah, Saudi Arabia. In 2006, he founded Adrian Smith + Gordon Gill Architecture (AS+GG), a firm dedicated to the design of high-performance, energy-efficient and sustainable architecture on an international scale. In 2008, he co-founded the MEP firm of PositivEnergy Practice, which specializes in the environmental engineering of high-performance, energy-efficient architecture. Before he started AS+GG, he was a Design Partner in the Chicago office of Skidmore, Owings & Merrill from 1980 to 2003 and a Consulting Design Partner from 2003 to 2006.

His work has shown an evolving interest in the use of vernacular and indigenous forms and compositions, together with state-of-the-art systems and technologies to integrate new buildings into the regional context. His designs are sensitive to each project's physical environment, taking into consideration conditions such as location, climate, geographical, geological, cultural, and social influences to achieve environmental sustainability. Over the last several years, his work has embraced the principle of "on site" power generation using the building's design to harvest power from the sun, wind, and geothermal conditions in order to reduce the building's reliance on local infrastructure. In many instances, this has had a dramatic impact on the expression of the architecture and has added an important influence to his philosophy of Global Contextualism.

Throughout his career, Mr. Smith has played an active role in international projects and developments. From 1971 to 1973, he was the Resident Project Architect for the Wills Hartcliffe project near Bristol, England. In 1989, he was selected to participate in the IV Hamburg Bauforum, to lead a team exploring alternative visions for the Speicherstadt district in Hamburg, Germany. In 1990, he participated in a team of 40 international architects and planners in the Zentrum: Berlin symposium, at the Bauhaus in Dessau, to discuss the challenges for the reunification of Berlin. He has also designed buildings in Bahrain, Brazil, China, Dubai, Saudi Arabia, Canada, England, Germany, Guatemala, Indonesia, Korea, Kuwait, Mexico, the United States (Chicago, Boston, Des Moines, St. Louis, Minneapolis, Washington D.C., Orlando, and New York City).

Mr. Smith was elected by the SOM Partnership to serve as the firm's Chief Executive Officer from 1992 to 1994. He also served as Chairman for the SOM Foundation from 1990 to 1995; Trustee to the Chicago Architecture Foundation in 1992 and 1999; President of the Chicago Central Area Committee in 1997 and 1999; Board member of the State Street Council from 1995; and Governor on the Board of the School of Art Institute of Chicago from 2002.

National positions include Lifetime Governor of the Urban Land Institute Foundation and member of the Urban Land Institute (1986 to present). He has served on numerous professional juries and committees, including the Chicago Chapter AIA Fellows Committee and the National AIA Large Firm Roundtable. He was Chairman of the National AIA Jury on Institute Honors (1987); the Progressive Architecture Awards Design Jury (1988); Jury Chairman of the Central States Region AIA Awards Program (1994); the 2000 Advisory Panel to the AIA Board of Directors for the Firm Award and Gold Medal Award recipients 2000); and Chairman of the AIA National Honor Awards for Architecture (2004).

He was keynote speaker at the Council on Tall Buildings and Urban Habitat (CTBUH) Fifth World Congress (1995); CTBUH World Congress Dubai (2009); CTBUH World Congress Chicago (2011); CTBUH World Congress Shanghai (2012); the ABN Amro symposium (1990); the Quaternario conference in Singapore (1991); and has lectured in Amsterdam, London, Buenos Aires, Prague, Frankfurt, Seoul, Shanghai, Hong Kong, Washington DC, Notre Dame, Chicago, New York, and other locations.

He was a trustee of the Building Experiences Trust Limited, a British organization devoted to furthering architectural education curricula from 1995 to 1998; the Royal Institute of British Architects British Architectural Library Trust Representative for the British Schools and Universities Foundation from 1994 to present; and has appeared in several documentaries including the BBC World Service's film *Chicago Architecture*, several episodes of *Chicago Tonight*; and the first two parts of the *Skyline: Chicago* film series.

Mr. Smith has been a registered architect in twelve states, the District of Columbia, the United Kingdom, Canada, and the National Council of Architectural Registration Boards, and is also an active member of the College of Fellows of the AIA, the Royal Institute of British Architects, the Ontario Association of Architects and The Architectural Institute of British Columbia.

During his tenure as Design Partner, projects under his leadership and direction have received more than 125 design awards including 5 international awards, 9 National AIA awards, 35 state and Chicago AIA awards, and 3 ULI Awards for Excellence (1989, 2005, 2008); and several Progressive Architecture Design Awards. His work has been exhibited at public museums in Chicago, Europe, South America, and Asia and ten of his projects are in the permanent collection of the Art Institute of Chicago.

Acknowledgments

From 1980 to 2003, I was Design Partner at the Chicago office of Skidmore, Owings & Merrill. From 2003 to 2006, I was Consulting Design Partner. In those roles, I was responsible for the concept and design implementation of all projects under my direction. Working closely with the studio head and senior members of each assembled team on each project, we established the design objective, design philosophy, form, materials, details, and strategies for the project's development throughout the design process.

The following list of team credits has been assembled to acknowledge the immense contributions made to projects under my design direction. Although every effort has been made to be as complete and thorough as possible, in some instances, these lists are partial because of the age of the project and incomplete records.

I want to thank everyone listed for their efforts, contributions, sacrifice of personal time due to intense work periods and tight schedules, and for their dedication to the art and science of making architecture. Without the millions of hours of their labor, the projects in this book would not have been possible.

I also want to thank Skidmore, Owings & Merrill and its many partners over the years for providing an environment of creativity and excellence that has attracted the brilliant architects, engineers, and other professionals that were so essential to the design of these projects. I also want to thank the current partners of SOM for their generous support of this publication.

I also want to Acknowledge Jocelyn Moriarty for the outstanding work on editing and transforming this edition from its initial version in 2006. By replacing the renderings and drawings with images of the now completed projects and reorganizing of the text and biography she has brought new life to this edition. She deserves much credit also for the new cover design. Thank you Jocelyn!

— Adrian D. Smith

Project Credits

7 South Dearborn

Chicago, Illinois, USA, 1999–2004
Client: European American Realty, Ltd.

Design partner	Adrian D. Smith	Senior structural engineer	Robert C. Sinn
Management partner	Richard F. Tomlinson II	Senior technical coordinator	Richard Smits
Structural partner	William F. Baker	Senior MEP engineer	Ermenegildo Di Iorio
MEP partner	Raymond J. Clark	Project manager	Robert Pigati
Studio head	Steven Hubbard	Project team	Dennis Rehill, Hun Sang Lee, Mark Pearson

10 Ludgate Place

London, England, 1988–1992
Client: Rosehaugh Stanhope Properties, Stewart Lipton

Design partner	Adrian D. Smith	Technical coordinator	Peter A. Weismantle
Management partners	Alan D. Hinklin, Thomas Fridstein	Structural engineer	Ronald Johnson
MEP partner	Raymond J. Clark	Project manager	Thomas Scheckelhoff
Studio head	Michael Karlovitz	Project team	Art Muschenheim, Roger Whiteman, Peter Weismantle, J. Marshall Strabala
Structural director	Srinivasa H. Iyengar		

201 Bishopsgate, The Broadgate Tower, and The Galleria

London, England, 1998–2008
Client: British Land
Development managers: 3M, Broadgate Properties, Railtrack Property

Design partner	Adrian D. Smith	Project team	Jane Cameron, Ping Jiang, Lin Kim, Yukiko Kuwahara, Lucas Tryggestad, Michael Grage, Paul Bielamowicz, Michael Pfeffer, Ingedia Gonzalez, Min Kim, Matthew Allen, Sara Beardsley, Jason Eiler, Yetunde Olaiya, Shara Castillo, Jayshree Kacholiya, Thomas Kinzl, Jonathan Rule, Jaaydeep Bhagat, Peter-Rene Menken, Bozina Drzystek, Gretel Clausen, Mathew Staublin, Patrizia Bischoff, Kevin Rodenkirch, Henry Lee, Enjung Chung, Lynn Kubin, Brian Schirmer, Mark Andersen, Ron Orelik, John Gislason, Wilfred Yang, Annmarie Gonzalez, Makus Mayerhofer
Management partner	Jeffrey J. McCarthy		
Structural partner	William F. Baker		
Studio head	Timothy A. Poell		
Project manager	Lynn Boeke		
Senior technical coordinators	Richard Smits, Peter A. Weismantle		
Senior structural engineer	Ronald Johnson		
Mechanical engineering	Jaros, Baum & Bolles		
Project manager	Edward L. Thompson		
Senior interior designer	Nada Andric		

Art Institute of Chicago, European Galleries Renovation

Chicago, Illinois, USA, 1987
Client: Art Institute of Chicago

Design partner	Adrian D. Smith	Studio head	Peter G. Ellis
Management partners	Bob Hutchins, Robert L. Wesley	Project manager	Don Ohlson

AT&T Corporate Center/USG Building

Chicago, Illinois, USA, 1986–1989; 1989–1992
Client: Stein and Company, Richard Stein

Design partner	Adrian D. Smith	Studio heads	Peter G. Ellis (AT&T), Steven Hubbard (USG)
Management partners	Bob Diamant, Robert L. Wesley		
Structural engineering partner	Srinivasa H. Iyengar,	Project managers	Neal Anderson, George J. Efstathiou
Senior structural engineer	William F. Baker	Plumbing engineers	Paul Conkel, Joseph Jamal
MEP partners	Raymond J. Clark, P. Gujral	Project team	Peter Brinckerhoff, Avi Lotham, Yusuf Shaikh

Banco de Occidente Headquarters

Guatemala City, Guatemala, 1978–1981
Client: Banco de Occidente

Design partner (Zone 1)	Bruce Graham	Structural engineering partner	Srinivasa H. Iyengar
Design partner (Montufar Branch and 9)	Adrian D. Smith	Project manager	Adrian D. Smith
		Senior interior designer	Patrick McConnell
Studio head	Adrian D. Smith	Associate architect/engineer	Holzheu and Hernandez

Bank Boston Headquarters

São Paulo, Brazil, 2000–2004
Client: Bank Boston

Design partner	Adrian D. Smith	Project manager	George J. Efstathiou
Management partner	George J. Efstathiou	Technical coordinator	Nancy Carreon
MEP partner	Raymond J. Clark	Interior designer for bank	Jaime Valez
Structural engineering partner	William F. Baker	Interior designer for lobby	Nada Andric
Studio head	Chris Harvey	Landscape architect	Isabel Duprat
Structural engineer	Chuck Besjak	Associate architect	Escritorio Tecnic Julio Neves S.C. Limitada

The Beijing Central Business District Master Plan Competition

Beijing, China, 2004
Client: Beijing Central Business District Development Co. Ltd.

Design partner	Adrian D. Smith	Project manager	Xuan Fu
Management partner	Jeffrey J. McCarthy	Project team	Yiwei Liu, Juan Betancur, Alex Martinez, Lin Kim, Hinsang Lee, Dave Walker, Brendan Gibbons
Planning partner	Philip J. Enquist		
Studio heads	Gordon Gill, J. Marshall Strabala		

BTV Headquarters Competition

Beijing, China, 2002
Client: BTV

Design partner	Adrian D. Smith	Studio head	J. Marshall Strabala
Management partner	Jeffrey J. McCarthy	MEP partner	Raymond J. Clark
Structural engineering partner	William F. Baker	Senior technical coordinator	Lou Oswald
Senior structural engineer	Chuck Besjack	Project manager	Xuan Fu
		Project team	Byungkoo Lee, Juan Betancur, Quicho Gou, Christopher Hurst, Pom Itarut

Burj Khalifa

Dubai, UAE, 2003–2008
Client: EMAAR

Design partner	Adrian D. Smith	Structural senior engineers	Ahmad Adbelrazak, Larry Novak, Stan Korista, Bob Sinn
Management partner	George J. Efstathiou		
Studio heads	Kenneth Turner, J. Marshall Strabala	Structural team	John Viise, Arif Ozkan, Brad Young, Ines Lam Kermin Chok, James Pawlikowski, Ken Neal, Francisco Valenzuela, Margaret Wtorkowski, Ahmed Lemghari, Alessandro Beghini, Arkadiusz Mazvrik
Project managers	Ed Thompson, Nancy Abshire		
Technical coordinators	Robert Forest, Peter Weismantle, Eric Tomich		
MEP partner	Raymond J. Clark	Architectural team	Alejandro Stochetti, Jin Woo Jang, Scott Kadiec, Sue Lee, Li Jin, Jihu Zheng, Luis Villafane, Si Wu, Bridgett Thomas, Daniela Dan, Tatsuhiko Shibata, Brad Wilkins, Hyejung Ryoo, Daniela Gherovici, Ryan Dent, Vanessa Newton, Kamil Krol, Mohammed Sheriff, Mark Tirikian, Peter Freiberg, Greg Smith, Joanna Hartman, Gabe Wong
MEP team	Roger Frechette, Joe Jamal, Gil Dilorio, Luke Leung, Anthony Dauginas, Fazal Mahmood, Marion Wnuk, Mir Hameeduddin, Ewa Gnyra, Michael Filar, Noriel Nicolas, Ishac Koussa, Stefanos Peroustianis, Ricardo Quintero, Debbie Chiu, Bob Eshoo, Jeff Boyer, Margaret Hamielec, Phil Sawyer, Dimitri Papastathis, John Nieman, Predag Ungureanu, Patrick O'Reilly, Valliy Dawood, Yalliy Dawood, Miguel Gonzalez, Aurelio Gonzalez		
		Senior interior designer	Nada Andric (for residential public spaces)
		Interior design team	Dan Bell, Lynn Kubin, Joshua, Fiedler, Babette Scheidt, Eunjung Cho, Jeremy Olbrys, Andy Wright, Scott Struik, Chris Ciraulo, Katey Knott, Jungsoo Kim
Structural engineering partner	Bill Baker		

Canary Wharf

London, England, 1998–2001
Client: Phase 1 – Olympia & York; Phase 2 – Canary Wharf Ltd.
Projects: Phase 1: FC–2; Phase 2: DS–1, DS–3, DS–4, HQ–1

Design partner	Adrian D. Smith	Technical coordinators	Bernie Gandras, Lou Oswald, (DS–1); Chris Pemberton, (HQ–1); Peter A. Weismantle, (DS–4); Jim Zamorski
Management partners	Jeffrey J. McCarthy (DS–1, DS–4, HQ–1); Robert Wesley (FC–2)		
MEP engineer	Raymond J. Clark (FC–2)	Project team (DS–1)	Byungkoo Lee, Matthias Schoberth, Olaf Detering, Chris Morton, Qichao Guo, Juan Betancur, Blanca Chavez, David Simoneau, Liliana Dori
Studio heads	G. Joseph Reibel, (FC–2); Marshall Strabala, (DS–1, HQ–1); Kenneth Turner, (DS–4)		
Structural engineer	D. Stanton Korista, (FC2)	Project team (HQ–1)	Dan Lew, Rugel Chiriboga, Juan Betancur, David Simoneau, Chris Morton, Paul Bielicki, Caldo Lopez, Antonio Caliz, Chi Leung
Project manager	Rogert Forest , Edward L. Thompson, (DS–1, DS–4, HQ–1)		

CCTV Headquarters Competition

Beijing, China, 2004
Client: CCTV

Design partner	Adrian D. Smith	Project managers	Ed Thompson, Xuan Fu
Management partner	Jeffrey J. McCarthy	Senior technical coordinator	Lou Oswald
Structural engineering partner	William F. Baker	Project team	Byungkoo Lee, Juan Betancur, Rugel Chiriboga, Qichao Guo, Andrew Blocha, Chris Hurst, Pom Itarut
MEP engineering partner	Ray J. Clark		
Studio head	J. Marshall Strabala		

Central Bank Headquarters

Jefferson City, Missouri, USA, 2002–2004
Client: Central Bank, Sam Cook

Design partner	Adrian D. Smith	Project team	Christopher Varone, Nicholas Kent, Sun Yoo, Jenny Elkus, Michael Grage, William Hodge, Mark Roeser, Jane Cameron, Brian Schirmer, Mark Andersen, Lawrence Novak, Raul Pacheco, Bob Eshoo, Stefanos Peroustianis, Marion Wnuk, Luis Ferrer, Antonio Sumulong, Margaret Wtorkowski, Ninoss Bewargis, David Callan, Richardo Quintero
Management partner	Richard Tomlinson		
Studio head	Timothy A. Poell		
Structural engineering partner	William F. Baker		
MEP engineering partner	Raymond J. Clark		
Technical coordinator	Peter Weismantle		
Project manager	William N. Larson		
Senior structural engineer	Robert Sinn		
Senior MEP engineer	Philip Sawyer		

Chemsunny Plaza

Beijing, China, 2002–2006
Client: Beijing Chemsunny Property Co. Ltd.

Design partner	Adrian D. Smith	MEP senior engineers	Luke Leung, Phil Sawyer
Management partner	Jeffrey J. McCarthy	Technical coordinators	Richard Smits, Yue Zhu
Structural engineering partner	William F. Baker	Project managers	Mark Ladd, Xuan Fu
Senior structural engineer	Chuck Besjack	Senior interpreter	Xuan Fu
Studio head	Kenneth Turner	Senior interior designer	Nada Andric
MEP partner	Raymond J. Clark	Interior designer	Eunjung Cho
		Project team	Ping Jiang, Ji Lin

China National Offshore Oil Company Competition

Beijing, China, 2003
Client: China National Offshore Oil Company

Design partner	Adrian D. Smith	Project team	Jane Cameron, Noel Michaels,
Management partner	Jeffrey J. McCarthy		Nicholas Kent, Michael Grage,
Studio head	Timothy A. Poell		Paul Bielamowicz, Lucas Tryggestad
Project manager	Xuan Fu		

Commerzbank Headquarters Competition

Frankfurt, Germany, 1991
Client: Commerzbank

Design partner	Adrian D. Smith	Structural engineer	Srinivasa H. Iyengar
MEP partner	Raymond J. Clark	Project team	Matthias Royal Hedinger,
Studio head	Larry K. Oltmanns		J. Marshall Strabala

Gateway XYZ

Chicago, Illinois, USA, 2005
Client: Chicago Central Area Committee

Design partner	Adrian D. Smith	Project team	Leslie Ventsch, Alex Martinez,
Studio head	Gordon Gill		Brendan Gibbons, Tristan Sterk,
			Yiwei Liu

General Motors at Renaissance Center

Detroit, Michigan, USA, 1996–2005
Client: General Motors

Design partner	Adrian D. Smith	Interior space programming	Donna M. Palicka
Management partner	Richard F. Tomlinson II	Civil engineering	Mike Fink
Planning partner	Philip J. Enquist	Project team	Don Stark, Si Wu, Eric Zachreson,
Structural engineering partner	William F. Baker		J.T. Hsu, Scott Sarver, Lin Kim,
MEP partner	Raymond J. Clark		Greg Beard, Dan Bell, Dane Rankin,
MEP engineers	Phil Sawyer, Gil Di Iorio		Rich Brunett, Bob Blohm, Marion
			Wnuk, Stefanos Peroustianis, Ed
Technical coordinators	Anwar A. Hakim,		Jiang, Noriel Nicolas, Joe Kurt, Kent
	Jorge Soler		Jackson, Mark Andersen, Claudia
Interior design	Nada Andric, Jaime Velez		Misi, Fernando Fen, Doo Yuon
Planning	Doug Voigt, Toni Griffin		Kum, Inyong Lee, Al Khoshaba,
Project managers	Thomas P. Kerwin, Jonathan		Wilfred Yang, Andrew Murray,
	Orlove, Bill Larson		Luke Leung, Ernesto Ocampo,
Structural engineering	D. Stanton Korista		Luis Ferrer, Yusuf Shaikh, Fazal
Studio heads	Todd D. Halamka, Timothy A. Poell		Mahmood, Hal Hutchinson, David
			Valaskovic, John Roukis

Jin Mao Tower

Shanghai, China, 1992–1999
Client: China Jin Mao Group Co.

Design partner	Adrian D. Smith	Senior structural engineer	Mark P. Sarkisian
Management partner	Thomas Fridstein	Senior electrical engineer	Riad J. Jamal
MEP partner	Raymond J. Clark	Senior mechanical engineer	Ermenegildo Di Iorio
Director of structural engineering	D. Stanton Korista	Electrical engineer	Paul Kwong
Studio head	Steven Hubbard	Civil engineer	Michael R. Fink
Interior designer	Nada Andric	Project managers	Tom Scheckelhoff, Paul De Vylder
Technical coordinators	Peter A. Weismantle,	Senior architects	G. Joseph Reibel, M. Karlovitz,
	Louis A. Oswald		Chris Harvey, Homan Wong

Jubilee Park Pavilion

Canary Wharf, London, England, 2004
Client: Canary Wharf Contractors, Ltd.

Design partner	Adrian D. Smith	Project managers	Edward Thompson,
Management partner	Jeffrey J. McCarthy		Jennifer Hollingsworth
Structural engineering partner	William F. Baker	Senior technical coordinators	Jason Stanley, Anwar Hakim
Studio head	Todd D. Halamka	Project team	Ryan Mullenix, Joanna Hartman,
			Gabe Wong

Kowloon Tower (Feasibility)

Hong Kong, China, 1997–2000
Client: Mass Transit Railway Corporation

Design partner	Adrian D. Smith	Consulting MEP engineer	Flack & Kurtz
Management partner	Thomas Fridstein	Consulting structural engineer	Ove Arup & Partners
Studio heads	Michael Karlovitz, Timothy A. Poell	Associate ME engineer	Daniel Chan & Associates Ltd.
Senior technical coordinator	Peter Weismantle	Vertical transportation consultant	Lerch, Bates & Associates
Project manager	Paul DeVylder	Associate architect	Dennis Lau

The Lakeshore East Master Plan

Chicago, Illinois, USA, 2001–2008
Client: Magellan Development, Joel Carlins

Design partner	Adrian D. Smith	Studio head, planning	Daniel R. Ringelstein
Management partner	Richard F. Tomlinson II	Project manager	Jeffrey Pivorunas
Planning partner	Philip J. Enquist	Studio head, architecture	Steven Hubbard

601 Congress Street

Boston, Massachusetts, USA, 2001–2003
Client: Manulife Financial, Real Estate Division

Design partner	Adrian D. Smith	Architectural and engineering team	Andrew Blocha, Andrew Murray, Gil Dilorio, Noriel Nicolas, Stefanos Peroustianis,
Management partner	Jeffrey J. McCarthy		
MEP partner	Raymond J. Clark		
Studio head	Todd D. Halamka	Associate architects	Stull & Lee, Inc.; David Lee and Tom Clasby
Structural engineering partner	William F. Baker		
Director of structural engineering	D. Stanton Korista	Site architect	Douglas P. Murray
Project manager design phase	Jeffrey Pivorunas	Local associate structural engineer	McNamara & Salvia
Project manager	Lynn Boeke	Local associate MEP engineers	R. G. Vanderweil Engineers, Inc. Joseph Tremble, Steve Collins, Rich Dean, and Dan Cook
Technical coordinators	Bernie F. Gandras, Wells Squire		
Project structural engineer	Dane Rankin	Landscape architect	Sasaki Associates, Inc.

Millennium Park

Chicago, Illinois, USA, 1998–2002
Client: City of Chicago; Lakefront Millennium Managers

Design partner	Adrian D. Smith	Project manager	Paul Decelles
Management partners	Robert Wesley, Thomas Kerwin	Project team	Henry Lee, Ross Blumker, Peter Kindel, David Wei, Jin Kim, Erich Stenzel, Les Ventsch, Richard Yiu, Chung Yeon Won, Jose Valeros
Planning partner	Philip J. Enquist		
Studio head	Leigh Breslau		
Senior technical coordinator	Jason Stanley		

Mitsui Headquarters Competition

Tokyo, Japan, 1989
Client: Mitsui Bank

Design partner	Adrian D. Smith	Studio head	Timothy A. Poell
Management partner	Thomas Fridstein		

Zifeng Tower (The Nanjing Greenland Financial Complex)

Nanjing, China, 2003–2008
Client: Greenland Development

Design partner	Adrian D. Smith	Sean Doyle, Michelle Laboy,
Management partner	Tom Kerwin	Bradlet Wilkins, Craig Kolstad,
MEP partner	Raymond J. Clark	Elena Birkenkemper, Fei Xu, Yiwei
Structural engineering partner	William F. Baker	Liu, Simon Lee, Junta Kato, Peng
Studio heads	Gordon Gill, J. Marshall Strabala	Chang, Kiet Ta, Alex Martinez,
Project manager	Robert Forest	Brendan Gibbons, Tracy Ting,
Technical coordinator	Bernie F. Gandras	David Mallory, Greg Denisuik,
Senior structural engineers	Chuck Besjack, Stan Korista	Matthew Staublin, Eyung Chung
Senior design architect	Juan Betancur	Cho, Christopher Cirilo, Julie Baeb,
Architectural team	Wei Wei Luo, Jose Valeros,	Leslie Ventsch, Brian McElhatten,
	Binh Truong, Yue Zhu, Jeff Stafford,	Wilfred Yang, Ines Lam, Stefanos
		Peroustianis, Gil Di Iorio,
		Phil Sawyer

NBC Tower at Cityfront Center

Chicago, Illinois, USA, 1985–1989
Client: Tishman/Speyer Properties

Design partner	Adrian D. Smith	Studio heads	John Burcher, Leonard Clagett
Management partner	Robert Diamant	MEP engineers	Ermenegildo Di Iorio, R. Joe Jamal
Directors of structural engineering	D. Stanton Korista, Ernest Makkai	Technical coordinator	John Martinkus
		Project manager	Hill Burgess

Olympia Center

Chicago, Illinois, USA, 1978–1982
Client: Olympia & York; Chicago Superior & Associates; Equity Financial & Management Company

Design partner	Adrian D. Smith	Director of structural engineering	D. Stanton Korista
Management partner	Robert Diamant	Structural engineer	Sarv Nayyar
Structural engineering partner	Fazlur Kahn	Technical coordinator	Robert Phelan
Studio head	D. Legge Lohan	Project manager	Neil Anderson
		Consulting MEP engineer	Jaros, Baum & Bolles

Palm Tower Dubai Competition

Dubai, UAE, 2003
Client: Palm Tower Development (Nakeel)

Design partner	Adrian D. Smith	Studio head	Kenneth Turner
Management partner	George J. Efstathiou		

Pearl River Tower

Guangzhou, China, 2005
Client: China National Tobacco Guangdong Company

Design partner	Adrian Smith	Interiors team	Nada Andric, Eunjung Cho, Jungsoo Kim
Studio head	Gordon Gill		
Senior designer	Jeffrey Stafford	Project team	Thomas Kerwin, Robert Forest, Yue Zhu, Fei Xu, Elena Berkenkemper, Daniela Ghertovici, ChunHang Lau, Jaydeep Bhagat, Weiwei Luo
Structural engineering team	William F. Baker, Charles Besjak, Brian McElhatten, Xuemei Li		
MEP team	Roger Frechette, Robert Bolin, Teresa Rainey, Jeffrey Boyer, Michael Filar, Michael Scotter, Jacek Mateja, Arvinder Dang, Kevin Cahill		

Pidemco Tower Competition

Singapore, 1995
Client: Pidemco Land Limited

Design partner	Adrian D. Smith	Studio head	Todd D. Halamka
Management partner	Jeffrey J. McCarthy	Project manager	George J. Efstathiou
		Project team	Gordon Gill, Don Stark, Si Wu, Ted Strand

Rowes Wharf

Boston, Massachusetts, USA, 1982–1987
Client: The Beacon Companies

Design partner	Adrian D. Smith	Studio head	G. Joseph Reibel
Management partners	Alan D. Hinklin, Robert Hutchins, James DeStefano	Technical coordinator	Richard A. Smits
		Civil engineering	W. Winscott
MEP partner	Raymond J. Clark	Project manager	John Kelsey
Director of structural engineering	D. Stanton Korista	Project team	Peter VanVechten, J. Gonzales, Steven Hubbard, Lee Ledbetter, Jean Rieger
Director of planning	Karen Alschuler		

Samsung Togok Feasibility Concept

Seoul, South Korea, 1994–2000
Client: Samsung Corporation

Design partner	Adrian D. Smith	Project manager	Edward L. Thompson
Management partner	Jeffrey J. McCarthy	Project team	Youngho Yeo, Gordon Gill
Studio head	Todd D. Halamka	Consulting architect and engineer	Samoo Architects & Engineers

Saudi Aramco Corporate Headquarters Complex

Dhahran, Saudi Arabia, 1991–1993
Client: Saudi Aramco

Design partner	Adrian D. Smith	Technical coordinator	Richard A. Smits
Management partner	Alan D. Hinklin	MEP partner	Raymond J. Clark
Director of structural engineering	D. Stanton Korista	Project team	Todd D. Halamka, Anwar Hakim, Nancy Carreon, Nada Andric, J. Marshall Strabala, Jorge Soler, Ron Johnson
Studio head	Larry K. Oltmanns		
Project manager	William N. Larson		

Shanghai Grand Project

Shanghai, China, 2005–
Client: Shanghai Grand Development Co.

Design partner	Adrian Smith	Interiors team	Nada Andric, Jung Soo Kim, Fey Xu
Studio head	Gordon Gill	Project team	Bernie F. Gandras, Juan Betancur, Brian Devinck, Sean Doyle, Michelle Laboy, Yong Mei, Robert Forest, Weiwei Luo
Structural engineering team	Stan Korista, Brian McElhatten, Wilfred Yang		

Trump International Hotel and Tower

Chicago, Illinois, USA, 2000–2008
Client: Donald Trump

Design partner	Adrian D. Smith	Project team	Sara Beardsley, Noel Michaels, Michael Pfeffer, Elizabeth Bishop, Jaydeep Bhagat, Ingedia Gonzalez, Min Kim, Roimonn Hepburn, Michael Grage, Jane Castillo, Yukiko Kuwahara, Shara Castillo, Dane Rankin, Al Khoshaba, Karl Pennings, Jeremy Kirk, Kermin Chok, Markus Mayerhofer, Shane McCormick, Roman Przepiorka, Brian Schirmer, Mark Anderson
Management partner	Richard F. Tomlinson II		
Structural engineering partner	William F. Baker		
Studio head	Timothy A. Poell		
Senior structural engineers	D. Stanton Korista, Robert Sinn		
Project managers	Ed Thompson, Nicholas Kent		
Senior technical coordinators	Peter Weismantle, Anwar Hakim		
Technical coordinator	Lucas Tryggested		

Tower Palace III

Seoul, South Korea, 1999–2002
Client: Samsung Corporation

Design partner	Adrian D. Smith	Senior mechanical engineer	Ermenegildo Di Iorio
Management partner	Jeffrey J. McCarthy	Senior civil engineer	Brian Schrimer
Structural engineering partner	William F. Baker	Studio head	Scott Sarver
MEP partner	Raymond J. Clark	Project manager	Edward L. Thompson
Senior technical coordinator	Bernie F. Gandras	Project architects	Dae Hong Minn, Andrew Myren
Senior structural engineer	Ahmad K. Abdelrazaq	Associate architect	Samoo Architects & Engineers
Senior electrical engineer	Joe Jamal	Landscape architect	SWA Group

United Gulf Bank

Manama, Bahrain, 1982–1987
Client: United Gulf Bank

Design partner	Adrian D. Smith	Project manager	William N. Larson
Management partner	William M. Drake Jr.	Senior interior architect	Patrick McConnell
Structural engineering partner	Srinivasa H. Iyengar	Senior structural engineer	D. Stanton Korista
Interiors studio head	Klaus G. Mueller	Civil engineer	Brian J. Schirmer
Technical coordinator	Frank E. Heitzman	Consulting engineer	Pan Arab Consulting Engineers
Studio head	Larry K. Oltmanns		

Washington University Psychology/Biology Laboratory

St. Louis, Missouri, USA, 1993–1995
Client: Washington University (Dick Roloff, Vice Chancellor)

Design partner	Adrian D. Smith	Technical coordinator	Gregory Soyka
Management partner	Robert L. Wesley	Project manager	Brian M. Jack
MEP partner	Raymond J. Clark	Structural engineer	Charles Besjak
Director of structural engineering	D. Stanton Korista	Mechanical director	Paul Kiessling
Studio head	Peter Van Vechten	Electrical engineer	Paul Kwong
Senior technical coordinator	Bernie F. Gandras	Piping engineer	Stefanos Peroustianis

Xiamen Post and Telecomunications Center Competition

Xiamen, Fujian Province, China, 1995
Client: Xiamen Post and Telecommunications

Design partner	Adrian D. Smith	Director of structural engineering	D. Stanton Korista
Management partner	Thomas Fridstein	Technical coordinator	Peter Weismantle
Project manager	Thomas Scheckelhoff	Senior designer	Gordon Gill
Studio head	Todd D. Halamka	Project team	Don Stark, Homan Wong, Si Wu, Doug Burcham

Awards

1980

National AIA, Honor Award, Banco de Occidente

1981

Chicago AIA, Honor Award, Banco de Occidente
Chicago Chapter AIA, Interior Architecture Award, Banco de Occidente

1984

Chicago AIA, Interior Architecture Award, Citation of Merit, First National Bank of Chicago
Architectural Design Citation, P/A Awards, United Gulf Bank

1986

Urban Design and Planning First Award, *Progressive Architecture* magazine 32nd Annual Awards (jointly with B. Graham, T. Beeby, and S. Tigerman)

1987

Chicago AIA, Distinguished Building Award, 222 N. LaSalle
Chicago AIA, Distinguished Building Award, Art Institute of Chicago Second Floor Gallery

1988

National AIA, Honor Award, United Gulf Bank
Chicago AIA, Distinguished Building Award, United Gulf Bank
Boston AIA, Urban Design Citation, Rowes Wharf
Chicago AIA, Citation of Merit, United Gulf Bank

1989

Chicago AIA, Divine Detail Honor Award, United Gulf Bank, October
Urban Land Institute Award for Excellence, Large Scale Urban Development/Mixed Use Award, Rowes Wharf
National AIA, Citation for Excellence in Urban Design, Rowes Wharf

1990

Chicago AIA, Distinguished Building Award, Rowes Wharf
Chicago AIA, Distinguished Building Award, NBC Tower

1991

Chicago AIA, Interior Architecture Certificate of Merit, 222 N. LaSalle
Urban Land Institute Award for Excellence, Large Scale Urban Development/Mixed Use Award, Rowes Wharf
National AIA, Citation for Excellence in Urban Design, Rowes Wharf

1992

Chicago AIA, Distinguished Building Award, Certificate of Merit, Unbuilt Design, 12/13 Broadgate
Chicago AIA, Excellence in Masonry Award, Silver Medal, NBC Tower
Chicago AIA, Ten Year Interior Architecture Award, Banco de Occidente
National AIA, Citation for Excellence in Urban Design, Rowes Wharf

1993

Alumni Lifetime Achievement Award, University of Illinois at Chicago, Architecture Alumni Association
Urban Land Institute Award of Excellence, Finalist, AT&T Corporate Center

1994

National AIA, Honor Award, Rowes Wharf, May
Chicago AIA, Distinguished Building Honor Award, 10 Ludgate

1995

University of Illinois, Alumni Achievement Award
Excellence in Engineering, ASHRAE, Jin Mao Tower

1997

Chicago AIA, Distinguished Building Award, Washington University Psychology/Biology Building,
St. Louis AIA, Honor Award for Architecture, Washington University Psychology/Biology Building

1998

National AIA, Honor Award for Urban Design, State Street Renovation
National AIA, Institute Honors Award, SOM Foundation

1999

International Union of Architects Beijing, Jin Mao Tower
Gold Prize of Shanghai Classical Buildings, Jin Mao tower by Shanghai Municipality

2001

AIA Chicago Chapter, Divine Detail Award: Special Recognition, Jin Mao

2002

AIA National Honor Award for Regional and Urban Design, Lakeshore East Master Plan

2003

National AIA, Interior Honor Award, Jin Mao Tower
Chicago AIA, Divine Detail Special Recognition, Jin Mao Tower
Chicago AIA, Interior Architecture Award, Jin Mao Tower
Chicago AIA, Interior Special Recognition, GM Circulation Ring

2004

Chicago AIA, Distinguished Building Award, Canary Wharf DS1

2005

Urban Land Institute, Award of Excellence, Millennium Park
The Chicago Athenaeum/Europe, American Architecture Award, Jubilee Park Pavilion at Canary Wharf
Korea Culture and Architecture Design Award, Presidential Award, Tower Palace III

2006

National AIA, Honor Award, Millennium Park Master Plan
Chicago AIA, Distinguished Building Award, 601 Congress Street

2007

AIA Chicago Chapter, Sustainable Design Award, Special Recognition, 601 Congress Street

2008

FIABCI, Prix d' Excellence Award: Master Plan Design, Lakeshore East Master Plan
Architectural Society of China, Design Excellence Award, Chemsunny Plaza
Middle East Architect Awards, Green Project of the Year, Masdar Headquarters, Dubai, United Arab Emirates
Cityscape Architectural Awards, Best Environmental Concept, Masdar Headquarters, Dubai, United Arab Emirates
2008 ULI Award of Excellence: the Americas, General Motors Renaissance Center, Detroit, Michigan

2009

The Chicago Athenaeum/Europe, American Architecture Award 2009, Matrix Gateway Complex

The Chicago Athenaeum/Europe, International Architecture Award 2009, Matrix Gateway Complex
CTBUH, 2009 Best Tall Building Europe, Broadgate Tower, London

2010

AIA Chicago, Design Excellence Award, Special Recognition, 201 Bishopgate and the Broadgate Tower
AIA Chicago, Design Excellence Award, Citation of Merit, Matrix Gateway Complex
AIA Chicago, Design Excellence, Unbuilt Catagory, Matrix Gateway Complex
CTBUH, 2010 Global Icon Award, Burj Khalifa
CTBUH, 2010 Best Tall Building in Middle East and Africa, Burj Khalifa
R+D Award for Sustainability, Chicago DeCarbonization Plan, Architect Magazine
P/A Award, Architect Magazine, Matrix Gateway Complex

2011

AIA Chicago, Unbuilt Design, Honor Award, King Abdullah Petroleum Studies and Research Center
AIA Chicago, Unbuilt Design, Citation of Merit, Dubai Bridge
AIA Chicago, Distinguished Building Award, Citation of Merit, Burj Khalifa
AIA Chicago, Interior Architecture Award, Citation of Merit, Public Areas at the Residences of Burj Khalifa AIA Chicago, Special Recognition Award, Burj Khalifa Level 153

2012

Texas A&M University School of Architecture, Outstanding Alumni Award
Chicago AIA, SustainABILITY Award, Chicago Central Area Decarbonization Plan

2013

Illinois AIA, Daniel Burnham Honor Award, Chicago Central Area DeCarbonization Plan
Texas A & M University, Honorary Doctorate of Letters Degree, 2013

2014

Chicago AIA, Design Excellence, Distinguished Building, Federation of Korean Industries
CTBUH, Best Tall Building Asia and Australasia, Finalist, Federation of Korean Industries
Middle East AIA, Merit Award, Non-Built Projects, Kingdom Tower

Bibliography

Publications

1980

Interior Design, May
Chicago Tribune, June
New Art Examiner, June
Des Moines Register, June 6
Des Moines Register, October 6, "Wards block plan unveiling set for today", Capital Square
Des Moines Tribune, October 7, "Proposed building for Ward block", "Plan Told for Ward Block", p. 1, Capital Square
Des Moines Register, October 8, "Developers reveal model for 'The Square'", p. 6A, Capital Square

1981

Chicago Tribune, January
Dodge Construction News, April 24
Chicago Sun-Times, May 1, "Chicago, Oak Park projects win architecture awards", Banco de Occidente, p. 14
Chicago Tribune, May 4, "1981 Architecture Awards: Two Chicago Firms Win", section 4, p. 14
AIA Journal, May, "Glazed Gallery Behind an Elegant Tower", pp. 175–182
Progressive Architecture, May, "SOM at Midlife", pp. 38–49
Focus, June 8
Chicago Tribune, June 26
The Builder, Capital Square
Chicago Tribune, July 16
Chicago Tribune, July 18, "Building Renovation Planned", 228 N. LaSalle, Business Section *Chicago Sun-Times*, July 21, "The Ticker", p. 60
Real Estate Advertiser, July 24, "Office Complex at 228 N. LaSalle Street", p. 1, 228 North LaSalle, p. 9
Realty and Building, July 25, "85 million office plan revealed for 228 N. LaSalle Street", 228 N. LaSalle, p. 2
Crain's Chicago Business, July 27, Chicago Business Diary
Real Estate News, July 27, "Announce Plans for Restoration and New Development at 228 N. LaSalle", 228 N. LaSalle, cover, p. 6
Chicago Sun-Times, July 30, "Wacker rehabilitation weds old with new", 228 N. LaSalle, p. 87
City Edition, July
Chicago Tribune, August 9, "Wacker-LaSalle corner gets mix of old, new", 228 N. LaSalle, Real Estate and Rental Guide
Chicago Sun-Times, August 21, August 24
Chicago Tribune, August 21, September 23, September 28, October 26
Chicago Tribune, October 18, "45 million complex in Des Moines", Capital Square, section 14, p. 2H
Annual of American Architecture, National AIA
Chicago Architectural Journal, Rizzoli, Vol. 2

1982

Chicago Tribune, January 7
Chicago Sun-Times, January 7
Buildings Journal, January 25
City Edition, Office of Mayor Byrne, January
Modern Construction, Republic of China, January
Inland Architect, May
Boston Globe, July 4, "Rowes, Fosters wharves out to bid", section A, p. 1
Chicago Tribune, August 1
Chicago Sun-Times, October 1
Crain's Chicago Business, October 17
Des Moines Register, October 17, "Expansions help fill new Des Moines offices", The Downtown Scene, Capital Square, p. 4F
Commerce, November
Interior Design, November 2, "Shops, Stores and Showrooms: First Place", pp. 182–185, "Adaptive re-use: first place," pp. 206–207, 919 N. Michigan, Art Institute of Chicago
Inland Architect, "100 Years of Vision," Vol. 26

1983

Space Design, Japan, February 2, Capital Square, Banco de Occidente
Chicago Sun-Times, February 24
Architecture and Urbanism, March 2, Bally at Switzerland, Madison Plaza
Des Moines Sunday Register, April 24, "Capital Square: a new focus for downtown", Capital Square, pp. 1CS–16CS, 1F, 1
Des Moines Register, April 25, "The Ball", Capital Square, p. 1T
Boston Globe, May 7, "2 developers vie for a $100m Rowes Wharf project", Rowes Wharf, Real Estate section. p. 1
Boston Herald, May 13, "Waterfront makeover reviewed", Rowes Wharf, p. 24
Inland Architect, May, "Little Journeys to the Office of Architects", pp. 9–29
Chicago Tribune, June 5
Engineering News Record, June 9, "Chicago builders borrow", Olympia Centre, pp. 28DC–28EC
Chicago Sun-Times, June 23, "Tenants Looking to the West—525 West Monroe", 525 W. Monroe, pp. 91–92
Chicago Tribune, June 26, "Chicago's New Master Plan", Arts and Books section
Chicago Tribune, June 27, "Substantial lease transaction pending at new downtown office high-rises", 525 W. Monroe
Chicago Sun-Times, June 30
Chicago Tribune, July 3, "2-personality tower on rise in North Loop", section 10, pp. 1–2
Chicago Sun-Times, July 24, "Making a Grand Entrance", Olympia Centre
Montgomery County Sentinel, October 7
Chicago Tribune, September 23, October 12, October 21, October 23
Dodge Construction News, October 24, "Loop Transportation Center", p. 6
Chicago Tribune, November 2, "Neiman-Marcus", Olympia Centre, Styles section, p. 1

Chicago Tribune, November 6, "First World's Fair Wish Granted", 1992 World's Fair, section 4, p. 14

Chicago Sun-Times, November 6

Christian Science Monitor, November 15, "City's architects carry on tradition of innovation", Olympia Centre, p. 10

Chicago Sun-Times, November 20, "Neiman-Marcus Building Reflects Chicago Heritage", Olympia Centre, Architecture section, p. 24

Chicago Tribune, December 15

Pioneer Press Quarterly, Winter, "Camera's Eye", Olympia Centre, pp. 14–15

1984

Chicago Sun-Times, January 24

Chicago Tribune, January 29

Focus, January

New Art Examiner, January, "Can Chicago Live Up to Its Past?", Olympia Centre, pp. 8–9

Progressive Architecture, January, "United Gulf Bank", United Gulf Bank, pp. 104–105

Chicago Sun-Times, February 10

Focus, February

Chicago Sun-Times, March 12, April 22, May 1

Inland Architect, March

Progressive Architecture, April

Gulf Mirror, May 3

Progressive Architecture, May

Inland Architecture, May

Al Mohandis, June 2, United Gulf Bank, Arab African Bank Headquarters, p. 19

Chicago Tribune, June 10

Inland Architecture, July

Chicago Tribune, September 16, "Never fear: America's future buildings won't all have postmodern excesses", United Gulf Bank, p. 1, "Arch Rivals", Olympia Centre, pp. 25–29

Focus, September

Inland Architecture, September

Boston Globe, November 11, "$3 billion in projects changing the cityscape", Rowes Wharf, pp. 22–23

Real Estate, November 16

Parking, November/December, "Chicago's Loop Transportation Center", 203 N. LaSalle, pp. 37–39

Chicago Tribune, December 4, "Chicago's own style takes stage at architecture show", section 5, p. 2

Chicago Tribune, December 23, "Olympia Centre: A Tasteful Giant for the Avenue", Olympia Centre, section 13, p. 11

Commerce, December

Yearbook of Architectural Design, Van Nostrand Reinhold Company

Chicago Architectural Journal, Volume 4, Rizzoli

1985

Progressive Architecture, January, 1992 World's Fair, pp. 140–144

Nikkei Architecture, February 11, Olympia Centre, Rowes Wharf, pp. 120–125

Progressive Architecture, February, "In Progress", pp. 47–48

Building Design & Construction, March, "A Building Revolution Under Glass", 525 W. Monroe, pp. 176–180

Boston Globe, May 17, "Rowes Wharf project is celebrated", p. 19

Focus, May, "Institute Announces Fellowships", Olympia Centre, pp. 3–4

Wall Street Journal, June 19, "Transit Adds Appeal to Chicago Building", 203 N. LaSalle, p. 33

Chicago Sun-Times, July 12, "AT&T developer list pared to 3", AT&T, p. 48

Chicago Sun-Times, August 12, "Construction readied on 60-story building", AT&T

Chicago Tribune, August 18, "New Materials and Systems used at Arborlake", Arborlake, section 16, p. 28

Chicago Tribune, August 18, National AIA, section 16, Real Estate

Chicago Tribune, September 8, "First of Three Arborlake Office Buildings", Arborlake

Chicago Sun-Times, September 10, "AT&T picks downtown site for HQ", AT&T, p. 1

Chicago Tribune, September 10, "Stein gets AT&T nod to build Loop Center", AT&T, p. 1 *Inland Architect*, September, "Speculating on LaSalle Street", 203 N. LaSalle, pp. 20–22

Waterfront World, September, "10 Years Later, Boom Begins in Earnest on Boston's Waterfront", Rowes Wharf, pp. 1–5

New England Construction, October, "Up/Down Speeds Pace at Boston's $180m Rowes Wharf", pp. 8–11

Chicago Tribune, December 16, "NBC picked cityfront for image, space, and equity", section 4, p. 10

Chicago Sun-Times, December 19, "Impressive Beginning for the North Loop", 203 N. LaSalle, p. 110, "Drive westward results in honors", 525 W. Monroe and 222 N. LaSalle, p. 111

1986

Chicago Tribune, January 2, Style section

Engineering News Record, March 20, "Boston project grows up and down", Rowes Wharf, pp. 64–65

The New York Times, May 4, "Harbor project lauded for scale", Rowes Wharf, National Notebook Section

Chicago Sun-Times, May 30, "AT&T's Revamp Detailed", "AT&T Signs Lease on Big Building", AT&T

Chicago Tribune, May 30, "AT&T, developer sign downtown lease deal", AT&T

Inland Architect, July

Chicago Tribune, August 17, "Signs for Success: Bigger is Better at Office Parks", Arborlake, pp. 1C–2C

Chicago Sun-Times, Fall, "LaSalle Street Goes West", 203 N. LaSalle, pp. 15–17

News Release, October 22

Chicago Tribune, October 23, "NBC Tower Groundbreaking", NBC, section 3, p. 1

Chicago Tribune, October 26, "Designs for Lawndale Center Take Commonsense Approach", section 3, p. 1

Chicago Sun-Times, Real Estate Report, October 28

Boston Globe, November 9, "Design Completed for 75 State Street", 75 State, Real Estate section

Chicago Magazine, November, Upfront section

Building Design Journal, December, "Like houses, corporate reflect the tastes and needs of the occupants within", AT&T, pp. 20–21

Chicago Magazine, December, NBC

Chicago Magazine, December, "Keeping Up With Architect's Skyline Changes in Chicago", NBC, p. 13

Chicago Tribune, December 7, "Olympia Centre's Success Reflected In Its Windows", Olympia Centre, section 16, p. 1

Chicago Architecture Annual: (4), AT&T, NBC, 75 State, 225 W. Washington, pp. 250–279

1987

Chicago Architecture Annual, Exhibition section

Post-Modernism, by Charles Jencks, Rizzoli, Rowes Wharf, p. 32, 239, and 249

Inland Architect, January

Progressive Architecture, January

Nikkei Architecture, "North American Waterfront Development", Rowes Wharf, pp. 46–81

Chicago Tribune, February 13

Boston Globe, March 21, "A Primer On Building in Boston", 75 State, Rowes Wharf

Chicago Tribune, March 22, "Moderne redux", AT&T, section 13, pp. 18–19

Boston Herald, April

Chicago Tribune, May 3

Detroit Free Press, May 3, "Harbortown brings a new focus downtown", "Riverfront rival slowly taking place", Harbortown

Chicago Sun-Times, May 8, "Art Institute to let new light shine upon Impressionist", Art Institute of Chicago, p. 17

Chicago Sun-Times, May 10, "Art Institute restores the Beaux-Arts glory of its European Galleries", Art Institute of Chicago, p. 1

Interior Design, May, 203 N. LaSalle

Boston Herald, June 14, "Hub's best-looking buildings", Rowes Wharf, p. D4

Real Estate Forum, July, AT&T

The New York Times, August 16, "Chicago Reshapes a Treasure", Goldberger's Architectural View, Art Institute of Chicago, p. 1

Boston Globe, August, "New touches help sell pricey condos", Rowes Wharf, p. 39

Boston Globe, August 24, "A New Opulence", Rowes Wharf, pp. 17–18

Abitare, August, "Chicago"

Focus, "Five Years of Interior Architecture", Banco de Occidente, First National Plaza, pp. 26–27

Boston Business Journal, September 21, "Rowes Wharf: A Splendid Addition to the City", Rowes Wharf, p. 168

Boston Globe, September 27, "Lots & Blocks", 110–120 Tremont

Space Design, September, "The Third Wave in Skyscrapers", 203 N. LaSalle, 222 N. LaSalle, AT&T, pp. 6–48

Chicago Sun-Times, Special Commercial Real Estate Report, Fall, NBC, pp. 12–14

Patriot Ledger, October 9

New England Real Estate Journal, October 13, "Foster's Court: an arch built 20th century way", Rowes Wharf

Boston Globe, October 13, "How Great Cities Used to Be Made", Campbell's review of Rowes Wharf, pp. 65–66

Boston Globe, October 20, October 21, October 24, October 25

Fortune, October 25

Boston Globe, October 29, "A Matter of Taste", Rowes Wharf

Patriot Ledger, "Waterfront Renewal", Rowes Wharf, p. 26

Concrete International, October, "Up-Down Construction Sails into Boston", pp. 43–47

Chicago Tribune, November 1, "Sound Structures", 222 N. LaSalle, Art Institute of Chicago, section 13, p. 14

Art New England, November, "The Rowes Wharf Project", Rowes Wharf, pp. 20–21

Metropolitan Home, November, Hot Properties, Rowes Wharf, p. 34

Boston Magazine, November, Style, Rowes Wharf, p. 330

Boston Globe, December 19, "The Lobby is Back", 75 State

Boston Globe, December 20, "Lots & Blocks", Rowes Wharf

Chicago Tribune, December 27, "Chicago Honor Roll", Arts section, p. 19

Chicago Magazine, December, "Spaces", p. 134

Conveyor, December, "NBC Headquarters", Cityfront Center

1988

New York Post, January 8, "Real Estate—The Best", Rowes Wharf

U.S. News & World Report, January 11, "Dressing For Success", p. 47

Observer, January 17, "In the Shadow of St. Pauls", Paternoster, p. 2

Chicago Tribune, January 24, "A Stitch in Time", 225 W. Washington

Progressive Architecture, January, "A Mixed Review for Rowes Wharf", Rowes Wharf, pp. 47–48

Architectural Review, January, "Unbuilt London/Bracken/Stag Place", pp. 15–17, "Power to the City", pp. 18–38, Paternoster

Building, January 29, "Tea Party Spectacular", Rowes Wharf, pp. 42–44

Metropolitan Review, January, "Ten Super Projects", AT&T, NBC, 222 N. LaSalle, pp. 15–42, "The Super Architects", p. 49

Inland Architect, January, "Deference and Dignity", 222 N. LaSalle, pp. 50–53

Boston Sunday Globe, February 21, "Tremont Street Turns the Corner", 110–120 Tremont, pp. 29–30

FYI, February, "On the Waterfront", Rowes Wharf, pp. 3–12

Progressive Architecture, February, "In Progress", 75 State, p. 40

Chicago Sun-Times, March 1, "Tower Planned", NBC

Boston Globe, March 13, "Will Gold Save Office Towers?", 75 State

Boston Globe, March 27, "Lots & Blocks", 110–120 Tremont

The New York Times, March 3, "Tapestries Warm Up Modern Buildings", "Homage to Louis Sullivan", 225 W. Washington, p. 19Y

Architectural Record, March, "Harboring Tradition", Rowes Wharf, cover, pp. 48–54

Architecture, March, "Case Studies of Structural Innovation", Rowes Wharf, pp. 88–89

Building Design & Construction, March, "Harborside Development Becomes an Instant Landmark", Rowes Wharf, pp. 48–54

The New York Times, April 10, "A Project That Weaves the Cityscape Together", p. 40

Constructor, April, Rowes Wharf, Award Issue

Boston Sunday Globe, May 8, "Lots & Blocks", "Waterfront", "Boston Waterfront Attractions", "Rooms with a (delightful) view", "Some Boston Hotels Do Cater to the Budget-Conscious", Rowes Wharf

Miami Herald, May 15, "Architects Begin Convention in New York", United Gulf Bank, p. 1H

Chicago Tribune, May 15, "Fight over library may be one for the books", Chicago Library, section 2, pp. 1–2

Chicago Sun-Times, May 15, "Library unveiling five designs", Chicago Library, p. 5

Chicago Tribune, May 22, "The Library Card", Chicago Public Library, pp. 20–21

Boston Globe, May 23, "The man who made Rowes Wharf fit in", ADS, p. 1

Daily Telegraph, May 25, "Lessons from the Windy City", Rowes Wharf, p. 16

Chicago Tribune, May 29, "Books vs. looks", Chicago Public Library, pp. 10–11

Architecture, May, "Tower Responds to a Demanding Climate", United Gulf Bank, pp. 186–187, "Multi-use complex that 'feels like Boston's waterfront'", Rowes Wharf, pp. 118–122

Progressive Architecture, May, "A Bow to Bahrain", United Gulf Bank, pp. 65–73

Architectural Review, May, "News & Reviews", Canary Wharf, p. 4

Inland Architect, May, "Seeking New Identities", 225 W. Washington, pp. 54–59

Iowa Architect, May, "Developing the Atrium", Capitol Square, pp. 18–21

Wall Street Journal, June 16, "Architecture: Boston Reclaims Its Waterfront", Rowes Wharf

Wall Street Journal, July 26, "Architecture: The Prince Had a Point", Bishopsgate, Canary Wharf, p. 24

Boston Globe, July 28, "30-story office tower seen for downtown", 110–120 Tremont, p. 45

Boston Globe, July 31, "A fashionable address", Rowes Wharf

Architectural Record, July, "CRSI Awards: 1987 Awards for Excellence in Concrete Structures", Terraces at Perimeter Square

Orange County Magazine, July, "History Lesson: Boston Harbor Hotel at Rowes Wharf", Rowes Wharf, pp. 17–18

Urban Land Institute Project Reference File, Volume 18, Number 14, Rowes Wharf

Crain's Chicago Business, August 1, "Public's Role Helps Waterfront Project Click", Rowes Wharf, pp. 15–17

Tab, August 9, "What's Up Docks?" Rowes Wharf, p. 1

Progressive Architecture, August, "Remaking Museums in Chicago", Art Institute of Chicago, pp. 35–38

The New York Times, September 11, "Even Chicago is not Immune to Fashion", 225 W. Washington, AT&T, p. 35H

Chicago Tribune, September 11, "Twenty-five Reasons Why Chicago is a Design Town", SOM

Chicago Tribune, September 28, "Lake Co. Shows the Way North", Arborlake, section 8, pp. 19–23, "The Loop is Bigger Than Ever", NBC Tower, pp. 12–16

House and Gardens, September, "Native Hostelry", Rowes Wharf, p. 78

Pension World, September, "Equity Investments In Land Development: The Sky is the Limit", Rowes Wharf, pp. 14–18

Architecture and Technology, September, pp. 9–25

Progressive Architecture, October, "Perspectives", Bishopsgate

Banker and Tradesman, November 9, 75 State

The Other Side of the Waterproof Membrane, November, Chicago Chapter AIA, United Gulf Bank

Metropolitan Review, November, "The New Chicago Skyscraper II", 222 N. LaSalle, AT&T, 225 W. Washington, pp. 30–35; "The SOM Tall Building Urbanistically Reconstructed", NBC, AT&T, 225 W. Washington, pp. 48–53

Chicago Tribune, December 18, "Award Winners", United Gulf Bank, pp. 14–15

Chicago Tribune, December 25, "Stunning lobbies a welcome value", 225 W. Washington, section 16, pp. 1–2

The New York Times, December 25, "Fashions in Bricks and Mortar Make Room for Conscience", Rowes Wharf, p. 32

Boston, Photographs by Santi Visalli, Rizzoli, pp. 15, 220–223

L'Industria Delle Costruzioni, December, "Two projects by Skidmore, Owings & Merrill", Rowes Wharf, pp. 28–39

Illinois Chapter American Society of Landscape Architecture Awards Issue 10, 120 & 222 S. Riverside Plazas, p. 13

Immel's New Guide to Bahrain, by Peter Vine, United Gulf Bank, p. 116

Community Builders Handbook Series Mixed Use Development Handbook, Urban Land Institute, Rowes Wharf, pp. 182, 203, 302, 320–321, Olympia Centre, p. 147

Cities Reborn, Urban Land Institute, second printing 1988, 75 State, p. 41

Places, Vol. 5 No. 4, MIT Press, "Public Presence in Form: The Station and the Wharf, Boston", Rowes Wharf, pp. 9–12

1989

Chicago Tribune, January 1, "Competitive Edgy", NBC, section 13, p. 20

Chicago Sun-Times, January 6, "Kup's Column", p. 44, "Billion-dollar neighborhood sprouting", NBC, Homelife section, p. 1

Business Week, January 9, "The Best of 1988", NBC, p. 129

Boston Herald, January 15, "'Best' bldg? It's Rowes Wharf", Rowes Wharf, p. D2

Chicago Magazine, January, "Off the Drawing Board and Onto the Streets", NBC, pp. 111, 124

Architecture, January, "Americans Abroad: Some Coming Attractions", Canary Wharf, pp. 64–65

Progressive Architecture, January, "36th Annual P/A Awards", Smith, pp. 65–125

Focus, "Distinguished Building Awards", United Gulf Bank, p. 16

Chicago, January, "Building The New City", Special Issue, NBC

Inland Architect, January, "Inside the Liveable City: The Atrium", 203 N. LaSalle, 222 N. LaSalle, pp. 40–41

Chicago Tribune, February 19, "Canadian, Dutch firms join to invade Chicago", Dearborn Tower, Real Estate section, p. 16C

Focus, February, "Architecture Chicago", Volume 6: The Divine Detail, pp. 69, 89, 95, 97, 119, 155

Chicago Sun-Times, March 19, "Cityfront Center: a $3 billion neighborhood", NBC, p. 4

Chicago Tribune, April 9, "AT&T on the move to new center", AT&T Real Estate section, pp. 4–5, "Building tension", SOM, ADS, Arts section, pp. 4–5, 22

Chicago Tribune, April 21, "NBC's 40-story peacock", NBC, section 13, p. 18

Boston Sunday Globe, April 23, "A cheer for 75 State Street—warts and all", 75 State, p. B6

Foundations, Spring 1989, "Boston: Innovation Gone Up-Side-Down", Rowes Wharf, 75 State

Chicago Tribune, June 18, "Shining spaces", Interior Architecture of Banco de Occidente, Near North Title Company, section 15, p. 6

New England Real Estate Journal, July 25, "TA Comm. signs lease for 10,688 s/f at 75 State", 75 State, section 14

Focus, July, "Ten Year Awards", Banco de Occidente, p. 8, "Certificates of Merit", Near North Title Company, p. 11

Prostyle, Summer, "Details", Rowes Wharf Photo, p. 3, "Exterior Wall Symposium Held in Chicago", ADS, p. 4

Estates Gazette, August 12, "Architects Today", Bishopsgate, pp. 20–21

The New York Times, August 13, "Proof That All That Glitters Is Not Vulgar", 75 State, p. 32H

Daily Herald, September 30, "WMAQ move could introduce new era in TV show production", NBC, section 2, p. 4

Chicago, September, "Et Cetera", AT&T, pp. 146–147

Building Design & Construction, September, "75 State breaks away from anonymity", 75 State, pp. 34–39

Inland Architect, September, "Urbane Renewal", Rowes Wharf, pp. 43–49

PCI Journal, September, "1989 PCI Professional Design Awards Program", Rowes Wharf, p. 24

Design Solutions (Journal of the Architectural Woodwork Institute), Fall, "State Street Lobby: Atrium On a Grand Scale", 75 State, pp. 57–60

Chicago Sun-Times Commercial Real Estate Report, Fall, "10 Buildings That Matter", NBC, AT&T, 225 W. Washington, pp. 8, 9

Post-Tensioning Institute, Fall, "Project News—A Total Concrete Building", NBC, p. 4

Chicago Tribune Magazine, October 1, "A moving experience", NBC, section 10, p. 10

Clarin, October 6, "Abren la muestra 'Los rascacielos de Chicago'", AT&T, p. 8

The New York Times, October 29, "In Chicago, A New Romanticism", AT&T, NBC, p. H39

Focus, October, "Divine Detail Award", "Honor Award", United Gulf Bank, p. 13

CAYC, October, "Rascacielos de Chicago", AT&T, p. 8

The New York Times, November 26, "A Yankee Upstart Sprouts in Thatcher's London", Canary Wharf, p. 37H

Chicago Sun-Times, December 8, "New retail center inside Cont'l", Continental Bank Renovation

Chicago Sun-Times, December 15, "The 'Yanklands'", Canary Wharf, p. 49

Focus, December, Olympia Centre

Urban Land Institute, December Awards Issue, "The 1989 ULI Awards for Excellence", Large-Scale Urban Development/Mixed Use Award, Rowes Wharf, p. 19

Stone World, December, "Marble Street leads the past into the future", 75 State, pp. 26–29

1990

Entrances, Urban Land Institute, Rowes Wharf

UIC Newsletter, Alumni Notes, January, Rowes Wharf, p. 6

Architecture, February, "Chicago On the Rise", NBC, AT&T, pp. 78–83

Progressive Architecture, February, "Perspectives", "Urban Critique: Cityfront Center", NBC, pp. 121–122

Compass, Winter, "Adrian Smith and Urban Architecture", pp. 20–23

Sarasota Herald-Tribune, March 11, "In Chicago, a New Romanticism Rises in Skyscrapers", NBC, AT&T, p. 9l

Chicago Sun-Times, March 12, "Super Structures", AT&T, NBC, USG, 525 W. Monroe, 222 N. LaSalle

Forbes, March 19, "Everything's negotiable", 500 W. Monroe, USG, AT&T, River Bend, 225 W. Washington, Dearborn Tower, NBC, pp. 70–74

Architect's Journal, March 28, "An Insight into the American way of architecture", Canary Wharf, Bishopsgate 12/13, pp. 38–56

Tribune, April 4, "In Context", ADS architectural philosophy, section 8, pp. 26–27

Architectural Record, April, "Rich as Rockefeller", NBC, pp. 68–73

Chicago Sun-Times, May 7, 500 W. Monroe, Real Estate section, p. 47

Metropolitan Review, May, "Green Architecture", 10, 20, 222 S. Riverside, pp. 50–51, Cityfront Center, pp. 52–53, "Canadian Broadcast Center", pp. 82–85

Chicago Sun-Times, June 11, "High Style", Real Estate Section, ADS Chicago buildings, pp. 41–42

Providence Journal-Bulletin, June 19, "New panache for mid-city site", Providence Place

Chicago Since the Sears Tower: A Guide to New Downtown Buildings, Molloy, Inland Architect Press, Art Institute (#8), 525 W. Monroe (#19), Olympia Center (#28), 203 N. LaSalle (#31), 222 N. LaSalle (#38), 225 W. Washington (#42), NBC (#50), AT&T (#52), 500 W. Monroe (#75)

Washington Post, July 14, "Cityscape", "Second City, On the Rise", New Chicago Architecture Exhibition, NBC, AT&T, pp. C1 & C9

Chicago Tribune, August 18, "Moderne Romance", AT&T, Section 13, pp. 12–13

Providence Journal, August 19, "A velvet glove and iron will", Providence Place, Business Section, pp. F1–F2

Focus, September, AT&T

Architectural Record, October, "Good Connections", AT&T, pp. 94–97

Chicago Tribune, October 17, "The Fabric of the City", AT&T, NBC, Section 7, pp. 10–11

Building Design & Construction, October, "New Roles, New Rules for the Development Game", AT&T, pp. 72–74, "Focus on Architectural Hardware", NBC, pp. 128–130

Chicago Tribune, November 25, "Winning Designs", Rowes Wharf, NBC, Section 13, p. 26

Focus, November, "1990 Awards", Rowes Wharf, NBC, pp. 11, 13

Providence Journal-Bulletin, December 10, "Sense of Place", Providence Place

American Society of Landscape Architects Bulletin, December, "1990 Illinois Chapter Merit Award Landscape Architectural Design", Harbortown, p. 27

Chicago Architect: Roads Not Taken, Volume 8, December, Chicago Chapter AIA, Yerba Buena, p. 55, CBC, p. 56, AT&T, p. 65, NBC, pp. 67, 98–99, Rowes Wharf, pp. 69, 94–95, 75 State, p. 70

1991

Consulting Specifying Engineer, "HVAC design The Computerized Way", AT&T, NBC, p. 2

Ufficiostile, January, Architettura Arredamento Design Ergonomia Office Automation, Berlin Zentrum, Annual 24, Number 1, pp. 73–89

Building, February 15, "Glad to be international: the secret of SOM's success", p. 23

Competitions, Winter, Volume 1, "Chicago Public Library: Chapter II", Chicago Public Library, pp. 4–9

Chicago Tribune Magazine, March 31, "Building on tradition", NBC, pp. 11–18

Structural Engineer, April 2, "Docklands—Canary Wharf", FC-2, pp. 129–133

Exterior Wall Systems: Glass and Concrete Technology, Design and Construction, ASTM, May 1991, "Contextual Intervention/Technical Invention", Rowes Wharf, NBC, FC-2, pp. 24–34

Berlin Heute, June, "Projects for the Future of Berlin", Berlinische Galerie, Frankfurter Allee, pp. 47–52

Chicago Tribune, July 26, "Rollin' on the river", section 5, p. 3

Chicago Access, Richard Wurman, "Loop", AT&T, pp. 15–16, "Architectural Highlights", NBC, p. 181

Chicago Sun-Times Magazine, September 10, "Tall order", AT&T, NBC, pp. 7, 15

Bauwelt, October 18, "66 Building Wishes for the Center of Berlin", Frankfurter Allee, Item 63

Financial World, November 12, "Big-Shoulders Buildings", AT&T, pp. 46–48

Chicago Sun-Times, December 2, "Commercial Real Estate", NBC, 500 W. Monroe, 222 N. LaSalle, p. 39

Baksteen, December, "De Buurtvriendelijke Wolkenkrabber", 75 State, pp. 4–7

The Language of Post-Modern Architecture, by Charles Jencks, Rizzoli International, 75 State, Rowes Wharf, pp. 176–177

1992

The Times (London), January 28, "Canary's towering triumph", FC–2, Life & Times section, p. 1

Chicago Flame, February 25, "The upward mobility of Adrian Smith", p. 3

Chicago Tribune, March 8, "The eminent domain", SOM, ADS, NBC, AT&T, Arts section, p. 18

Architects Journal, June 24, "Working in Berlin", Frankfurter Allee, SOM, p. 52

Chicago Architecture Foundation 1993 Engagement Calendar, NBC

Boston Globe, July 5, "Where the City Meets the Water", Focus section, Rowes Wharf, pp. 63–65

City Changes: Architecture in the City of London, Architecture Foundation, 10 Ludgate, pp. 28–29

Chicago Tribune, July 19, "The highs and the lows", Arts section, 222 N. LaSalle, p.10

Energy Focus, July, Rowes Wharf

Building Design (London), September 18, "Learning at Ludgate", 1, 10, and 100 Ludgate

Chicago Tribune, September 23, "Going Global", Commercial Real Estate section, pp. 6–9

The Independent (London), September 30, "The last word in American accents", 1, 10 and 100 Ludgate, Architecture section, p. 19

Architecture, October, "Chicago Development Moves Out of the Loop", AT&T, pp. 26–27

Estates Times (London), October 16, "Berlin won over by SOM designs", Frankfurter Allee, p. 1

Chicago Tribune, October 25, "Deco delights", AT&T, NBC, Home section, p. 1

Ascent, Fall, "Using the Team Approach", Canary Wharf, NBC, Rowes Wharf, United Gulf Bank, pp. 8–17

Washington Times, November 22, "Chicago was always in the architecture loop", "Put the City Up" Exhibit, NBC, p. D2

Bauwelt, December 4, "Broadgate und Ludgate," Broadgate, Ludgate

World Architecture Review (Japan), No. 28, SOM Special Issue, Rowes Wharf, Banco di Occidente, United Gulf Bank, AT&T, NBC, 75 State, Broadgate, Canary Wharf, pp. 9, 25, 27–30, 38, 44

1993

Estates Gazette, January 16, "Right place but the wrong time", Ludgate Place, pp. 55–57

Chicago Architecture Foundation Memo Book, February, Washington University Psychology Building, p. 84

Northern Illinois Real Estate, March, "New Kid on the Block an Inviting Addition", p. 11

Stone World, March, "Admiring Canary Wharf's stone plumage", FC–2, pp. 35–46

A History and Directory of the College of Fellows, April, National AIA, ADS

Habitat Ufficio, April, Volume 61, "Dossier-Skidmore, Owings & Merrill", AT&T, USG, pp. 62–62

Inland Architect, May, "Last of the Towers", USG, AT&T, pp. 48–53

Chicago Architecture and Design 1923–1993, June, Art Institute of Chicago, AT&T, 203 N. LaSalle, ADS, pp. 27, 67, 324, 471

Focus, July, "Excellence in Masonry Award Winners", AT&T, USG, p. 13, "Project Spotlight", 500 W. Monroe, p. 15

Freitag, August 6, "Heldenverehrung verboten", Chicago Architecture & Design 1923–1993 Exhibit, p. 21

Progressive Architecture, August, "10 Ludgate", p. 88

Chicago Tribune, September 5, "Asia offers tall possibilities for area architects", Jin Mao, section 7, p. 1

Chicago Sun-Times, September 14, "Vested Interest", Continental Bank Renovation, pp. 8–9

Chicago Sun-Times, September 22, "Profile", ADS, p. 20

Architecture, September, "Commonwealth Edison", East Lake Substation, p. 159

Yapi (Turkey), September, "Skidmore, Owings & Merrill", 10 Ludgate, Canary Wharf, United Gulf Bank, Bishopsgate, pp. 47–72

Chicago Tribune, October 5, "Rising Career", ADS, Business section, p. 1

Architecture, October, "Industrial Gothic", 10 Ludgate, pp. 72–79

Ludgate, Broadgate Properties PLC, 1, 10 and 100 Ludgate

Urban Land, October, "A Tale of Two Cities", Rowes Wharf, 75 State, pp. 17–26, 37

Focus, November, "The Notebook", ADS, p. 14

Architecture Today, by Charles Jencks, Harry Abrams, Inc., Revised and Enlarged Edition, Rowes Wharf, p. 300

Cityscapes Boston: An American City Through Time, Campbell & Vanderwarker, Rowes Wharf, 75 State, pp. 110, 121

Marquis Who's Who in America, 1994 edition, ADS

A Guide to Recent Architecture, Hardingham London, Artemis, Canary Wharf, FC–2, 10 Ludgate, pp. 182, 187, 298, 299

The Best of British Architecture 1980–2000, E & FN Spon, Noel Moffett, Canary Wharf, FC–2, p. 59

London Architecture: Features & Facades, by Matthew Weinreb, Phaidon, 10 Ludgate

Waterfronts: Cities Reclaim Their Edges, by Ann Breen & Dick Rigby, McGraw-Hill, Rowes Wharf, pp. 115–119

World Cities, (London by Ernst & Sohn, Academy Editions), Canary Wharf, 10 Ludgate, 100 Ludgate, pp. 150–159

1994

Aberdeen's Magazine of Masonry Construction, January, 10 Ludgate

Chicago Tribune, February 1, "Coming up with perfect plans" Rowes Wharf, section 1, p. 18

Chicago Tribune, February 6, "Duel in the Sky" Jin Mao, section 10, pp. 12–19

The Architects' Journal, February 9, "New City Architecture Awards", Ludgate, p. 8

Focus, February, "How's Business?", "Chicagoans Win AIA Honor Awards", Jin Mao, Washington University Psychology Building, Rowes Wharf, pp. 5, 8

AIA Memo, February, "Honor awards reflect diversity in profession", Rowes Wharf, p. 13

Jiefang Daily, March 5, "High, Higher, Highest-Asia makes to build world's highest building everywhere", p. 12

Tagesspiegel, March 5, "Ein Hauch von Chicago in der Frankfurter Allee", Frankfurter Allee

Time International, March 7, "Anthems for The Millennium", Jin Mao, pp. 60–61

Insites, Spring, Chicago Architecture Foundation, "Architecture Around the World Ball", p. 7

Building, April 1, "Eighth Wonder of the World", pp. 14–15

Chicago Sun-Times Commercial Real Estate Magazine, Spring, "Special Export", Jin Mao, p. 7

Estates Times, April 15, "News", Jin Mao, p. 3

Architecture, May, "Distinction in Place", Rowes Wharf, pp. 105, 108

Shanghai Star, May 13, "American Architect Designing Jin Mao", Jin Mao, p. 5

Focus, June, "The Notebook", 10 Ludgate, p. 18

Newsweek, July 18, "Towers Rise in the East", Jin Mao, p. 60

Toronto/Chicago (German), "Stadtplanung und Stadtentwicklung", NBC, p. 54

AIA Guide to Boston, Second edition, Rowes Wharf, 75 State, pp. 57, 59, 68, 102, 104–105

Architectural Record, July, "The Great Leap Skyward", Jin Mao, pp. 32–33

Wen Hui Bao (China), July 14, "Urban Construction: Emphasis on Cultural Context", Jin Mao, p. 7

Student Life, September 9, "Where does this go?", Washington University Psychology Building

Chicago on Foot, Fifth edition, NBC, pp. 133–134, AT&T, p. 66, 500 W. Monroe, p. 98, 10 & 120 S. Riverside, p. 96, 222 S. Riverside, p. 93, Olympia Centre, p. 139

Chicago Tribune, October 3, "City architects' group passes out '94 honors", 100 Ludgate, Tempo Section, p. 2

Focus, October, "Distinguished Building Award", 10 Ludgate, p. 16

Time+Architecture, Vol. 32, No. 3, "Jin Mao Building, Pudong New Area, Shanghai", Jin Mao, pp. 2–4

Focus, November, "AIA Chicago Honors Design Award Recipients", ADS, p. 7

Metropolis, November, "Sears Tower", Jin Mao, pp. 25–26

Architecture Chicago, Volume 12, Distinguished Building Award, 10 Ludgate, pp. 82–83

Building, April 1, "Eighth Wonder of the world"

1995

Chicago Tribune, February 10, "Block busters?", 600 N. Michigan Block, section 1, p. 25

Xin Min Evening, February 21, "China's Tallest 'Pagoda'—A Glance at the Jin Mao Building", Jin Mao

Xin Min Evening, February 25, "Jin Mao Building Has a Solid Foundation", Jin Mao, p. 2

Progressive Architecture, March, "Asia Bound", Jin Mao, pp. 43–46

The Times, January, Council on Tall Buildings & Urban Habitat Newsletter, p. 1

Property Review, February/March, "Competing for the World's Tallest Building", Jin Mao, pp. 26–29

Illinois Quarterly, March/April, "Alumni Achievement Award Winners Announced", ADS, p. 12

Jie Fang Daily, April 18, "Builders on the Hot Soil of Pudong", Jin Mao, p. 3

Chicago Sun-Times, June 8, "State Street Sidewalks to Make Room for Traffic", State Street Renovation, p. 47

RIBA Journal, June, "Architecture as Part of the Global Economy", Jin Mao, p. 11

The New York Times, July 2, "The Great Asian Steeple Chase", Jin Mao, Section 4, p. 1

Habitat and the High Rise: Tradition and Innovation, 1995, Council on Tall Buildings & Urban Habitat, AT&T, p. 38, Jin Mao, p. 485, p. 488

Wen Hui, July 3, Jin Mao, p. 3

The New York Times, July 18, "From Debacle to Desirable", Canary Wharf, p. D1

Architectural Design, July–August, Vol. 65 No. 7/8, "Reaching for the Skies", Jin Mao, p. 96

Wen Hui, August, "The Tallest Commercial Building in China Has 88 Floors", Jin Mao

Jie Fang Daily, September 21, "The Placing of Concrete in the Foundation Mat of Jin Mao Building Starts", Jin Mao, p. 2

La Nacion, October 11, "VI Bienal, un exito esperado", ADS, section 5, p. 4

Chicago Sun-Times, October 22, "The Bears Mean Bucks for Chicago's Economy", Soldier Field, pp. 24–25

Crain's Chicago Business, October 23, "Soldier of fortune", p. 1, "Unless they get a defense, that's SOM bullish prediction", Soldier Field, p. 8

Chicago from the River, by Joan V Lindsay, NBC, p. 14, AT&T, pp. 40–41

Chicago Sun-Times, November 7, "Cleveland Latest Victim", Soldier Field, p. 92

Chicago Sun-Times, November 9, "Bears Mean Business, City Told", Soldier Field, p. 55

Chicago Sun-Times, November 16, "Which Plan Will Play?", p. 1, "Pipe Dream of Planet Park is a Universe Away From Here", Soldier Field, p. 123

The Times, November 16, "How the stadium proposals stack up", Soldier Field, p. D-3

Xiamen Economic Daily, December 8, "Tallest Building of the Century on the Lu (Egret) Peninsular To Rise", Xiamen Posts and Telecommunications

Chicago Sun-Times, December 13, "City Tries to Get Bears Talking Again", Soldier Field, p. 22

Hong Kong Standard, December, "Ho in $23b plan for super-island", Macau Entertainment Complex

1996

Asia-Pacific Space Design, January 2, "Skidmore, Owings & Merrill", Ludgate, Canary Wharf, AT&T, United Gulf Bank, Olympia Centre, Rowes Wharf, pp. 46–51

SCMP, January 3, "Developer says sky's the limit in Pudong", Jin Mao

Chicago Tribune, January 20, "Restoring State as a great Street", State Street Renovation, section 1

Chicago Tribune, January 24, "That Great Street un-malled", State Street Renovation, section 1

The New York Times, February 1, "Chicago Gives a Pedestrian Mall the Boot", State Street Renovation, p. A10

AIArchitect, February, "SOM: A Model of Resilience", Rowes Wharf, p. 1

Urban Land, February, "State Street: Reviving the Heartbeat of the Loop", State Street Renovation, pp. 14–19

Interiors, February, "In Xiamen: A flower tower?", Xiamen Post & Telecommunications, p. 9

Building Design & Construction, March, "Chicago launches Loop revitalization plan", State Street Renovation, p. 11

Chicago Sun-Times, April 1, "Chicago Architects Turn to Scraping Asia's Sky", Jin Mao

Civil Engineering, June, "Tall Buildings Triumph", Jin Mao, pp. 21–22, "Chicago Returns Traffic to Pedestrian Mall", State Street Renovation, p. 14

Building Design & Construction, June, "U.S. designers building a towering presence in Asia", Jin Mao, pp. 11–12

Chicago Sun-Times, June 11, "State Street rehab is back on schedule", State Street Renovation, p. 6

AIArchitect, June, "The SOM 24 Celebrate 25!", SOM, p. 1

Architectural Record, July, "Filling in the Missing Link", Washington University Psychology Building, pp. 84–85

Architecture, September, "Exporting Experience", Jin Mao, pp. 155–165

Landmark Chicago: The city of Modern Architecture, September, Chicago Athenaeum, NBC Tower, p. 23, AT&T Corporate Center, p. 28

Chicago Daily Defender, October 16, "Lighting up State Street", State Street Renovation

Asian Wall Street Journal, October 17, "Asian Cities Worth Living In", Jin Mao

Midwest Real Estate News, October, "Historic State Street gets new lease on life", State Street Renovation, p. C–3

Chicago, October, "Chiefs of State", Frontlines, State Street Renovation, p. 25

Eleven, WTTW Chicago Member Magazine, November, "Can Chicago Preserve Its Architectural Heritage?", ADS, p. 6

Chicago Tribune, November 1, "Holiday revival", State Street Renovation, section 3

Chicago Tribune, November 9, "Send-off set Friday for a reopening of State Street", State Street Renovation

Chicago Sun-Times, November 10, "Old magic, new look on Loop's State St.", p. 1, "A great street's rebirth", p. 20, "Most malls have failed to save downtowns", "State Street's new direction", Metro section, State Street Renovation

Chicago Tribune, November 10, "Things in-between", State Street Renovation, p. 1

Chicago Tribune, November 15, "New look suits State Street's future, section 1, p. 32; "Field's chief sees great profits from new State Street", section 3, p. 3; "Stately street", section 5, p. 1; "Celebrate on State—no hard hats needed", State Street Renovation

Chicago Sun-Times, November 15, "Ceremony to mark State Street opening", "City's heart starts to beat anew on State", State Street Renovation

Chicago Sun-Times, November 16, "Daleys help with a dazzling reopening", State Street Renovation

Telegraph, November 16, "State Street, that open street", State Street Renovation

Daily Herald, November 18, "'Sunset' star shines at State Street celebration", State Street Renovation

Chicago Tribune, November 19, "Some find oldtime magic on new State", State Street Renovation, section 2, p. 3

Chicago Tribune, November 24, "Altered State", State Street Renovation, section 1, p. 22

U.S. News & World Report, November 25, "The Automobile Returns to State Street", State Street Renovation

Chicago Tribune, November 25, "Thumbs up for improved Lake Shore, State Street", State Street Renovation, p.1

Chicago Tribune, November 27, "The grand return of a great street", State Street Renovation, Section 1, p. 1

Daily Herald, November 30, "State Street's reputation in no danger of slipping", State Street Renovation

Chicago Sun-Times, December 1, "Renowned firm was instrumental in State Street renovation", p. 7SS, "State Street lights up holiday season with traditional flair", p. 2SS, State Street Renovation

Chicago Tribune, December 1, "State Street crowds a dream come true", State Street Renovation

Era of High-Rise: Concept of Optimum Structure in Chicago, Olympia Center, p. 36

Chicago Sun-Times, December 3, "Merchants merry", State Street Renovation

Chicago Sun-Times, December 5, "Gimme shelter", State Street Renovation

Daily Herald, December 16, "State Street, that new great street, has ...", State Street Renovation, section 3, p. 1

1997

Wall Street Journal, January 3, "Ten Top Towers: The Pros Make the Picks", AT&T, p. B10

Chicago Tribune, January 3, "Gaining on great?", State Street Renovation

Architecture, January, "State Street, that Great Street", State Street Renovation, p. 31

Chicago Magazine, January, "Street Smart", State Street Renovation, pp. 47–48

American Planning Association, January, "'That Great Street' Hopes for a Comeback", State Street Renovation, pp. 12–15

Bâtiment, March–April, "Shanghai World Financial Center & Jin Mao Building", Jin Mao, pp. 11–12

Urban Land, May, Asia Supplement, "State-of-the-Art Building in Asia", Jin Mao, pp. 24–26

Chicago Sun-Times, June 18, "Spire vs. Antenna: New AT&T ranking revives tower dispute", AT&T Corporate Center, p. 8

Jung Ang Ui-Bo, "Conditional Approval of Samsung Kangnam 102-story building", Samsung

Place, Summer, State Street Renovation,

Pocket Guide to Chicago Architecture, by Judith Paine McBrien, W.W. Norton & Co., Inc., pp. 43, 70, 99, 101, 128

The New York Times, July 20, "GM Begins a Game of Musical Chairs", Renaissance Center, p. Y27

Engineering News Record, July 21, "More Record-Holders in the Ranks", Jin Mao, p. 8

Urban Land, August, "Main Streets on the Comeback Trail: Lessons from Chicago's State Street, State Street Renovation, pp. 31–32

Jiefang Daily, August 24, "No. 1 Building in China", Jin Mao Tower, p. 5

Construction Times, August 25, "Congratulations", Jin Mao Tower, p. 4

Jin Mao Tong Xun (Jin Mao News), August 28, Jin Mao Tower (by Shanghai Jin Mao Construction)

Hemispheres (United Airlines), September, "Tower Power", Jin Mao Tower, pp. 76–85

Crain's Chicago Business, September 1, "Chicago's Who's Who", ADS, p. WW48

Crain's Chicago Business, September 8, "Skidmore exhibit sketches 15 years of design history", ADS, Jin Mao, NBC Tower, AT&T Corporate Center, p. 38

Chicago Tribune, September 15, "China's No. 1 Building is World's 4th Tallest", Newsmakers section, Jin Mao

Chicago Tribune, October 17, "Architects select year's best in design", Washington University Psychology Building

Seoul in the 21st Century: The Role of the High Rise Building, Architectural Institute of Korea, "Architecture as Firmness, Commodity & Design", pp. 57–63

A Point in Space as an Organizing Force, St. Louis AIA, October 28, Washington

University Psychology Building, p. 4

Chicago Tribune, December 15, "State Street renovation gets national recognition," State Street renovation, Tempo section, p. 6

Chicago Tribune, December 25, "Wacker tower may bode new wave", 301 Wacker, Business section, p. 1

1998

Architectural Record, February, "Skidmore Sweeps AIA Awards Again", State Street Renovation

Chicago Tribune, February 3, "Busy State Street is bustling with new possibilities", State Street Renovation, p. 1

University of Richmond Architecture, February, Vernon May, Psychology Building

Silver Kris, March, "Buildings with Brains," Jin Mao, pp. 37–40

Corporate Real Estate Executive, April, "Shanghai's Building Booming" Jin Mao, pp. 38–42

Architectural Record, May, "AIA 1998 Honors & Awards", State Street Renovation, p. 127

ENR–Engineering News-Record, May 18, "View From the Top" (cover story), Jin Mao, pp. 24–28

Chicago Sun-Times, July 5, "Architecture often soars in spite of its occupants"

Chicago Sun-Times, September 11, "Loop Needle Wins City OK"

Chicago Tribune, September 11, "Plan Commission Oks 82-story Loop Tower"

Crain's Chicago Business, September 11, "The Chicago Plan Commission approved a proposal to build 82 story office tower at 7 S. Dearborn."

Metropolis Magazine, November 1, "From Mass to Membrane", King Abdul Aziz Airport

Civil Engineering News, November, "Skyscrapers–Spiraling Facade Highlights Xiamen Building" p. 16

Shanghai Today/Pudong, November, "Jin Mao: a pagoda for the 21st Century", pp. 22–23

The Wall Street Journal/The Property Report, December 2, Significant '98 Properties, "Five Exciting New Projects–Bold Developers See Opportunities in Big Cities World-Wide", p. B10

San Francisco News, December 21, "World's tallest building proposed for Kowloon"

The Fifth International Conference on Tall Buildings, 1998, Proceedings: Volume I, Edited by Y.K. Cheung, A.K.H. Kwan, "Kowloon Landmark Tower", pp. 78–86, "Design and Construction of China's Tallest Building: The Jin Mao Tower-Shanghai", pp. 139–144, "A Tower for the Twenty-First Century: Xiamen Posts and Telecommunications Building", pp. 177–180

1999

Metropolis, January, *"Cual es mas alto?"* "With a challenging Chicago skyscraper on the horizon, its antenna raises questions over bragging rights", 7 S. Dearborn

Chicago Tribune, January 17, section 7

Chicago Sun-Times, February 22, "Leaping into the Millennium", p. 16

The New Yorker, "Accidental Piazza" by Robert Polidori

The Wall Street Journal, Marketplace, March 17, "From Paddy Fields to Skyscrapers—A Glittering Hotel Rises in Shanghai's Pudong District"

Dialogue Magazine, April, "An Investigation into the Synthesis of Modern and Traditional —the Jin Mao Building, Shanghai"

Milwaukee Journal Sentinel, May 3, "Graceful Design Helps revive Chicago's State Street"

Whitney Gould Building Design Magazine, May 7, "Dockland Delights. Does Canary Wharf produce the finest corporate architecture in the world? Architects on both sides of the Atlantic seem to think so."

Asian Architect & Contractor, May, "Intelligent Building Supplement Landmarking Shanghai: Jim Mao Building"

Chicago Tribune, June 7, "New Plan for Tallest Building"

The New York Times, July 13, "Another Entry for King of the Sky"

Chicago Sun-Times, July 21, "Architects Criticism stirs high-level heat"

Civil Engineer, August, "Chicago Group Files Plans for World's Tallest Building" p. 12

Newsweek, August 16, "Who Says Size Doesn't Matter?"

USA Today, September, "High hopes, Chicago skyscrapers would be world-beater"

World Architecture 79, September, "SOM on a Shang-High Jin Mao Building, Pudong, Shanghai, People's Republic of China", p. 67

Newsweek, August 16, "How Big Is It? Building Up, Not Out, Reaches New Heights", p. 8

Crain's Chicago Business, September 6, "Who's Who", p. 67

World Architecture, September, "Winds of Change", "Planting the Future", The Mile High Club"

Chicago Tribune, September 12, "Fall spotlight on Architecture", section 7, p. 7

Building Design, August 10, "Chicago to tower again"

Architectural Record, August

Architectural Record, September, "Most contemporary architects have callously abandoned the social agenda set by the founders of Modernism", pp. 49, 50

Chicago Sun-Times, September, "Hopes are high for 7 S. Dearborn"

Chicago Tribune, September 22, "Hope's going up again for 'tallest' building"

Chicago Tribune, September 29, "City Council OK's world's tallest building"

Chicago Tribune, September 30, "Tallest building gets OK and some rivals", section 7, p. 1

Chicago Tribune, October 1, "A skyscraper for tourists? Cud you repeat that?"

The Christian Science Monitor, October 1, "Chicago's bid for 112 stories of glory"

The Economist, October 2–8, "Back on top of the world"

Milwaukee Sentinel, October 3, "Sensible design will count more than world height title"

ENR Magazine, October 4, "Chicago expected to OK plan for 1,550-ft-tall skyscraper", p. 11

ENR Magazine, October 11, "Chicago Approves Plan For 1,550-Ft-Tall Skyscraper", p. 9

Time, November 1, "It's a Tall World, After All", p. 38

Chicago Sun-Times, November 4, "Gift for the Century", p. 6

Collected Papers of Habitat and the High-Rise Tradition and Innovation, "Contextualism in a Multi-Cultural Society", pp. 3–5

Collected Papers of Habitat and the High-Rise Tradition and Innovation, "Intelligent Building Systems for the Jin Mao Building", p. 323

World Architecture, November, "Checking In"

Architecture, November, "Chicago's Tower Envy"

Building Design & Construction, "Does Size Still Matter?"

Extreme Engineering, December, "The Sky's the Limit", p. 66

Architecture, December, "Skyscraper Panic", p. 89

2000

Civil Engineering, January 6

WIRED, January, "Chicago Reclaims the Heavens"

New Zealand Design TRENDS, Vol. 15, No. 15, "Five star's feng shui", p. 46

Building Design & Construction, January, "Renaissance Center renovation", p. 9

Architectural Record, January, "Rising at the heart of Shanghai's new business district, the Jin Mao Tower designed by SOM reflects the new face of China", p. 82

National Geographic World, February

Popular Mechanics, March, "The Sky's The Limit", p. 57

Planen, Bauen, Wohnen, February 4, "Den Stolz züruck nach Chicago bringen", p. 79

PROJETO Design, February, "Nova sede do BankBoston, na zona sul paulistana, pretende ser 'oasis urbano'", p. 80

College of Architecture and the arts UIC, "Architecture"

Chicago Tribune, March 12, "Architecture"

Innovation, March, "Höchstform"

SPACE 88, "Skidmore, Owings & Merrill LLP—7 S. Dearborn Building in Chicago, U.S.A.", p. 158

Financial Times, April 15, "The world's tallest buildings", p. 53

Projeto Design, Maio, "Arquitetura de pagodes inspira formas do predio mais alto da China", p. 74

World Architecture, June, no 87, "Walking on water", p. 56

Elle Décor, August, "Sky High", p. 44

Architectural River East and Historical Plaza Cruises, 7 S. Dearborn

Chicago Tribune, September 20, "Downtown proposal thinks big, big, bigger", p. 1

Building Images: Seventy Years of Photography at Hedrich Blessing, ATT/United States Gypsum, p. 166

PORTFOLIO, The Art Institute of Chicago, "Skyscrapers: The New Millennium", p. 4

UrbanLand, September, "Park It Here", p. 36

re intériouro cree 2000, "Tour 7 South Dearborn, Chicago Tour Jin Mao, Shanghai Tour Kowloon MTR, Hong Kong", p. 42

Architectural Record, November, "Ambitious Development Proposed for Downtown Chicago"

SOM Evolutions (Recent Work of Skidmore, Owings & Merrill LLP) 2000, Jin Mao Building, pp. 68–73

Jin Mao Tower: Design, Strategy and Construction, China Construction Industry, August

A View From the River, by Jay Pridmore, Pomegranite Communications

2001

Chicago Tribune, January 5, "AIA Awards for Interiors—Jin Mao Tower"

The Wall Street Journal, January 19, "Towers of Power", p. W13, Jin Mao

FOCUS, newsletter of AIA Chicago, February, "Chicago Well-Represented in National Design Awards"

FACE The East, March, "Asia's Tower of Power"

The New York Times, March 2, "Stun-Gun Reality, Magnificent In Its Artifice"

Estates Gazette (London), March

Chicago Sun-Times, March 16, "Lakeshore East plan approved", p. 50 N

Chicago Sun-Times, March, "Developer Building North and South"

Architects' Journal, March

Domus, April, "7 South Dearborn"

Architectural Record, May, "American Institute of Architects Honor Awards", p. 129

House & Garden, June, "Reach for the Sky"

World Architecture, June, "The $30,000 question ...", p. 78

Skyscrapers: The New Millennium, John Zukowsky (ed), Prestel Publishing, pp. 112, 134, 141

The Tampa Tribune, August 20, "Vertical Extreme"

Chicago Tribune, October 15, "Making buildings terror-proof", p. 1

Anuario Arquitetura & Engenharia Os Melhores Profeissionais—Os Melhores Produtos, p. 230

The Architectural Review, October, "View", p. 28

Canary, Winter, "The Architecture of Canary Wharf", (supplement guide)

Encyclopedia Britannica, Year in Review, "Architecture and Civil Engineering", Jin Mao, p. 164

Domus, September, "The tower and the city"/"The tower breaks out of the box", pp. 44–51, "The Chicago School", p. 97

2002

Grid, April, "Midwest Movers"

Facility, Ano V, "Nova sede do BankBoston"

Chicago Sun-Times, June 27, "Revised Trump tower picks up civic support"

Projecto Design, July, BankBoston

Chicago Tribune, July 31, "Redeemed"

Architectural Record, September, "Design modified for SOM's Trump Tower Chicago"

Architecture and Urbanism (A+U), November, pp. 39–42, 57, 142–143.

The New York Times, November 14, "Shanghai Polishes Up Its Rough Edges", House & Home section

Through the Lens, The Images Publishing Group, Jin Mao, p. 78

Os Rios e as Cidades (The Rivers and the Cities), by Nobuyoshi Chinen and Pier Luigi Cabra, Bank of Boston

World Architecture 149, November, pp. 16, 17, 23, 24, 25, 26, 27, 28, 29, 30, 31, 32–36, 46–51

Urban Land, November/December, "Modernist Vocabulary", pp. 114–121

Pro Architect Monograph #24, Adrian D. Smith, FAIA

In The Loop, Spring, The School of the Art Institute of Chicago, "The Art of Architecture", p. 10

2003

BuildingEnvelopes.org, Jin Mao Building

Daylighting Performance and Design, by Gregg Ander, FAIA, 2nd edition, Wiley

Focus, "Two Chicago Firms in Green Exhibition at National Building Museum", Manulife Financial

Popular Science, March, "How High Will They Build?", pp. 60–71

Sky High: Vertical Architecture, by Chris Abel, Royal Academy Books, pp. 105, 111

Brasil: Contemporary Architecture, (mini CD-ROM), The Embassy of Brazil

Concept magazine, April 4, "Skidmore, Owings & Merrill", pp. 52–61,

Gulf News (Online Edition), May, "Emaar opens registration for Burj Dubai"

Chicago Sun-Times, June, "Skidmore to design next 'world's tallest'—in Dubai"

Architectural Record, July, "SOM designs world's tallest tower for Dubai developer", p. 30

Identity, August/September, "Tall Order", p. 79

AW (Architecture World), no. 100, "Pro Architect Adrian Smith", pp. 120–131

Chicago Tribune, September 24, "Trump Unwraps Building Plan", p. 1, "Improved Design Wrapped In Promises"

A+U Architecture and Urbanism, 03:12, pp. 53, 80–83, CCTV

Architectural Record, December, "So far, so good with design for Trump's new Chicago tower", p. 22

Skyscrapers.com, "Skidmore, Owings & Merrill (SOM)"

Tall Buildings, The Museum of Modern Art, pp. 138–143, 170–175

Environmental Design + Construction, September/October, "Architecturally Integrated Photovoltaics", p. 28

Skyscrapers, by Antonino Terranova, Barnes & Noble, Jin Mao

2004

Sky High Living, Contemporary High-Rise Apartment and Mixed-Use Buildings, The Images Publishing Group, Olympia Centre, 7 S. Dearborn, pp. 30, 229

Construction Week, Feb–March, "World's Tallest", p. 13

Metropolis, April, "Tall, Taller, Tallest", pp. 148–150

Chicago Tribune, April 18, "Chicago's Bold Rebirth"

Architectural Record, May, "Upcoming building projects help establish a new design tradition", p. 95

Urban Land Magazine, May, "A New Lakefront Neighborhood in the Heart of Downtown Chicago", p. 65

Chicago Tribune, May 26, "UAE tower to surpass 2,000 feet"

Chicago Sun-Times, June 14, "From fountain to Rookery, survey notes 'best of best'"

Urban Land Institute, "Beyond Oil", August 2004, p. 36

New York (NY) Newsday, August 1, "Reaching for the sky"

Fachthemen, "GM Football—Vestibule of the General Motor's Headquarters, Detroit", pp. 552–561

Remaking the Urban Waterfront, Urban Land Institute, p. 55

The New York Times, September 15, "G.M. Helps to Drive a Detroit Revival"

The Slatin Report, September 15, "Mideast Taller Tale"

Skyscrapers, by Andres Lepik, Prestel Publishing, pp. 22, 126–127, 148–149

Shanghai—Architecture & Urbanism For Modern China, pp. 85, 113

Focus, October, "Distinguished Building Awards", AIA Chicago, p. 7

Midwest Construction, October, "Walking Through Chicago's Millennium Park"

AW (Architecture World), "Adrian D. Smith, Skidmore, Owings & Merrill LLP"

Architectural Record, November, "7 South Dearborn", p. 57,

La Derniere Heure (Les Sports), December, "Des Belges au sommet mondial", p. 6

Standaard, December, pp. 50–51

Business Times, December 9, "Emaar awards Burj Dubai Tower deal to Samsung"

De Morgen, December 10, "Hoogste gebouw ter wereld kan nog hoger", p. 16

Gazet Van Antwerpen, December 10, "Toren van 705 meter 'sleutel op de deur'", p. 15

Le Soir, December 10, "Besix vise trés, trés, trés haut a Dubai", p. 16

Het Laatste Nieuws, December 10, "Wij, Belgan, bouwen hoogstetoren ter wereld Strasf, HE" p. 5

Le Vif (L'Express), December 17, "Construction Plus haut", p. 12

Korean Central Daily (Toronto, Ontario), December 10, 11

Time, December 27, "Kissing the Sky", pp. 170–173

2005

Taiwan Architect, no. 353, "Adrian Smith, A Sky City-Interview with Adrian Smith", pp. 96–103

Metropolis Magazine, January, "City, Rereaching for the Stars", pp. 84–85

Intelligent Building, no. 3, p. 74

Morocco Times.com, January 2, "UAE The world's tallest skyscraper will be in Dubai in 2008"

The Economist, "Tall Story Dubai's dream, every vertigo sufferer's nightmare"

Canada News.com, March, "Dubai skyscraper to bring world's tallest structure to the Middle East"

Chicago Sun-Times, March 23, "Sky's the Limit"

AME Info, March 28, "Burj reaches defining moment as world's tallest building begins to rise"

The Virginian-Pilot, March 31, "Higher Ground"

Visionary Chicago, Chicago Central Area Committee

Netscape News, March 30, "Dubai Looks to Build Tallest Skyscraper"

Time, April 25, "Kissing the Sky", pp. 46–53

Hong Kong Engineer, July, "Dubai takes on the super-high rise challenge"

Space, Asia's Super-Tall Buildings, pp. 75, 76, 95, 98

The Observer, July 31, "Dizzy Heights", 201 Broadgate

Cityscape (The Official Preview Magazine), August, "Burj Dubai Rises and Rises", p. 10

Id+ (Living Design), September, "Virkelighedens Xanadu", p. 84

Communication Arts, September, Tall Buildings, Jin Mao

Greenroofs, September 28, "Category: Intensive Industrial/ Communities, project: Millennium Park, Chicago, Illinois"

RIBA World, no. 387, September 30, "The Sky's No Limit"

Chicago Architecture and Design, by Jay Pridmore & George Larson, Harry Abrams, Inc., pp. 206–210, 272, NBC Tower, Millennium Park

Architectural Record, "Tall Tales"

Architecture of Skyscrapers, by Francisco Asensio Cerver, Watson-Guptill Publications

AIArchitect, September 8, "SOM's Adrian Smith Honored for Service to Comm. Cancer Center"

Chicago Sun-Times, November 27, "The Man of Steel Able to Leap Tall Buildings", p. 1D, 5D

Business Week Online, December, Jin Mao

2006

Architectural Record, December, "SOM's Pearl River," p. 172

Bâtiment, December, "La tour mixte, signal urbain au coeur de la ville de demain?"

Chicago Sun-Times, "Architect's dream project," p. 31A

I4design, September, "Green with Envy," p. 67

Wallpaper, August, "Peak Performance," p. 91

Metropolis, July, "Super Tall and Ultra Green," pp. 106–107

Architectural Record, June 15, "Not innovative? SOM'S Skyscraper Projects in China Tell a Different Story"

Dwell, June, "Shanghai," p. 112

The Charlotte Observer, June, Pearl River

Ark, June, Burj Dubai

Focus, AIA Chicago, May, Pearl River Tower—Guangzhou China, p. 24

Architect, May, "Arabian Heights," pp. 126–133

Architectural Record, April 27, "SOM aims to build a zero-energy office tower in Guangdong"
Business Week, March, "Dubai's Architectural Wonders"
ARX (Building), March, Jin Mao, p. 106
Sheridan Road Magazine, "Leaping Tall Buildings...In a Single Bound," p. 42
Mercedes Magazine, Pearl River
High Society Magazine, "Burj Dubai," p. 118
Engineering Tall Buildings Conference, brochure, Burj Dubai, Trump, Jin Mao
Denver Museum of Nature and Science, Burj Dubai
Chicago Magazine, Shangri-la

2007

Metropolis, November 8, "Beyond the Spectacle"
The Chicago Tribune, November 7, "Developers embracing 'green' to gain an edge," p. 3
Sunday Times, November 4, "City Salvation"
Gulf News, September 5, "Ground Breaking"
Chicago Sun-Times, October 12, "Tall order for tower," p. 57
Blueprint, October, "A New Practice with a Zero Energy Approach", p. 47
Bund Pictorial, October, "The Work of Adrian Smith"
The Architect's Newspaper, "Imitation of Life," 05 September, 2007
Chicago Magazine, September, "Chicago Architecture in 2020," p. 94
GQ, September, "Green Giants," pp. 221–222
The Chicago Tribune, August 19, "How to build today's supertalls"
Architectural Record, August 17, "The Skyscraper: Still Soaring"
The Big Project, Issue 7, "Viewpoint: Sustainability has deep roots," pp. 74–77
UIC Alumni Magazine, July/August, "Unfinished Business," p. 14
Chicago Sun-Times, August 16, "Sears Tower hires green architects," Business briefs
El Tiempo, July 28, "En flores se inspiró Adrian Smith para diseñar la torre más alta del mundo: el Burj Dubai"
Chicago Sun-Times, July 24, " Chicago Architect Says World's Tallest Building Still Growing"
CNN Traveller, May/June, "World of Tomorrow"
GULF Life, May, "High, Higher, Highest," pp. 34–38, 40,42
JAM: Art, Architecture & Design, Spring/Summer, "Interview: large-scale mixed-use and supertall; The American architect Adrian Smith," pp. 31–35
Chicago Magazine, February, "A New Order," pp. 62–65, 98–104
The American Magazine, January/February, "Lust for Height," p. 16
Business Times, January 17, "Burj Dubai is 100 Stories High," p. 1
Urban Land, January, "Managing Risk Before and During Construction," p. 142
Metropolis, January, "Parting Company," pp. 30, 32
The Big Project, Issue 2, "King Abdullah Economic City: Honored for Service to Comm. Cancer Center"
Id+, "Saudi's single largest private sector investment," pp. 34–43

2008

Millionaire, December Issue 11, "Yearning to soar," pp. 36–43
Living Design, Winter 2008, "Den Gronne Skyskraber," pp. 34–36
Residence, Number 7, "Renast i varlden," p. 72
Green Source, November/December, "Urban Harvest", pp. 108–113
The Columbus Dispatch, November 30, "Tall tales: ever-higher buildings reflect solutions for the future"

The New York Times, November 19, "A new wind is blowing in Chicago"
Globe and Mail, November 11, "A building with an energy all its own"
The Chicago Tribune, November 3, "Skyline on pause: Credit crunch leaves Spire, other towers short"
identity, November, "The future is now", pp. 106–110; "Green giants," pp. 112–113
Solares Bauen, November, "Masdar-Hauptquartier Bei Abu Ahabi Von AS+GG Architecture: Ultra Green," pp.80–81
Cityscape Magazine, November, "Cityscape Dubai: the regional reality", pp. 30–33; "New look for old", pp. 40–42 GEO, November, "Masdar City: Die Null-Emmissions-Stadt in der Wuste"
Travel + Leisure, November, "New American Landmarks," p.221–230
The National, October 30, "Architectural 'exuberance' could slow"
Metropolis, October, "Innovation from the Innovators" Globe and Mail, October 18, "Market panic? Bring it on" Business Week, October 15, "Undaunted, skyscrapers reach higher"
Building, October 14, "The tallest building in the world: the contenders"
World Architecture News, October 9, "Meraas Development taps Adrian Smith + Gordon Gill for megaproject"
The National, October 8, "Tall Buildings put us on the map, says Burj Dubai architect"
Building, October 8, "Sears tower set for L85m green makeover"
The Chicago Sun-Times, October 8, "Developers turn to rentals in downturn"
The Chicago Tribune, October 7, "Chicago architects plan more towers in Dubai"
Khaleej Times, October 7, "Cityscape $1 trillion showcase," p. 1
The National, October 6, "Dubai sees no reason to stop scraping skies"
Building, October 3, "Burj Dubai: Top of the world"
Crain's Chicago Business, September 1, 2008, "Who's Who: Chicago's Power", p. 18
The Chicago Tribune, August 28, "Getting the inside story on the Pearl River Tower, billed as the world's greenest skyscraper"
The Wall Street Journal, August 20, "Skyline Gets Facelit Ahead of Asian Games"
International Herald Tribune, August 12, "Rising in Dubai: Adrian Smith's Vision of Green: taller and getting taller"
New York Times, August 10, "Reaching for the clouds in Dubai," p. 24
The Chicago Tribune, August 5, "Why do the Olympics start on 8-08 at 8:08 pm? For the same reason that many Chinese skyscrapers are 88 stories tall"
BPM, Issue 91, Summer 2008, "Masdar," p. 12
Limited Edition, Summer 2008, "Adrian Smith; The Master of Skyscrapers," pp. 18–22
Shanghai: The Architecture of China's Great Urban Center, p. 66–67
Chicago Public Radio, "Architects Float Idea for Bridge"
The Big Project, Issue 10, "Geometrics of the Desert Flower"
The New York Times, June 15, "Scraping the sky and then some," p. 20
The Chicago Tribune, June 15, "Chicago Architect Walter A. Netsch Dies at 88"
Architect, June 8, "Positive Energy," p. 74–79
AIArchitect, June 6, "Adrian Smith, FAIA, RIBA"
Crain's, June 2, "Smith & Gill Wins Dubai Deal," p. 21
Focus, June, "The Rise and Rise of the Superscraper," pp. 34–42
Chicago Architect, June, "The Next Big Thing," pp. 32–35
The Sunday Times, May 11, "Dinosaurs bite the dust," p. 10
Gulf News, May 9, "Dubai Gives the Necessary Freedom Designers Need"
Architectural Record, May 7, "Smith + Gill Tapped for Ultra-Green Project," p. 29
Gulf News, May 4, "Dubai: City of Supertowers"
Modern Design, May, "The 11 Hour and the Carbon Conflict: Smooth Operator," p. 75
Gulf Life, May 1, "Head in the Clouds"
Khaleej Times, April 28, "Man of Many Storeys"
Real Estate Forum Magazine, April 8, "Abu Dhabi Sustainable Project Moves Forward," p. 8

AIArchitect, April 4, "Beyond Zero: Adrian Smith + Gordon Gill Architecture's Desert Experiment"
Middle East Architect, April, "Sprawl to Tall," pp. 14–15
Engineering News-Record, "Building sector needs reeducation," p. 10
Regina Leader Post, March 12, "Architects Building New Cities"
Emirates Business 24/7, March 7, "Giving Shape to Big Ambitions and Tall Buildings Around the World"
Skyscrapers, March, "Post-Modernism and the Rise of the Middle East," p. 108–109
Building, February, Issue 8, "The Middle East green building challenge"
Financial Times, February 27, "Walkable, Pleasant, Urbane, Hot"
The Chicago Tribune, February 24, "Sweet New Start for Chicago Architect," Section 5
Chicago Public Radio, February 22, "Radio Interview"
The Chicago Tribune, February 22, "'Green' Light for Chicago Design"
Enjeux Les Echos, January, "Adrain Smith; Paris-La Defense a Besoin d'une tour de 500 m de haut"

2009

Engineering News-Record, December 9, "Design team held to competition promises"
The Plan, December, "Abu Dhabi: A new metropolitan city emerges from the desert," p. 53
The New York Times, October 20, "New agency to lead global energy push"
The Architect's Newspaper, October 14, "They might be giants: Willis Tower," p. 15
The Toronto Star, October 10, "Towering Example"
Maktoob Business, October 9, "Burj Dubai to open Dec. 2, chairman says"
cnn.com, October 8, "Sexy architecture alive and well in the Middle East"
Business, September, "Green giant," p. 9
The Chicago Tribune, September 11, "Adrian Smith: building to the stars like never before"
RIBA Journal, August/September, "The color of money," pp. 44–50
Architecture + Urbanism, August, "Relationship between design and construction", pp. 30–33
The Chicago Tribune, June 25, "Sears Tower plans hotel, self-greening"
The Chicago Sun-Times, June 25, "Lofty 'green' renovation for Sears Tower"
Wall Street Journal, June 25, "Big hotel planned next to Sears Tower"
Crain's, June 24, "Sears Tower owners propose 5 star hotel"
The New York Times, June 24, "Sears Tower to be revamped to produce most of its own power"
Urban Land Middle East, Spring, "Burj Dubai", pp. 54–55
Science Illustrated, March/April, "Building Towards the Clouds", pp. 36–43
Architectural Record, March 4, "Is the Green-Building Market Recession-Proof?"
ABC News, March 9, "Burj Dubai: Architectural miracle in the desert"
Blueprint Magazine, February 11, "Reject the Dubai Clichés,"
Midwest Construction, February 1, "In a Stalled Economy," p. 23
Riscaldamento Climatizzazione Idronica, February, "Biomimetica per edifici," pp. 68–74
Medill Reports, January 29, "Local architects plan an eco-bridge to complete Burnham's plan"
Engineering News-Record, January 19, "Green-retrofit work thrives in uncertain economic times", p. 22
Space, January, "Clean Technology Building," pp. 86–90

2010

Fortune, "World's greenest skyscraper"
GreenSource, December, "The rise of retrofit," pp. 106–113
inhabitat.com, October 29, "Korean Tower Boasts One of World's Most Efficient Solar Facades"
The New York Times, September 25, "Planning a Sustainable City in the Desert"

Architect Magazine, August, "2010 Award for Sustainability: Chicago Central Area Decarbonization Plan"
Ecolibrium, July, "Desert Star," p. 7
B1 Magazine, June, "Sustainable Excellence: Masdar," pp. 36–41
Metropolis, June, "Skyline: Willis Tower," p. 83
The National, May 26, "Masdar showcased at a Smithsonian Institution's museum"
Perspectives, April, "Building for change," pp. 84–87
RICS Buisness, March, "Power tower," p. 7
Architect, March, " Burj Khalifa curtain wall," pp. 23–24
Crain's, March 1, "In going green average isn't good enough for Willis Tower"
Eco-Structure, February 25, "Adrian Smith + Gordon Gill Architecture Offers a Low-Carb Plan for Chicago"
inhabitat.com, February 22, "Adrian Smith + Gordon Gill hatch massive plan to decarbonize Chicago"
World World Architecture News, February 18, "AS+GG completes first phase of Chicago DeCarbonization Plan"
The Architect's Newspaper, February 11, "Unveiled: Federation of Korean Industries."
The New Yorker, February 8, "Castle in the Air," pp.62–64
Archone, February 1, "Former student Adrian Smith '66 designs world's tallest building"
Brownbook, January/February, "Building Big," p. 71
Architect, January 20, "What if an entire city could be housed under one roof?" pp. 60–63
The Chicago Sun-Times, January 20, "Architect defends his stature"
The Orange County Register, January 18, "San Clemente gave architect of world's tallest building a foundation"
e-architect, January 11, "Chicago architect Adrian Smith's Burj Khalifa, world's tallest building, opens in Dubai"
The National, January 9, "Sky is still the limit for architect"
The Providence Journal, January 7, "Superman, meet Dubai's superscraper"
The Lake Forester, January 7, "Sky-high: Lake Forest's Adrian Smith designs world's tallest building in Dubai"
Spiked, January 7, "What's wrong with towering ambition?"
Emirates Business, January 5, "The impossible transformed into reality"
Khaleej Times, January 5, "Meet the architect of the world's tallest tower"
The Chicago Tribune, January 4, "The Burj Dubai: New world's tallest building shows that nothing succeeds like excess"
The New York Times, January 4, "Dubai opens a tower to beat all"
The Chicago Tribune, January 3, "The tallest building ever (brought to you by Chicago)"
The Los Angeles Times, January 1, "The Burj Dubai and architecture's vacant stare"
Vertical Density, January, "Torre Meraas," pp. 212–213
Architecture Now, Vol. 7, January, "Skidmore, Owings & Merrill: Burj Khalifa," pp. 432–437

2011

Hospitality Style, Winter, "Q+A: Adrian Smith," p. 56
The Nashville Post, November 3, "Giarrantana unveils trio of proposed skyscrapers"
Tall Buildings, November, "KOPOJIEBCKNN POCTOK"
Sphere, Autumn, "Arabian Heights"
Homes & Lifestyle, Autumn "Dubai's Comeback," pp. 13–17; "IM Interview: Adrian Smith," pp. 18–21
The Lake Forester, October 27, "Tall order"
Perspective, October, "Reigning over the sky"
Sciences et Avenir, October, "En Image: Plu pres du ciel"
Southeast Asia Building, September/October, "Adrian Smith + Gordon Gill Architecture wins competition to design Wuhan Greenland Center"
DFUN Magazine, September, "World of Great Towers: Kingdom Tower"
Chicago Architect, "People + Places: Kingdom Tower"

The Chicago Tribune, September 9, "Trump's tower a symbol of a post-attack revival"
The Wall Street Journal, September 8, "The skyscraper as a pillar of confidence"
The Los Angeles Times, September 4, "Skyscrapers remain powerful symbols, post 9/11"
Perspective, September, "Higher up in the wind"
B1, September, "Kingdom Tower"
Bloomberg, August 30, "Kingdom Tower architect grapples the wind at 3,000 ft"
Metropolis, August 16, "Move Over, Burj Khalifa"
New York Magazine, August 14, "Higher"
Construction Week Online, August 13, "King of Skyscrapers"
The Sun, August 12, "King of towers hits the heights"
The Gulf Today, August 11, "A Bird? A Plan? It's Kingdom Tower!"
NPR, August 8, "World's tallest building to be built in Saudi Arabia"
Red Eye, August 3, "3,280"
The Times of India, August 3, "At 1000m, Jeddah to have world's tallest tower"
The Wall Street Journal, August 3, "Saudis plan world's tallest tower"
The Huffington Post, August 2, "Kingdom Tower: Adrian Smith talks designing world's tallest building"
msnbc, August 2, "World's tallest building coming to Saudi Arabia"
Popular Science, August 2, "Saudi's set to build Kingdom Tower, soon to be the world's tallest building"
The Chicago Sun-Times, August 2, "Chicago firm designing new tallest building"
The Telegraph, August 2, "Saudi Arabia takes step to build world's tallest tower"
Emirates Business 24/7, August 2, "Kingdom Tower to top reigning champ Burj Khalifa"
World Architecture News, August 2, "AS+GG Confirmed to design world's tallest tower"
The Chicago Tribune, August 2, "Chicago architecture firm to design world's tallest tower"
Globe and Mail, August 2, "Saudi thrusts forward with plan for world's tallest tower"
The Baltimore Sun, August 2, "Chicago architecture firm to design world's tallest tower"
The Washington Post, August 2 , "Saudi presses forward with plans to build world's tallest tower, outdoing neighbor Dubai"
Architectural Record, August, "On the Boards: Wuhan Greenland Center"
Civil Engineering, August, "Wuhan Greenland Center"
Identity, August, "High Life"
The Wall Street Journal, July 8, "Architect Q&A: The State of Super-Tall Towers"
World Architecture News, June 24, "Adrian Smith Wins 2011 Lynn S. Beedle Lifetime Achievement Award from the CTBUH"
Construction Week, June 23, "Burj architect gets lifetime achievement award"
World Architecture News, June 21, "Adrian Smith + Gordon Gill, Thornton Tomasetti and PositivEnergy Practice to design world's fourth tallest building"
inhabitat.org, June 21, "AS+GG Aerodynamic Wuhan Greenland Center to be World's 4th Tallest Building"
e-architect, June 21, "Wuhan Greenland Center Tower"
One, Spring/Summer, "(Re)Conceiving Cities," pp. 13–15
Archone, May 17, "College of Architecture names eight 2011 Outstanding Alumni: Adrian Smith"
Nissan Technology Magazine, April 28, "2025: The future of mobility and our future cities"
Crain's, March 7, "Crain's 2011 Coolest Chicago Offices: Adrian Smith + Gordon Gill Architecture"
Archone, March 4, "Adrian Smith visits students, presents Rowlett Lecture"
The Battalion, February 25, "Aggie reaches for the sky," pp. 1, 5
The Architect's Newspaper, January 17, "Smart Grid City"
That's Shanghai, January, "The architect's architect," pp. 28–29

2012

Beyond Magazine, December 26, Tianfu Ecological City, "A Shining Example of the Urban Future;" Qintai International Center, "Form Follows Performance: Qintai Center"
Beyond Magazine, December 18, "Efficient Streamlined Design"
Net Zero Energy, December, "A Guide for Commercial Architecture"
Chicago Architect, November/December, "2012 SustainABILITY Awards: Citation of Merit, Chicago Loop Decarbonization Plan"
Areas Globales, November 27, "Reduccion de las emisiones de carbono en el area central de Chicago"
Arab Construction World, November, "The Kingdom Tower: Middle East's New Landmark"
Crain's Chicago Business, November 16, "Overseas planning gigs: A closer look"
Design Boom, November 6, "Adrian Smith + Gordon Gill: Qintai International Tower, Wuhan"
Surface Asia, November, "Seoul Searching: the Dancing Dragons in YIBD"
Concept Magazine, Special Issue 2012, "Yongsan International Business District: Dancing Dragons"
Men's Book Chicago, Fall, "The Visionaries: Hitting the Heights," pp. 90–91
Wired, October 30, "From AT&Ts to iPhones: Early Sketches of 10 Iconic Objects "
New York Magazine, October 15, "9 Experiments in Large: Jeddah, World's Tallest Building"
World Architecture News, October 3, "AS+GG strikes the right note"
Ideat, October, "Special Architecture: Kingdom Tower"
Chicago Architect, September-October, "Built to Scale"
Zenith Business Report, September-October, "Starship to Riyadh," pp. 10–12
The Wall Street Journal, September 22, "Designing Towers to Catch the Sky"
Architect Magazine, September 21, "The Architect 50"
Northwest Tourism, September, "Dimensional Life—Delicate Space," pp. 27–33
Civil Engineering, September, "Ancient Architecture Inspires Contemporary Tower Complex"
MADE, September, "Yongsan International Business District: Dancing Dragons"
Architect Magazine, August 22, "Dancing Dragons"
Perspective, August, "Dancing in the dragon hills"
Building Design + Construction, August, "Mixed-Use Towers in Seoul Awake the Dancing Dragons"
idesign Travel, August, "Wuhan Greenland Center," pp. 59–65
IDT, August, "Wuhan Greenland Center"
Beyond Magazine, August, "Dragon Dancing Twin Towers"
Southeast Asia Building, July/August, "Adrian Smith + Gordon Gill Architecture designs Dancing Dragons, a two-tower complex for Seoul's Yongsan International Business District"
Architectural Update, July 18, "Vantone Center, Tianjin AS+GG"
Crain's, June 28, "High-rise, low-carb buildings offer new ideas for sustainable skyscrapers"
B1, June, "Dancing Dragons Towers"
Green Architecture Now 2, June, "Adrian Smith + Gordon Gill Architecture: Head Offices of the Federation of Korean Industries
World Architecture News, May 11, "Enter the Dragons: Architects unveil twin Korean towers with lizard-like 'scales' of glass that let the buildings 'breathe'"
Building Capacity, May, "A Taste of Living Future 2012"
Men's Book Chicago, Spring, "On Top of the World," pp. 42–44
Nox, Winter-Spring, "Dualidad Geometrica"
The Chicago Sun-Times, March 14, "Development buzz at Reese site"
The Construction Index, February 28, "Challenger emerges for China's tallest tower record"
China Daily, February 28, "Bigger is better, developer decides midway"
Bloomberg News, February 27, "Chinese Tower May Add Floors to Become World's Tallest after Burj Khalifa"

China Daily, February 27, "Wuhan Greenland Center to be China's tallest building"
CRI English, February 27, "Wuhan Mulls Tallest Building in China"
RIBA Journal, February, "United Arab Emirates: Burj Khalifa, SOM"
The Epoch Times, January 31, "China's Risky Skyscraper Extravaganza"
The Chicago Tribune, January 4, "The Burj Khalifa two years later"

2013
Green Buildings, December, "Expo—2017," pp. 16–21
B1, October, "Expo 2017 Pavilion," pp. 38–39
ArchOne, February 11, "Alumnus who designed world's tallest building to receive honorary doctorate degree"
Popular Science, February 15, "Rise of Supertall"
The Daily Telegraph, February 15, "World's best architects vie to make their mark on Sydney"
U Magazine, February, "Never Ends"
Southeast Asia Building, January/February, "Adrian Smith + Gordon Gill Architecture wins competition to design Qintai Center, new corporate headquarter in Wuhan, China"*PM Network*, January, "Closing Credits"
World Architecture News, January 7, "A slice of life in Chengdu"
Perspectives, January, "A Solution for All"
Evolo Magazine, Asian Edition, January, "Chengdu Tianfu District Great City"

2014
Bloomberg BusinessWeek, March 24, "Shedding the Vortex," pp. 92–95
Kohkoku, March, "Higher than Higher," p. 138
Architectural Record, March, "Big Bigger Biggest," pp. 114–115
Architectural Record, March, "Towering Ambition," pp. 94–101
The Chicago Tribune, February 23–27, "The Global City: Designed in Chicago, Made in China"
Greater Middle East, January 8, "Thought Leaders: Adrian Smith, AS+GG Architecture"
The Skycourt and Skygarden: Greening the Urban Habitat, January, "Dancing Dragons," pp. 188–191
Architect, January, "Architecture and the 3rd Industrial Revolution," pp. 100–103
OC South Magazine, November, "The Sultan of Skyscrapers," pp. 66–69
Luxury Magazine, Fall, "Skyscrapers: Race for the Clouds," pp. 214–226
Chicago Architect, May–June, "Answers to Zurich: Adrian Smith, FAIA," p. 74

Lectures, Juries, Panels, Exhibits, Committees

1981
Juror: Skidmore, Owings & Merrill Foundation, Fellowship Grant Program

1982
Jury: Skidmore, Owings & Merrill Foundation, Fellowship Grant Program
Member: Board of Directors, Chicago Architectural Assistance Center
Member: Mayor's Council to Light Up Picasso and Chicago Civic Center
Member: Subcommittee to the Women's Board of The Art Institute of Chicago to Light Up Distinguished Buildings and Sculptures in Chicago

1983
Member: Central Area Committee Task Force for New City Plan for Chicago
Fellow: Architectural Society of the Art Institute of Chicago

Participant: Cornell Symposium on Computer Usage in Architecture
Member: Chicago Architecture Foundation
Jury: Chairman, Senator Richard A. Newhouse Model Building Competition

1984
Fellow: Elected Fellow, National AIA
Panel: Bright New Cities Program
Judge: Sacred Arts IV All-Media Art Exhibition
Member: Design Task Force, 1992 World's Fair Charette at Los Angeles
Panelist: Sculpture in Chicago, South Loop Planning Board

1985
Jury: Chairman, University of Illinois at Chicago School of Architecture Alumni Association
Lecture: Design Program Contemporary Architecture: The Reconstruction of the City, Illinois State AIA Conference
Exhibit: *150 Years of Architecture*, Museum of Science and Industry

1986
Exhibit: Barat College
Exhibit: Grinnel College
Exhibit: McCormick Place, AT&T, Graham Foundation
Exhibit: *New Chicago Skyscrapers*, The Merchandise Mart, Chicago
Exhibit: *Work Space*, The Centre de Creation Industrielle, Paris
Jury: AIA Jury on Institute Honors, Washington, DC
Jury: Young Architects Award, National AIA Design
Panelist: BOMA Conference, June 29–July 2
Panelist: Chicago Chapter AIA Young Architects Seminar
Participant and organizer: ULI Charette, Housing & Community Center, Lawndale

1987
Exhibit: July, November, New Chicago Skyscrapers
Exhibit: University of Illinois At Chicago School of Architecture Alumni Show
Jury: Chairman, November 9–10, National AIA Jury on Institute Honors, Washington, DC
Jury: October 15, Michigan AIA, Detroit, Michigan
Speaker: May 6, "American Architecture Today: A Regional Expression", Washington Design Center, Capital Design Week
Panel: June, "Emerging Voices: The Young, Bright and Talented Minds in American Design", Neocon 19 Program, Merchandise Mart
Lecture: August, Symposium on Modern Architecture, Merchandise Mart
Panel: September 25, "Updating the Chicago Architectural Tradition", Indiana Society of Architects
Exhibit: University of Illinois, *Designing a World's Fair*, 1992 World's Fair

1988
Exhibit: Competition Scheme 9H Gallery, Paternoster
Exhibit: *The 1909 Plan of Chicago*, Chicago
Lecture: January, Visiting Critic, University of Nebraska
Speaker: February, Visiting Critic, University of Nebraska

Lecture: May 26, Chicago Chapter AIA, Cultural Center, Chicago Library

Exhibit: May 19–June 21, Chicago Public Library Entry, Cultural Center, Chicago

Exhibit: July 6, *The Divine Detail*, Chicago Architectural Center, United Gulf Bank

Exhibit: July, *New Chicago Skyscrapers*, Archicenter, AT&T, NBC

Exhibit: September 7, *Renovating Urban Space*, Ikekbukuro Sunshine City, Japan

Jury: October 2–4, 36th *Progressive Architecture* Awards Program Design Jury, Stamford, Connecticut

Panel: October 6, "The Canary Wharf Project", *Progressive Architecture*, New York, Canary Wharf

Exhibit: *Design For Culture*, Gallery of Design of the Merchandise Mart, Chicago, Art Institute of Chicago

Lecture: October 26, "Works in Progress", Merchandise Mart

1989

Exhibit: June–December, *99 Chicago Architects*, (Portuguese-American Meetings On Contemporary Art) Calouste Gulbenkian Foundation, Porte & Lisbon, Portugal, 110–120 Tremont

Lecture: Tishman Research Symposium, April 10, "Contextual Intervention/Technical Invention"

Lecture: Boston Architectural Center, May 10, "Rowes Wharf", Centennial Lecture Series, "Conversations about Boston Architecture: Is there an emerging style?"

Participant: September 4–8, Hamburger Bauforum, Hamburg, Germany

Panel: Concept Chicago '89, October 5, "Why Do High Rises Look the Way They Do?"

Exhibit: September 18–October 20, *New Chicago Skyscrapers*, 1989 Buenos Aires Biennale, Buenos Aires, Argentina, Europe, Asia, and Australia

Jury: *Design Wars!*, October 17, NOVA, Chicago Public Library Competition

Panel: October 23, Cervantes Convention Center Expansion Review, St. Louis

1990

Jury: March 21, Florida AIA, January, Chicago

Exhibit: March 13–May 19, *On The Waterfront: Site-Sensitive Building On The Chicago River*, Friends of the Chicago River, Archicenter, 222 N. LaSalle

Exhibit: June 26–July 22, *New Chicago Architecture*, Mid-America Committee & Chicago Athenaeum, Washington, DC, AT&T, USG, 225 W. Washington, 500 W. Monroe, NBC

Exhibit: July 23–December 31, The Chicago Skyscraper: *Selections from the Permanent Collection*, Art Institute, Galleries 9 & 10, 203 N. LaSalle, NBC

Member: Chairman, SOM Foundation

Participant: September 30–October 1, Zentrum: Berlin Charette, Berlin, Germany

Lecture: October 3–5, National AIA Conference, Corporate Architects Committee, AT&T Case Study and Tour

Lecture: Boston, October 7, National AIA Design Conference—Urban Waterfronts, "Rowes Wharf"

Lecture: October 9–10, "Know Your Chicago", NBC

Lecture: October 24–25, Zentrum: Berlin International Symposium, Berlin, Germany

Exhibit: October 20–December 22, *Chicago Designs: Fashion, Photography, Architecture*, Chicago Cultural Center, AT&T, NBC

Moderator: November 1, "The 'Art' of Development", ULI Conference, Chicago

Participant: *Perspectives*, NBC, "Skyline: Chicago Part I: The Chicago River", ADS Chicago Works

1991

Exhibit: January 22–June 30, *New Chicago Architecture*, Chicago Athenaeum & Metropolitan Review, Chicago Athenaeum, AT&T, USG, 225 W. Washington, 500 W. Monroe, NBC

Exhibit: June, *Projects for Berlin*, Berlinische Galarie, Frankfurter Allee

Lecture: Prague, June 18, "New Work", Chicago Athenaeum & City of Chicago

Exhibit: 1991–1993, *New Chicago Skyscrapers*, (Prague, Berlin, Sweden, Warsaw, Toronto, Budapest), AT&T, USG, Dearborn Tower, Riverbend, P–3, NBC, 500 W. Monroe

Lecture: Singapore, July 19, "Contextual Intervention/ Technical Invention", Quaternario

Lecture and tour: Chicago Chapter AIA Interior Architecture Fall Tour Program, October 23, Continental Bank Renovation

1992

Participant: *Perspectives*, NBC, "Skyline: Chicago, Part 2: The Loop", 222 N. LaSalle

Lecture: Chicago Architecture Foundation Auxiliary Board Dinner, June 16, NBC

Lecture: National AIA Convention, June 19, Rowes Wharf

Lecture: International, Tile Exposition, June 26, Broadgate 12/13, 75 State, NBC, AT&T, 10 Ludgate

Member: Trustee, June 26, Chicago Architecture Foundation

Exhibit: London, *City Changes: Architecture in the City of London 1985–1995*, May 22–August 21, 10 Ludgate

Exhibit: Helsinki, *American Skyscrapers*, September 1–17, AT&T, NBC

Exhibit: Berlin, *Ringprojekt Frankfurter Allee*, October 22–November 12, Community Project Presentation, Frankfurter Allee

Exhibit: Washington, DC, *Put the City Up: Chicago Commercial Architecture, 1820–1992*, Chicago Architecture Foundation, November 20–March 15, AT&T, NBC

1993

Exhibit: March 30–May 29, *New Chicago Architecture*, Chicago Athenaeum, King Faisal Foundation, Commerzbank, East Lake Substation

Exhibit: Harold Washington Library, *Put the City Up: Chicago Commercial Architecture, 1820–1992*, Chicago Architecture Foundation, May 15–July 17, AT&T, NBC

Exhibit: Art Institute of Chicago, *Chicago Architecture and Design 1923–1993*, AT&T, Central Area Plan, Cityfront Center, NBC, East Lake Substation, 1992 Chicago World's Fair

Exhibit: June 17–July 31, *Portraits of Famous American and Italian Architects*, Chicago Athenaeum

Member: Chicago International Biennale Committee, Chicago Athenaeum

Participant, International Design Education Clinic, Building Experiences Trust

Member: Urban Land Institute Urban Development/Mixed-Use Council, July 1

Jury, July 22, Chicago Chapter AIA, Design Excellence Twenty-Five Year Award

Lecture: September 30, "Skidmore, Owings & Merrill: New Projects", Chicago Athenaeum

Exhibit: September 1–October 23, *Skidmore, Owings & Merrill: New Projects*, Chicago Athenaeum, Washington University Psychology Building, Jin Mao Hawaii Globe, King Faisal Foundation, East Lake Substation, Frankfurter Allee, Commerzbank, Dearborn Tower, 10 Ludgate, King Abdul Aziz International Airport

Member: Chief Executive Officer, SOM, October, Two-Year Term

Member: Trustee, Building Experiences Trust, November

1994

Member: February, British Architectural Library Trust Representative, British Schools & Universities Foundation, Royal Institute of British Architects

Member: March 4, Architectural Society of Shanghai, China

Member; April, Governor, Urban Land Foundation

Member: November, National AIA, Large Firm Roundtable

Jury: September, Chairman, Nebraska AIA

Jury: September, Chairman, Central States AIA

Jury: September, Chairman, Nebraska AIA Brick

Lecture: October 12, "A 'Firm' Foundation", AIA Chicago 125th Anniversary Lecture Series

Exhibit: November, *New Chicago Architecture 1994*, Chicago Athenaeum, Jin Mao, Washington University Psychology Building

Committee: December, Chicago Cultural Center Foundation Benefit

1995

Lecture: January 18, "Jin Mao", Chicago Architecture Foundation Lunchtime Seminar

Architecture Alumni Association Honorary Director, University of Illinois at Chicago, two-year term

Lecture: May, Special Session Speaker, ABN AMRO Bank, Fifth World Congress, Council on Tall Buildings & Urban Habitat

Lecture: May, Fifth World Congress, Council on Tall Buildings & Urban Habitat, Contextualism

Speaker: May, Streeterville Organization of Active Residents, Michigan Avenue

Speaker: June 5, "Stars by Night" Chicago Architecture Foundation, ADS riverfront buildings

Speaker: June 7, Greater State Street Council Membership Meeting, State Street Redevelopment Project

Speaker: October 7, VI Bienal de Arquitectura de Buenos Aires, Museo Nacional de Bellas Artes, Argentina, Contextualism

Exhibit: October 5–11, VI Bienal de Arquitectura de Buenos Aires, Museo Nacional de Bellas Artes, Banco di Occidente, 10 Ludgate

Speaker: October 19, University Club of Chicago Architecture Series, SOM and Contextualism

Member: November, Director, Greater State Street Council, three-year term

1996

Honor: Architects and Designers Council, 1996 Honor Award Encouraging Excellence: Pritzkers, May 14, Washington, DC

Member: May, Vice President—President Elect, Chicago Central Area Committee

Member: September, Executive Committee, Greater State Street Council

1997

Lecture: August 26, "Seoul in the 21st Century: The Role of the High-Rise Building", Architectural Institute of Korea

Exhibit: November 9–30, São Paulo Biennale, Sao Paulo, Brazil, *New Chicago Architecture*, Xiamen Post and Telecommunications, Jin Mao

1998

Exhibit: May, São Paulo Biennale, Chicago, *New Chicago Architecture*, Xiamen Post and Telecommunications, Jin Mao

1999

Panel: September 23, TRANSACT '99 Conference—Urban Land Institute, "Staying Two Steps Ahead of the Office Market: Positioning for the Next Five Years."

Lecture: November 12, Chicago AIA, 1999 Professional Development Conference, "Super Tall Buildings"

Member: Council, 1999 Board of Directors, Landmarks Preservation Council of Illinois

2000

Exhibit: January, *The Museum of Science and Industry, Tall Tales*

Lecture: March 15, The Chicago Architecture Foundation, "Skyscrapers by Skidmore"

Exhibit: December 9, 1999 to February 28, 2000, Chicago Architectural Foundation, *The Art of the Long View*

Exhibit: Museum of Contemporary Art, *100 Years of Architecture*

Exhibit: August, The Art Institute of Chicago, *Skyscrapers: The Next Millennium*

Panelist: March 25, The Mayors Institute on City Design

Lecture: April 7, Solar Business Opportunities in the Building Sector Executive Conference in Copenhagen, Denmark, "Sustainable Design Principles"

2001

Panel: May 18, AIA National Convention, Denver, Jin Mao

Lecture: May 15, Royal Institute of British Architects (RIBA), "Tall Storeys? Has Sky Scraper Development at last come of age?"

Lecture: September 6, International Conference on Tall Building, Universität Leipzig, Germany, "Trends in Tall Buildings"

Panel: October 15, Council on Tall Buildings and Urban Habitat (CTBUH), Chicago

Lecture: November 9, Symposium—Architectural Institute of Korea (AIK)

2002

Lecture: October 20, 1st National Bank/Bank One Symposium, "Chicago is History," UIC

Panel: March 5, Real Estate Media, "The Second Annual Real Estate Chicago Architectural Roundtable"

Lecture: October 18, AISC, "Tall Buildings & Sustainability"

Panel: AIA National Convention, Urban Design Awards

Special Consultant: World Exposition Architectural Design & Research Center, Shanghai Xian Dai Architectural Design (Group) Co., Ltd.

2003

Exhibition: Green Exhibition at National Building Museum, Washington DC

Juror: Chairman of the 2004 National Awards Jury for Architecture, Interior Architecture Regional & Urban Design and The Twenty-Five Year Award (AIA)

Speaker: August, CAF River Cruise, architectural commentary

Speaker: "Waterfront Development and Planning", Lisbon

2004

Juror: AIA Philadelphia Design Jury

Design panel: The School of the Art Institute of Chicago

Exhibit: *Great Chicago Places & Spaces*, May 21–23, The Trump International Hotel & Tower: Creating a New Landmark for Chicago

Lecture: The Art Institute of Chicago, "Trump Tower and Other Super Tall Structures"

Collection: The Art Institute of Chicago, March, 7 South Dearborn Street drawings accepted and added in the collection of the AIC

Exhibit: Museum of Modern Art (MOMA), New York, Jin Mao, 7 S. Dearborn
Exhibit: The Art Institute of Chicago, *Unbuilt Chicago*, 7 S. Dearborn
Exhibit: *Visionary Chicago Architecture* (Chicago Central Area Committee)
Forum: Der Traum Vom Turm Hochhäuser: Mythos—Ingenieurkunst—Baukultur NRW—Forum Kultur and Wirtschaft, Düsseldorf

2005
Juror: Jury Chair, AIA Honor Awards
Exhibit: Feb–April, *GRATTACIELI: Architecture Per IL XXI Secolo*, Lucca
Lecture: May 12, Visionary Chicago Architecture
Lecture: October 17, Council on Tall Buildings Urban Habitat, New York, "Burj & Trump Tower"
Lecture: Chicago Architecture Conference and Product Show (Association of Licensed Architects), November 8, "Burj Dubai, World's Tallest tower—An Architecture and Structural Discussion"
Lecture: November 21, "Technology and Memory", University of Illinois at Chicago
Lecture: August 17, "Filling the Void: Renewing the Urban Fabric", Notre Dame
Lecture: September 27, "Burj & Trump Tower", Chicago Architectural Foundation
Exhibit: November, MOMA, *Tall Buildings*
Lecture: December 2, "Trump Tower", Illinois Real Estate Alumni Forum

2006
Lecture/speaker: 24 March, SFT Architecture Convention, Munster, Germany
Lecture: "Mr. Adrian D. Smith: Lecture on Recent Work and Philosophy of Architecture and New Firm Ambitions," Tianjin, China

2007
Lecture: May, "Global Environmental Contextualism." AT Kearney All-Hands Corporate Headquarters Meeting, University Club, Chicago, May
Lecture: May, "Pearl River Tower: Designing a Zero Energy Building." AIA Convention, San Antonio, Texas,
The National Organization of Minority Architects Symposium UIUC, 20 April, Champaign, IL

2008
Exhibit: September–November, Chicago Architecture Foundation, "Boom Town," Masdar Headquarters, Chicago, IL
Lecture: September, "Climate Change, Urgent," MIT Department of Architecture, Cambridge, Massachusetts
Lectures: October, "Supertall, Super Sustainable" and "Masdar Headquarters: Setting the Project Benchmark", Cityscape World Architecture Congress, Dubai, United Arab Emirates,
Panel: November, "Trends in Global Architecture." University of Chicago, Graduate School of Business, Chicago, Illinois

2009
Lecture: May 18, "Masdar Headquarters," Spotlight on Design, National Building Museum, Washington DC
Lecture: October 23, "Decarbonization of Our Central Cities," Council on Tall Buildings and Urban Habitat Conference,

2010
Lecture: November 3, "Toward the Zero-Energy City," Illinois Institute of Technology, Chicago,

2011
Jury: World Architecture News, Urban Design Sector
Interview: October 29, "Lake Forest-Lake Bluff Historical Society: Local Legend Award," Gorton Community Center, Lake Forest, Illinois
Keynote Address: October 10, "The Evolution of an Idea," CTBUH 2011 World Conference, Seoul, Korea
Lecture: May 19 "The Future of Sustainable Design," Corner Symposium on Climate Change, Chicago's Field Museum
Lecture: April 14, "Toward the Zero-Carbon City," with Gordon Gill, Northwestern University
Lecture: February 18, "Toward Sustainable Cities," John Miles Rowlett Lecture Series, CRS Center for Leadership and Management in the Design and Construction Industry at Texas A&M University,
Lecture: April 14, "Toward the Zero-Carbon City," Northwestern University
Lecture: May 25, "The Future of Sustainable Design," Chicago Field Museum, Corner Symposium on Climate Change

2012
Lecture: December 12, "Small World, Big Projects," CAF Lunch Talk, Chicago, Illinois
Lecture: September 19, "From Jin Mao to Kingdom: Search for an Asian Supertall Vernacular," CTBHU 9th World Congress, Shangai
Lecture: September 18, "Current Works: Adrian Smith + Gordon Gill Architecture," Archina, Shanghai, China
Lecture: May 19, College of Fellows 2+2 Convention Program, AIA National Convention, Washington, DC
Lecture: March 82011, "Toward Zero Carbon: The Chicago Central Area DeCarbonization Plan and Other Sustainable Initiatives, " Northwestern Climate Change Symposium, Evanston, Illinois

2013
Panel: November 13, "The Next Cycle: Capitalizing on New Trends," Kellogg Real Estate Conference, Museum of Contemporary Art, Chicago, Illinois
Lecture: November 7, "From Chicago to the World: A Review of Chicago's Architectural History and the Lessons for Global Projects of Tomorrow," ULI Fall Meeting, Chicago, Illinois
Lecture: October 2, "Supertall Towers & Green Cities," The Robie House Series on Architecture, Design and Ideas, Logan Center for Arts, University of Chicago
Lecture: February 13, ULI YL Leadership Series, AS+GG Offices, Chicago, Illinois

2014
Panel: January 15, "Supertall, Supergreen: Judith Dupre, Adrian Smith and Rick Cook: Architectural Explorations in Book Series Event," New York Public Library, Stephen A. Schwarzman Building, Margaret Liebman Berger Forum
Exhibition: June 7–November 23, *Absorbing Modernity: 1914–2014*, Kingdom Tower, Masdar Heaquarters, Great City Chengdu, Venice Biennale, Venice, Italy
Lecture: June 11, "Supertall Towers and Green Cities," Neocon 2014, Chicago, Illinois
Presentation: September 29, "Density Study and Green Cities," Leadership Summit on Sustainable Design hosted by the Design Futures Council, Salt Lake City, Utah

Photography Credits

Unless otherwise credited, photography, renderings and drawings are © Skidmore, Owings & Merrill LLP.

Adrian Smith portrait pages 1 and 504 by Brian Briggs

Art Institute of Chicago, European Galleries Renovation
Photography: Hedrich Blessing Photographers

AT&T Corporate Center/USG Building
Photography: Steinkamp Ballogg Photography Inc.

NBC Tower at Cityfront Center
Photography: Hedrich Blessing Photographers

Rowes Wharf
Photography: Nick Wheeler Photography

Washington University Psychology/Biology Laboratory
Photography: Nick Merrick, Hedrich Blessing Photographers

Banco de Occidente Headquarters
Photography: Nick Wheeler Photography

Olympia Center
Photography: Timothy Hursley, The Arkansas Office (page 52); Hedrich Blessing Photographers (pages 53, 57)

United Gulf Bank
Photography: Hedrich Blessing Photographers

Saudi Aramco Corporate Headquarters Complex
Photography: Steinkamp Ballogg Photography Inc.

Commerzbank Headquarters Competition
Photography: Hedrich Blessing Photographers

Jin Mao Tower
Photography: Gartner Photography (page 87); Hedrich Blessing Photographers (pages 89, 92, 94 top left, top right, and bottom left, 96, 97 right, 98-99, 101, 102, 103–105, 108 left, 109); China Jin Mao Group (pages 93, 97 left, 107); Heudorfer (pages 94 bottom right, 108 right)

Pidemco Tower Competition
Photography: Steinkamp Ballogg Photography Inc.

10 Ludgate Place
Photography: James H. Morris

Chemsunny Plaza
Photography: Adrian D. Smith (pages 123, 125, 129 left, 131-133); Tim Griffith (pages 127, 129 right); Robert Leslie (page 130)

Xiamen Post and Telecommunications Center Competition
Photography: Steinkamp Ballogg Photography Inc.

General Motors at Renaissance Center
Photography: Justin Maconochie, Hedrich Blessing Photographers

Burj Khalifa
Photography: James Steinkamp (pages 159) Tim Griffith (pages 160, 162, 163, 167, 170, 175, 177, 183, 189-191, 193, 198, 200, 206, 207, 209, 211-213, 215-217, 220, 223, 226, 227); Adrian D. Smith (pages 201, 203, 204)

Zifeng Tower (The Nanjing Greenland Financial Complex)
Photography: Steinkamp Ballogg Photography Inc. (pages 229, 231, 234, 236, 237, 239-241, 247) Adrian D. Smith (page 238, 244); Qihua Liu (pages 245, 246, 252, 253)

601 Congress Street
Photography: Peter Vanderwarker Photographs

Trump International Hotel and Tower

Photography: Tom Rossiter (pages 271, 278, 279, 282, 284, 285); James Steinkamp (pages 273-277, 283); Hedrich Blessing Photographers (page 281)

7 South Dearborn

Photography: Steinkamp Ballogg Photography Inc.

Pearl River Tower

Photography: Tim Griffith (page 293, 294, 300, 302-309); Steinkamp Ballogg Photography Inc. (page 298, 299)

Gateway XYZ

Photography: Steinkamp Ballogg Photography Inc.

Jubilee Park Pavilion

Photography: H.G. Esch

Kowloon Tower (Feasibility)

Photography: Steinkamp Ballogg Photography Inc.

Samsung Togok Feasibility Concept

Photography: Steinkamp Ballogg Photography Inc.

Tower Palace III

Photography: H.G. Esch

201 Bishopsgate, The Broadgate Tower, and the Galleria

Photography: Richard Leeney Photography (page 361, 363, 373, 374, 375); Adrian D. Smith (pages 364, 366, 368, 372) James Newman (page 377)

Central Bank Headquarters

Photography: Steinkamp Ballogg Photography Inc. (pages 383, 384 right, 385, 386, 388); Ezra Stoller Associates (page 384 left)

DS–1, Canary Wharf

Photography: H.G. Esch

HQ–1, Morgan Stanley European Headquarters

Photography: H.G. Esch

DS–4, McGraw-Hill European Headquarters

Photography: H.G. Esch

Mitsui Headquarters Competition

Photography: Muromachi

Bank Boston Headquarters

Photography: Steinkamp Ballogg Photography Inc. (pages 427–440, 441 top left and right, 443); Gearte Photography (page 441 bottom left);

CCTV Headquarters Competition

Photography: Steinkamp Ballogg Photography Inc.

The Lakeshore East Master Plan

Watercolor renderings: Michael McCann

Millennium Park

Photography: Steinkamp Ballogg Photography Inc; Watercolor renderings: Michael McCann

Steps Toward Sustainability

Photography: Nick Wheeler Photography (page 489); James H. Morris (page 490 top and bottom left); Adrian D. Smith (page 490 bottom right); Nick Merrick, Hedrich Blessing Photographers (page 492 top); Steinkamp Ballogg Photography Inc. (pages 492 middle and bottom, 496 bottom); H.G. Esch (page 494 left); Peter Vanderwarker Photographs (pages 494 middle and right, 496 top)

The information and illustrations in this publication have been prepared and supplied by Adrian D. Smith. While all reasonable efforts have been made to ensure accuracy, the publishers do not, under any circumstances, accept responsibility for errors, omissions and representations express or implied.